THE HISTORICAL ARCHAEOLOGY OF BRITAIN,

c. 1540–1900

Frontispiece: *Statue of Neptune standing within a former lake and mill pond belonging to the copper master, William Champion. The statue is encrusted with zinc slag from Champion's Warmley brass, copper and zinc works near Bristol. (© D. Cranstone)*

THE HISTORICAL ARCHAEOLOGY OF BRITAIN, *c.* 1540–1900

RICHARD NEWMAN

WITH DAVID CRANSTONE AND CHRISTINE HOWARD-DAVIS

SUTTON PUBLISHING

First published in the United Kingdom in 2001 by
Sutton Publishing Limited · Phoenix Mill
Thrupp · Stroud · Gloucestershire · GL5 2BU

Reprinted in 2001

British Library Cataloguing in Publication Data
A catalogue record for this book is available from the British Library.

ISBN 0-7509-1335-5

Typeset in 10/13pt Bembo Mono.
Typesetting and origination by
Sutton Publishing Limited.
Printed and bound in England by
J.H. Haynes & Co. Ltd, Sparkford.

CONTENTS

NOTE

Reference to counties within the text are all to the pre-1974 historic counties. Not only does this represent the contemporary county structure for the period under discussion, but UK local government changes in the 1990s rendered redundant the post-1974 county structure. The present structure appears still fluid and is unfamiliar, unappreciated and little understood.

CHAPTER ONE

INTRODUCTION

The archaeology of Britain after *c.* 1540 is an enormous topic and any book attempting to deal with it needs to be clearly scoped. Initially the authors of this present volume had intended to provide an update to David Crossley's seminal work published in 1990, *Post-Medieval Archaeology in Britain*, though the date range of our book, while overlapping, is not identical. In concept it was hoped to produce a similar review of topics, but with a concentration on those aspects covered in least detail by Crossley. To some extent these initial intentions are still mirrored by the following text, but at the outset it became obvious that so much new work had been done since the first publication of Crossley's book that it was now impossible, outside an encyclopaedic volume, to encompass all, or even most, of the aspects of the archaeology of the period 1540–1900 in anything other than a summary manner. The geographical coverage also differs in our text in comparison to most other reviews of British archaeology. Its emphasis on the north and west of Britain not only reflects the authors' experiences and interests, but is a deliberate attempt to redress the biases of much 'British' archaeological writing, which has an anglocentric and southern bias (Gaimster 1994, 287). In covering a period which saw the growth of an Atlantic economy and the industrialised areas of northern England, central Scotland and south Wales, a focus of interests away from the south-east of Britain is justified.

Crossley observed how post-medieval archaeology had grown in Britain since the 1950s (Crossley 1990, 1). By 1990 it had long had its own society, founded in 1967, the Society for Post-Medieval Archaeology (SPMA), with its own journal and published research agenda (SPMA 1988). Much of the data gathered for post-medieval archaeology, however, was recovered in the course of multi-period investigations in which the post-medieval deposits formed the uppermost or most recent levels and were often accorded only cursory examination (SPMA 1988, 1). This situation has altered dramatically in the past decade. Not only has there been a considerable shift in the attitudes of many academic archaeologists with regard to the importance of post-medieval archaeology, but the system within which much archaeological research is undertaken in Britain has changed radically, and to some extent in favour of post-medieval archaeology.

From the 1960s through to the 1980s the majority of archaeological projects carried out in the United Kingdom could be classed as rescue archaeology, with work often undertaken as an emergency response to a potential destructive threat from new development. During the 1980s, and particularly following the advent of competitive tendering for archaeological projects, this work became more structured and more closely linked into the planning framework. The advent of Planning Policy Guidance (PPG) Note 16 in 1990 ensured that archaeological remains were always a material consideration in the planning process (DoE 1990). This has placed post-medieval remains on a more equal footing with those of other periods, preventing them from being ignored through academic prejudice or disposed of quickly as a pragmatic response to budgetary and time constraints. Moreover, the increased reliance on non-invasive techniques such as desk-based studies and earthwork surveys, as the initial response to the evaluation of the archaeological resource prior to the consideration of a planning application, has led to a proportionately greater recording of post-medieval remains. Put simply, more recent remains are more likely to be evidenced in documents and as surface features.

Following PPG 16, Planning Policy Guidance Note 15 established archaeological landscapes and historic buildings as matters of material consideration, requiring assessment and evaluation of their merits through the planning process, and where necessary recording, if developments were to be allowed which would alter or destroy them (DoE and DNH 1994). PPG 15 has in part addressed one of the research priorities defined by the SPMA in 1988. Then it was stated that 'it remains a matter of concern that many worthwhile but unlisted buildings may still disappear without record. Planning permission for alterations to historic buildings should be conditional on provision being made for recording prior to or during such operations' (SPMA 1988, 2). Given the nature of Britain's historic building stock, and the preponderance of post-medieval features within the landscape, it is obvious that the post-medieval period would be the greatest beneficiary of PPG 15.

One of the issues of concern for Crossley was the variability in publication and lack of synthesis (1990, 5). Little has changed in this respect. In common with the data from other archaeological periods, the bulk of the reporting on all this new planning-process-inspired archaeological endeavour is now confined to unpublished client reports accessioned into local Sites and Monuments Records. This 'grey literature', as it has come to be known, is of highly variable quality and accessibility. For reasons of time and expense no systematic attempt has been made here to synthesise the results of this literature with regard to post-medieval archaeology. Reference is made to projects reported on in the 'grey literature' of those organisations with whom the authors have been most closely associated. Much new and unpublished work is contained within this sample, but it represents only a fraction of the data available within the total 'grey literature' resource. As with Crossley's work in 1990, some of the references to unpublished projects are derived from the brief summaries in the 'Post-medieval Britain and Ireland' section of *Post-Medieval Archaeology*; unfortunately, while these record that work has taken place, the relevance and meaning of the results can often be difficult to establish.

In addition to the great increase in data relating to the period, post-medieval archaeology has been the subject of growing theoretical reassessment. For three decades up to 1990, the developments in general archaeological theory could be claimed for the most part to have been ignored by the practitioners of post-medieval archaeology. Both the new 'scientific' (processual) archaeology and later post-processual archaeology seemed to pass by post-medievalists in Britain. Archaeological theory appears to have been viewed as relevant primarily to prehistorians. In part this may have been a fault of some of the British progenitors of theoretical archaeology, who seem to have taken a primarily prehistoric stance in the application of archaeological theory. Moreover, the inaccessibility of the language of the theorists, an acknowledged problem (Hodder 1991), may have been off-putting to archaeologists more familiar with history and architecture than with social anthropology. Perhaps also, as Palmer and Neaverson have suggested (1998, 3), the nature of much post-medieval archaeological work, being small-scale and site-based, has not lent itself to the application of the more expansive elements of archaeological theory. Above all, the sheer quantity and diversity of the material record for the post-medieval period have been the greatest obstacles to the post-medieval archaeologist breaking away from being a mere collector and recorder of items. In addition, the subject is a young one and perhaps had to mature sufficiently before engaging with mainstream archaeological theory. The neglect of theory in post-medieval archaeology can be claimed, nevertheless, to have been detrimental to its development.

Too much post-medieval archaeology has been object-fixated. There has been too little recognition that the post-medieval archaeologist deals with material culture for the insights it sheds on people and their social relations. It is fundamentally a period-based study of humanity, not things! Criticisms of the lack of a theoretical framework have been particularly levelled at industrial archaeology, with its concentration on the functional and technological rather than on the social and cultural (Johnson 1996, 12; Clark 1995, 45–8). Although the critique can be taken too far, as a full appreciation of the social meanings of consumption cannot be gained without understanding the processes of production (*see* Chapter 5).

The evidence we use to gain insight into the past is located in the present. As Barrett has argued, statements about present-day evidence need to be theoretically informed in order to produce meaningful insights about the past, in part because we do not have unprejudiced viewpoints, but regard the past through a gauze of present-day, culturally derived prejudices (1990 31, 34). This is the basic tenet of what has been termed critical archaeology (Leone *et al.* 1987; Shennan 1986; Potter 1992). We, the observers of the evidence, can never review it entirely objectively (Wrathmell 1990, 37–40), and therefore should acknowledge the fact that, like the producers of the evidence we observe, we are 'culturally informed and knowledgeable agents' (Barrett 1990, 35). We require the use of theoretical approaches to acknowledge our observational prejudices and utilise them in a positive way.

During the 1990s post-medieval archaeology has embraced mainstream archaeological theory, most clearly demonstrated by Matthew Johnson, a medieval and post-medieval scholar, who has recently published arguably the most accessible British introduction to archaeological theory (1999c). In the study of buildings a number of influential works have appeared which have gone beyond the functional to explore the meaning of structures, and have used spatial analysis to examine social organisation (Parker Pearson and Richards 1993; Johnson 1993a). In particular, hierarchical and gender relationships have been illuminated by the study of spatial division and use. Matthew Johnson (1996) and Paul Courtney (1996; 1997a; 1997b) have both shown how the study of the items of everyday life can elucidate our understanding of the mechanisms of capitalism and the development of a consumerist society, and some attempt has been made to examine a theoretical framework for the study of designed landscapes (Locock 1994) and of post-medieval landscapes in general (Newman 1999). Even industrial archaeology now has advocates of a more theoretically framed approach which will produce insights into human behaviour beyond the economic and technological (Palmer and Neaverson 1998, 3–8).

Ironically, given the late acceptance of theoretical approaches by post-medieval archaeologists, many of the concepts and ideas used by their theoretically inclined colleagues in Britain were pioneered in the United States among archaeologists working with evidence pertaining to the period from the sixteenth to the nineteenth century (Glassie 1975; Deetz 1977; Beaudry 1988). In America the archaeology covered by this timespan is termed historical archaeology, a title adopted for this book. We are well aware that in a British context historical archaeology could be taken to refer to the archaeology of all periods after the Iron Age; indeed, the renowned American historical archaeologist, Robert Schuyler, defined historical archaeology as the study of material remains from any historic period (Orser and Fagan 1995, 6). In this sense it is the archaeology of literate societies. Post-medieval archaeology under such a definition is a subdivision, with historical archaeology being a type of archaeology whose genesis begins at different times across the globe (Orser and Fagan 1995, 7). Current views of the old American definition of historical archaeology consider it to be chronologically narrow, and it is certainly definitionally incorrect for much of the Old World (Andren 1998; Funari *et al.* 1999). While it is difficult to argue with the broad logic of this more inclusive definition of historical archaeology, its use in the title of this book, in preference to the geographically exclusive post-medieval, is intended to convey chronological, cultural and methodological meanings that would be understood by both Old and New World archaeologists.

Although textual evidence such as the Vindolanda tablets undoubtedly provide a valuable context within which to study the material culture of the northern frontier of Roman Britain, there is a clear distinction between the availability and potential usefulness of historical sources during the Roman period and much of the medieval period in Britain, and that during the sixteenth to nineteenth centuries. For the most part documentary sources remain scarce before the mid-sixteenth century, and are heavily biased towards the activities of the social elite. Medieval documents provide little basic information about the living conditions of the majority, their daily life, their belief systems or their psyche. The domination of documentary evidence over material remains has, in the view of many archaeologists, held back the study of medieval archaeology in particular, preventing some of the more revealing anthropologically inspired observations that have, of necessity, fuelled debate in prehistoric archaeology. Archaeology has been seen as dancing to history's tune, subordinated to the primacy of the historical record and thus constrained by that record's political and ideological prejudices (Champion 1990, 92–3). Using post-processual approaches to interpret the archaeological evidence, it has been argued, enables the exploration of those issues which are not generally enlightened by documents (Austin 1990). This allows the development of a distinct archaeological approach to the study of medieval life, rather than the use of archaeology to support historical research objectives. It is further argued that such an approach should be valued equally with documentary research, and the two applied in a twin-track methodology (Austin 1990, 76). These views could also be applied to post-medieval archaeology, although the written record expands so much along with the ownership of books that it can itself be studied as material culture.

From the mid-sixteenth century the documentary record expands enormously, though many important activities of everyday life continued to generate few records (Crossley 1990, 2). Nevertheless, the documentary record after the mid-sixteenth century stands in marked contrast to that before it. Documents are increasingly written in the vernacular and cover far more of the everyday aspects of social and economic life, though the historical record remains dominated by the elite since they were more likely to be literate or able to employ literate people. From the mid-sixteenth century there was an increase in printed works, some of which came to reflect occasionally and often obliquely on the activities and lifestyles of the 'common man'. The late sixteenth and early seventeenth centuries also saw the development of recognisably accurate maps, soon followed by more accurate graphic depictions of landscapes and buildings. This huge growth in size, scope and – to an extent – reliability of the documentary record justifies the subdivision of medieval and post-medieval within the broader genre of historical archaeology within Britain.

The historical information cannot be ignored. It must be accommodated and must be *a*, but not *the*, primary evidential source in the discussion of any post-medieval archaeological topic. Even so, despite the greater scope and coverage of the post-medieval documentary record in comparison to the medieval, the lives of the majority are hardly illuminated by it (Crossley 1990, 2). Women, children and the poor are for the most part excluded from the historical record, but a critical and interpretative examination of post-medieval material culture sheds light upon their lives. The Reformation, the Renaissance and European imperial expansion around the world are all historical themes crucial to the appreciation of the early post-medieval period, but we should remember Edmund Blackadder's statement to his servant: 'to you, Baldrick, the Renaissance was just something that happened to other people' (BBC 1992). For the majority, living their lives in the shadow of major historical processes, such developments were unperceived and not critical to their lives. Archaeology can illuminate the history of the Baldricks.

If a twin-track approach, giving equal weight to archaeological and historical research, is considered the way forward in the study of medieval archaeology (Austin 1990, 76), the increased wealth of written sources from the sixteenth century onwards requires the subordination of historical data to the demands of an archaeological research agenda. This is not to deny that archaeologists and historians are part of the same research process, chasing the same goal – of course they are; it merely allows archaeology to have a different perspective (Hundsbichler 1997, 48–9). In this approach the documentary record provides a context, but not a strait-jacket, within which to examine and explore the meanings of the material culture observed. By this means post-medieval or later historical archaeology is truly text-aided (Orser and Fagan 1995, 16).

When James Deetz used historical archaeology as a definition, he imbued it with meanings which reflected the archaeological study of the global spread of European culture since the fifteenth century (Orser and Fagan 1995, 11). To an extent the choice of the term historical archaeology for this present work, in preference to post-medieval, is intended to reflect this as well. The impact of European global expansionism, as reflected in material culture, was not a one-way process but dynamically interactive, affecting the colonisers as well as the colonised. The culture of Britain was hugely affected by its global relationships. Hence the use of the term historical archaeology within this book is intended to reflect both a theme and a methodology. It reflects a study of British material culture within the context of an increasingly literate society and at a time of rapidly expanding horizons, and it is also a review of text-aided archaeology.

It must be confessed that neither definition immediately requires a date range of 1540–1900. Date ranges are chosen primarily for pragmatic purposes, essentially to make the subject matter digestible. They are always, at least to an extent, arbitrary, a convenience rather than an imperative. Although the term historical archaeology does seem particularly apposite to describe the archaeology of Britain after the mid-sixteenth century, it can be applied to the medieval period as well. Indeed an argument can be made for replacing the descriptions medieval and post-medieval archaeology with historical archaeology, thus removing the artificial boundaries erected by such imposed periodisation (Champion 1990, 92). The labels medieval and post-medieval are constructs, convenient for producing bite-sized chunks of history but potentially stifling of creativity by encouraging an academic retreat into period-bounded laagers (Courtney 1997a, 9, 10; Crossley 1990, 2).

The date range for this present study, though cutting across previously defined and accepted periodisation, and others that could be justifiably defined, is itself no more than a convenient construct, but one, nevertheless, that can be seen as having some internal consistency and continuity. The mid-sixteenth to twentieth centuries in Britain are culturally dominated by three major interlinked historical trends: capitalism, consumerism and colonialism (Orser 1996; Johnson 1996). The start date 1540 is one of many which can be considered historically significant in the change from a medieval to a post-medieval world in various parts of the west (1450 and 1492 are others that might be chosen), but such dates are of limited practical value in relation to changes in material culture (Verhaeghe 1997, 27). The entire span of the fifteenth and sixteenth centuries can be seen as a period of transition in Europe, from a world that was recognisably medieval in 1400 to one that was something quite different in 1600 (Gaimster and Stamper 1997). Indeed, as many of the themes covered in the ensuing chapters will reveal, a convincing argument could be made for viewing the archaeology of the period 1350–1660 as a cohesive period (Johnson 1996), one which witnesses the birth of capitalism, setting the stage for the 'long eighteenth century' and the 'revolutions' which led to the development of the 'modern' world. Yet such a view would be simplistic; attributions of change or continuity in any period definition are aspects of hindsight and not necessarily contemporary perceptions. Equally, the recognition of a period of transition is the product of present-day attitudes and views and would not have been comprehensible to contemporaries. To define the fifteenth and sixteenth centuries as a period of transition creates a new bounded timespan and implicitly accepts the periodisation of medieval and post-medieval in order for there to be a transition from one to the other. While acknowledging these difficulties of definition and perception, the usefulness of periodisation is accepted, and thus, if a study is to be compartmentalised into timespans, it must have a start date.

The mid-sixteenth century in western Europe was a time of significant developments in material culture. Major changes had taken place in ceramic production for example, with new and more sophisticated types being acquired from the domestic and foreign markets (Barton 1992; Gaimster 1994). Growing commodification in the sixteenth century led to an increase in the number and diversity of portable objects of all types (Verhaeghe 1997, 33), and the overseas discovery of new lands with new crops led to the creation of new fashions, resulting in additions to the material cultural assemblage; perhaps the most obvious example is the clay tobacco pipe. A similar situation can be found with more static elements of the cultural resource. It has long been claimed that the later sixteenth century witnessed a revolution in the nature of vernacular housing in England (Hoskins 1953). Although the initial thesis has been criticised and revised (Machin 1977; Platt 1994), there can be no doubt that major changes had occurred in many regions, so that the domestic building stock in 1600 was quite different in terms of its structure from that of 1400. However, although the transition from an open-hall tradition to a closed, three-cell, lobby-entry form of house may have been completed in Suffolk in the second half of the sixteenth century (Johnson 1993a, 64), in other regions such as Lancashire the situation was very different. Changes in building traditions graphically illustrate how developments in material culture often cannot be considered to have a consistent national perspective. Elsewhere in Europe it has been noted, for example, that while the increase in furniture sophistication and diversity mirrored to an extent the ceramic situation, in some areas such as Brabant simpler forms of furniture in the 'medieval' tradition were still favoured into the seventeenth century (Verhaeghe 1997, 33). Nevertheless, despite considerable local variations in the adoption of developments in material culture, at a national and European level trends can be perceived. With this perception the mid-sixteenth century can be seen as a period which witnessed both the culmination and initiation of many of the developments which collectively make post-medieval Britain distinct from medieval Britain.

If any particular date can be seen as symbolic of these changes for much of Britain it is 1540. The completion of the process of suppressing the monasteries in England and Wales marks an event of major significance to the psyche of the majority of the populace of those countries, and one that was to become physically represented by changes in the landscape. Symbols of

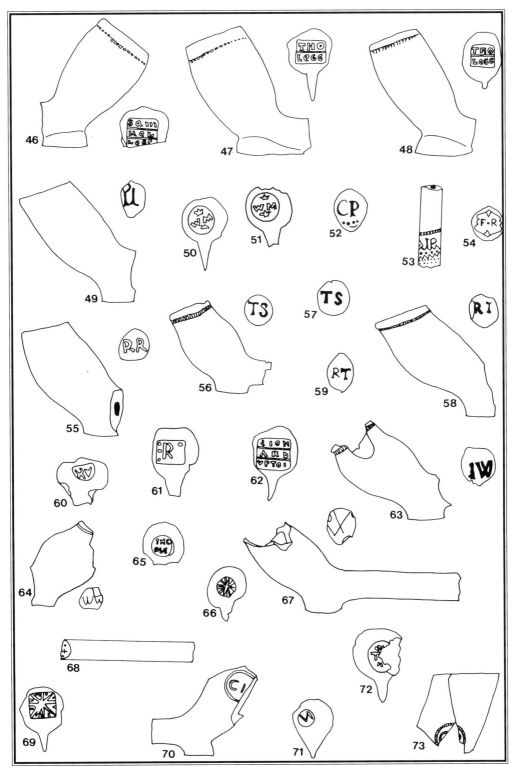

Stamped clay tobacco pipe bowls from Llanmaes, south Wales. The pipes not only provide good dating evidence but convey information concerning industry, trade, global contacts, lifestyles and even health. (© C. Newman)

ecclesiastical authority became ruins or were incorporated into houses intended to represent secular power. The destruction of the power of the medieval church, the investment of the gentry in new landed estates and the advancement of monarchical power are all represented by the Dissolution. These are key themes in the creation of a new post-medieval world. However, even an event like the Dissolution did not have a uniform effect throughout Britain – Scotland after all was a distinct kingdom whose chronology and experience of religious reformation was different.

The termination of this present study in 1900 may be considered even more arbitrary and contentious than its commencement date. To many, including at least originally the SPMA, the period after 1750 is considered to be distinct from that which preceded it (Gaimster 1994, 283–4). Most frequently the archaeology of this period is regarded as industrial archaeology, 'defined as the study of the tangible evidence of social, economic and technological development of the period since industrialisation, generally the last 250 years' (Palmer and Neaverson 1998). This is not a uniformly accepted definition, and others have claimed that industrial archaeology is a near-synonym for post-medieval archaeology or that it equates with the archaeology of early modern capitalism (Campion 1996, 847). While accepting elements of all these definitions, industrial archaeology is not regarded in this present work as a period-specific discipline. It is seen rather as a thematically based method of archaeological inquiry dealing with industrialisation, its remains and associated features. No period distinction is drawn here between industrial and post-medieval. Industrial archaeology is simply one of the themes, along with buildings and landscape archaeology, that form part of the narrative of the period 1540–1900. It is indisputable that the quantity, diversity and symbolic importance of industrial remains is greater in the period 1540–1900 than at any previous time.

By 1900 the process of industrialisation was complete throughout Britain and its consequences were manifest. Many areas of countryside were affected by widespread and quite large-scale extractive industries, new industrial towns had developed and mass-produced commodities were available nationally. Transportation had been revolutionised and its benefits extended to the masses, enabling the breakdown of vernacular traditions as building materials could be easily transported around the country, and everywhere the medieval traditions of house building had been replaced. Similarly, open-field farming had finally been replaced and enclosure was triumphant. These two phenomena – the closure of space within houses and the enclosure of fields – have been seen as symbolic of change from a medieval to a modern world view (Johnson 1993a, 165–76). In some areas these processes were well under way, particularly for the wealthy, in the sixteenth century, but in many others they were not completed for all classes until the late nineteenth century.

The end of the Victorian Age makes much sense as a terminus. We are probably too close to the twentieth century's cultural detritus to be able to focus clearly on the nature of its archaeology. Moreover, the development of the telegraph, the telephone, photography and, at the end of the nineteenth century, the internal combustion engine, all had profound effects on material culture and everyday life, most of which were not fully realised until much later in the twentieth century. Above all, however, by 1900 the major themes that had influenced material culture since the sixteenth century, if not for some two hundred years earlier, had reached a form of conclusion. Capitalism, consumerism and globalisation, though all remained influential on material culture in the twentieth century, had, along with Britain's national power and prestige, reached a zenith. They would be challenged by socialism, anti-imperialism and environmentalism during the twentieth century, and the response to, and effect of, these challenges is part of our lives today.

Much has been made in this introduction about the application of theoretical approaches to historical archaeology. None of the contributors, however, would claim to be an archaeological theorist, and for a consistently theoretically informed view of the post-medieval period one should look elsewhere, Matthew Johnson's *An Archaeology of Capitalism* (1996) for example. Even if much archaeological theory is little more than the explicit articulation of a researcher's prejudices, it nevertheless has value. It is important to make a clear statement defining a researcher's agenda. Two fundamental assumptions underlie the foregoing review of the historical archaeology of the period 1540–1900: first, that changes in material culture occur at different times in different places dependent on social circumstances, and secondly that the relationship between these elements is not linear but dynamic and iterative.

The adoption of changes in material culture are locally driven and influenced by locally pertaining social factors. This localism in cultural response was broken down during the mid- to later nineteenth century, sometimes deliberately, as in the case of the suppression of the Welsh language, a process which deepened and accelerated for much of the twentieth century. The current vogue for regional identity is in part a backlash to these developments. Even so, one of the conclusions revealed by this study is that, taken in total, the material culture of Scotland is different from that of England and Wales in a way that is indicative of a separate national identity. Within specified localities changes in material culture are adopted at different times according to social circumstances. However, new or higher-quality aspects of material culture are not necessarily adopted first by the wealthiest, with an attendant trickle-down effect through time. The previously mentioned adoption of post-medieval furniture styles in Brabant is a case in point; here it was the wealthiest who clung to older styles longest because, it is argued, of class conservatism (Verhaeghe 1997, 33). Similarly, in the United States plantation sites have revealed perceived higher-status tablewares among the slaves' quarters than at the main house, the explanation advanced being that the acquisition of such objects was more important for defining status among slaves than it was for the slave-owners (Adams and Boling 1989). The very concepts of trickle-down and class emulation of material culture are questioned by the ensuing study, and an alternative thesis begins to emerge of a triumphant middle class, who come to share power with the landed elite and whose values are imposed through material culture on the poor. Yet archaeology also reveals patterns of resistance to middle-class values, with an adherence to traditional rural lifestyles within the growing urban environments, even in the late nineteenth century.

This present work, in comparison to Crossley's 1990 volume, has a different period remit, evolved from a reconsideration of the nature of the subject matter. It is influenced by the application of theories of archaeological interpretation as applied in British historical archaeology during the 1990s, though it does not claim to be adding to that body of work. Moreover, the examination of the issues covered within this current volume is structured within a thematic framework based on the divisions generally self-imposed on archaeological fieldwork and professional affiliation: landscape, buildings, industrial and artefacts. Each theme is broken down into easily referenced topics, and greatest weight is given to those only touched on by Crossley or where recent research has greatly changed perspectives in the past decade. Each topic is developed chronologically. Some topics, such as urbanism, recur under different themes, and the authors' attempts to avoid repetition may require the reader to cross-reference between chapters. Together the themes present a cohesive, though not comprehensive, view of the archaeology of Britain during the sixteenth to nineteenth centuries.

CHAPTER TWO

BUILDINGS OF SECULAR AND SPIRITUAL AUTHORITY

BUILDINGS ARCHAEOLOGY IN PRACTICE

Much of historical archaeology's material resource still remains unburied and plainly observable within the fabric of the existing building stock. A significant proportion of the occupied and utilised buildings of Britain date to the sixteenth to nineteenth centuries, and as far as houses are concerned as many as 60 per cent pre-date the twentieth century. Since these buildings form part of the present social and cultural environment they are still evolving as they are added to, altered and adapted to suit changing circumstances of ownership and use. The analysis and interpretation of these buildings and their development can provide historical archaeologists with their most significant resource for shedding light on the past. These buildings are the 'megafauna' of the material culture of the sixteenth to nineteenth centuries. Their form, decoration and adaptation reflect the aspirations, cultural affinities and social relations of the people who owned, lived, worked and died in them (Hillier and Hanson 1984; Johnson 1993a, viii–xi).

Post-medieval buildings took many forms. Indeed, the expansion of the variety of building types is one of the characteristics of the growth of material culture during the sixteenth to nineteenth centuries. As well as an increase in specialised forms of agricultural and industrial buildings, new types of public and corporate buildings appeared. In rural areas new prisons, poor-houses and schools appeared, mainly from the late eighteenth century. In and around towns theatres, market houses, court houses, judges' lodgings and almshouses were appearing in the sixteenth and seventeenth centuries. Later, in the nineteenth century especially, town halls, civic halls, club houses, learned and working-men's institutions, libraries, municipal baths, hospitals and lunatic asylums all grew in number, reflecting changes in both social attitudes and legislation, and the requirements of competitive corporate pride. The nature of the urban fabric was both added to and defined by the number and character of its civic, institutional, charitable and leisure-orientated buildings. Asylums in particular illustrate the social pressures behind the adoption of new and very expensive forms of building. An Act of 1808 provided for the establishment of pauper lunatic asylums, an indication of a desire for a more humane approach to insanity, although few counties introduced asylums before further legislation in 1829 (Chalklin 1999, 80). By 1847 there were 21 in England and Wales, growing to 102 by 1914 (Taylor 1996, 15). Located on the outskirts of towns, these enterprises tended to be massive in scale because they not only encompassed institutional patient care but also had to cater for the complete social needs of inmates, so that within the building complex all the many functions of an urban community might be present. Like workhouses, with which they were often associated, their

Blackburn Workhouse, later the Queen's Hospital, as shown on the first edition Ordnance Survey map, dominating the higher land to the south of the town. (© Lancashire County Council)

massive size and often prominent location on the urban fringe served as a warning to a town's working classes of the consequences of intemperate and immodest living (LUAU 2000a). Sometimes cheaply built, they might use innovative techniques, such as the structural use of corrugated iron as at Hatton Hospital near Warwick (LUAU 1996a), in order to equate scale with limited budgets (Taylor 1996, 16–7).

This great increase in building types to an extent reduced the physical impact of religious buildings within the landscape, particularly in some towns, as they were dwarfed by the

Detail from a Buck print of Peterborough, 1731, showing the medieval abbey's dominance of the townscape.

enormous scale of some of these new building forms, whether they were lunatic asylums, textile mills, dock warehouses or town halls. This can be seen as part of a process of 'secularisation' of the landscape, which reflects a changing moral climate and social structure, with traditional and customary forms of obligations and outlooks being eroded or replaced (Reed 1983, 183–4). There is a degree of accuracy in this view, and the authority of at least the Established Church in society, as reflected in the physical dominance of medieval church architecture, was reduced during the eighteenth and nineteenth centuries. The mid-eighteenth-century Buck brothers' print of Peterborough, for example, shows a townscape massively dominated by the cathedral (Hyde 1994), but this was a scene that was not repeatable in the industrialised town a century later. Moreover, the use of space and its implications for control, and the social meanings embodied in these new types of building, are part of the new moral and philosophical map created by the industrialising society of the later eighteenth and nineteenth centuries (Markus 1993). Nevertheless, it can be too easy to sense an expression of the triumph of the modern, rational and secular over the medieval, superstitious and spiritual in the eighteenth-century expansion of secular buildings, and a perception of decay and neglect in ecclesiastical structures. The eighteenth century witnessed the building of new places of worship to accommodate the sects of the New Dissent. This increased into the nineteenth century when the Anglican Church underwent a religious revival and an unprecedented period of church building and refurbishment began. The nineteenth-century expansion in church activity was in part an attempt by the middle classes to control the lifestyles of the labouring classes, many of whom clung to traditional rural habits and traditions (Reed 1983, 189–92), even within urban environments. (This theme is discussed in detail below.)

For the most part the archaeological study of buildings has been concentrated on particular groups. Domestic, military and ecclesiastical buildings are, along with industrial structures, those which have received most archaeological attention: they are, for example, the only groups of buildings referred to in Whyte's brief overview of the post-medieval period, produced for *The Archaeology of Britain* (Hunter and Ralston 1999). They are perhaps also the most significant groups of buildings in terms of their embodied meanings in relation to developing post-medieval society. Some other groups of structures, such as farm buildings, are now receiving detailed archaeological attention in mainstream literature (Brunskill 1987; RCHME 1997). Other areas, such as corporate and public buildings, are less well served by synthesis, but recent publications, such as the RCHME's books on hospitals and workhouses (Richardson 1998; Morrison 1999), have begun to fill the gap. Even so, the relative lack of archaeological, as distinct from architectural or social, studies of these structures ensures that the focus of this current review will be on houses, military buildings and places of worship.

THE MEDIEVAL LEGACY

As late as 1550 much of the building stock of all types was likely to be fifteenth century or earlier in date. Social need, attrition through time (Currie 1988) and perhaps, to some extent, limited constructional longevity led to the replacement of much of the medieval domestic building stock during the post-medieval period. Others survived, but their usage changed and their later development did not reflect their original purpose. An interesting example of this is Arlington Row, Bibury, in the Gloucestershire Cotswolds, where a large structure with an apparently industrial origin was built in the late fourteenth to fifteenth centuries, but was converted and subdivided for domestic use in the sixteenth century (Moore 1994). Medieval buildings of higher social status, such as some castles and most places of worship, in contrast to the majority of lower-status sites, continued to be occupied and used throughout the period of study. Changing social circumstances, however, led to changes in function among these buildings too, as old structures were adapted to new uses. Even where buildings were abandoned, the ruined phase of their history, which for some structures still surviving today can represent more than half their existence, is often as significant as their earlier occupied history (Wood 1996, 154). The relevance and importance of the post-medieval evolution and history of buildings of medieval origin are often overlooked. For many of today's surviving structures, four hundred years of post-medieval accretions, alterations and conversions to new uses have assisted in creating their present appearance and relationship to their surrounding environs.

Castles

The medieval castle incorporated two primary roles: it was a noble residence intended to impress and to portray kinship with a chivalric past and aristocratic lifestyles (Coulson 1979), and it was also a military stronghold. The precise primary function, or contemporary perception of that function, would have varied from castle to castle dependent on location and ownership, and would have changed through time as a result of changing circumstances. Most castles were private residences, and in England at least, apart from those in the Scottish Marches, were seldom required to act as strongholds during the Middle Ages (Johnson 1996, 123). While some continued to perform this function during the sixteenth century, many were abandoned; indeed, perhaps no more than 35 per cent of the castles observed by Leland in *c.* 1540 were lived in (Thompson 1987a, 104). Unsurprisingly, given a castle's principal use as a residence, the main reason for their abandonment seems to have been not military but domestic. Castles were hardly suitable to meet the requirements of privacy and comfort demanded by the elite by the end of the fifteenth century (Thompson 1987b, 209).

The military value of medieval castles is considered to have been seriously diminished, if not extinguished, by advances in gunnery in the late fifteenth and early sixteenth centuries (Coad 1997, 159), although doubt has been cast on the military value of all but first-rank medieval fortifications, before the advent of gunpowder and gunnery, in the face of superior siegecraft (Coulson 1979, 74, 82). There can be no doubt, however, that when gunnery could be deployed its effect was dramatic. The damage caused by English artillery to Edinburgh Castle in the siege of 1573 led to massive rebuilding in the next half-century, changing the late medieval castle into the substantially post-medieval fortress and garrison visible today (Driscoll and Yeoman 1997, 234–6). Even so, castles, together with some of the less obviously martial great houses that replaced them, continued to have a perceived and sometimes real military significance well into the post-medieval period. Even abandoned castles in the sixteenth century were still considered to have military value (Thompson 1987b, 208). No matter how ineffective their medieval fortifications might be when threatened with sixteenth- and seventeenth-century ordnance, castles could continue to function as strongholds where troops could be mustered and munitions and goods stored largely safe from attack by small enemy forces not equipped with heavy field guns.

The continued military importance of castles is demonstrated by the pattern of their abandonment, being most frequent in regions of little martial threat. In Scotland and the borders, where reiving and family feuds made for less secure conditions, tower-houses and castles continued to be maintained and occupied, and in some instances built, throughout the sixteenth century and into the seventeenth (Thompson 1987a, 122–5). Indeed, it was not until the eighteenth century in some cases that they were given up for more comfortable accommodation (Tabraham 2000, 63). In some instances medieval castles were modified to take account of new military imperatives; defences could be reduced in height or strengthened by the addition of massive earthen banks (Coad 1997, 159), and gun-ports and platforms were added. Following the Scottish raid of 1513 the defences at both Norham and Wark castles on the Tweed were improved, with gun-ports included in the rebuilding of masonry defences (Crossley 1990, 107; Kenyon 1977). Gun-ports were also inserted into the defences of Caerlaverock Castle in Dumfries. On a more elaborate scale new continental concepts of fortification were added to existing medieval defences. Excavations at the Scottish royal castle of Stirling revealed a likely mid-sixteenth-century augmentation of its southern defences by the addition of angle-pointed fortifications of Italianate design and a barbican-like wall probably associated with a gatehouse dating to the reign of James IV, 1473–1513 (Ewart 1980, 23, 36). These were destroyed following a further remodelling of the defences in the early eighteenth century.

The continued perceived military significance of medieval fortifications is best exhibited by their treatment during the English Civil War. There was a widespread reoccupation of castles and refurbishment of defences at the onset of military activities (Thompson 1987b, 210), while at some sites, such as at Wigmore in Herefordshire in 1643, the defences were destroyed to prevent garrisoning. In Wales, Raglan Castle, a mid-fifteenth-century fortified residence built on the site of a presumed earlier stronghold, was subjected to siege in 1646, and the subsequent defeat of its royalist garrison has been seen as marking the end of the 'first Civil War' (Taylor 1950, 21). Although designed primarily as a symbol of the prestige of the Herbert family and not as a military stronghold, nevertheless it was considered to be eminently defensible in the mid-

Sixteenth-century gun port within the curtain wall at Norham Castle, Northumberland. It was built after the Scottish raid of 1513.

seventeenth century. Its Great Tower, detached and surrounded by a moat, was clearly constructed with security as a primary consideration, as it was designed with both arrow-slits and gun-ports on its ground floor (Taylor 1950, 44). Lord Herbert was one of the main financiers of the royalist cause, and his treasury, housed in the Great Tower, was crucial to the royalists' military efforts. Prior to the siege he strengthened the castle's defences by the addition of gates and outworks (Kenyon 1982). Despite the use of siege artillery by the Parliamentarians, the garrison held out for three months and only surrendered when it became clear that there was no hope of relief. After the siege the defences were slighted, and the Great Tower, which had survived daily bombardment relatively unscathed, was partially destroyed by the traditional siege technique of undermining (Taylor 1950, 22).

Another fifteenth-century castle, Lathom House, the Lancashire home of the Earls of Derby, was similarly utilised during the Civil War. Initially besieged unsuccessfully by parliamentary forces in 1643–4, it was later taken and razed to the ground (Wood 1996, 143). Its destruction was evidently so comprehensive that the exact location of the castle has been disputed until recently. Work by the Lancaster University Archaeological Unit identified the probable site of the castle under the ruined remains of the eighteenth-century mansion at Lathom. Fabric analysis of that structure has revealed that sufficient masonry from the fifteenth-century castle must have been available in the eighteenth century for it to have been re-used in the later structure. Thus the complete demolition and site clearance of the fifteenth-century castle was partly the result of post-siege dismantling and partly the product of eighteenth-century building activities.

Elsewhere in Lancashire other castles were successfully besieged with varying fates. The two fifteenth-century castles at Greenhalgh and Thurland were both slighted, the former being almost totally destroyed, but the latter surviving to form the basis of a later mansion. A similar fate befell Hornby. Clitheroe, already partly ruinous in 1608, was further demolished in 1649 (Wood 1996, 143–4). Such stories can be told about many medieval castles and later great houses throughout England; the neighbouring Yorkshire castles of Pontefract and Sandal (Crossley 1990, 117), and the Tudor mansion built within an earlier medieval ringwork at Basing House, Hampshire (Harrington 1992, 24–5), are all examples of fortified sites destroyed as a result of the Civil War and where archaeological investigation of relevant deposits has been undertaken.

The English Civil War had a profound effect on the survival of medieval structures in Britain, particularly in England and Wales. Their slighting, mainly after 1646, ruined many examples of great medieval architecture, reducing their significance to little more than useful sources of building stone for perhaps a century. In contrast, many castles in Scotland survive today in a far better condition because they escaped slighting and remained occupied for longer. The desire of the parliamentary military and the later Commonwealth government to undertake the systematic destruction of royalist castles and great houses cannot simply be dismissed as a vengeful assault on the material wealth of their opponents, but must reflect a contemporary perception of the military value of such structures. Indeed, the second Civil War clearly exposed the risks of leaving defensible castles empty or manned by small garrisons. To ensure they were denied to a potential enemy meant they had to be rendered useless as fortifications, and so there was a further flurry of orders for slighting in 1648–9 (Porter 1994, 130), with the last demolition orders being issued for Chirk Castle in 1659 (Thompson 1987a, 145). Although the destruction of the castles can be regarded as confirmation of their continuing military significance into the mid-seventeenth century, it also physically represents the end of that significance, not only for the ruined structures but for most of the surviving examples as well.

The medieval castle was adapted or used for other non-military functions both before and after the English Civil War. Many castles continued to fulfil the function of prestige houses, but the requirements for comfort and display were different in the later sixteenth century from what they had been even a century earlier. In some areas, such as parts of Scotland, the need for defence could not be abandoned, so at castles like Caerlaverock Renaissance-style prestige accommodation was built in the early seventeenth century within the circuit of the still functional modified medieval defences. Elsewhere, wholesale rebuilding was often required to accommodate sixteenth-century requirements, and much medieval fabric was lost in consequence. At Old Beaupre Castle in the Vale of Glamorgan, a late thirteenth-century castle was largely remodelled in the late sixteenth century to form a courtyard-plan house with attached farm. Later additions are for the most part absent, perhaps because much of the site fell into disuse when Old Beaupre was abandoned as the principal residence of the Bassett family after the Civil War. The family fortunes did not recover, and the site and the estate of which it had formed the caput were sold in 1709 (Hague 1973, 8). To the west of Old Beaupre, at Oxwich Castle in the Gower peninsula, another courtyard house was erected on the site of a late medieval castle, incorporating some medieval structural elements. Excavation and structural analysis has indicated two phases of building, one dating from the early to mid-sixteenth century and the other to the mid- to later sixteenth century (Blockley 1997, 124–5). By 1632 Oxwich Castle was being let, and by the early eighteenth century its status had declined to that of a tenanted yeoman farm; it is not surprising, therefore, that by the mid-eighteenth century, as evidenced on a Buck print, the site was partially ruinous (Courtney 1997c, 134). A few baronial castles remained as elite residences, such as Alnwick, Berkeley,

Powis, Skipton and Warwick. All are still occupied, and though substantially altered they remain recognisably medieval castles.

Other castles were adapted to alternative uses. Some lost their military function yet maintained their administrative or judicial significance. Kidwelly in south Wales housed a judicial court in the early seventeenth century, possibly within a sixteenth-century hall (Kenyon 1986, 11). Still other castles were reused because of the security offered by strongly built structures. St Briavels Castle near Lydney in Gloucestershire is one of the smallest royal castles and was the home of the Constable of the Forest of Dean. By the later seventeenth century and into the eighteenth century the castle operated as a prison. Though extensively modernised in the seventeenth century, the castle fell into dilapidation in the eighteenth century, with its keep collapsing in 1752, and it remained largely ruinous until restoration at the beginning of the twentieth century (Cooke 1913; Hart 1995).

Early seventeenth-century Renaissance-style house built by the Maxwell family within the defences of Caerlaverock Castle, Dumfries.

Another royal castle, though much larger and more important than St Briavels, also continued to function in the post-medieval period both as a centre of jurisdiction and as a prison. Lancaster Castle had undergone campaigns of building from the twelfth to fifteenth centuries, and by the sixteenth century was already an amalgam of different periods and styles of building. As well as being a stronghold, it had always functioned as an administrative and judicial centre and presumably as a place of incarceration. It retained these latter functions in respect of the Duchy of Lancaster, and the county of Lancashire, throughout the post-medieval period, and for these reasons it was maintained and repaired (White 1993, 22). In the late eighteenth century the county justices decided to rebuild Lancaster Castle to provide better accommodation for the gaol and the county government and court. New accommodation was built for male and female prisoners and a new curtain wall erected, and at the end of the century an impressive complex of courts and county offices, including a new Shire Hall, was completed in a neo-Gothic style (Dalziel 1993, 122–3). Further building work was undertaken in the nineteenth century, but the constraints of the plan and nature of a still essentially medieval structure limited the efficacy of efforts to render the buildings suitable for use as a nineteenth-century prison (Winstanley 1993, 156). Sadly, and to what should be the shame of the twenty-first-century Home Office, Lancaster Castle remains a prison to this day.

The most important royal castle/prison of the sixteenth and seventeenth centuries was the Tower of London. As well as an incarceration facility, it was also an archive, a treasury and a magazine. At the end of the sixteenth century it was still considered vital to the defence of the city of London (Parnell 1983, 337). A century later these functions were all considered

The later medieval gatehouse of Lancaster Castle, still the entrance to a functioning prison.

sufficiently valid to merit refortifying the Tower. Not all the recommendations and plans put forward were implemented, but many new gun-platforms for artillery were added to the defences. However, by 1714 these modifications were considered to be ineffectual, with many of the gun-placements regarded as 'useless' and being of appearance value only. Although further modifications to the defences were made, it is clear from contemporary reports that the Tower was no longer an effective military establishment, but had become of ceremonial significance only (Parnell 1983, 350–1).

Royal castles often had a different post-medieval history from baronial ones. The reduction in the martial role of the nobility hastened the decline in the importance of fortified strongholds in much of England and Wales from the late fifteenth century. The depredations of the Civil War and its aftermath physically concluded the process, but royal castles often survived, sometimes as judicial centres with incarceration facilities, occasionally, as at Dover or Edinburgh, as military strongholds, and exceptionally at Windsor as accommodation for the royal household. At the latter, although it was modernised to become a palace fit for late seventeenth- and eighteenth-century monarchs, its essentially medieval character was consciously retained as a symbol of the link with a monarchical past (Brindle and Kerr 1997, 48–9). In the earlier nineteenth century this iconic character was 'enhanced' (Brindle and Kerr 1997, 54–5). Unlike the role of the medieval nobility, that of the Crown in central government was modified but not removed, and hence the vestigial remnants of medieval power were symbolised by the continued use of royal

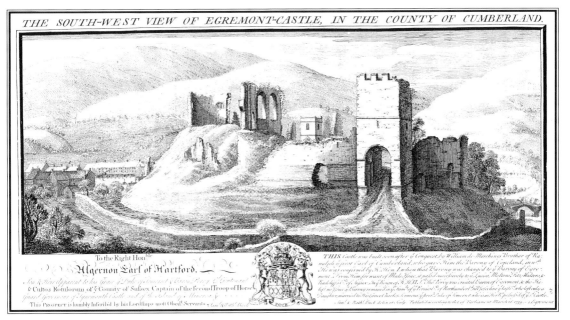

The Buck brothers' view of Egremont Castle, Cumberland, 1739. This castle was used as a prison and courthouse during the sixteenth and seventeenth centuries.

castles. Of course, these medieval structures were substantially modified and were never ideal for the uses to which they were put, and many new purpose-built structures – garrisons, fortresses, court houses, prisons and palaces – were erected. Yet the expansion in need and the cost of meeting it for all such purpose-built establishments must have ensured that the value of some of the royal medieval castles remained high, and so they continued to be used and survived. Nevertheless, while to an extent a pragmatic response to circumstances, the survival of royal castles as traditionally functioning buildings through to the present day is also a material anachronism, which can perhaps be seen as an expression of an anachronistic surviving monarchy.

Most castles had been ruined by the eighteenth century by a combination of abandonment, entropy and masonry pillaging, or by deliberate slighting. Slowly the ruins attracted the attention of antiquarians, and a new value was attached to medieval castles, that of 'heritage'. The growth of antiquarianism has been recorded elsewhere (for example Schnapp 1993, 122–219), but one event in particular marks this development: the refounding of the Society of Antiquaries of London in 1717. Its first secretary, and perhaps the greatest of all antiquarians, was William Stukeley, and it is he who is credited with inspiring the artists and engravers Nathaniel and Samuel Buck to commence their programme of recording antiquities in England and Wales (Hyde 1994, 18–19). The sites recorded in their engravings completed between 1724 and 1741 are primarily castles and monasteries. Earlier commissioned and subscription-sponsored engravings of secular subjects, such as those of Johannes Kip, tended to be of contemporary aristocratic residences. The Bucks' views, and their subscribers and patrons, indicate that the interests of the literate and wealthy now embraced their medieval heritage, an impression reinforced by the contemporary revival of Gothic elements in architecture. What had once been an integral feature of government and the physical expression of wealth and power had become romantic ruins, yet they still connected their owners and admirers with an ancient and perceived chivalric past. As such they were recreated as follies within landscape parks, those eighteenth- and nineteenth-century symbols of prestige. The new meanings and values attributed to the ruined castles in the eighteenth and nineteenth centuries ensured a degree of protection, and hence the survival of the remains into the twentieth century, when state protection was extended to the majority.

Monasteries, Preceptories and Granges

The suppression of the monasteries in England and Wales between 1536 and 1540 made available for secular use a huge number of previously Church-owned buildings, as well as the landed estates that went with them. As Crossley has pointed out, the Dissolution had two principal effects on the building of elite houses: it provided structures for conversion and it made available suitable sources of building stone for use elsewhere (1990, 53). The presence of monastic buildings exercised a considerable influence on the distribution of elite houses (Crossley 1990, 53), particularly in the richer and more populous areas. In poorer, less hospitable environments, where there was less interest in acquiring the buildings, monastic ruins tend to survive today, as for example at Rievaulx and Byland in the North York Moors (Williamson and Bellany 1987, 60). There were many reasons for acquiring former monastic buildings for conversion to secular mansions. They were conveniently situated to serve as the centres of the newly secularised landed estates. Large buildings designed to impress could be adapted relatively cheaply, avoiding the greater expense of building from new. Moreover, many of the new owners of former monastic property were from families whose rise to prominence was relatively recent, and so occupation of an ancient site and building could have been regarded as bestowing on them an air of antiquity and heritage. There were various approaches to conversion, but one of the most popular was to use the claustral ranges as the basis for a courtyard house, as at Newstead Priory, Nottinghamshire (Williamson and Bellany 1987, 118), though the demolition of the church was often stipulated by the suppression commissioners to prevent reuse by dissident Catholics. At Newstead, as elsewhere, the church was used as a quarry for building materials. Similarly at Audley End, Essex, and Vale Royal, Cheshire, great houses were built around the claustral ranges of former monasteries (Crossley 1990, 53). Recent work at Vale Royal has shown that its new owner, Thomas Holcroft, followed closely the instructions of the suppression commissioners, leaving only the south and west ranges of the cloisters as the basis for a new house (McNeil and Turner 1988, 66–7).

In some instances the monastic church was saved to become the local community's church, though the conventual buildings were removed. This was particularly the case where the monastery was attached to a settlement which had no alternative church. At Gloucester the church of St Peter's abbey became the new cathedral, and the same happened at Chester and Peterborough. At Tewkesbury, near Gloucester, the local community petitioned to be allowed to retain the abbey church as the parish church, as they did at Romsey, Hampshire, and as a result both these small towns possess churches of a size and magnificence unrelated to the importance of the settlement. The church at Cartmel in Lancashire-over-Sands, which had always functioned as the parish church, was kept for parochial use. In addition, some of the conventual building range, including a gatehouse, was retained as part of the village fabric, the medieval structures gradually being disguised by later frontages.

In Scotland the monastic orders were spared the Henrician suppression. Even so, the mid-sixteenth century witnessed increasing criticism within Scotland of the Catholic Church, culminating in 1560 when the Scottish Parliament abolished the mass and rejected the supremacy of the papacy (Fawcett 1994, 118). This did not lead to the immediate end of Scottish monasticism, though the removal of the trappings of Catholicism from monastic buildings often amounted to mob vandalism and looting, and in some cases caused considerable permanent damage. Urban-based friaries in particular seemed to have suffered badly (Fawcett 1994, 120). It was not until 1587 that the Scottish monarch followed his earlier English counterpart and seized the monastic properties through the Annexation Act. Following this, a pattern of secular conversion of buildings emerged similar to that previously observed in England and Wales. Unless monastic churches served a local parish they tended to be demolished or allowed to decay into ruination, with the conventual buildings being used to form elite residences, as at Arbroath. At Holyrood and Dunfermline new royal palaces grew out of former abbeys (Fawcett 1994, 121). The

Blocked doorway within a former monastic range at Cartmel, Lancashire. The range now forms commercial and domestic accommodation.

process of secularisation did not progress as smoothly or as rapidly as it had in England. At Sweetheart Abbey, Dumfries, an abbot remained in residence until 1608 under the protection of the local Catholic lords, the Maxwells. Later in the seventeenth century part of the abbey became used as the parish church of New Abbey, the previous church being on an island in a lake situated 1.5km from the settlement of New Abbey (Richardson 1995, 11). In 1731 a new church was built against the south wall of the nave. Although the abbey continued to be a focus for worship within the community and a place of burial for members of the Maxwell family, local inhabitants nevertheless pillaged the ruins for building stone, particularly in the eighteenth century, and many of the houses of New Abbey incorporate fragments of the monastic buildings. The threat to the survival of the ruined monastic church at Sweetheart led in 1779 to local efforts to ensure that the building was preserved as 'an ornament to that part of the country' (Richardson 1995, 11)

In the eighteenth century a growing concern for the value of monastic remains as antiquities was evident throughout Britain, with many ruined monastic buildings being considered as suitable subjects for engravings, for example. In Scotland this led to the removal of some later additions to the monastic buildings where they were used for continued worship. The use of Dunfermline, Melrose and Jedburgh as parish churches was abandoned in part because this would allow the removal of post-medieval fabric, and thus facilitate the appreciation of the medieval remains (Fawcett 1994, 122). At Sweetheart the church built among the monastic ruins in the eighteenth century was demolished in 1877 (Richardson 1995, 11).

Sweetheart Abbey, Dumfries, is an early example of a ruined medieval building being protected as a monument.

The monasteries were not the only church properties secularised throughout Britain. Other monastic sites, such as granges and preceptories, became new secular farms. Here the changes were perhaps less dramatic, since such properties had served a primarily economic function as agricultural estate centres, and the buildings were already suited for farming. Moreover, such properties had often been in secular hands since the fourteenth century, when the monastic orders began to lease out their farms. Nevertheless, in most cases the secularisation of granges and preceptories, with the consequent programmes of modernisation in response to changed domestic and farming requirements over the following centuries, has meant that little medieval monastic fabric survives at such sites. At Newland Park in Yorkshire, a former Hospitallers' preceptory, the buildings were converted over two centuries into a mansion, with some conventual buildings surviving into the eighteenth century (LUAU 1997a).

Much monastic property was situated in towns, especially the friaries. As in the countryside, most monastic town property came into the hands of the wealthy, and during the mid-sixteenth century, particularly in London, the buildings were converted for use as elite urban palaces (Schofield 1993a). For example, Holy Trinity Priory, Aldgate, was given to Thomas Audley, and later became known as Duke's Place, although the choir, aisles and eastern chapels were converted into tenements (Schofield 1984, 145–8; Morris 1989, 378). Similarly, the Austin Friars precinct went to William Paulett and became Winchester Place. There were difficulties in developing constricted urban sites, already full of stone-built structures, which shaped the way in which these sites developed, in contrast to the rural sites which were redeveloped as spacious mansions. At the Charterhouse, adoption of the double court layout, as seen at Hampton Court, could only be achieved by placing the two courts at an acute angle to the street entrance (Schofield 1993a, 29). Nevertheless, in spite of restrictions, it can be seen that attempts were made to adapt the sites to the fashions and requirements of sixteenth-century elite residences (Schofield 1993a, 33).

In provincial towns the redevelopment of urban monastic sites proceeded at a slower pace. Investigations of the Carmelite Friary in Newcastle-upon-Tyne showed that, though partly demolished in the sixteenth century, the site was not fully redeveloped until the nineteenth century (Harbottle 1968; Crossley 1990, 80). At Chester, St Werburgh's Abbey was founded as the cathedral church of the new diocese of Chester in 1541. Little immediate change occurred to the buildings, but this is unsurprising considering the continuity of personnel between the monastery and the cathedral chapter (Thacker 1995, 21–2). Gradually, however, the ex-monks were replaced and a combination of reduced finances and neglect of clerical duties appears to have led to a deterioration in the fabric of many of the precinct buildings (Thacker 1995, 26–7). By the early 1570s the former monastic refectory housed a grammar school, but by 1578 it was derelict and seems not to have undergone extensive repairs until 1613, when it was again occupied by the grammar school (Thacker 1995, 32–3). The northern half of the outer court of the abbey was, by the seventeenth century, not a desirable place, because of the close proximity of a brewhouse (Thacker 1995, 35). In general the former abbey precinct seems to have been neglected for much of the sixteenth century, and was in a poor state by the early seventeenth century. The 1630s witnessed a programme of restoration, but the occupation of Chester by parliamentary forces in 1646 saw the destruction of many of the old conventual buildings, along with the rebuilding work of the previous decade (Thacker 1995, 34–5, 43).

Parish Churches

The greatest resource of still-functioning medieval buildings surviving in Britain today are the parish churches. In the sixteenth century they were among the most significant, ancient and durable buildings in regular use in the majority of communities. Their continued use over many centuries ensured that few were formed of fabric of a single period, most having undergone repeated periods of redesign, rebuilding and repair. It is thus necessary to view their post-medieval development as part of a continuum of adaptation. Even so, the post-medieval period witnessed a major change in the nature of the church and its liturgy; ushered in by the Reformation, this change inevitably left its mark on the physical remains of the church.

The Reformation itself, which gripped all of Britain in the sixteenth century, did not have a huge impact on the parish church, at least in England and Wales. The government of Edward VI (1547–53) did engage in some iconoclasm, and its commissioners were responsible for the removal of much church plate, though whether this was a wholly doctrinal response to the changes in the celebration of communion or a matter of financial expediency is a matter of debate. In general, however, doctrinally inspired change to medieval church fabric and fittings appears to be limited in the sixteenth and early seventeenth centuries. The Protestant doctrine of justification by faith alone (Solafidianism) removed much of the incentive for benefactors to endow churches with new fittings and fabric (Gilchrist and Morris 1996, 117). The reaction against the veneration of saints also had an effect. Statues, icons and relics were in many cases removed from churches, and private chapels, chantries and fraternities all fell into disuse. Some of these changes may have resulted in alterations to the church fabric, particularly in parishes lacking in money; parts or all of the chancel and transepts were allowed to decay or were demolished, as happened in a number of instances in East Anglia, and processional doorways may have been blocked (Gilchrist and Morris 1996, 117). Internally, rood screens were removed and altars replaced by communion tables (Gilchrist and Morris 1996, 120). Overall, however, such an historically momentous change seems to have left little obvious trace in the physical development of the parish church, especially with regard to new additions in contrast to neglect.

There are a number of possible explanations for the apparent lack of sixteenth- and early seventeenth-century physical evidence for doctrinal changes in parish churches. Firstly, it is difficult to distinguish sixteenth-century building works from either fifteenth- or earlier seventeenth-century work, though some features, such as straight-headed mullioned windows, have been regarded as Elizabethan (Simmons 1959, 41). Throughout these years church architecture was dominated by the Perpendicular style (RCHME 1987, 46), though this very conservatism would appear to be indicative of the limited impact of the Reformation on church building development. Indeed it may reflect the considerable conservatism detectable in popular religion, with, in many regions, a continued adherence to traditional beliefs in the sixteenth century (Duffy 1992, 479). The prodigious church rebuilding that had been undertaken in the preceding century must have also reduced the needs and incentives for new works (Gilchrist and Morris 1996, 117; Duffy 1992, 132). Immediate post-Reformation church modifications are likely to be under-represented in surviving church fabric because of Victorian modernisations (Morris 1989, 400–3). It has been estimated that less than 2 per cent of the eight thousand surviving pre-Victorian churches in England remained largely untouched by nineteenth-century restoration (Gilchrist and Morris 1996, 116).

The earlier seventeenth century experienced an increase in church modernisation and rebuilding, though this may have been more for social than doctrinal reasons. Some contemporary documents survive recording the reasons for alterations to church fabric. Most frequently these related to the desire for more space and comfort on behalf of the leading families of the parish (RCHME 1987, 46), evidenced in the introduction of family pews. The general embellishment of churches with new woodwork in the decades preceding the Civil War may be a reflection of the need of an emerging squirearchy to express itself, but also may reflect changes in the Anglican Church, particularly during the archiepiscopate of William Laud. The Laudian church supported Arminianism, which encouraged the revival of ceremony and reintroduced elaborate furnishing and even wall painting. In 1633 Laud decreed that the altar should be placed against the east wall and introduced the communion rail (Gilchrist and Morris 1996, 120). The effect of Laud on reversing the puritanical trends of the preceding years is difficult to assess, as much of the work he inspired was undone in Puritan backlashes in the 1640s.

It was in the middle years of the seventeenth century, assisted by the Civil War and Interregnum, that Puritanism gained control of the Anglican Church, and it is perhaps then, rather than during the Edwardian Reformation, that Protestant iconoclasm had its most serious impact on the appearance on medieval churches. Much of the obliteration of medieval decoration, such as the whitewashing of the frescoes at Kempley (Gloucestershire), is likely to be attributable to the Puritan period, though archaeologically this is frequently difficult to ascertain. In Scotland it can be argued that the changes to the church interiors dictated by a reformed church came earlier, but here it is also difficult without documentary evidence to date the changes beyond a general attribution to the post-Reformation periods of 1560–1700 (Dunbar

1996, 128). The situation may have been different in Wales as well, where prevalent royalist sympathies and a weak Puritan tradition may have cushioned the effects of mid-seventeenth-century iconoclasm (Parkinson 1996, 150). These traditions may explain the remarkable survival of late medieval rood screens in the central Welsh marches. The most lasting impact of Puritanism on medieval churches, however, was the change it wrought in people's attitudes to the buildings. The Puritans opposed the veneration of the church as a holy place (Morris 1989, 437), and this seems to have had an impact on the entire Protestant establishment. From the mid-seventeenth century until the mid-nineteenth century respect for the church as a building was greatly diminished (White 1962, 4).

The lack of reverence for church buildings could manifest itself in seemingly contradictory ways: it could lead to an easy acceptance of wholesale modernisation, as might be inferred from the restoration of Homington Church in Wiltshire in 1794 (RCHME 1987, 54), or to neglect and decay. Overall the later seventeenth and eighteenth centuries do not seem to have witnessed a great deal of reconstruction of medieval churches in England and Wales, and in some cases even maintenance does not seem to have been adequate. At Pulloxhill Church, Bedfordshire, the steeple fell down in 1653, the tower was ruinous by 1668, the nave was abandoned by the early eighteenth century and roofless by the 1740s. Although the mid-eighteenth century saw attempts to raise money for repair, and the chancel was rebuilt and enlarged for use as a church, it was not until 1845–6 that the entire church was rebuilt (Pickford 1996, 155–9). In west Yorkshire and in Shropshire medieval churches appear to have been neglected in favour of building new churches (Ryder 1993, 79–90; Friedman 1996a, 1996b). A survey of standing churches in south-east Wiltshire showed that, while it was not an 'age of utter neglect', the eighteenth century was a period which for the most part was characterised by limited repair to ageing parish churches, with only the aristocracy undertaking ambitious works (RCHME 1987, 54–6). Their sponsored works were inspired largely by selfish reasons of familial glorification through the provision of elaborate private mausolea and monuments, or the enhancement of vistas from their mansions (RCHME 1987, 56–9). When new work was undertaken on the fabric of the church, it was not universally welcomed. One of the earliest uses of neo-Gothic in church restoration – at Hereford Cathedral, by Wyatt in the late eighteenth century – was criticised in the *Gentleman's Magazine* for its negative effect on the primarily Romanesque church (Friedman 1996b, 112). Elsewhere the impact of classical elements introduced into medieval churches could be equally displeasing and lacking in harmony to both contemporary and modern eyes.

Scotland had a different post-Reformation church history from that of England and Wales, and by the eighteenth century its surviving medieval church fabric formed parts of structures that were distinct to the country. Scottish medieval churches, in any case, had a different building tradition from those south of the border. Many of the rural churches were simple, relatively unadorned buildings, and most Scottish buildings had avoided the extravagances of the English Perpendicular. The present lack of medieval fixtures and fittings within Scottish churches is attributed to the destruction wrought during the Reformation (Yeoman 1995, 43, 52), which was more populist than its English counterpart and consequently may have been more devastating in its initial stages. Nevertheless, the overall physical impact of the Reformation in Scotland seems to have been similarly gradual and accumulative (Dunbar 1996, 128; Green 1996, 133). As in England, iconoclasm peaked in the mid-seventeenth century. The Ruthwell Cross, for example, an Anglo-Saxon sculpture considered idolatrous, was broken up in 1642 following an edict of the General Assembly. Unlike in England and Wales, however, where the dominant and state-sponsored form of Protestantism was of a mild and unradical nature (except during the Interregnum), in Scotland the more radical Presbyterianism predominated. In 1690 the Revolution Settlement made the Presbyterian Church the Established Church in Scotland (Green 1996, 134). Throughout the seventeenth and into the eighteenth century churches were modified to meet the needs of Presbyterian doctrine and aesthetics, so that by the mid-eighteenth century many Scottish medieval churches had been rebuilt as the characteristic Presbyterian church: white-harled, plain, narrow rectangular buildings with a belfry (Green 1996, 134–5). By this time surviving medieval remains were probably rarer and more fragmentary than elsewhere in Britain.

The apathy of the eighteenth century was replaced in the nineteenth century by a renewed burst of church building and modernisation of existing buildings. The impact of the nineteenth century, and in particular the Victorian period, on surviving medieval churches cannot be underestimated. The explanations behind this phenomenon are many and interacting. The population was expanding, creating a need for new churches. The established churches were in competition with nonconformist denominations to win new congregations. The government willingly assisted the established church – starting with An Act to Promote the Building, Repairing or Otherwise Providing of Churches and Chapels in 1803 – since in the wake of the French Revolution radical religion, especially among the lower classes, was seen as potentially connected to radical social and political thinking (Curl 1995, 21). Around 1830 the Anglican Church was forced to realise that it was unpopular in comparison to nonconformity, particularly in the burgeoning industrial areas (Parkinson 1996, 145). New church buildings were the principal strike weapon of a religious arms race. With new buildings being erected in modern styles, pressure was placed on existing ageing buildings to counter the attraction of the new. Overall, the surge in church refurbishment in the nineteenth century is a sign of religious revival, and, in the earlier nineteenth century at least, an establishment reaction to radicalism.

Initially, nineteenth-century church refurbishments were undertaken in a variety of architectural styles (Gilchrist and Morris 1996, 121), including Gothic. This style, based on Decorated and Perpendicular later medieval English architectural fashions, was even used in Scotland, where the styles employed were alien to the Scottish tradition (Green 1996, 138). Despite the decorative elements, no matter which style was used for the redesigned churches, the basic layout remained that of a reformed church focused on pulpit preaching (Morris 1989, 431). The true Gothic Revival, which gathered momentum in the 1830s, went in tandem with the revival in the fortunes of the Anglican Church and a move towards a more Anglo-Catholic form of worship, which became reflected in the design of the new and restored churches. Church building and restoration were physical expressions of an Anglican religious revival, and Gothic architecture came to be seen as the essential style in which to express this renewed spirituality.

As early as the 1820s the government-appointed Commissioners for Building New Churches were beginning to advocate the adoption of the Gothic style (Curl 1995, 22). The early nineteenth century saw the publication of a number of antiquarian studies of medieval buildings which influenced contemporary architects. By the 1840s Gothic, in particular the Decorated style, was coming to be seen as the truest form of Christian architecture. The influential architect Augustus Pugin, a convert to Roman Catholicism in 1834, believed Gothic to have been an invention of Christian culture and that it symbolised Christian beliefs (Morris 1989, 431; Curl 1995, 30). At Oxford and Cambridge influential architectural societies concerned with church architecture were set up in the 1830s (Curl 1995, 28–9). In 1844 the Cambridge Camden

Society ruled that the Decorated style was best suited to meet the doctrinal needs of Christian (i.e. Established Church) doctrine (Morris 1989, 435). These societies became associated with a major Anglican doctrinal theoretical development. Taking its name from the publication the *Tracts of the Times*, Tractarianism was at the doctrinal heart of the Anglican revival. It moved Anglicanism much closer to Roman Catholicism, leading to a re-emphasis on ceremonial and ritual; architecturally the chancel became more important, with the altar becoming the focus of the Communion (Parkinson 1996, 145–6). In 1845, following accusations that the two learned societies were advocating Roman Catholicism, the Camden Society became the Ecclesiological Society (Curl 1995, 29) and the Ecclesiological Movement was founded.

Inevitably it is tempting to view the Tractarians' interest in high medieval architecture as symbolic of a desire to return the Established Church to medieval and thus pre-Reformation roots. The accuracy of such a view is debatable, but certainly those on the more evangelical wing of Anglicanism seemed to make this connection, as can be judged from Dr Francis Close's argument in 1844 that the restoration of churches correlated with the 'restoration of popery' (Curl 1995, 29). Despite such opposition, what Richard Morris has called the 'architectural McCarthyism' (1989, 436) of these High Anglican architectural movements gathered momentum. Between 1846 and 1853 Henry Bowman and Joseph Crowther compiled *Churches of the Middle Ages*, a book which purported to be a record of Gothic-style churches and was used as a source book for church restorations (Hyde 1997, 22–3). In reality the book was a style guide presenting churches as the architects wished them to be rather than how they actually were when recorded. Nantwich parish church in Cheshire, for example, is depicted as an unadulterated fourteenth-century interior, similar to the appearance of the restored church in 1861, yet at the time of recording it was very different, as other depictions of the church show. Before restoration it had the layout of an auditory church, a large pulpit in the nave, which was galleried, and a chancel sealed and barely visible, but this was not the interior shown in the book – instead a notional medieval appearance was provided which served as a blueprint for a facsimile reconstruction of a medieval interior (Hyde 1997, 24–5).

Under the influence of the Ecclesiological Movement, most original medieval churches were revamped and modernised, often with the imposition of wholly uncharacteristic and inappropriate Gothic architectural elements. In Scotland apses were added to many churches in the later nineteenth century, though the apse was rare in the Scottish architectural tradition (Green 1996, 141). In Wales an alien architectural style was imposed on many small rural churches (Parkinson 1996, 146). Everywhere medieval fabric and fittings were lost as a consequence of the adoption of a Church-approved medievalism. Add to this the disruption caused by new facilities, such as heating, gas lighting and the widespread insertion of organs, and churches were not only gutted but acquired new additions, such as boiler rooms (Green 1996, 140; Gilchrist and Morris 1996, 121). The effect of Gothic-style church restoration in the late nineteenth century was not entirely a negative one, however. The use of Perpendicular Gothic was very appropriate for the many medieval churches built in this style. Consequently some later nineteenth-century rebuildings produced churches in which the architectural elements are far more harmonious than in those structures with earlier inserted features. Manchester Cathedral, originally built as a parish church in 1422 and restored and enlarged in 1882, is an excellent example, and the nineteenth-century workmanship at Bristol Cathedral also blends well with its medieval architecture. The restoration process removed many of the additions and modifications which could be associated with the Reformation and more radical strains of Protestantism. It

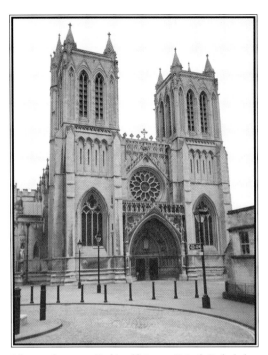

Nineteenth-century Gothic additions to Bristol Cathedral blend well with the original medieval architecture.

rediscovered and restored some of the hidden and partially destroyed medieval antiquities, such as the Ruthwell Cross. Yet ironically, for all its historicism and interest in the medieval past, the Ecclesiological Movement did more to destroy the original fabric of that past than any outbreaks of Protestant iconoclasm ever did.

The passion for Gothic architecture cannot be seen in purely doctrinal terms, however, as its influence was extended across Anglican, Presbyterian, Unitarian, Roman Catholic and other denominations. Some of the principal influential church architects of the period were not Anglican: Pugin and Hadfield were Catholics and Bowman was a Unitarian. What may have begun as a manifestation of an Anglo-Catholic, philosophical outlook became a popular fashion avidly supported by the moneyed classes, seemingly ever willing in a denominationally competitive environment to endow their chosen churches with new fittings, stained-glass windows and the like. In turn Gothic became the accepted architectural norm for most Christian buildings in Britain.

New Religious Buildings

New Church Buildings in the Sixteenth, Seventeenth and Eighteenth Centuries

The period between the later sixteenth century and the early nineteenth century is generally considered to be one, at least in England and Wales, when there was no large-scale construction of new churches (Ryder 1993, 79). This view is an oversimplification, for while the Reformation does appear to mark the end of the late medieval church building boom, there were from the late seventeenth century regional and particularly urban-based significant episodes of church building. The sixteenth and seventeenth centuries, though a time of enormous doctrinal shifts in the Established Church, did not experience a major overhaul of the parochial system in England and Wales, nor was there a dramatic increase in population. Many churches had been newly built or recently rebuilt. Thus there was not a great need for the erection of new churches. New church building tended to be confined to chapels-of-ease, erected to fill in gaps in local coverage, or to landowner-sponsored proprietary churches (Gilchrist and Morris 1996, 118). As a consequence they were generally small. Architecturally they tended to be relatively simple representations of the late Perpendicular style. Specific local circumstances might lead to the building of a new parochial church, as at Taynton in Gloucestershire. There the medieval church was damaged during the Civil War and its replacement was erected on a new site. The original church was positioned within what had become a deserted small nucleated settlement, but the new church was more centrally located within the parish to facilitate better access for the dispersed population (Newman 1988). In Scotland parochial reorganisation in the seventeenth century led to the establishment of new churches (Dunbar 1996, 129). Despite a lack of variation in the liturgical requirements of the church in Scotland at this time, these churches varied greatly in plan form. The simple rectangular nave form based on medieval precedents was common, but some plans appear to have been derived from continental models, as for example the cruciform plan adopted at Lauder Church, Berwickshire, built in 1673–4 (Dunbar 1996, 129).

It was in London that the opportunity arose to build new churches in numbers and on a grand scale. The Great Fire in 1666 destroyed many medieval churches, and Sir Christopher Wren was given the brief to rebuild them. St Paul's Cathedral is of course his most famous monument, but he rebuilt many of the city's churches in the then fashionable Baroque Classical style. These churches were also designed to suit the prevailing Protestant liturgy, being built on an auditory plan (Gilchrist and Morris 1996, 118). Most were completely rebuilt, though at St Mary-at-Hill he retained the existing north and south walls with their sixteenth-century windows (PMA 1992, 97–8). The decrepit nature of many of the surviving medieval churches, and the influence of Wren's new church designs, led to further medieval church replacement in and around London in the late seventeenth and early eighteenth centuries.

The evidence for the refurbishment of existing churches indicates that the eighteenth century was not a period of great religious expression in architecture. Even so, population growth and a desire among the church endowers to build new edifices in a classical style led to pulses in new church building in some regions and in the expanding urban areas. There is evidence to suggest that the building boom in London, led by Wren and his disciple Nicholas Hawksmoor, encouraged provincial emulation. This process has been noted even as far from the capital culturally and geographically as the more Anglicised parts of north Wales (Parkinson 1996, 152). In Shropshire in the earlier eighteenth century the late seventeenth-century metropolitan churches appear to have been the inspiration behind the conversion of medieval churches to a classical style and the building of new churches. St Alkmund's medieval church in Whitchurch collapsed and was replaced in 1711–13 by a church that seems to owe its inspiration to Wren's St James's Piccadilly, built 1676–84 (Friedman 1996a, 86–8). In Leeds the interest of members of the local elite in the works of Wren undoubtedly facilitated the rise of classically inspired church building there. In the early eighteenth century members of Leeds Corporation's Pious Uses Committee visited Wren and his churches (Friedman 1996b, 5). As a consequence of their resultant enthusiasm, twenty-four new churches and chapels were built within 5 miles of the centre of Leeds during the eighteenth century, all in the classical style (Friedman 1996b, xv, 170). There seems to have been little interest in the maintenance of medieval buildings. Decaying, and presumably expensive to maintain, they did not fit with the image of a modern expanding community, whereas new classically conceived buildings did (Friedman 1996b, 10–11). In Shropshire the very neglect of much of the existing church fabric seems to have contributed to the need to build new churches. St Chad's medieval church in Shrewsbury was allowed to fall into ruin, and in 1789–92 it was replaced by a Georgian circular church at the forefront of contemporary classical design (Friedman 1996a, 93–4).

Much new church construction obviously relates to the expansion of particular settlements, and, where not too altered by later developments, their architectural style and layout are indicative of the prevailing building and liturgical fashions of the day. These churches may to some extent be a reflection of local religious zeal, but they are certainly a symbol of economic

St John the Evangelist Church, Blackburn, was built in 1789 in the classical style.

and corporate success. Indeed, it is through the endowment of churches that civic pride appears to be principally expressed in the eighteenth century (Friedman 1996b, 1). Liverpool owes its growth as a city primarily to the Atlantic trade of the eighteenth century, and in the nineteenth century the city's churches reflected this. Liverpool was not made a parish until 1699, at which time it had one medieval church; by 1824 it had two parish churches and a further sixteen non-parochial churches. Of these, nine were purpose-built in the eighteenth century, while a further two were built as dissenting chapels in the early eighteenth century but had been acquired by the Established Church by 1800. The remaining six churches were built in the early nineteenth century (Baines 1824, 166–9). In contrast, in neighbouring Southport all the churches apart from the medieval one date to the nineteenth century, when the town grew as a seaside resort (Anon 1922). Consequently Southport has a far more uniform Gothic appearance to its ecclesiastical architecture than does Liverpool.

Nonconformist Chapels and Meeting Houses

Churches independent of the Church of England were established in the sixteenth century, with Horningsham Chapel in Wiltshire, built for the Longleat Estate in 1566, claiming to be the oldest (Banton 1952), but it was not until the late seventeenth century that large numbers of non-Established-Church meeting houses were erected. Until the Restoration of Charles II the more radical strands of Protestantism were largely contained within the Established Church. Indeed, during the Interregnum Presbyterian ministers gained control of many parish churches and chapels-of-ease, and they and their sympathisers in the congregations only reluctantly ceded control of these buildings back to the Established Church in the later seventeenth century. In 1662 the Act of Uniformity was passed in England and Wales. This sought to ensure that all ministers conformed to the set patterns of worship prescribed in the Book of Common Prayer and administered rites in accordance with the Anglican Church. Those who refused to acknowledge this Act were *de facto* nonconformists and were to be ejected from their benefices. About two thousand ministers were deprived of their livings in this way. Some dissenting ministers and congregations managed to retain control of their churches for years, and in some cases, as at Toxteth Park in Liverpool, even had their occupancy recognised under the Act of Toleration in 1689, when their churches were licensed as nonconformist preaching houses (Halley 1869, 151).

For most the reaction against the Presbyterian tradition in the Church of England led in the later seventeenth century to dissenting communities abandoning existing churches and seeking

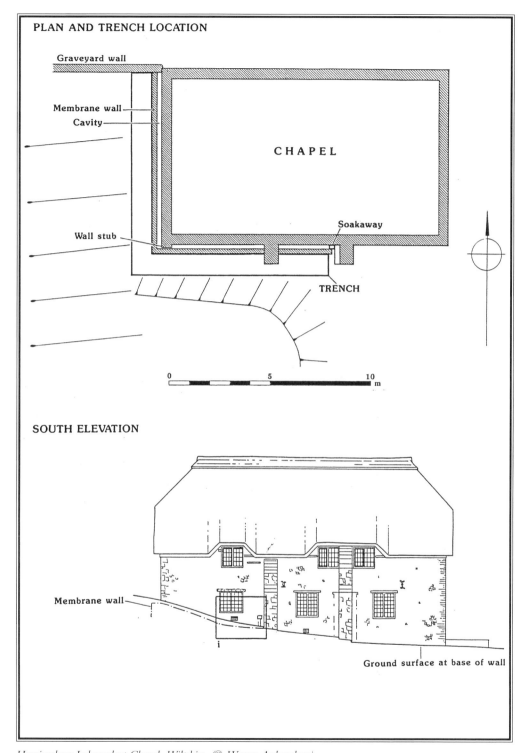

PLAN AND TRENCH LOCATION

Graveyard wall

Membrane wall

Cavity

CHAPEL

Soakaway

Wall stub

TRENCH

0   5   10
m

SOUTH ELEVATION

Membrane wall

Ground surface at base of wall

Horningsham Independent Chapel, Wiltshire. (© Wessex Archaeology)

Quaker Meeting House, Lancaster. This is typical of the plain vernacular style adopted by the Society of Friends during the eighteenth century.

alternative accommodation for their worship. In Scotland this did not happen, as the Presbyterians remained ascendant, and in 1690 the Revolution Settlement made the Presbyterians the Established Church in Scotland and left the Episcopalians as the dispossessed outsiders. Initially, in England and Wales, the dissenting congregations, under the threat of specific prosecution and general persecution, and without the benefit of legal recognition of their places of worship, met in private houses and barns. After the Act of Toleration, however, meeting houses were established in most places where dissenters had a significant presence.

The congregations of what became known, after the advent of Methodism, as the Old Dissent were divided between the Presbyterians, Independents, Baptists and the Society of Friends (Quakers). The early meeting houses of all these sects tended to be simple vernacular-style buildings, like the Congregational chapel at Horningsham, which is a simple stone and thatch building in the local tradition. Similarly the Presbyterian meeting house at St Nicholas Street, Ipswich, was built in the local style of rendered timber-framing, and was admired by Defoe as the then best example of a meeting house (Stell 1998, 44). There may be a number of reasons why this was the case. To some extent the choice of a humble architectural style may have been doctrinally inspired and reflected religious values of plainness and simplicity. In an early nineteenth-century history of Preston the eighteenth-century Friends' meeting house in Friargate was described thus: 'the building possesses all that plainness and simplicity which distinguishes that highly respected sect of Christian people' (Tulket 1821, 78). Even so, a study of the Friends' meeting houses in north-west England concluded that in plan they mirrored local domestic architecture (Butler 1978). This is for the most part also true of their external appearance. This may reflect a lack of money to hire specialist architects or a conscious desire not to (Friedman 1996b, 126). A domestic appearance could be seen as reflecting the humble nature of their worship and a wish not to make the building special. It may also indicate among some of the congregations a desire not to draw attention to themselves by making their buildings appear overtly religious. While the presence of a dissenting congregation could not be kept a secret, a retiring aspect may have been considered a way of reducing possible offence.

Until the passing of the Riot Act of 1715, when the wrecking of meeting houses was made a felony, dissenters' meeting houses were under a real threat from mob attack (Morris 1989, 397). Thus a plain vernacular style and a secluded situation, often down a back lane at the rear of established properties, were the norm for many early nonconformist meeting houses. Barton Street Presbyterian chapel in Gloucester was built in 1700 on a restricted city centre site, probably in the garden of a house which would have concealed it from the street (Stell 1998, 41). The location of the buildings, however, particularly in urban contexts, may have been more influenced by their insertion into crowded towns, reflecting a lack of funds to compete for the most desirable properties (Morris 1989, 397–8). Long after the acceptance of nonconformity, chapels were still built on back plots because of high land prices and crowding on street frontages.

The middle of the eighteenth century saw the rise of the New Dissent, with itinerant preachers, leading to the development of congregations of Wesleyans, Swedenborgians and Moravians among others. They were able to exploit deficiencies in the parochial system in areas such as the north-west of England, where huge parishes with only a sparse provision of chapels-of-ease left many communities without a convenient place of worship. The radical Protestant teachings of these sects also appealed to the inhabitants of areas such as the Pennine valleys, where manufacturing, particularly of textiles, was growing in the eighteenth century (Stell 1994, xxi). The cloth workers were operating in a new social context, largely free of the obligations and constraints which traditionally bound the agricultural labourer and small farmer. An independent religion not tied to the ambitions and outlook of the landed estate owners was likely to appeal.

Throughout the later eighteenth century the appeal of nonconformity grew, particularly in the newly industrialising regions where the Anglican Church was slow to respond to the development of new communities. In the later eighteenth century a new confidence was expressed in the architecture of the meeting houses and chapels. The vernacular style of most meeting houses was replaced by what Parkinson has termed artisan Georgian (1996, 153). The preaching house, with its pews and galleries focused on the pulpit rather than on the altar, was well suited to the adaptation of Georgian domestic architecture, a simple rectangle with symmetrical features. The principal external features that distinguished the late eighteenth- and early nineteenth-century dissenting chapels as specialised buildings were the use of round-arched windows and in many cases the presence of twin adjacent entrances to allow the separate entry of men and women. Such gender differentiation was often expressed in internal seating arrangements in many dissenting congregations. The standing evidence indicates that meeting houses built in towns were more impressive and ostentatious than those in the countryside. This may be a result of architectural competition among the various Christian denominations, or may simply reflect the greater wealth and prestige of many urban congregations. It affected even the Society of Friends. A stark contrast can be made between the meeting house in the small county town of Lancaster and those in the expanding cities of Leeds and Manchester. In Lancaster the building is plain, and though rebuilt it preserves the simplicity of the late seventeenth-century original and is similar to contemporary meeting houses in the surrounding countryside. In Leeds and Manchester by the 1830s the Society was meeting in grand, if austere, classical-style structures which had replaced earlier, more modest buildings (Friedman 1996a, 134; Stell 1994, 114).

Of all these early dissenting chapels, many of which have long been abandoned or superseded, only one has been extensively investigated by excavation. Goodshaw Baptist Chapel at Rawtenstall, Lancashire, was built in 1760 in the local vernacular style and is a simple rectangular, galleried preaching house. Survey and excavation revealed the many changes the chapel went through in its 103 years as a functioning place of worship, including evidence of long-abandoned external stairs giving access to the galleries (Brandon and Johnson 1986).

The Nineteenth-century Christian Building Boom

Eventually the Established Church in England and Wales recognised the threat posed by nonconformity. Areas as diverse as Cornwall and Leeds were considered by Anglican clergymen to have been lost to Methodism by the early nineteenth century (Lake *et al.* 1997, 26). In 1803 legislation was passed to promote the building of new churches. A government-appointed Commission for Building New Churches was established by statute in 1818. The churches erected as a consequence of this Act and the subsequent legislation of 1824 are often known as Commissioners' churches (Curl 1995, 21). New Anglican churches began to appear throughout

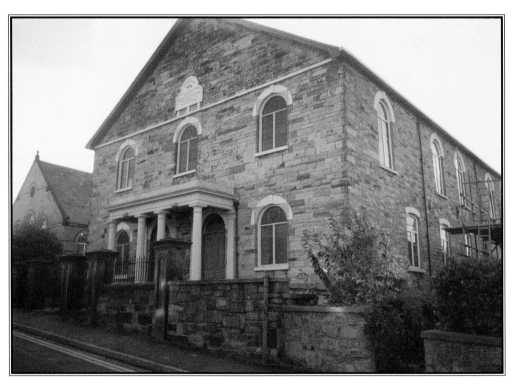

Rhosllanerchrugog Calvinist Methodist Chapel, near Wrexham, originally built in 1776 and rebuilt in 1837. It is typical of the classical architecture favoured by Methodist sects. (© R. Hammond)

England and Wales, particularly in the expanding urban areas. In the London borough of Kensington alone it was claimed that in the twenty years preceding 1872 forty-three new churches were built (Curl 1995, 50). The mill town of Burnley in Lancashire had one medieval Anglican church in 1800, but by 1900 it had a further eight Anglican churches (Pevsner 1969). By the mid-nineteenth century new Anglican churches were invariably built in the Perpendicular Gothic style, as this became the accepted architecture of the Anglican Church and reflected its move away from the pulpit-centred auditory church to a more medieval style of worship focused on the altar. In Scotland the Established Church, though less threatened by nonconformity, was equally faced with a need to provide for the rapidly growing population, particularly in urbanising industrial areas. New churches in the early nineteenth century were built in both neo-classical and Gothic styles, though by the middle of the century, under the influence of English architectural trends, Perpendicular Gothic was the most favoured style (Green 1996, 137–8).

In addition to an Anglican revival and the ongoing expansion of nonconformity, the Roman Catholic Church experienced its own revival after the Roman Catholic Relief Act of 1829. In 1793 Roman Catholics were allowed freedom of worship and began to build some new churches (a few were built earlier). Generally, as with nonconformist chapels, these buildings were relatively plain and discreet, presumably in an attempt not to attract attention or cause offence (Curl 1995, 19). After the 1829 Act, however, with professed Roman Catholics admitted into the political establishment, the brake on church building was removed, and by the end of the nineteenth century most towns had a Roman Catholic church. It was in the urban areas that the Church faced its greatest challenge, as from the mid-nineteenth century in towns such as Glasgow, Liverpool and Manchester they filled with Irish Catholic labourers (Green 1996, 142). Since Roman Catholicism wished to establish links with its usurped medieval heritage, and Augustus Pugin, the leading exponent of Gothic architecture, was a Catholic convert, it is unsurprising that Catholic church building was largely in the Gothic style and that some of the best examples of nineteenth-century Gothic belong to the Catholic Church. Later in the nineteenth century much of the inspiration for new churches was derived from continental medieval examples, again emphasising Catholicism's antiquity and also its European, as opposed to Anglocentric, roots (Curl 1995, 37–40).

In Scotland, perhaps because Presbyterianism was the dominant denomination, the primarily English- and Welsh-based nonconformist churches had only a limited impact (Green 1996, 142). However, Scotland had dissenters of its own, and in 1843 a large number of ministers of the Church of Scotland broke away to form the Free Church. Known as the Disruption, this secession resulted in large numbers of new churches, as each parish was split between the two kirks. The secessionist churches in general followed the prevailing style of the Church of Scotland, which by the mid-nineteenth century was Gothic. The doctrinal division between the two Churches does not seem to have developed a specific architectural expression, although the buildings of the Free Church tended to be relatively plain and unflamboyant versions of Gothic architecture, befitting their austere Presbyterianism (Green 1996, 138–9).

The division and definition of the nonconformist Churches into a wide variety of sects by the early nineteenth century are claimed to be linked to a preference for distinct denominational styles in architecture. It is likely that such distinctions were regional and always marked by exceptions. In Wales it is argued that Welsh dissenting congregations favoured classical architecture in the nineteenth century, whereas incoming English congregations favoured Gothic

(Parkinson 1996, 153); similarly Welsh-speakers appear to have been distinguished in Pembrokeshire cemeteries by the choice of classical-style gravestones (Mytum 1999). In Lancashire there is a clear preference among Methodists of all persuasions, throughout most of the nineteenth century, for classically inspired buildings. The same pattern has been noted in Cornwall (Lake *et al.* 1997, 29). In contrast other sects, such as the Unitarians, happily embraced Gothic, erecting chapels which looked outwardly identical to contemporary Anglican churches. Perhaps this indicates more concern among the Methodists (as among Welsh-speaking dissenters) for appearing distinct from the Anglican Church. Since Gothic was deliberately chosen by Anglicans as a style in order to establish a link with a medieval and Roman Catholic past, it should not be surprising that it was shunned as a style by many nonconformist congregations (Gilchrist and Morris 1996, 123).

What does seem strange is that so many dissenting chapels, especially in the mid- to late nineteenth century, were built in the Gothic style (Curl 1995, 112), particularly as nonconformist rites were not well suited to the long nave and chancel plan of most Gothic churches. A striking example is the huge Baptist church at Paisley, near Glasgow, built in 1894 (Green 1996, 142–3). The flamboyant Gothic of this primarily English- and Welsh-based sect starkly contrasts it with the plain and relatively simple buildings favoured by most Scottish churches. Clearly the choice of architectural style was not simply governed by doctrine and denominational affiliation, and other statements were being consciously made by congregations in their architectural preferences. Principal among these seem to have been ethnic/cultural allegiance, but status and acceptance were also important. By the mid-nineteenth century nonconformists occupied positions of economic power and political influence at national and local levels – they had become part of the establishment. Borrowing the architectural devices of the establishment's traditional church was a means of physically expressing their integration and 'coming of age'. Even for the classically rooted Methodists, however, increasing elaboration is noticeable in their buildings in the later nineteenth century, as they built in more ornate Italianate styles, and this too suggests that they were displaying their ability to compete architecturally with other denominations (Lake *et al.* 1997, 32).

Whatever architectural style was chosen, the most elaborate chapels were those of the wealthiest and largest congregations. The Wesleyans, among whose adherents many in the nineteenth century would have been considered middle class, built solid, restrained, Georgian-style preaching houses in the early nineteenth century, and later branched out into elaborate Italianate and Renaissance designs. In contrast, the Primitive Methodists, who had ceded from the Wesleyans and were a largely working-class sect lacking resources, had limited architectural ambitions.

Synagogues

Permission to meet to worship was granted to a small group of Jews in 1656, and from then on Jews benefited from the various legislation that permitted increasing religious toleration through to the mid-nineteenth century (de Lange 1984, 169). In the eighteenth century London had two synagogues, one each serving the Sephardic and Ashkenazim communities (Johnson 1991, 15) but by the mid-nineteenth century there were eight (Jamilly 1992, 22). By then a number of synagogues had been built throughout Britain, located primarily in the largest cities and ports, such as Bristol and Manchester, reflecting the Jews' largely urban distribution and trading connections. In London the spread of synagogues into the suburbs (de Lange 1984, 169), away from the East End, probably reflects the 'middle-class' character of many Jews who, along with their middle-class brethren of other faiths, moved away from the industrialised city centres. The rise in toleration and fortune is exhibited also in building styles, which as with dissenters had been simple and discreet initially, but later became statements with exuberant architecture and prominent locations (Jamilly 1992). The architectural style of synagogues by the mid-nineteenth century was eclectic, seemingly in a deliberate attempt to distinguish them from Christian buildings. The Princes Road synagogue in Toxteth, Liverpool, built in the 1870s, is a mix of Gothic, Byzantine and Moorish styles (Curl 1995, 113). The choice of Byzantine and Moorish styles may have been a conscious attempt by synagogue architects to link the British synagogues to a Jewish medieval and Mediterranean past.

POST-MEDIEVAL MILITARY BUILDINGS

The continued construction of military buildings in the post-medieval period is associated with a number of developments, including the establishment of standing military forces, the importance of the Navy, and the threat from (in the English government's perception) the Scottish Highlands. The technical evolution of post-medieval fortifications, however, is primarily related to the need to accommodate and counter artillery (Crossley 1990, 106). Unlike castles, which were often privately owned and multi-functional, post-medieval military buildings were usually state-sponsored and increasingly specialised, leading to a variety of different building types. The broad outlines of these developments, primarily based on upstanding and documentary evidence, has been given by Andrew Saunders in *Fortress Britain* (1989). The contribution of below-ground archaeology has been more limited (Coad 1997, 159), but it is growing.

Continental Influence on Early English Artillery Fort Design

The need to deal with the use and threat of artillery had exercised late medieval designers of fortifications, but it was not until the reign of Henry VIII (1509–47) that new forts, purposely designed to cope with artillery, began to appear. In 1539 a programme of coastal defence was instigated along the south coast. The forts thus built were based on German designs with round bastions in a concentric plan. This form was already considered obsolete on the continent (Crossley 1990, 107–8), where it had been replaced by the *trace italienne* defensive system. *Trace italienne* fortifications were defensive systems utilising angular bastions with dependent, usually earthwork, enclosing fortifications, providing defence in depth and flanking fire (Saunders 1989, 53–5). Earthwork defences were particularly important as they could absorb the impact of artillery better than walls, though they could prove to be problematic. At the English fort of Balgillo in Scotland, which fell to Scottish forces in 1550, the earth ramparts kept sliding into the ditches (Caldwell and Ewart 1997, 109). The Henrician coastal forts have been criticised for being backward, but excavations at Camber Castle in Sussex have suggested that this might not be the case. Italian influence on the fortifications has been indicated by evidence of rectangular forward works for each bastion and a further octagonal-plan retaining wall for a rampart outside the upstanding curtain wall (Crossley 1990, 108; Coad 1997, 161–2).

The influence of continental developments in fort design can be seen in Scotland too. At Eyemouth, Berwickshire, the English established a *trace italienne* fort in 1547. Abandoned in

1550, it was reoccupied by French forces between 1557 and 1559 (Caldwell and Ewart 1997, 61). Excavations indicated that the principles of the *trace italienne* system were not well employed, and the English fort in general was not well designed. The slighted English defences were reused by the French, who substantially strengthened the overall defensive capacity of the site (Caldwell and Ewart 1997, 108–12). The overall impression gained from the two campaigns of fortification is that the English were constructing a site to function for only a few years, but the French were building in a more permanent fashion (Caldwell and Ewart 1997, 112).

English Military Buildings and the Navy

As an island nation the English perceived hostile threats as likely to be aimed primarily at their eastern and southern coasts. The southern and south-eastern coasts were regarded as particularly vulnerable as they were the nearest to England's most likely enemies, briefly the Spanish, but in the longer term the French and the Dutch, its greatest commercial and imperial rivals. Fort building continued through the sixteenth century, particularly around the new dockyard towns (Coad 1997, 162), but it was not until the later seventeenth century that a building campaign similar to Henry VIII's was undertaken. The Dutch raid on the Medway in 1667 underlined England's weaknesses in relation to coastal defence (Smith 1993, 56). Following the raid, improvements were made to the defences of the Medway and at Portsmouth and Plymouth (Saunders 1989, 83). New forts were built to defend Chatham, one at Cockham Wood and the other at Gillingham (Smith 1993, 57). Cockham Wood was a cannon battery, arranged in two tiers, with corner bastions at the waterside and at the gatehouse/redoubt on the landward side. The battery was designed not simply to be functional but to impress as well, and thus perhaps to reassure. The redoubt was built in a highly decorated, ornate style, clearly intended for display (Smith 1993, 64). This may also account for the blocks of Purbeck marble found on the adjacent beach and seemingly derived from the former battery, although its principal building component was brick (Smith 1993, 74). Other responses to the Dutch raid included the erection in 1667 of ill-armed blockhouses at Tilbury and Gravesend on the Thames (V.T.H. Smith 1994).

Further attention was paid to England's south coast defences in the later eighteenth and early nineteenth centuries when it was once again the French who were the enemy. Following an invasion scare in 1778 the Thames and Medway were once more the focus of attention. A new gun battery, New Tavern Fort, was built on a zigzag plan in the early 1780s to provide flanking cover for the Gravesend blockhouse (Smith 1996, 285). Possibly erected on the site of the 1667 Gravesend blockhouse (V.T.H. Smith 1994, 50), it was initially built with its rear open to the land, but after complaints of trespass and cattle entry a wall was added to the rear in 1795, on the basis of documentary evidence and a dated brick (Smith 1996, 288). The wall included musket loops, but as it was only 0.5m thick it was clearly never intended as anything other than a security barrier and was of no real defensive value (Smith 1996, 288). The Napoleonic period saw the adoption of gun batteries as the principal means of deterring raids on harbours, although they were not intended to defend the coast against invasion. In the event of an invasion, the local populace was expected to engage in a 'scorched earth' policy, including the flooding of Romney Marshes (Saunders 1989, 141). There, however, this radical policy was abandoned in favour of a defensive line intended to contain an invading force within the marsh. Consequently between 1804 and 1809 the Royal Military Canal was built from Seabrook to the River Rother, to provide a defensive barrier and communications link in case of a French invasion (Greatorex 1995).

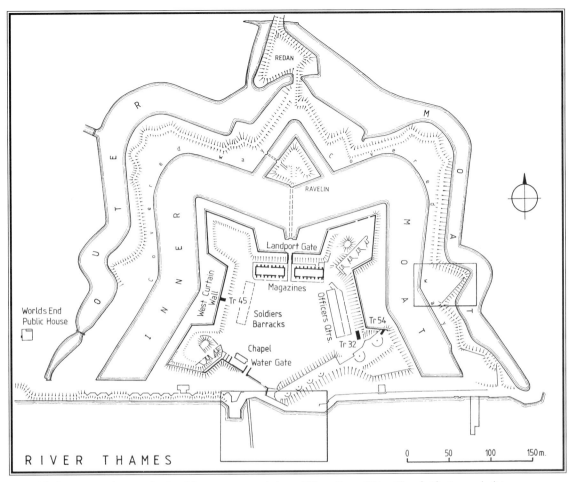

The late seventeenth-century bastioned fort on a pentagonal plan at Tilbury, Essex. This artillery fortification was built in response to the Dutch raid of 1677. (© Society for Post-Medieval Archaeology)

The importance of defending the naval dockyards continued to be uppermost in military thinking during the French Wars, emphasising Britain's dependence on naval power. At Plymouth various defensive improvements were made, including the erection in the 1780s of redoubts on Maker Heights, in order to deny an enemy the opportunity to use this higher ground as a base for bombarding the naval installations (Evans 1999). These defences, like others erected in the Napoleonic Wars, continued to be the basis of Britain's fortification strategy until the mid/late nineteenth century, when improvements in artillery rendered most of them redundant (Evans 1999, 65). Shell-fire, better-armed and protected ships, rifled guns, the development of concrete and submarine mines all influenced the way in which coastal defences were perceived in the later nineteenth century. As a consequence a Royal Commission was established to review Britain's defences, and its recommendations, delivered in 1859, influenced the country's fortifications policy for the remainder of the nineteenth century (Saunders 1989, 171–90). In the later nineteenth and early twentieth centuries, as the threat of hostilities was perceived as shifting from France to Germany, Britain and the other Great Powers embarked on an unprecedented period of fortification construction. In Britain efforts were concentrated on protecting its ports and command of coastal seaways rather than on frontier lines; the remains of this activity are abundant but are only now beginning to attract serious archaeological attention.

From the late seventeenth century military building works did not simply consist of forts, blockhouses and redoubts. On the site of the relinquished Greenwich Palace, a royal naval hospital was established. Like the defences of the dockyard towns, this is also indicative of the importance of the Navy in the late seventeenth century. Begun in 1696, the hospital evolved as four blocks of roughly equal size (Bold 1999, 33), with much of the initial design work being undertaken by the foremost architects of the day, Christopher Wren and Nicholas Hawksmoor (Bold 1999, 34–5). Although specifically intended to accommodate the Navy's invalids, the hospital buildings were clearly also designed to impress, and appear to represent an attempt by the Crown to rival the magnificence of royal endowments elsewhere in Europe.

Military Works in Scotland

Although the accession of James VI of Scotland to the English Crown in 1603 put an end to centuries of national rivalry between the two countries, the political difficulties of the Stuarts ensured that military conflict in Scotland continued. While the First English Civil War had little impact on Scotland, the execution of their king by the English Parliament led to the Scots proclaiming his heir, precipitating open conflict with the English Commonwealth in 1650–1. The defeat of Charles II's royalist, and primarily Scottish, forces in the Second Civil War was a harbinger of things to come, both of conflicts between a pro-Stuart Scotland and an anti-Stuart England, and of the savage nature of the pacification and military occupation of Scotland. Oliver Cromwell instituted a programme of fortress/citadel building, establishing five permanent fortresses at Ayr, Leith, Perth, Inverlochy and Inverness, and twenty less permanent supporting forts (Saunders 1989, 104). This was the first such programme of state-funded conquest fortifications, designed for internal suppression, since the Edwardian castles in Wales in the late thirteenth century. As in Wales, these Scottish fortresses were a symbol of English military dominance. The forts were designed to the best contemporary principles of European military fortifications, with projecting flanking angle bastions in a system of in-depth defence.

The Restoration of Charles II to the English throne represented a victory for Scottish interests, but the Stuarts' dynastic problems continued, and the difficulties caused by the later accession of Charles's Catholic-sympathising brother led to renewed conflict. In 1688 James II of England and VII of Scotland was deposed by both Scottish and English Parliaments and the crowns offered to William and Mary of Orange. Unfortunately, not only was there a residual loyalty in Scotland to a Scottish dynasty but many of the Highland clans were still Catholic or Episcopalian and favoured James for his religious views. They were also opposed to the Presbyterianism of the Scottish Established Church and of the dominant Highland clan, the Campbells. Consequently, a Highland schism developed into the Jacobite cause and became a source of national insecurity for both Scotland and England. The ensuing conflict between the Jacobites and the Williamites, with the latter the victors, led to renewed efforts to garrison the Highlands. A new fortress, Fort William, was built at Inverlochy, revamping the earlier Cromwellian defences (Tabraham and Grove 1995, 40). The symbology of this act increased through the garrison's participation in the massacre at Glencoe, becoming seared in Highland folk memory (Tabraham and Grove 1995, 41–2).

The Treaty of Union of 1707 extinguished the existence of Scotland and England as national political entities. That and the final end of the Stuart royal dynasty with the death of Queen Anne and the offering of the throne of the combined kingdoms to George Ludwig, Elector of Hanover, further estranged Highland society from the Anglicised Scottish Lowlands and England. While opposition to the House of Hanover and support of the Jacobite cause were not exclusive to Scotland, it was there, in the Highlands in particular, that it was mixed with a fear of change to a traditional society and an antipathy towards 'foreign' influence. Consequently the earlier eighteenth century witnessed a series of Jacobite uprisings, supported to varying degrees by one or more continental powers, culminating in the defeat of the Highland forces of Prince Charles Edward Stuart at Culloden in 1746.

In order to control the Highlands the Hanoverian army had to have a widespread presence, therefore they needed troops to be stationed in outposts away from the fortresses. The outposts were part barracks, part defensible strongholds, and usually consisted of previously existing fortified houses, modified to be suitable for an army garrison. A typical example is Corgarff Castle in Aberdeenshire, which consists of a modified sixteenth-century tower-house surrounded by a star-shaped wall (Tabraham and Grove 1995, 101–2). New fortresses were also built, such as Fort Augustus. Erected between 1729 and 1742 (Tabraham and Grove 1995, 78–9), it consisted of four projecting corner angle bastions connected by curtain walls and encompassing various buildings including barrack blocks. Indeed, the need to house a standing army in circumstances that catered for their security was one of the major developments of early eighteenth-century military architecture.

Barracks

The development of a standing army from the later seventeenth century led to the erection of barracks. Initially troops were billeted in local settlements. However, the concept of lodging troops within forts and in other military buildings was well established by the Civil War, but the structures were not usually designed as living accommodation or for permanent occupancy (Saunders 1989, 5–7). In the siege of Edinburgh Castle in 1689 the Jacobite garrison took refuge from the artillery of the forces of William of Orange in vaults beneath the Half-Moon Battery. In 1989 the skeletons of fifteen young men, likely to date to this period, were found in a temporary cemetery within the Inner Bailey; they were probably the victims of the unhealthy and insanitary conditions experienced during the siege (Tabraham and Grove 1995, 37–9). In Scotland the need to house troops among a hostile population, as in the Highlands, led to a requirement for secure purpose-built accommodation such as was constructed at Fort William in 1710 (Tabraham and Grove 1995, 51). Defensible barrack blocks were erected in the Highlands at Bernera, Kilwhimin, Inversnaid and Ruthven following the 1715 rising (Saunders 1989, 109). They were built to control the population and to provide secure bases for the army. They were instruments of suppression and symbols of Scotland's loss of independence.

Purpose-built barracks first appear in the late seventeenth century in London and at the key naval stations at Tilbury, Portsmouth and Plymouth (Saunders 1998, 8–9), with the earliest surviving example being the Foot Guards' barracks at Hampton Court, built in 1689 (Saunders 1998, 13). Their basic design was established then and remained fairly consistent for two centuries as large, rectangular, strongly built blocks. These barracks were established where security needs required an available garrison, but elsewhere troops continued to be billeted on

Berwick-upon-Tweed army barracks, originally built in the eighteenth century to serve the needs of both the garrison and the town.

the local populace. This system was unpopular. At Berwick-upon-Tweed the continuous imposition of troops on the town led to ceaseless complaints against billeting. Lacking suitable military buildings for use as lodgings, the soldiers were housed in taverns and alehouses, hardly a situation conducive to good military discipline (Grove 1999, 5). Indiscipline, drunkenness and the unpopularity of billeting led to the first purpose-built accommodation for troops at Berwick-upon-Tweed in 1719 (Reed 1983, 199). Barrack blocks like these provided conditions that today would be considered cramped and relatively insanitary, though similar to those experienced by modern-day inmates of some of Her Majesty's prisons. Even so, in contemporary terms the accommodation was adequate. Being housed in blocks, with limited points of access and egress, ensured that soldiers could be easily controlled.

By the 1790s the perceived threat of the crowd and revolutionary sedition encouraged the building of strategic barracks in England in the industrial towns such as Manchester, Nottingham and Sheffield (Douet 1998, 43). Like the Highland barracks, these were also instruments of suppression. Some, like Fulwood in Preston, Lancashire, became centres of military administration as the army became increasingly organised on a local basis, with brigades raised within regional territories. Throughout the nineteenth century barracks proliferated in response to Britain's imperial military needs, and by the end of that century most larger towns had their own local barracks (Douet 1998, 167–9).

CHAPTER THREE

HOUSE AND HOME

The most common form of building type in the archaeological record is the house, the most important and essential material structure in human life. It served as a container for many of the other cultural items owned by its inhabitants, it provided shelter and security and its size, layout and appearance could indicate status and wealth. It should not surprise then that the archaeological study of houses is key to the study of material culture. Since Johnson's seminal work on the housing of western Suffolk, the wider potential of the meanings of domestic architecture has been more fully realised by archaeologists. Houses are seen not only as representing economic and technological changes in society but also as containing cultural and social messages as well. They are the physical expressions of successive generations of householders, representing their values, beliefs and aspirations (Johnson 1993a, 1–3).

MEDIEVAL RESIDENTIAL BUILDINGS

Medieval domestic buildings, albeit frequently adapted and updated, would have dominated the appearance of many towns until the later seventeenth century. In some rural areas too, elite houses and some domiciles of lesser status would also have been relatively prolific.

Palaces

England in particular abounded with great houses by the mid-sixteenth century, many of them built in the previous hundred years. The early sixteenth century was a particularly busy time for the erection of new polite houses or the rebuilding of existing ones (Johnson 1992, 46). In part this was a response to a desire to display conspicuous wealth within a competitive geopolitical environment, but it was also an attempt to incorporate new tastes in comfort and concepts of private and public space (Crossley 1990, 48). This process is exemplified in the palaces of Henry VIII. With an established and static court, his palaces were all close to London, the more provincial rural palaces being allowed to decay. The term 'palaces' is here used in the sense of a royal residence, the nature of which could vary considerably, and is not applied in the strict sense in which it was used in the fifteenth and sixteenth centuries (Thurley 1997, 93–4). Under Henry VIII new palaces were built or existing buildings acquired and refurbished as at Nonsuch, Whitehall, Bridewell and New Hall. These new structures joined older medieval buildings like Clarendon, Woodstock and Westminster.

Westminster Palace, like other medieval palaces such as Greenwich, had been built together with a major church to service the spiritual needs of the royal family, in this case Westminster Abbey. The abbot was the largest landowner in Westminster, and the dominant structure of the abbey in relation to the palace encapsulates the medieval view of the relationship between temporal lords and God. Henry VIII's building of Whitehall Palace and his suppression of the monasteries changed this view (Thurley 1997), physically expressing the radical alteration in his concept of kingship in comparison to his predecessors. Though only a few hundred metres from Westminster Palace, Whitehall became the centre of a newly enriched royal estate. It was indicative of the secularisation of Westminster and led to the physical separation of the executive from the administrative arm of government. The space previously required for the royal domicile became occupied by Parliament and a variety of royal courts, the government departments of their day (Thurley 1997, 96–7). Since Westminster Palace had always been a seat of monarchical government as well as a residence, it is unsurprising that once its residential function lapsed it continued in its role as a centre of government.

The Scottish Crown, much poorer than its English counterpart, could not afford the lavish expenditure on new palaces. The principal palace continued to be Holyroodhouse in Edinburgh, which was, however, rebuilt from 1503 under the direction of James IV. Following the Union of the Crowns in 1603, the Stuart dynasty abandoned direct rule in Scotland for rule from the comfort of south-east England and its plethora of late medieval royal residences. Consequently the interest in the maintenance of Scottish royal residences waned. Holyroodhouse remained the principal residence of the monarchy when in Scotland, and it was rebuilt in 1671–8, but this was only in response to the burning down of James IV's palace.

Henry VIII's royal residences may have been more of a burden than a boon to his descendants. The Crown had many more palaces than it needed or probably could afford. As early as the reign of Edward VI Bridewell, built between 1515 and 1523, was converted into a prison. Excavations have demonstrated that though it was damaged in the Great Fire of 1666, Bridewell remained substantially intact until demolition in 1803 (James 1990, 156; Schofield 1984, 134–6). Elizabeth I is noted for not having built a major palace or substantially rebuilt an existing one, probably because there was no need for her to do so. She had an abundance of buildings, and her monarchy was sufficiently similar to her father's in protocols and functions not to require the radical remodelling of the spaces within which it operated (Thurley 1993). This may have been a deliberate policy, intended to give Elizabeth greater credibility within a patriarchal society by emphasising continuity and directly associating her own identity with that of her father (Johnson 1999a, 84).

In the Stuart period and the eighteenth and nineteenth centuries some new royal residences were built, but most of the older ones had decayed or been demolished. Unlike Westminster, most medieval royal palaces were largely residences, and thus there was less reason to retain them. A few, like Greenwich, were adapted, being substantially rebuilt in the seventeenth and eighteenth centuries (Bold 1999). Some were sold, while others found new uses, if only temporarily, for example Nonsuch was occupied by the Admiralty in the late seventeenth century. Still others, like Clarendon, a long way from London, were allowed to decay (James 1988, 10). Similar fates of abandonment and ruination befell many of the other palaces. Elsyngs was demolished in 1608, while Eltham gradually decayed in the seventeenth century, as did the late medieval manor house of Otford (sold to Sir Robert Sidney in 1601) and Grafton, one of the few royal residences outside the home counties; Nonsuch had been demolished by the end of the seventeenth century, Oatlands by 1650 (Crossley 1990, 49–52; Colvin 1982). In some cases the sites were redeveloped, such as the Tudor and Jacobean Somerset House. Here excavations in 1999 showed that far more of the palace survived the redevelopment of the 1770s, when Somerset House was remodelled as Georgian-style government offices, than was previously thought.

The Great Houses

The medieval great houses of the nobility and wealthier gentry survive today in considerable numbers, though sometimes only as ruins or as archaic elements within buildings of a superficially later appearance. Their greater suitability to the needs of aristocratic life in the post-medieval period, in comparison to castles, may have contributed to their survivability. There are around seven hundred surviving medieval great houses today, of which most are still roofed and many inhabited; in contrast there are around five hundred surviving castles, of which the majority are ruinous (A. Emery 2000, 3). The distinction between a castle intended primarily for a military function and a great house intended primarily as a residence is not always clear; in the north of England, for example, most great houses can be described as fortified (Emery 1996, 3). Many were developed from earlier defensive sites, as at Alnwick and Bamburgh in Northumberland, or the courtyard houses of Old Beaupre and Oxwich castles in south Wales. During the fifteenth century tower-houses appeared throughout Britain; primarily residential, they were nevertheless defensible (A. Emery 2000). In northern England, even more so in Scotland, and to a lesser extent in Wales, the continuing need for a defensible habitation was recognised into the early sixteenth century. Whether to meet a perceived threat or as a conscious design allusion to a feudal, military inheritance, the influence of medieval fortifications on elite house design is evident in the tower-houses and fortified halls of northern Britain in particular, and in the courtyard houses of the south.

Courtyard houses like Knebworth House in Hertfordshire, dating to the early sixteenth century, were built with gatehouses lacking ornamentation to give the impression of a defensive structure (Smith 1992, 46). The principal entrance to the hall was on the opposite side of the courtyard, and facing into it. Thus such houses were inward-looking, with the main display elements facing into the courtyard (Johnson 1996, 120). Knebworth House was rebuilt in the later sixteenth century, but its layout and inward-looking characteristics were retained (Smith 1992, 47). These late medieval great houses can be considered to be conservative in style, utilising layouts and architectural devices that had been in use since the fourteenth century, but, as Johnson has recently argued, in the early sixteenth century they were the focus of 'new scales of conspicuous consumption' (Johnson 1996, 133).

The earlier sixteenth century witnessed a building boom among the elite (Howard 1997). In Suffolk twenty-three of the twenty-six surviving elite houses dating to 1400–1700 were built or remodelled in the early sixteenth century (Johnson 1992, 46). At Acton Court, Gloucestershire, survey and excavation has revealed a medieval residential complex, which was redesigned into a courtyard-style house in the mid-sixteenth century. Much of the medieval fabric, though not all the medieval architectural elements, was removed in a later sixteenth-century remodelling (PMA 1986, 346–7). The importance of wealth display in the geopolitics of the Tudor court was realised not only in the palaces of the monarch but also in the elite houses of the courtiers. Machicolations and gatehouses in particular were added to existing houses. The new gatehouses and other surfaces were often decorated with heraldic devices (Johnson 1992; Johnson 1996, 133–4). The messages communicated by the architecture of the elite houses seem to relate to traditional social values, or, as Johnson put it, themes of hospitality, deference and community (Johnson 1996, 134). Associations were consciously made with a medieval martial past, though within the context of buildings clearly lacking in contemporary military value. These links with the medieval roles of the elite must reflect the desires of the house owners, many of whom in the early sixteenth century were newly elevated to the elite, to emphasise continuity and tradition. The decline of the importance of the values expressed in earlier sixteenth-century architecture led to the decline of the houses themselves. Though many were adapted and modernised, others were abandoned in favour of new, more fashionable houses, whose architecture conveyed more up-to-date messages. Many originally medieval elite houses were downgraded in status to farmhouses, as at Acton Court and Oxwich Castle (PMA 1986; Blockley 1997).

In the far north of England medieval elite residences such as the castles of Alnwick, Chillingham and Raby, or the Bishop of Durham's Bishop Auckland Palace (Emery 1996), remained the principal seats of the local aristocracy throughout the post-medieval period. While it should be remembered, as Cooper has recently emphasised, that 'at any given time few houses are modern, and most people make do with at best the piecemeal adaptation of the houses of their ancestors' (1999, 4), for the elite their homes were expressions of their dominance and their relationship with society. Thus the retention of medieval residences may reflect the zenith in the fortunes of most of the northern English aristocracy. The Dacres, Nevilles and Percys were at their height of power and fortune in the fourteenth and earlier fifteenth centuries, when their homes would have been among the foremost in Britain. Though these families survived the Wars of the Roses, warfare and economic decline took their toll during the fifteenth century (Emery 1996, 19). Tudor antipathy towards powerful nobles and the failure of the Northern Rebellion in 1569 further reduced their circumstances. Faced with political competition from newly powerful families in the post-medieval period, they may have viewed their medieval houses as links to a more glorious past. Although perhaps lacking the motivation and resources to replace these medieval great houses with more up-to-date but equally prestigious buildings, over time internal layouts and décor were modernised, but the basic medieval structure, architecture and symbolism of these houses remain.

At the level of the manorial house, medieval buildings survived and were adapted in the post-medieval period. In the northern counties of England and in Scotland tower-houses and fortified halls – usually with an attached tower and barmkin (an enclosing courtyard wall) – not only survived into the sixteenth century but were still being built, particularly in the Scottish lowlands. There has been much discussion over the nature and definition of these structures (Ramm *et al.* 1970; Dixon 1979, 240), though little of it would have been understood by contemporaries. To them they were simply the fortified residences of local lords which varied in design and scale but all shared the same purpose: to act as defensible residences. Some, like Bonshaw Tower in Kirtleside, Dumfries, were equipped with gun loops, though whether these were of more than symbolic/deterrent value is questionable (Maxwell-Irving 1994, 55). The necessity for these structures was peculiar to border society, where a lack of direct royal control, centuries of national warfare, isolated communities and local family rivalries resulted in continuous family feuding and cattle raiding (reiving). This ended following the accession of James VI of Scotland and the deportation of the principal malcontents (Dixon 1979, 250). The building of such structures ceased in the seventeenth century even in Scotland, though many continued in occupation. Drumcoltran Tower in Dumfries, built in the later sixteenth century, was remodelled in the eighteenth century before being replaced as a residence by a later eighteenth-century farmhouse built adjacent to it (Stell 1996, 112).

Further south, in Westmorland and north Lancashire, fortified manorial residences had ceased to be built by the sixteenth century. Although designed as defensible structures, presumably in response to fears of Scottish raids, these buildings were clearly elite residential structures incorporating multiple rooms on more than one storey, and in many instances boasted enclosed fireplaces with chimneys. Their history and survival varies from manor to manor, as can be demonstrated by the history of a group of neighbouring structures in Westmorland. Sizergh Castle, the home of the Strickland family from the fourteenth to the twentieth century, is a mansion, the core of which is a fourteenth-century tower and hall. The hall was remodelled in the later sixteenth century and then refenestrated and battlemented (to match the tower) in the eighteenth century. Nearby Levens Hall, the home of the Stricklands' rivals, the Redmaynes, appears to have been a late

Late fifteenth-century tower house at Orchardton, Kirkcudbrightshire. This had an unusual rounded tower and was occupied throughout the sixteenth century.

medieval fortified manor house. It was remodelled in the late Elizabethan period and most of the medieval fabric was removed. The presumed earlier tower seems to have influenced the Elizabethan building, however, which included a new four-storey tower, purely as an architectural affectation (Emery 1996, 248–9). To the south of Levens is Heversham, which survives as a fifteenth-century hall, remodelled in the sixteenth, with an adjacent tower allowed to become ruinous (Emery 1996, 211). Nearby Beetham Hall is a fourteenth-century hall with

Levens Hall, Westmorland. This minor country house developed in the sixteenth century around a medieval fortified manor house.

attached tower. The building complex was surrounded by a defensive wall incorporating arrow loops and a defended gateway. The hall ceased to be the main residence in 1693, when a new farmhouse was built and the hall became downgraded for use as a barn (Emery 1996, 189–90). Elsewhere, these buildings continued as elite residences forming the basis for Gothic Revival-style structures. This is the case at Hellifield Peel in Yorkshire, where the medieval tower-house forms the core of an eighteenth-century Gothic mansion (Ryder and Birch 1983).

Lesser Medieval Domestic Buildings

Below the level of the great house lay a variety of buildings serving as domiciles in medieval Britain. These varied both in regional distribution and social attribution, but in general they can all be considered to follow a single basic plan. They were rectangular, and the principal or only room (the hall) was open to the roof. In the past, surviving examples of medieval buildings were considered to be rare and most were thought to have been replaced by more durable buildings during the post-medieval period. This stance is no longer valid. Medieval domestic buildings have been shown to be far more durable than previously thought, and it is clear that until at least the later seventeenth century many rural houses, though perhaps substantially modified, were likely to have been of medieval origin. Modifications included the flooring over of open halls and the addition of chimneys. Usually chimneys were added to the gables, but in some areas, such as the Welsh borders, they were built internally, perhaps because it was considered easier to do so in a timber-framed house (Wiliam 1978, 88).

The challenge to the concept of the medieval peasant house as an impermanent hovel has been recently neatly summarised by Jane Grenville (1997, 151–6). Excavations at West Whelpington, Northumberland, in the 1970s indicated that peasant houses built from the thirteenth century in clay-bedded stone would have been capable of standing for centuries (Wrathmell 1984, 30). That these buildings did not last into the post-medieval period was not a result of their lack of durability but of Scottish devastation and consequent temporary settlement abandonment. Reoccupation of the settlement led to construction of similar buildings in the fifteenth century which were replaced in the mid-seventeenth century, not because of poor building techniques but to accommodate new housing requirements. In one case a building was modified to meet the new needs (Wrathmell 1984, 30; Jarrett and Wrathmell 1977). Subsequent work on the excavated evidence from Wharram Percy in Yorkshire (Wrathmell 1989) and documentary analysis of late medieval buildings throughout the north-east of England demonstrated the durability of these structures (Harrison and Hutton 1984).

Work in south Wales has yielded similar results to those from the north-east of England. Excavations at the site of a farmhouse demolished in the mid-nineteenth century at Cwmcidy near Barry revealed that the building had originated in the late thirteenth to early fourteenth century as a structure built of clay-bedded stone (Griffiths and Thomas 1984). Original internal dimensions of approximately 12.7m × 5m accord well with contemporary peasant houses from nearby deserted settlements, though the excavators suggested that the Cwmcidy house may have been initially subdivided by means of archaeologically unidentifiable partitions, creating a through-passage between the opposed doorways (Griffiths and Thomas 1984, 23). In the late sixteenth or early seventeenth century a thick cross-wall containing a fireplace was inserted, dividing the ground space into two equal cells. There was some evidence for a newel stair integral to the construction of the fireplace, which indicates that ground space subdivision was

Post-medieval wattle partition at Old Abbey Farm, near Warrington. (© Lancaster University Archaeological Unit)

accompanied by conversion of the house into a two-storey dwelling (Griffiths and Thomas 1984, 20–1). Further minor alterations and modifications appear to have been undertaken in the course of the eighteenth century, but the building was never 'Georgianised' or brought up to the standard of a contemporary newly built farm.

Late medieval peasant structures at deserted settlements in south Wales such as Cosmeston have been shown by excavation and experimental reconstruction to have been similarly well built and durable (Newman 1987). Only the failure of the settlements within which they existed led to their abandonment and thus the potential for their archaeological recovery. Elsewhere, in more successful settlements, such buildings would have continued and been adapted. This very adaptation and survivability may make them difficult to recognise without detailed fabric analysis – a factor commented upon at Cwmcidy – raising questions about the precise dating of the origin of many surviving, ostensibly early post-medieval, houses in the Vale of Glamorgan (Griffiths and Thomas 1984, 25–8).

The continuation and adaptation of medieval non-elite domestic buildings is an archaeologically demonstrable phenomenon in areas with an early stone building tradition, but it was also a feature of buildings in areas of traditional timber building. As well as the dated (or datable) extant buildings, such as Wealden houses in south-east England or the later cruck-built halls of the Welsh borders, archaeological investigations of superficially much later buildings can reveal medieval origins. At Risley, near Warrington, fabric analysis of a standing structure, documentary research and excavation following demolition have revealed a complex building history. The misleadingly named Old Abbey Farm was not a former monastic property but the moated demesne farm of the sub-manor of Pesfurlong. Originally built in the thirteenth century as an aisled hall, a two-storey cross-wing was added in the mid-sixteenth century. The medieval house had timber-framed walls, but from the early seventeenth century these were gradually replaced by brick, in at least four distinct phases over a period of a little more than a century. The progressive nature of the renovation and some of the structural details suggest that some of the joints of the frame were failing and that the timber-frame was therefore replaced out of necessity rather than designed intent. Here then may be an example of structural instability prompting renovation, but even so the medieval building was repaired rather than replaced. A chimney was also inserted in the seventeenth century, but it was not until the early eighteenth century that the open hall was floored over. Further modifications took place during the eighteenth and nineteenth centuries, including the addition of a rear outshut and the rebuilding of the north wing to accommodate stock (Heawood forthcoming a).

Old Abbey Farm, Risley, is of particular interest as its building history seems to closely mirror the fluctuating documented fortunes of its owners and inhabitants. Initially a small manorial site, the house at Old Abbey Farm was within the local vernacular tradition, though it was probably of a better quality than could be afforded by all but the wealthiest peasant. By the mid-sixteenth century the farm seems to have lost its manorial status, and by the end of the sixteenth century it was let to tenants. Nevertheless, it was still a superior quality dwelling in comparison to those inhabited by the majority of the populace in contemporary north-west England. By the mid-seventeenth century it would certainly have been considered archaic and uncomfortable by anyone with the slightest pretensions, and in the eighteenth and nineteenth centuries it was a typical dwelling of a middling tenant-farmer. Towards the end of the nineteenth century, in the midst of agricultural depression, the farmhouse seems to have been teetering on the threshold of a rural slum. The simultaneous decline in status of the inhabitants and the social context of the building perhaps explains the observable piecemeal nature of the renovations and improvements during the post-medieval period, and ironically may in part be responsible for the survival of the evidence for the medieval origins of the building (Heawood forthcoming a).

It is quite clear that structural instability does not seem to have been the primary reason for the apparent lack of medieval, non-elite, rural domestic buildings surviving today. Many may be unrecognisable without detailed analysis, and recent work has indicated that where research is undertaken more medieval low-status dwellings survive than is appreciated (Grenville 1997, 156). Even so, there would have been many more surviving in the early seventeenth century than there are today. Their abandonment and/or replacement by more recent buildings was a result of regionally distinctive social factors; changing agricultural conditions were proposed at West Whelpington and changing use of space is offered as an explanation for the poor survival of pre-Black Death houses in Kent (Wrathmell 1984; Pearson 1994). Currie's (1988) modelling of attrition rates similarly proposes social factors as the primary reason behind poor survival rates rather than any flimsiness of construction, though he also highlights fire as a major culprit over time, and this must certainly be true where timber buildings predominated, particularly in urban environments. In rural situations, however, it is most likely, as Wrathmell simply summarised, that 'rebuilding occurred when circumstances and needs changed' (1984, 30).

Today medieval town houses, often heavily disguised under later refacings, survive in those former medieval towns which avoided destructive redevelopment as a result of industrialisation, fire and war damage, or later twentieth-century planning policies. In the sixteenth and seventeenth centuries medieval urban housing, albeit adapted, altered and extended, would have comprised the bulk of the housing in many towns. Built in timber, stone or a combination of the two, towns such as Chester, Lincoln, Salisbury, Southampton, Worcester and York would by the sixteenth century have consisted of durable and serviceable medieval buildings. Moreover, the population decline of the later medieval period, with at best only a sluggish recovery in the sixteenth century, would have provided little incentive for the building of new town houses. Many towns in Britain, as on the continent, went into economic decline during the period 1400–1600. Consequently, whether in major towns such as Winchester or minor urban centres such as Cowbridge in south Wales (RCAHMW 1988, 508–13), the early post-medieval period witnessed very little new building in towns. There was, however, much refurbishment and rebuilding of existing structures (Schofield 1997, 141), a process that has been demonstrated by excavations in Norwich (Atkin *et al.* 1985, 247–8).

By 1500 the building of open halls within towns appears to have been universally abandoned (Brunskill 1997, 128; Schofield 1997, 136). The flooring over of halls and in some cases their subdivision into smaller rooms during the sixteenth and seventeenth centuries is well attested. In many towns back-to-back chimneys replaced the open hearth in the late medieval period, and were common in London by 1500 (Schofield 1997, 139). With the construction of chimney stacks within the main body of the house, the separate kitchen of the grander houses went out of favour in some towns during the sixteenth century (Schofield 1997, 139). Also during the sixteenth century, communication between storeys was focused on a single stair which led to all floors from the ground. Sometimes located adjacent to the main entrance to the building, and by the seventeenth century connecting to landings or galleries, these stairs would have changed the perception of the upstairs, potentially increasing its importance from a secondary space reached through the downstairs reception rooms to an alternative destination (Schofield 1997, 139). Contemporaries were very conscious of this 'modernisation' process, and property owners required tenants to improve their houses accordingly. At Worcester in 1580 a condition of the lease of a house in Edgar Street from St Michael's churchwardens to Giles Patrick was that he should undertake 'edifyinge the chimneyes making of flores, steyers seelinges wyndowes and other necessaries' (Hughes 1980, 282). By the later sixteenth century there was a clear idea of the features considered fundamental to a town house.

While attrition, particularly by fire, and by the late seventeenth century an increasing desire to replace old buildings with new buildings influenced by polite rather than vernacular architecture both took their toll on the medieval domestic building stock, many structures survived in continuous habitation into the nineteenth century. At Oxford an extra-mural part of the town, first settled in the twelfth century, exhibited excavated evidence of a fourteenth-century structure having been continuously occupied until demolition in the mid-nineteenth century to make way for the building of the Ashmolean Museum (Andrews and Mepham 1996).

POST-MEDIEVAL RESIDENTIAL BUILDINGS

Elite Houses

Much has been written by architectural and art historians on the post-medieval houses of the elite, that is the nobility and the wealthier gentry (particularly significant are Girouard 1978 and Airs 1994). It is not the intention to repeat these works here but rather to summarise the main areas of recent, particularly archaeological, research. The development of elite architectural styles and their relationship to examples of standing buildings has received much previous attention, as noted by Crossley (1990, 56). Archaeologists can be accused, however, of ignoring this class of monument (West 1999, 104). With a few notable exceptions (Johnson 1992, for example), archaeologists have not taken the opportunity to explore how elite houses, as cultural constructs, might reflect the changing attitudes and relationships of their inhabitants. The wealthiest members of society in the sixteenth and seventeenth centuries, as today, generally had more than one residence. Since their wealth tended to be based on the productivity of their landed estates, a country house there would be one residence. In addition, a town house in London would be necessary while they pursued a career as courtiers, and later to accommodate them when they functioned as Members of Parliament or attended the House of Lords. Further town houses might be located in the principal market towns serving their estates, such as the Earl of Derby's house in Preston, Lancashire. Such towns, until the Reform Acts of the nineteenth century, were often also politically subservient to the estate owners. Other town houses were established in the eighteenth and nineteenth centuries in fashionable resorts such as Bath, Cheltenham and Brighton. Thus the elite had a series of houses, each serving as a domicile but also fulfilling differing functions related to aspects of the family's lifestyle.

Country Houses

While the country house did function as the administrative centre of a rural estate, it was rarely designed with the needs of efficient estate management as the primary consideration. The term 'country house' cannot be used as a generic appellation for all rural residences of large landowners (Clemenson 1982, 56). A true country house had a specific purpose, which was to reflect the owner's superior position in society. As such, necessary farm buildings were architecturally integrated with the house or located elsewhere and screened from it. The house frequently had far more rooms than could possibly be used by the family or their friends. It was thus expensive to run and consequently in many instances was never adequately heated and difficult to maintain, so that the owners would often prefer to live in their smaller, more convenient town houses. The country house was not primarily built to provide comfortable accommodation for its inhabitants, but was principally used for display, to impress; it was a status symbol, and as such its architectural composition and image were all-important (Girouard 1978).

It is frequently stated that increased comfort was one of the factors influencing the development of elite housing in the early post-medieval period, and this is used as an explanation for a number of developments in the physical appearance of the house. For example it is argued that the encasing of timber-framed houses in brick was partly motivated by a desire for increased comfort (Crossley 1990, 62). This hardly seems credible, however, since the exclusion of draughts can be achieved far more cheaply and effectively by other means. The principal means of improving housing comfort – enclosed hearths with chimneys and window glass – were widely available to the elite (though not to other social classes) in the late Middle Ages. While these devices were, of course, included in country houses, their design, layout, heating arrangements and room size all mitigated against comfort being a major factor in their development.

The country house had its origins in the great houses of the later Middle Ages, many of which were built for similar purposes of image and impression. In England the lingering links to a military noble past, still evident in late medieval houses such as Lathom House or Herstmonceux,

Floors Castle, near Kelso. Designed by William Adam for the 1st Duke of Roxburgh in 1721, and remodelled by William Playfair in the mid-nineteenth century, this country house both displays the family's wealth and reflects a connection with their Ker ancestors' martial past.

were abandoned in the later sixteenth century in favour of houses like Longleat or Wilton (both in Wiltshire), lacking military associations but influenced by fashionable design elements taken from classical architecture. The century-long transition from late fifteenth-century great house to late sixteenth-century country house is complex but undoubtedly expressive of the changing attitudes and sense of self within the elite.

The sixteenth century witnessed considerable change in the composition of the elite. Many of the old feudal families had been reduced as a consequence of the dynastic disputes of the previous century. New elite families had arisen, aided by the new opportunities provided by the Tudor court and the massive land sales consequent upon the Dissolution of the monasteries. In the earlier sixteenth century the newly built or remodelled great houses appear to have been deliberately designed to provide links with a medieval past (Johnson 1992, 50–1). Medievalism in architectural style and the use of feudal symbolism can be taken as giving the great landowners what Johnson has described as 'a sense of class identity they did not, in fact, share' (Johnson 1992, 51). Why this changed in England and Wales (though not in Scotland) in the later sixteenth century can only be speculated upon, but these changes seem to reflect a conceptual shift in the view of many members of the elite about their relationship to the wider world (Cooper 1997, 115).

The late sixteenth-century country mansion was quite different externally from its early sixteenth-century equivalent. Although a few were castellated, most bore little evidence of a pseudo-military medieval influence. For the most part, instead of being inward-looking, courtyard-style houses with the display elements concentrated towards the courtyard, they were outwardly expressive, particularly through the front elevation (Cooper 1997; Smith 1975, 230). Even where the houses were of medieval origin and based on a courtyard design, they were remodelled to be outward-looking to the gardens and surrounding parkland, as happened at Tredegar House in south Wales in the later seventeenth century (Apted 1977). From the 1570s elite country mansions were increasingly symmetrical in layout and frontage. Architectural embellishments reflected classical influences rather than the late medieval Perpendicular style, even where old-fashioned courtyard styles were used, as at Kirby Hall, Northamptonshire (Johnson 1996, 139). A number of explanations accounting for these developments have been offered. The Renaissance is frequently cited as influencing the change from Tudor Gothic to classical architectural style in the later sixteenth century (Crossley 1990, 56; Platt 1994, 104). As has been recently emphasised, however (Cooper 1997, 121), this may have been a factor in terms of a general appreciation of classical forms rather than direct foreign influence. In part, as a consequence of war and anti-Catholicism, the Elizabethan period saw a decline in continental influence which was not revived until Inigo Jones (Cooper 1997, 121; Platt 1994, 104).

Perhaps the underlying reasons for change lay in the increase in the gentry as members of the elite, and the growing confidence of this class in the later sixteenth century (Cooper 1997, 118–20). Whereas previously there had been a need to create a link with the perceived traditional medieval past, by the later sixteenth century the increased influx of newcomers into the ruling class, and the decline in relative authority of the old aristocracy, may have made associations with a feudal and chivalric past unnecessary. Indeed, Queen Elizabeth's antipathy towards the feudal and military associations of the nobility, particularly following the rebellion of the northern earls in 1569, may have discouraged ambitious courtiers from building houses with architectural associations with a medieval past. Instead of reflecting military and medieval influences, mansion architecture came to reflect good order in its regularity, and education and sophistication in its classical influences (Cooper 1997, 122–3). Emerging in the later sixteenth century, the new gentry houses formed a distinct group of buildings by the mid-seventeenth century (Mercer 1954). They were often smaller than the earlier aristocratic houses, utilising a regular, squarish double-pile plan which has been explained as allowing the maximum display for limited resources (Smith 1975, 229; Smith 1992, 78). They were also more convenient and economical in use of space and heat retention (Cooper 1999, 142). Along with the change in the nature of the country house came an increase in their numbers, as the gentry grew in size and power; there was a consequent increase in the number of resident squires, and thus the requirement for country seats (Cooper 1999, 56).

A compact, usually cubiform symmetrical structure, often with wings, became increasingly common during the seventeenth century, appearing in elite houses in southern England in about 1650 and about thirty years later in the north (Smith 1992, 78; RCHME 1986, 83). In England and Wales by the late seventeenth century the classical conventions that first appeared in mansion architecture a hundred years previously had been refined in use. Many of the early classically influenced houses such as the Duke of Suffolk's Audley End, which was internationally acclaimed in the early seventeenth century, came to be seen as too exuberant and vulgar (Platt 1994, 73–5). A century of increased continental contact had led to an increased understanding among architects and some of their patrons of the principles underlying classical architecture. The late sixteenth-century classically influenced houses were seen as being ostentatious in their decoration, with classical motifs and elements being superficial and incorrectly utilised in buildings that lacked a classical form or plan. Indeed it is still considered that the classical style was not well understood at this time and it is clear that behind the façades and the detailing, internal layouts were often rooted in the traditions of late medieval great houses (Platt 1994, 75;

West 1999, 108–9). Evidence for this can be seen in mansions like Montacute House, Somerset; built in the 1590s, it has a mix of architectural styles lifted from continental pattern books and, following medieval tradition, it was originally focused on a Great Hall (West 1999, 109). Late sixteenth- and early seventeenth-century country mansions often still had a great hall, usually dividing the family rooms from the service wing. Though usually only used for grand occasions when size and display were important, it still preserved its medieval form and conditioned the layout of the house (Girouard 1978). The new house forms, adopted by the gentry in particular, lacked these hierarchical design elements with a concentration of display elements in a specialised internal space; instead the entire building was an item of display (Cooper 1999, 56).

In Scotland medieval-influenced building styles lasted much longer for elite housing, partly reflecting the need to maintain a stronghold aspect during the sixteenth century. This was also reflected in the houses of the lesser gentry and freehold farmers, where tower-houses and bastles were built because of the insecurity of the region (Crossley 1990, 62). As with these lesser buildings, many of the elite houses continued to be built with barmkins, even into the seventeenth century in areas where there can have been no military need for them. Excavations at Craigievar Castle, Aberdeenshire, confirmed the presence of just such a wall, as recorded on eighteenth-century maps, at this house built in the early seventeenth century (Greig 1993). Yet here, and at other nearby elite houses in the Grampian region in the early seventeenth century, there can have been little need for such defensive structures, and their building must relate to custom rather than necessity. These buildings show an unbroken continuity of development with the castles of the later Middle Ages, but they should not be considered necessarily backward-looking nor military in nature. There is evidence to suggest that some of these elite houses incorporated the latest architectural features from the continent: at Pitsligo, Fyvie, Inverugie and the Palace of Huntly, evidence of French-inspired Renaissance architectural forms and devices abound (McKean 1991, 369–70). This should not surprise, as throughout the sixteenth century the Scottish royal family and aristocracy enjoyed close political links with France. Indeed, the elite castle-style houses of Scotland, such as Traquair House (Peeblesshire), are similar to continental great houses like the French châteaux, and like them their purpose was one of display (McKean 1991, 386–8). They were mock-military creations intended to impress and to link their owners with a martial past but not intended for contemporary military use. By the later seventeenth century the Scottish fondness for medieval castle architecture was waning. The Earl of Strathmore, owner and renovator of Glamis Castle, a massive tower-house with extensions, wrote 'such houses are worn quyt out of fashione, as feuds are, which is a great happiness, the cuntrie being generally more civilised then it was of ancient times' (Apted 1986, 94). While such views accurately reflect to an extent a continued need in the sixteenth century for some Scottish aristocratic residences to have a military function, they have contributed to a false modern Anglocentric view that Scottish elite architecture was backward in comparison to that in England.

In the eighteenth century the Anglo-Welsh and Scottish fashions in country house construction moved closer, undoubtedly assisted by the union of the two kingdoms and the greater success of the anglophile owners of Scotland's landed estates. Scottish mansions built in the classical style were indistinguishable from the great houses of England. One of the best examples of this is Hopetoun House, near Edinburgh, built in 1699–1703 with a new façade added by William Adam in 1748. Indeed the cross-fertilisation in country house design between England and Scotland in the eighteenth century is best exemplified by the Adams family,

Lyme Park, Cheshire. The house and grounds were repeatedly remodelled in the eighteenth and nineteenth centuries to maintain a fashionable appearance.

architects who famously worked on mansions in both countries (McWilliam 1979, 356). The revival of castle-style building in Scotland in the second half of the eighteenth century is linked to the Gothic Revival in England. Built in the 1740s and 1750s for Archibald Campbell, Duke of Argyll, Inveraray Castle intentionally portrays the Campbells' feudal and military associations. It is, however, quite distinct in style from the late medieval Scottish castle houses, having been designed by the English architect Roger Morris, an early perpetrator of the Gothic Revival style and designer of Clearwell Castle in Gloucestershire. The enthusiasm for motifs and embellishments associated with castle architecture resurfaced, vigorously, in the nineteenth century. At Abbotsford, Roxburghshire, Sir Walter Scott, whose stories were rooted in Scottish history, folklore and traditions, built a house that reflected these interests. Using William Atkinson, another architect famous for Gothic buildings in England, he built a house that alluded to Scottish medieval architectural traditions and in doing so helped to start a fashion that became known as the Scottish Baronial style (Girouard 1979, 113–14).

During the eighteenth century changing elite attitudes led to houses designed for social gatherings and entertainment. Upton House, Tetbury, in Gloucestershire, was built in 1752 and is an example of a house where the strings of apartments were replaced by communal rooms. A defining feature in country house design of the later eighteenth century was the layout of the communal rooms in a way that allowed a group to progress around the house in a circular manner (Kingsley 1981, 12). Many great houses were remodelled during the eighteenth century to reflect these new trends in taste, often in conjunction with a major remodelling of their surrounding grounds, as at Lyme Park and Tatton Park, Cheshire. Together the house and grounds formed in the eighteenth century islands of fashionable modernity and planning within an often unplanned and ancient landscape. They provided a physical impression of dominance by a class sharing common interests and culture (Cooper 1999, 326), where landownership had replaced lordship as the mechanism for sustaining that dominance.

Even so, many country houses, once built, were often allowed to become old-fashioned. The considerable expenditure involved in building a country house acted as a deterrent to future major rebuilding. For this to occur there had to be a coincidence between strong motivation for rebuilding with the availability of significant resources. These circumstances were most likely when a family was increasing in wealth and importance, when the desire to reflect their status was matched, at least partly, by the resources available to realise their ambitions. Where these circumstances were absent, major remodelling of houses tended not to take place. Thus the appearance of a country mansion tends to reflect the period at which a family achieved its greatest significance and was at its most wealthy.

RURAL VERNACULAR HOUSES

Whether they were built as new structures or converted from existing medieval buildings, the post-medieval period witnessed enormous changes in the design of vernacular dwellings and the use of domestic space. These changes happened at a variable rate dependent on the social class of the inhabitants, the geographical region, whether the building was in an urban or rural environment, rates of attrition of the old housing stock, local requirements for new housing to meet population expansion and 'accidents of history' such as changes in estate management. The characteristics of the post-medieval house and the huge change it symbolised in relation to its medieval antecedents were defined many years ago (Hewett 1973). Primarily involving the insertion of a fireplace and chimney stack, the flooring over of the open hall and the subdivision of living space, these changes indicate considerable differences in the use of the house and signify changes in concepts of domestic living and spatial use within society. Extra usable space was gained and comfort increased, but patterns of flow and usage were also altered, affecting and conditioned by changing social relationships. Entrance arrangements were altered to provide increased control and to facilitate social exclusion. The lobby-entry, which provided a heat-efficient form of egress for houses with central chimneys, ensured that the hall and parlour could be entered independently (RCAHMW 1988, 372). This arrangement may have been adopted when the parlour was transferred to the entry end of the house, in order to provide it with greater privacy in the later sixteenth and early seventeenth centuries – a time when the social gap between householder and domestic servants was increasing (Mercer 1975). The decisions required to change the nature of a house are social ones based not only on pragmatic needs but also on desire and aspiration. The changes reflected in the adoption of the post-medieval house required investment indicative of major motivational forces affecting the householder as consumer (Wilk 1990).

Building Post-medieval Houses

The development of rural vernacular housing in the post-medieval period has been dominated by the concept of the Great Rebuilding (or rebuildings). This concept, first advanced by W.G. Hoskins (1953), sought to explain the occurrence of houses dated to the late sixteenth or early seventeenth century as the earliest domestic buildings in many areas of southern Britain. This Great Rebuilding was associated with the ending of the medieval building tradition and saw the introduction of enclosed fireplaces, the roofing over of the open hall and the multiplication of rooms. This concept was modified as it was realised that the southern English model did not fit other areas where the timescale for the appearance of the earliest non-elite durable houses was different (Machin 1977). Using the evidence of inscribed date-stones, Machin concluded that

Farmhouse at Hodnet, Shropshire. Built in the later sixteenth century, this is a typical farmhouse associated with the 'Great Rebuilding'.

rural building nationally peaked around 1700. This view too has been challenged (Johnson 1993b), and it has been shown that it biases the discussion to areas of stone-building tradition. Moreover, a date-stone is often not contemporary with the origins of a building, and in the case of dated improvements may cover a range of improvements over many decades (Alcock 1983).

The challenges and modifications to Hoskins' theory have led to the view that there were a number of regional rebuildings that operated at different times for different social groups. A study of date-stones in south Lonsdale, Lancashire, where their use on farmhouses is prolific, concluded that a 'great rebuilding' happened for the yeoman class after 1660, following in the wake of their social betters some decades earlier (Garnett 1987, 73). Similarly, in south Wales there is evidence for gentry and yeomen acquiring post-medieval houses in the Vale of Glamorgan before 1640, but in the Blaenau (upland region) this seems not to have happened until the later seventeenth century, and in the Gower peninsula not until the eighteenth century (RCAHMW 1988, 22–3). The picture is further complicated by differences between social classes, for it would seem that in the Vale the husbandman and perhaps labouring classes did not acquire post-medieval-style houses until the later seventeenth century (Newman and Wilkinson 1996, 229).

It can be argued that the timing of the Great Rebuilding was subject to both regional and social variation. In south-east England the open hall had ceased to be built by 1500, in the west Midlands and the Welsh borders it survived throughout the sixteenth century, surviving into the later seventeenth century in northern England and into the nineteenth century in west Wales and parts of Scotland (Brunskill 1997, 52). Put very simply, for non-elite housing the gentry of the south-east of England experienced the introduction of the post-medieval house first and the rural poor of north-western Scotland last. Such a view is, of course, an oversimplification. Indeed the acquisition of post-medieval-style housing is subject to so much social and geographical variation, and is affected by so many historical processes from industrialisation to the Highland Clearances, that the concept of a Great Rebuilding is perhaps no longer meaningful or useful. Currie, arguing for the balancing of phases of construction with an understanding of building loss, pointed out that waves of rebuilding may be illusory (1988, 6). As has already been demonstrated, many late medieval buildings were highly durable. Many more than are known were probably converted to meet new needs, while others would have been replaced out of necessity brought about by damage through fire or flooding or as a consequence of settlement change. Nevertheless, Hoskins' view that most early surviving domestic buildings in England were at least modified or newly built between 1500 and 1700 holds true (Pearson 1998, 168). What is not entirely clear is how much this relates to the processes of building creation during that period or to the processes affecting the survival and continued use of earlier buildings.

Dated doorway to a farm building at Middleton-in-Lonsdale, Westmorland, indicative of yeoman aspirations.

The view that there were post-medieval regional rebuildings related to the need to replace poorer-quality medieval peasant housing has persisted, and Currie's interpretation has been challenged (Mercer 1990; Smith 1990). It is argued on the basis of surviving upstanding buildings that high-quality durable peasant houses appeared in southern England, the west Midlands, East Anglia and the Welsh border from the fifteenth century (Mercer 1990, 1; Smith 1990, 4). This ignores the below-ground evidence from south Wales and north-east England which clearly reveals the presence of durable stone-built medieval peasant houses from the fourteenth century (Griffiths and Thomas 1984; Newman 1987; Wrathmell 1984, 1989). While it is accepted that in areas such as the English limestone belt, stone-built houses erected after 1570 may have totally replaced earlier durable timber-framed structures, it is considered unlikely that the same happened in the north of England in the later seventeenth century, when many of its farmhouses seem to have been built (Smith 1990, 4). Excavation evidence from the north-east clearly demonstrates that this is not a sustainable argument, and there is no reason why this should not also be true of the north-west, though too little excavation of medieval peasant structures has been carried out to support this contention. A survey of houses at Low Row, Swaledale, however, indicated that a seventeenth-century stone dwelling had superseded a timber-framed building (Currie 1990, 8). The evidence from the north-west's towns indicates that until as late as *c.* 1800 they contained substantial late medieval timber-framed structures that were then replaced by new stone and brick buildings. It was not a lack of durability that led to their removal but complex social factors involving fashion, status, social competition and modernity.

In areas of the west and north of Britain it is also argued that the standard of late medieval non-elite houses could not have been high because they were all removed in the sixteenth and seventeenth centuries to be replaced by housing that was considered to be poor by sixteenth- and seventeenth-century contemporaries (Mercer 1990, 1). Certainly this may be true for the Highlands and islands of Scotland, where sixteenth- to seventeenth-century buildings often seem to have consisted of little more than oval or sub-rectangular single-cell structures built of dry-stone or turf (Caldwell *et al.* 2000, 62), though their replacement with more substantial dwellings often did not occur until the eighteenth century. In northern England and Wales, however, there is much evidence for the existence of substantial and durable vernacular domestic structures by the late medieval period. Work at sub-manorial sites such as Risley has shown that some elements of medieval buildings do survive encased in later building work in houses in these areas. Moreover, the criticism of the quality of structures surviving in the sixteenth and seventeenth centuries (which may include buildings from earlier periods) cannot be taken to imply that earlier buildings were necessarily of even worse quality. At Cosmeston in south Wales, peasant buildings abandoned in the fourteenth and fifteenth centuries were of better quality, judged on their excavated remains, than structures built there in the sixteenth century. What is more, houses built there in the eighteenth and nineteenth centuries were little different in plan and floor space from those erected in the thirteenth and fourteenth centuries. Of course the relative contemporary social status of the inhabitants of these dwellings may not be comparable, and the social context within which they lived certainly was not.

The vernacular threshold, the point at which vernacular structures were erected in permanent materials, was passed for peasant houses throughout much of England and Wales in the later medieval period (Brunskill 1971, 28). However, this does not imply that all peasants within any given area crossed this threshold or that there could not be a later regression from this threshold for the poorest classes. The increase in the landless poor in the sixteenth and seventeenth centuries led to extensive squatting on wastes, and there is clear evidence that the huts and hovels occupied by the squatters could often not be regarded as durable buildings. A 1787 survey of such houses in the Forest of Dean reveals 13 per cent to have been insubstantial structures built of mud, turf or rushes (Newman 1988). These were structures that perhaps contained an enclosed fireplace but were in other respects inferior to late medieval peasant dwellings in the area. The nature of impermanence, and indeed the whole concept of a vernacular threshold, is open to question, however (Pearson 1998, 173). In northern and western Scotland, where apparently impermanent materials such as straw and turf were used for much longer than was the case generally in England, structures built in the sixteenth century of seemingly impermanent materials were still in occupation in the nineteenth century (Walker and McGregor 1993, 9).

A lack of durability is unlikely to be the primary reason for the rebuilding of houses in the post-medieval period. It is clear that time and chance did play a major role in the survival or otherwise of individual buildings during the post-medieval period (Currie 1990, 7). Nevertheless, there are observable regional patterns of post-medieval building throughout Britain, and these require explanation. In much of north-west England, gentry houses, vicarages, farmhouses and even labourers' cottages were built in mortared and often rendered stone in the period 1600–1730 (Machin 1977; Garnett 1987). There are geographical variations within this

Trial trench exposing the remains of a post-medieval house at Cosmeston, near Cardiff. Other than evidence for the use of lime plaster, the excavated remains are similar to those of medieval peasants' houses within the settlement.

region; based on the evidence of date-stones, the principal period of post-medieval rural building would appear to be the 1690s in Westmorland, whereas in south Lonsdale, Lancashire, it is twenty years earlier (Garnett 1987, 59). There is also social variation, the lesser gentry building their houses in the earlier seventeenth century, yeoman farmers mainly after the Restoration (Garnett 1987, 60). The ability of the yeomanry to invest in these houses is evident, though there is no obvious reason for an increase in their available wealth between the early and later seventeenth centuries (Garnett 1987, 70–1, Marshall 1980). Rather than increasing wealth, there is some evidence to suggest a refocusing of investment by the house builders away from goods and perhaps into the building of the home. They appear to be more economically active, and house renewal may have been seen as a long-term family investment (Garnett 1987, 71–3).

If the means to build new homes were available for some time before construction took place, and necessity was not the driving force behind building, then consumer choice must have influenced the point at which new homes were built. What were the motivational forces at work behind the post-medieval erection of new houses or the rebuilding of old ones? In the Anglo-Scottish border area houses now commonly called bastles were built in the late sixteenth and early seventeenth centuries. These were small, defensible structures, usually with a byre in the basement and living accommodation above, and generally built by wealthier farmers (Ramm et al. 1970; Ryder 1992). The motivation for building these structures may in part have been derived from the late sixteenth-century border disturbances, but since many were built after the cessation of reiving activity a more complex explanation is necessary. It has been suggested that the ending of border raiding led to an increase in wealth among the farming classes, who were then able to afford to build fortified houses in anticipation of a resumption of border disturbances (Dixon 1979, 250). Here the motivation to build such homes may have been present in the later sixteenth century, but for many the resources to do so were not available until the reason for building defensible structures had ceased.

In west Gloucestershire there are many houses that originated on squatter holdings in and around the Forest of Dean. Date-stones and architectural style indicate that the majority of these

Former squatter's cottage at Netherend, Gloucestershire.

houses are early to mid-nineteenth century in date, though many of the encroachments were much older than this. While it is possibly true that squatters initially lacked the money to finance their building works (Taylor 1992, 26), it was perhaps not lack of resources but lack of motivation that led to their buildings often being impermanent. In the early nineteenth century the commons, upon which the squatters' encroachments were made, were enclosed, and as a consequence the encroachments were legalised (Newman 1988). With legal recognition of their holdings, the squatters embarked upon the rebuilding of their houses secure in their tenure. There was little change to their economic circumstances, but until legal recognition of their holdings the incentive to invest in their houses was lacking. This is a specific and crude illustration of motivation, as is the rebuilding of many Scottish houses in the late eighteenth century as a result of agricultural and estate management changes (Naismith 1985). Where such major stimuli to investment in housing were not present, more subtle reasons must be sought for the building of durable post-medieval houses.

The appearance of rural house types dated to certain periods throughout Britain is far more complex than can be explained by simply proposing a Great Rebuilding (or rebuildings). Specific local and/or class-related circumstances triggered the investment in new building or rebuilding in some areas. Medieval buildings do survive in some areas dependent on attrition rates, and the historic buildings which survive today do not necessarily represent a replacement of the medieval housing stock. Much new building was undertaken to cope with population growth between the sixteenth and nineteenth centuries, though the relationship between population growth and rural building expansion is also a complex one (Taylor 1992).

The concept of a rebuilding driven by a desire to replace poorly built earlier buildings or of a series of regional rebuildings inspired by increased wealth may no longer be sustainable, and a more complicated picture is emerging (Johnson 1997, 13–14). Nevertheless, between the sixteenth and nineteenth centuries, at all levels of society, housing very different from its medieval precursors was adopted. This housing is indicative of a significant change in modes and patterns of domestic life. In the United States students of English colonial archaeology defined a contrast between the symmetrical classicism of the Georgian house and the organic unsymmetrical form of the 'pre-Georgian, medievally-derived house' (Deetz 1977, 43). They argued that the symmetrical, structured Georgian house was symbolic of a shift to a more structured rational existence, less communal and more individualistic (Glassie 1975, 182–93; Deetz 1977, 43).

Along the earliest European-settled parts of the eastern seaboard of the United States, culture in general is seen to have developed away from what were essentially medieval English roots in the early seventeenth century and to have been reintegrated in the eighteenth century into an Anglo-Georgian culture (Deetz 1977, 39–43). England is seen as undergoing a similar change. This is a very different view of the nature of post-medieval building from that exemplified by the concept of a Great Rebuilding. In its distinction between a folk building tradition and an Anglo-Georgian classical tradition, too much emphasis is placed on linking the folk tradition to the idea of a peasant/medieval culture. If the folk tradition in the United States is considered to be the same as the vernacular tradition in Britain, it can be seen that it is not, in the seventeenth century, medieval in context. The medieval building tradition and the lifestyles it represented had been changing since the fifteenth century, and these changes were reflected in the regional vernacular building traditions of the sixteenth and seventeenth centuries. Although houses of this period are sometimes referred to as sub-medieval, they are not characterised by the open plan and communal spaces of the medieval building, but rather share the subdivision and growing room specialisation of their Georgian descendants.

Johnson, in his examination of rural housing in western Suffolk, advanced the theory that many of the assumptions underlying the process of 'Georgianisation' during the eighteenth century may be part of a longer-term process originating in the fifteenth century (1993a, xi). He argues that the late medieval/early post-medieval house underwent a process of 'closure', in which the house became less open to the community and more closed, exclusive and private. This is signified by structural changes such as flooring over the open hall. Certainly this process can be seen in elite houses from the fifteenth century (Courtney 1996, 90). Externally, the timber-frames are hidden under rendering and unavailable for conspicuous display; internally, open hearths are closed off into fireplaces and gradually diminished in size and symbolic importance, roofs are hidden from view by ceilings and open spaces are divided and segregated (Johnson 1993a, 111–19). The world of work is also seen as being isolated from home life by the later seventeenth century and the household role of women marginalised (Johnson 1996, 8).

The Georgian building should then be seen as the culmination of a long process of development reflecting changes in society. Gradually the layout of houses had been rationalised and became more structured until the Georgian house emerged with a symmetrical layout, functionally distinct rooms, and a separation of male and female activities and of family and servants (Johnson 1996, 83). This view identifies the Georgian house plan as an evolutionary development rather than an imposition from without. Although the adoption of classical architectural style was inspired by influences outside Britain, the façade and the plan often did not match in Britain until after the Restoration. In the later seventeenth century the Renaissance house became available to social strata below the elite. Its ideal was the 'compact cubiform building' and this was exemplified by the double-pile house plan which began to be used for farmhouses from the early eighteenth century (Brunskill 1997, 82–3). In this context the double-pile house can be seen as an evolutionary development from the continuous outshut plan, one of a number of plan variants which added additional rooms in depth to the basic two-cell plan of many rural post-medieval houses (Brunskill 1997, 56–84). The Georgian house plan can thus be seen, in part, as a vernacular development.

The End of the Vernacular Tradition

The eighteenth century witnessed the gradual adoption of the Georgian house plan for all types of house other than those of the rural and urban poor. It has long been seen as indicating the end of the vernacular tradition and regional distinctiveness (Barley 1961, 243–4), but this is an overstatement of its impact. Not only does it ignore the widespread adoption across regions of pre-Georgian house plans, and a general lack of external distinctiveness not related to building materials among pre-Georgian houses, it fails to acknowledge adequately the continued use of local materials into the nineteenth century. Moreover, this view fails to contend with the evidence for a continuance of the vernacular tradition into the early nineteenth century, as exhibited by regionally distinctive specialised house types such as Pennine weavers' cottages and the upland farmers' laithe houses. Nor does it take sufficient account of the continuance in parts of Wales and Scotland into the nineteenth century of the folk building tradition among the rural poor. For those who could afford it, however, there was a uniformity of architectural style. This was facilitated by the emergence of the literate builder who could reproduce designs from published style guides which began to appear in the late seventeenth century (Barley 1961, 243). While the Georgian house plan and classical-style architecture may not have ended regional distinctiveness in building, there is no doubt that consumer preference was being expressed in the building of a Georgian-style house. A neat, classical-style house was perceived as a sign of good taste and refinement. For a farmer its possession was a status symbol and facilitated his identification with a national class of people. They were also an expression of relative wealth (Woodforde 1978, 68–9).

It is not until the mid-nineteenth century that regional distinctiveness in building styles is finally lost, particularly among the houses of the poor. The increasing provision of housing by an employer or a developer/speculator for the working classes, combined with the availability of ubiquitous building materials, finally extinguished the vernacular tradition. It was a lengthy process, however. In the small town of Redcar, Yorkshire, for example, most houses were still thatched in the mid-eighteenth century; thatch had been replaced by tiles fifty years later, but many of the houses were still mud-walled (Sherlock 1999, 177). It was not until the mid-nineteenth century that non-vernacular, architect-designed houses were built for the town's working classes as the town developed in response to the railways (Sherlock 1999, 179). Navigable waterways and, particularly, railways provided access to national markets for factory-made bricks and Welsh roofing slate. The spread of non-local building materials and the ending of the vernacular tradition are linked, but the connection is a more complex one than might at first be supposed. For example, from the late sixteenth century pantiles were exported from the Netherlands and Denmark for roofing in England and Scotland. In Norfolk by the late eighteenth century, pantiles were the most common roofing material, though they were noticeably more popular close to the coast (Lucas 1998b, 83). Until the later eighteenth century these were largely continental imports, yet so widespread was their use in the county that they can be considered a distinctive feature of the local vernacular tradition, eventually spawning a local pantile industry (Lucas 1998b, 89).

The Houses of the Middling Sort

The rural 'middle class' was largely composed of the lesser gentry, yeoman farmers and the clergy. It is usually their houses that are under consideration when regional periods of rebuilding are identified, and the literature abounds with worthy studies of the development of house plans and architectural form. It was this class in England and Wales that in the mid- to late seventeenth century moved away from traditional, locally based housing styles to a largely non-vernacular style of building usually designed and built by professional architects and builders. The typical, though by no means the only, house type built for middle-class rural housing in this period was the double-pile house. Consisting of a double depth of rooms, with the ground floor layout broadly mirrored on the first floor, entry from the outside was no longer directly into a room, but via a doorway set centrally in the frontage into a vestibule leading to stairs at the rear of the

The vicarage at Dymock, Gloucestershire, is a fine example of an eighteenth-century double-pile house.

house. Double-pile houses were built for the gentry in the later seventeenth century (Barley 1979). By the end of the century they were being adopted for parsonages (Barley 1979, 269), and by the second decade of the eighteenth century for farmhouses (Brunskill 1997, 84). In the earlier eighteenth century the design became widespread in the south of England, though it was adopted later in the north. Many examples were erected in the later eighteenth century for new farms associated with parliamentary enclosure (Alcock 1996, 148).

The influences on these new house plans were both vernacular and derived from the Renaissance houses of the elite. The entrance arrangements, for example, developed from the lobby entry form which appeared in East Anglia in the sixteenth century, in the Welsh borders in the late sixteenth century and in south Wales and the south Midlands in the earlier seventeenth century (Alcock 1996, 135; RCAHMW 1988, 372–3). Though for the most part the stair was removed from the centre of the house to the rear, and in some areas such as north-west England this led to the development of the long, centrally situated staircase window to illuminate it. Such features are regionally specific and, although appearing within so-called 'Georgian' houses, they are evidence of continuing and developing vernacular traditions for some aspects of middle-class housing. These new 'Georgian' house plans increased the level of social filtration that could take place following entry into the house. The staircase, facing the entrance and visible immediately to a visitor, allowed for conspicuous status display in its design and decoration. Though these houses had vernacular influences they were now clearly distinct from lower-status houses. In Warwickshire, about 1700, these houses were symmetrical and often brick-built; while containing some vernacular decorative details such as chamfered and stepped ceiling beams, they were clearly different from houses of the lower classes which remained timber-framed (Alcock 1996, 152).

In Highland Scotland the social structure was different from that in England and Wales, and a more feudal and ancient form of society persisted into the eighteenth century. Within the township of Lianach in Perthshire a house of seemingly eighteenth-century origin from artefactual evidence, and possibly the home of a principal tenant, was excavated and shown to be a two-celled longhouse (Stewart and Stewart 1988). With irregular stone walls bedded in clay, one cell formed the dwelling and the other a byre. There was some evidence to suggest that the roof was supported by earth-fast crucks (Stewart and Stewart 1988, 307). The construction techniques and layout of the building would not have been out of place in parts of England and Wales in the thirteenth century. The artefactual assemblage, however, apart from a relative lack of pottery, is not dissimilar to that from a late seventeenth- or early eighteenth-century husbandman's house in south Wales (Newman and Wilkinson 1996). The building was also larger than the others in the settlement, and was the only one with an internal division and more than one entrance. All this suggests that it was a socially elite building within the context of the settlement (Stewart and Stewart 1988, 310).

In some areas the changes in social structure as reflected in building design were less marked than in others. In Westmorland, for example, communal spaces continued to feature in houses until the eighteenth century. The farmer often housed his farm servants within his own home, eating with them as he shared their workload (Hayfield 1995). The Wharram Research Project has identified a range of farm workers' accommodation in the Yorkshire Wolds. Servants' wings, kitchens and dormitory accommodation can be recognised in a number of surviving farmhouses (Hayfield 1995). From the mid-nineteenth century the relationship between farmer and servant appears to have changed, and farmers seem to have attempted to distance themselves from their workers. Extensions were built as dining rooms for the farm servants, separating their eating arrangements from the family's (Hayfield 1995, 26). In the later nineteenth century in other regions new types of accommodation evolved. In many areas it had long been common to house male farm workers in lofts above the stable or other farm building, sometimes in dormitory-style accommodation (Nash 1989, 57). In north-west England parts of barns were converted, or extensions to them built, to provide domestic accommodation for farmhands. These were known as 'paddy houses', reflecting the ethnic origin of many of the rural labourers in the region in the later nineteenth century. They can be physically distinguished from the rest of an agricultural building range by their small domestic-style windows and gable-end chimneys.

The Houses of Cottagers and Smallholders

In relation to Wales, Eurwyn Wiliam argued in 1988 that since at best only 5 per cent of the population of Wales could be considered to be part of the gentry, their houses tell us less about ordinary society and culture than the homes of their tenants and others less elevated on the social scale (Wiliam 1988, 5). Even when account is taken of the merchants, tradesmen and yeoman farmers that made up the lower middling orders, the vast majority of the population is excluded. This is true not only for Wales but for the rest of Britain in general as well. Ordinary smallholders and labourers are rarely represented in the documentary record, and yet archaeology, which could throw light on their pasts, has primarily been used to investigate the lives of the elite minority, largely to the exclusion of the rest. To an extent this has been an accident of survival:

Hill House Farm, Taynton, Gloucestershire. This is a typical one-up, one-down seventeenth-century cottage. Few such unaltered examples survive today.

the above-ground standing fabric of past housing tends to be the most heavily invested in, the most architecturally appreciated, the most easily adapted and above all the most continually useful. The houses of the poor tend not to survive above ground, particularly from before the eighteenth century. Surviving houses are those that continued to meet the needs of their inhabitants, and the poor often did not enjoy houses which would do this until the nineteenth century. The investigation of the below-ground remains of such housing has not been extensive. Indeed, considerably more archaeological information is known about the housing of the medieval peasant than about their post-medieval smallholder and labourer descendants.

It has been claimed that until the nineteenth-century urban growth and the development of urban working-class housing all classes occupied similar houses, particularly in the Georgian period, when standard designs were used and the difference in house-owner wealth was represented only by size (Cave 1981, 223). Such a view ignores the evidence of the vast majority of dwellings – those which were occupied by the smallholders and labourers. The level of investment in the housing of the rural poor in comparison to that of the wealthier land-holding classes was significantly lower. A study in Cumberland and Westmorland has shown that where labourers' cottages were financed by landlords or employers, the late seventeenth-century cost of erecting suitable housing varied between £7 and £20 (Tyson 1993). The cheaper houses appear to have been one-up, one-down, with the more expensive perhaps two-up, two-down. None of these houses appears to have lasted for much more than a century before being abandoned or replaced by better housing. In comparison, a contemporary local double-pile house cost £64, and an architect-designed, classical-style town house over £500 (Tyson 1993, 26). Yet, despite the considerable discrepancy in the cost of the housing of these rural labourers in comparison with their middle-class contemporaries, the examples cited were probably at the quality end of the housing provision for many of the rural poor. In terms of cost they compare favourably with mid-nineteenth-century urban workers' housing; in St Helens, near Liverpool, a dwelling valued at £6 was considered to be likely to house 'a very respectable class of person' (Jackson 1979, 134). These estate-sponsored workers' cottages at least had materials and labour provided for their construction. One of the most significant differences between the houses of the middle classes and those of the rural poor was in the matter of who built them. Unlike farmhouses, the dwellings of the smallholders and landless labourers in the sixteenth to eighteenth centuries were not generally designed and erected by professional builders, but were constructed by the prospective inhabitants (Wiliam 1995, 23).

Since there are few surviving examples of cottages that are earlier than the eighteenth century, it has long been suggested that the houses of the rural poor lacked durability, being poorly built of poor-quality materials (Brunskill 1997, 86–8; Wiliam 1995, 23). The notion that the dwellings of the poor were all impermanent structures is, as already demonstrated, open to question. Certainly they lacked resources in comparison to the more wealthy. Even in the later eighteenth century in England, and the nineteenth century in west Wales, some squatters were still building homes in easily obtained but impermanent materials. Lack of security of tenure, not only for squatters but also for some leaseholders and even tied labourers, would have acted as a disincentive to investment in housing. Thus it seems, as a number of authorities have concluded, that impermanent building techniques related to social circumstances continued alongside more permanent building methods in the same region (Smith 1983, 34). However, poor contemporary survival is not a conclusive argument in favour of a past lack of durability. In Scotland the occupation of blackhouses into the twentieth century and the remains of houses in fermtouns, depopulated in the eighteenth century, both indicate that simple post-medieval structures using turf and dry-stone walling could survive for many generations (Walker and McGregor 1993). Similarly, in Cardiganshire and Carmarthenshire many small nineteenth-century mud-built cottages survive today (Wiliam 1995, 26–8). Parts of such homes would have been frequently replaced, but this can be seen as maintenance rather than rebuilding. While the use of materials such as turf and straw may necessitate frequent repair, they also facilitate its ease and make it less of a burden.

The rural poor acquired 'post-medieval' houses suitable to their long-term needs at a relatively late date. At Llanmaes in south Wales excavations revealed the remains of buildings interpreted as husbandmen's or labourers' houses; there was some evidence of smithing at one of the properties. The least-disturbed structure consisted of stone walls bedded in clay (a technique used in the area since the thirteenth century) surrounding a mortar floor (Newman and Wilkinson 1996, 196). The building had an enclosed hearth, stairs to an upper storey and evidence of a ground floor partial partition. Built in the later seventeenth century, it resembled a very small version of the lobby-entry-type houses commonly built by the gentry and yeomanry in Glamorgan during the seventeenth century (Newman and Wilkinson 1996, 199, 229; RCAHMW 1988). This plan continued to be used for many cottages throughout south Wales into the early nineteenth century (Wiliam 1988, 26). The houses at Llanmaes were clearly durable, and designed to emulate the dwellings of their social superiors, yet few similar contemporary houses of their status appear to survive in the area, though there are many larger farmhouses of the period. Although Llanmaes seems to provide examples of the acquisition of post-medieval houses by the poorer classes, they still did not survive the eighteenth century but were abandoned. In Glamorgan part of the reason for the lack of such surviving cottages may be the abandonment of the rural areas by labourers and smallholders emigrating to the developing industrial settlements. This is a documented process that began in the early eighteenth century, when the Llanmaes houses were abandoned, and continued until the mid-nineteenth century (Newman and Wilkinson 1996, 229–30).

The partially excavated remains of a husbandman's property at Llanmaes, south Wales. The house is towards the top of the excavated area and was entered via a carefully cobbled yard.

The general lack of archaeological data concerning the housing of the 'common people', particularly in rural areas, causes difficulties when trying to develop and apply theories of social organisation and cultural evolution based on the evidence of housing. Matthew Johnson's ideas about the social implications of changes in house layout and design in the fifteenth to eighteenth century, for example, are provocative and valuable, but they are only applicable in those geographical areas, and among those social groups, where such changes in housing occurred (Johnson 1993a; Johnson 1996, 79–80). Patterns of circulation, and social and gender relations were less likely to change when the space within which they were enacted remained unaltered. Except for Scotland, the evidence for housing of the poorest and largest part of British society comes largely from the writings of seventeenth- to nineteenth-century travellers and social commentators, and from eighteenth- and nineteenth-century artists' depictions and nineteenth-century photographs. These indicate that for many poorer people houses continued to be simple, single-storey, single-room dwellings, in some instances well into the nineteenth century (Newton 1976). If it is accepted that the physical evidence of these homes both reflected and conditioned the lifestyles of those who inhabited them, it becomes clear that the post-medieval period witnessed an increasing divergence in the lifestyles of the poor and wealthy. This was reflected not only in their access to consumer goods but also in the way in which housing reflected and constrained familial, gender and social relationships. These material differences between the poor and the wealthy would have accelerated and solidified the processes of social stratification that are so evident in the post-medieval period.

Single-storey buildings continued to be built during the post-medieval period. They were built on the commons by squatters throughout England in the sixteenth and seventeenth centuries and in established settlements as the dwellings of labourers. In west and north Wales single-storey, single-cell houses were common into the nineteenth century, such as those known as tyddyn in Caernarvonshire. While these are likely to have had enclosed fireplaces and chimneys in the nineteenth century, in the eighteenth they would still have had open hearths (Wiliam 1995, 30, 35). In west Wales, certainly from the mid-eighteenth century, these cottages tended at least to have two rooms (Wiliam 1995, 35). In the Highlands in the early eighteenth century even a well-built, new, relatively commodious specialised dwelling like a ferryhouse (part inn, part ferryman's home) was single celled, single storeyed and unceilinged, with an earth floor (MacKie 1997, 246–8, 280–1). Its specialised nature was indicated by the enclosed hearths in each gable. In the Highlands, however, this might be a building comparable to those inhabited by the less-well-to-do minor clan gentry, and was certainly a more luxurious home than those of the tenant farmers (MacKie 1997, 281).

Such houses were not confined to the Celtic fringe. They were present in the eighteenth century in Lancashire and Yorkshire, for example (Brunskill 1977, 71; Newton 1976; RCHME 1985b). In west Yorkshire examples of originally single- and double-cell cottages built in stone can be found dating from the seventeenth and eighteenth centuries, with some later brick examples (Newton 1976; RCHME 1986, 183–4). On a visit to the fishing hamlet and developing seaside resort of Blackpool in 1788, William Hutton wrote that the older cottages 'were formed of clay, plastered upon wattles, the roof and the whole fabric being supported upon crooks [sic], and the interior open to the thatch, which was generally of rush in place of straw; and they contained a large capacious chimney, above which was erected what was termed a soot loft, the depository of lumber, forming a canopy over the family hearth' (Farrer and Brownbill 1911, 242). In Carnforth, north Lancashire, many cottages in the early eighteenth century were open to the roof, and at least one had an open hearth (LUAU 1998, 108).

Travellers' and antiquarian accounts should not be taken at face value. Often the very fact that such buildings were deemed noteworthy is likely to indicate that they were unusual within a district. The accounts of English travellers in Scotland and Wales are particularly suspect as they often contain racist overtones. Some authors may have exaggerated the poverty of the conditions in order to contrast the barbarity of the natives with the civility of the English (Wiliam 1988, 33). Even so, it is clear that for many of the poor, particularly in the north and west of Britain, housing conditions were little different from those of their medieval forebears. Where most of the family time was spent outdoors, there may have been little need for change. During the eighteenth century major social changes had an impact upon the life of the rural poor, resulting in changing housing requirements and opportunities for new housing. From the eighteenth century the ability of the poor to erect dwellings, or to occupy houses erected on their behalf, which still survive today, reflects the huge contemporary social changes that affected them.

The eighteenth and early nineteenth centuries saw estate rationalisation and the coalescence of landed wealth in fewer hands. Parliamentary enclosure was complementary to this. While these processes meant misery for some of the poor, they offered others opportunities. In parts of England and in much of Scotland old settlements were abandoned and new ones established, complete with estate workers' cottages with symmetrical frontages and central doorways. Even where wholesale settlement replanning did not take place, new workers' cottages were often considered essential to the well-being of an estate. The enclosure of the commons provided many squatters with the opportunity to gain secure tenure of their holdings, giving them motivation to rebuild their homes. The growth of industry altered the settlement geography in some parts of Britain, and in areas such as the southern Pennines provided employment to supplement smallholdings and encouraged the building of new types of cottage suitable for accommodating weaving. Among the poor, as previously in the wealthier classes, a desire developed to separate the private domain from the public. In two-room cottages, one space became used more for public activities – the hall/kitchen – and the other for more private ones – the bedroom, or in some instances the parlour (Brunskill 1997, 86). In Scotland in the nineteenth century it has been noted that even in two-celled cottages, one room would be reserved for visitors and special occasions (Carruthers 1993, 32). The world of men in the loomshop was separated from the world of women in the parlour/kitchen. Despite these developments, and the tendency for cottages in general to become multi-roomed during the eighteenth century, houses remained small and were therefore often overcrowded, necessitating a continued difference in attitude to family life and privacy from that espoused by the more wealthy. Moreover, the front door often still opened into the main room ensuring that this space remained a welcoming, inclusive one. This is in contrast to the vestibule/hallway of the middle-class Georgian house, where the visitor was segregated from the main body of the dwelling before being taken to the appropriate private room according to business and status.

The box bed was one way in which the cottager could gain some privacy when rooms were still in multiple use and occupancy. In Welsh single-storey cottages, lofts may have developed as a result of boarding over two box beds placed back-to-back. This space, known as a *croglofft*, could then be boarded at the front and accessed by a ladder, forming a separate storage or sleeping area (Wiliam 1988, 26–7). In Scotland a single-storey cottage recorded at Torthorwald, Dumfries, is typical of many rural Scottish cottages in the eighteenth century. Cruck-framed with stone walls and a thatched roof, it was single-cell with a clay-and-lath canopied chimney hood over a gable-end fireplace (Fenton and Walker 1981, 8, 22). The single-storey house type remained a common feature of rural housing in the later eighteenth and nineteenth centuries in west Wales and Scotland. By then they were usually built of at least two rooms, with an enclosed fireplace and externally perhaps exhibiting some influences from polite architecture. Even in remote St Kilda houses with mortared walls, more than one room and an enclosed fireplace were introduced after 1860 (Emery 1999a, 166–7). In Scotland, even after the rebuilding of much of the cottagers' housing stock between *c.* 1750 and *c.* 1860 (Naismith 1985, 30; Gauldie 1974, 50), the single-storey cottage remained the dominant form of housing for the rural poor everywhere. The influence this has on the appearance of today's Scottish countryside is very noticeable, marking a clear difference between the character of the rural landscape of English Cumberland and neighbouring Scottish Dumfriesshire, for example.

It has been claimed that the greater majority of the rural population of Britain in the nineteenth century were still living in the traditional cottages built by their ancestors (Gauldie 1974, 49). This is not a sustainable view. The dating of surviving cottages and the evidence relating to estate reorganisation and the rebuilding of squatter houses indicate that this was not the case. The increase in the rural population in many areas also clearly suggests that new housing must have been built to accommodate them. Throughout England single-storey cottages were largely replaced in the eighteenth and early nineteenth centuries. Some of the new houses were

Late eighteenth- to nineteenth-century single-storey cottage at Auchindrain, Argyll. (© Lancaster University Archaeological Unit)

variants of the double-pile plan, while some were developments of half-lofted cottages. Some were built in rows, others singly or as semi-detached pairs. Until access to a rail link was available they were generally built using local materials. Externally they were unpretentious, and only the window styles reflected prevailing architectural fashions. Nevertheless, though many of the homes of the rural poor were rebuilt or newly built during the eighteenth and early nineteenth centuries, the quality of the housing continued to be generally low. A partially excavated example of a single-cell nineteenth-century cottage at Cosmeston in south Wales indicates that the living conditions, in terms of space and dwelling comfort, were little different from those experienced by their medieval ancestors whose dwellings had been excavated nearby. Enclosure, rising population and harsh employment conditions reduced the ability of the poor to build their own houses from available local resources (Williamson and Bellamy 1987, 162). Labourers were forced to seek accommodation provided by landlords at high rents in cheap and badly made houses.

To moralising reformers, the state of rural cottages in the mid-nineteenth century was as much a matter of concern as the state of the dwellings of urban workers. Small size and the lack of room specialisation were of particular concern, because this precluded separate sleeping areas for the male and female members of a household and was thus considered a cause of immorality. In the Highlands and islands of Scotland conditions were often little different from those considered inadequate by observers 150 years earlier. In Wales it was often the more modern cottages that were most scathingly criticised, being considered less roomy and having thinner walls than the more traditional cottages (Wiliam 1988, 25–6). The cottages of west Wales were attacked, but those in south Wales were considered particularly poor, and in the view of one observer they endangered the entire moral fabric of society in Llantwit Major, in the Vale of Glamorgan (Wiliam 1988, 26). Poor-quality cottages were also a problem in the heartlands of England. In counties such as Dorset, Norfolk and Shropshire cottages were condemned for being too small, overcrowded, having mud floors, being damp and lacking privies, and were considered a disgrace for estate owners (Williamson and Bellamy 1987, 163; Bettey 2000, 47). A Royal Commission report of 1867 typifies the middle-class reaction to the conditions experienced in rural cottages. Of particular concern was the effect of a lack of privacy on decency and morality: 'with beds lying as thickly as they can be packed, father, mother, young men, lads, growing and grown-up girls altogether; where every operation of the toilet and of nature, dressing, undressing, births and deaths, is performed, each within sight and hearing of all' (Kaufman 1907, 60). A witness to a later Royal Commission in 1885 described a good cottage as one which was weatherproof, had access to clean water and a sound floor, but he considered that throughout Britain the majority of agricultural workers lacked such cottages (Gauldie 1974, 55). Interestingly, when viewed from this practical standpoint, room subdivision and privacy were not considered primary issues.

Not all rural cottages were badly built and cramped in the nineteenth century. Many of the great estate owners realised the benefit of investing in their workers' cottages. By providing decent cottages they tied their workforce more firmly to them and counteracted the attraction of the burgeoning industrial areas. Again the importance of appropriate buildings to the creation of a righteous, well-behaved and worthwhile workforce was paramount in the motivation behind investment in labourers' housing. The Duke of Bedford commented in 1895 that 'good and comfortable cottages, in which the decencies and dignity of human life may be maintained, generally imply that they are inhabited by good and efficient labourers' (Mitson and Cox 1995, 30). On the Yarborough estate in Lincolnshire between 1850 and 1875, estate workers' cottages were erected that survive as desirable homes today: brick-built, two-storey, of varying sizes but usually with at least five rooms and situated in generous garden plots (Mitson and Cox 1995, 34–44). In such homes the values of the middle classes – privacy and decency, family and gender segregation, a structured and ritualised domestic life – could be instilled into rural labourers.

It is likely that, as in urban areas, the fear of moral degradation and its perceived resultant consequences for social order and economic output was as important in the gradual improvement in the standards of poor rural dwellings in the late nineteenth and early twentieth centuries as any practical concern for the well-being of the rural labourer. The problem of rural housing, consisting for the poor of badly built small cottages, lacking room specialisation and basic facilities, was not finally addressed until the advent of local authority social housing in the twentieth century.

URBAN AND INDUSTRIAL HOUSING

The subject of post-medieval urban and industrial housing has received scant attention from archaeologists until recently. All too often the remains – both standing and below ground – of dwellings of this period have been, and continue to be, removed, with no, or inadequate, recording. Industrial workers' housing in particular has only begun to be studied by archaeologists in the past twenty years, and little, outside the work of the RCHME in West Yorkshire (1985), has been published fully. Even so, many non-archaeologists have written about workers' housing. Throughout the nineteenth century and into the twentieth social reformers like Friedrich Engels commentated on British industrial workers' housing. While writers in the early 1970s bemoaned the lack of published material on the history of 'working-class' housing and the relative paucity of local studies (Chapman 1971, 9), their work demonstrated the considerable growing interest. Subsequent local studies have greatly extended the geographical coverage of the subject (Lowe 1977; Roberts 1977; Timmins 1977, 1979, 1993).

Industrial Workers' Housing in Rural Areas

Much of the early development in industrial workers' housing was not in towns and cities but in rural settlements and dispersed across the wider countryside. Aside from market-dependent crafts and finishing trades, much industrial activity was not urban-based. Extractive industries were dependent on geology, and iron-making on the availability of water power and wood supplies. Fuel supply and/or water power and supply were often the overriding locational factors for many other industries in the early post-medieval period. Those seeking employment in these industries required housing close to the centres of production. The nature of this housing was in part dictated by the type of industry in which the householder was employed, but was also influenced by landscape/topographical constraints (themselves a result of industrial location), patterns of landholding and other local socio-economic factors, such as the nature of the prevailing vernacular tradition.

Before the eighteenth century the concept of purpose-built industrial workers' housing would have been for the most part incomprehensible. Much industrial activity was domestically based and took place in adapted, primarily domestic spaces. Outside the urban-based crafts, few labourers engaged in industrial activity full-time but participated in it as a by-employment, while also engaging in agriculture either as hired hands or on their own land. Even workers in the iron industry, one of the most centralised and mechanised of pre-eighteenth-century manufacturing activities, would have laboured elsewhere part-time because of the seasonal and necessarily periodic nature of an ironwork's operational life. Thus there would be little distinction between the dwellings of an agricultural labourer and a rural industrial worker because such a social distinction did not exist. Until the eighteenth century the housing of industrial workers in the countryside formed part of the general housing stock of rural areas, largely indistinguishable from other housing and developing within the same local vernacular traditions.

Nevertheless, some industries caused new housing to arise in some areas during the sixteenth and seventeenth centuries. The iron industry, generally based in remote wooded locations, of necessity had to create new settlements for its workers. In the Forest of Dean in 1635 the housing of the workers in the Crown's ironworks was included in an inventory of those works (Newman 1988, 375). The labourers' housing appears to have consisted of small thatched cottages, seemingly only one-storey high and presumably similar to the Sussex ironworkers' cottages of around 1600, which were said to be small cottages roofed with clods and turf (Schubert 1947, 371–2). Of the better cottages described in more detail, the furnace-keeper's house at Cannop furnace was said to be a timber-built cabin covered with boards, and the hammerman's house at Lydbrook forge was timber-built with a stone chimney, but being only a single storey and measuring 30ft (9.23m) by 20ft (6.15m), its floor size was less than that of many excavated medieval peasant houses. In contrast, the clerk's house at Bradley forge was stone-built with a tiled roof, three storeys high and with ground floor dimensions of 56ft (17.23m) by 20ft (6.15m) (Newman 1988, 375–6).

In Sussex in the sixteenth and seventeenth centuries, and in west Gloucestershire some hundred years later, new settlements arose associated with the iron industry or other wood-dependent industries. These were often unplanned and unregulated squatter settlements encroaching on the common wastes, usually with the tacit approval, if not active encouragement, of the local manorial lords. Judging from the documentary evidence, however, within these settlements there does not seem to have been any difference between a part-time industrial worker's cottage and that of a part-time hired agricultural labourer. Similar encroached landscapes occurred elsewhere in Britain. At Coalbrookdale, Shropshire, during the seventeenth and eighteenth centuries the steep slopes of the Severn gorge were colonised with squatter encroachments housing a population of industrial workers including coal-miners, potters and clay tobacco-pipe makers (Trinder 1982, 33). Initially, it can be assumed that the houses were no better than those of other squatters. Industrial workers also squatted on common land in the north of England, particularly labourers associated with extractive industries (Caffyn 1983, 173–4). As with the iron-workers of the Forest of Dean, their homes were single-storey, simply built structures utilising local materials. Such structures continued to be built in northern England into the nineteenth century, so that as late as 1838 the cottages of the region could be described as being 'of one storey and generally of one room' (Caffyn 1983, 173; Newton 1976, 65). A similar situation prevailed with regard to industrial workers' housing in much of Wales. In the west, from Carmarthenshire to Caernarvonshire, one-storey, two-celled houses were commonly built by the rural poor between 1750 and 1850, and houses of this type were adopted for industrial workers (Lowe 1977, 10). The design was so persistent that it found its way into urban terraces; as late as the mid-nineteenth century the industrial suburb of East Pennar, Pembroke Dock, had rows of single-storey, two-celled houses built very much in the style of the local vernacular tradition (Lowe 1977, 53).

Not all rurally situated industrial workers' housing remained so simple in design and unspecialised in nature. In the textile manufacturing districts, and particularly in the West Riding of Yorkshire and in central and east Lancashire, new forms of housing developed in the eighteenth century. The mechanisation of spinning and carding made cotton yarn available in much greater quantities, encouraging growth in textile production in the later eighteenth century. By the 1780s purpose-built weavers' housing was springing up throughout the central Pennine region (Porter 1980, 81). Weaving required a well-lit room in which to work the loom and space to store yarn and cloth. Existing houses were adapted, with roofs being raised and new large windows inserted to provide better light for the working spaces; farmhouses adapted in this way are known from the Saddleworth and Delph districts near Manchester. Elsewhere other local vernacular adaptations to domestic buildings occurred in response to textile manufacture. In the woollen-cloth-producing district of Kendal in Westmorland wooden spinning galleries were added to existing farmhouses. This feature is found to a lesser extent elsewhere, for example at Ruthin, Denbighshire.

The long window is the most distinctive architectural feature of the purpose-built weaver's cottage of the central Pennine region. They developed from the vernacular-style mullioned windows, still common in the region into the mid-eighteenth century, though the mullions of weavers' cottages tended to be square and flat-faced rather than splayed and recessed. The windows often had six to eight lights, and in west Yorkshire illuminated a second- and/or third-storey room. Such houses dating to the eighteenth and early nineteenth centuries survive in many villages of the central Pennines (Porter 1980, 82). A variant of these weavers' houses developed in central Lancashire in the Blackburn/Bolton district. There, first- or second-floor loomshops were rare; instead the loomshop was at ground-floor level or housed within a cellar (Porter 1980, 83; Timmins 1977, 20). Often these were lit by three-light mullioned windows, as at Dawber's Lane, Euxton (Timmins 1977, 67). Houses with such an arrangement are therefore much more difficult to distinguish as weavers' cottages, although sometimes such windows were placed together in long rows (Timmins 1979, 261).

An early eighteenth-century house with upper-storey loomshop, Delph, near Manchester. Changes in the nature of the brickwork may indicate that this was a later addition.

The late eighteenth-century weavers' cottages were built from local materials; in an upland rural situation these had stone-flagged roofs and watershot stone walls. In West Yorkshire they consisted in the main of a ground-floor living room with a bedroom above which would have doubled as a loomshop (Caffyn 1983, 174; RCHME 1985b, 47–8). In central Lancashire the loomshop might be in the cellar or might share the ground floor with the living room in an early version of the two-up, two-down industrial worker's dwelling (Timmins 1993, 104–6). In both instances the house types and characteristics were regional variants of industrial workers' housing developing within vernacular traditions (Timmins 1993, 104). There was a lack of specialisation in room function, and the living-room in particular would have been the multi-purpose centre of family life, being used for relaxation, food preparation, cooking, eating and a variety of other domestic tasks and social interactions.

As with Coalbrookdale or the valleys of south Wales, the textile districts of the Pennine uplands were topographically restricted, and this influenced the character of housing. The linear nature of valley-side building encouraged the erection of rows of cottages. Much of the housing was provided by speculators developing relatively low-value land. Building on steep slopes often meant that the backs of houses were unlit. One way of achieving higher densities of housing in popular weaving districts, where development land was at a premium because of adverse topography, was the construction of dwelling-and-underdwelling housing. The underdwelling was accessed from the down-slope and its back was built into the hillside; above it was erected a two-storey dwelling, accessed from the up-slope (RCHME 1985b, 15). Good examples of such housing can be seen on the banks of the Spodden brook at Whitworth (Lancashire). Such blind-back and back-to-earth houses in terraces may be seen as part of a process that culminated in the widespread adoption of back-to-back dwellings as the norm for housing industrial workers in the nineteenth century. The back-to-back house was first erected in the industrial villages of the Pennine weaving districts in the late eighteenth century. At Huddersfield Road, Thongsbridge, in west Yorkshire, a row of two-and-a-half-storey cottages with upper-floor loomshops has a datestone of 1790 (RCHME 1985b, 16). In Yorkshire, blind-back and back-to-back housing, usually of the one-up, one-down variety, was certainly not exclusive to textile workers in the late eighteenth and early nineteenth centuries, and similar cottages were built in rural areas for iron workers, miners and quarrymen (Caffyn 1983, 176).

Small terraces of weavers' cottages ceased to be built as factory-based power-loom weaving superseded handloom weaving and separated the work place from the domestic space (RCHME 1985a, 55). Before this happened, however, purpose-built weavers' cottages, particularly in terraces, had contributed much to the landscape and settlement pattern of the central Pennines. Villages such as Belthorn and Tockholes near Blackburn owe much of their evolution to the erection of terraces for handloom weavers (Timmins 1979, 270). These were, of course, also built within towns, and indeed a number of newly emerging urban areas within the central Pennines in the early nineteenth century, such as Heptonstall, Hebden Bridge and Todmorden, owe their growth to the development of weavers' housing.

Extractive industries were a major factor in developing new rural communities in the post-medieval period. The housing associated with these industries was often of the most basic sort; in Scotland conditions appear to have been particularly bad because until the end of the eighteenth century many miners were bonded labourers (Gauldie 1974, 66). Throughout Britain, however, probably until at least the early nineteenth century, most housing associated with extractive industries would have consisted of single-storey structures with either one or two rooms (Brunskill 1997, 90). There are many reasons for this; often, particularly in the case of coal mines, the workings would be leased from a local landowner so that the mine owner had little interest in investing in anything other than the mine (Gauldie 1974, 65). Frequently mining ventures were highly speculative and the operational life of a mine could be very short. In the Forest of Dean, in part resulting from the tradition of free-mining, the operations remained small and under-capitalised well into the nineteenth century (Hart 1971, 265–9). There the houses of the miners and quarrymen were squatter cottages erected on the waste by the labourers themselves. A survey of 1787 makes it clear that most were single-storey cabins often built of relatively impermanent materials such as turf (Newman 1988, 375). As with other squatters, the miners and quarrymen built better housing following the enclosure of the squatted wastes and their gaining of more secure rights of occupancy. Moreover, the mid-nineteenth-century expansion of mining in the Forest of Dean and the formation of better-capitalised mining companies led to the investment in colliery housing and the creation of new settlements, the largest of which was the town of Cinderford.

Even in the eighteenth century, quarry- and mine-owners did provide some housing. Lord Bathurst owned quarries at Pillowell in the Forest of Dean, and in the late eighteenth century he paid six shillings for the erection of a cottage on the common waste to house a quarry worker (Newman 1988, 369). The Penrhyn slate quarries in north Wales, which supplied much of the roofing slate used in later nineteenth-century industrial housing throughout Britain, resulted in the creation of a number of new settlements. The design of dwellings and the allocation of land for housing was controlled by the Penrhyn estate, and the houses favoured by the estate for the quarry labourers were single-storey dwellings with a *croglofft* (Lowe 1977, 62), such as housed most Welsh rural labourers. Similar buildings housed industrial workers, such as the lead-miners of Cwmystwyth in west Wales, as late as 1835 (Lowe 1977, 10). Pairs of one-and-a-half-storey cottages, which were a direct development from the eighteenth-century croglofft cottages, continued to be built for the Penrhyn quarry at Mynydd Llandegai as late as the 1870s (Lowe 1977, 62).

In the Durham area, coal-miners' housing in the earlier nineteenth century tended to consist of a single room and a garret (Emery 1992, 149), though there was a variety of plan types during the nineteenth century (Brown 1995, 296). The houses were often built quickly on badly drained sites (Brown 1995, 292). Sanitation and drainage were rudimentary; the Durham mining village of South Hetton had no privies in 1842 and only one for 154 dwellings in 1892 (Emery 1992, 154). As late as 1887 a report on public health found coal-mining settlements to be 'foul, priviless, ill-watered, unscavenged, overcrowded lairs' (see Gauldie 1974, 64). Even so, during the nineteenth century it became essential for colliery owners, particularly in the Great Northern Coalfield, to provide reasonable quality houses if they wished to attract and retain miners (Gauldie 1974, 64–5). For example, the Nostell Priory estate in Yorkshire built forty-seven terraced cottages at Long Row between 1860 and 1865 to house workers in its colliery (RCHME 1985b, 69). Miners' cottages throughout the northern coalfields in the later nineteenth century tended to be brick-built with thin Welsh slate roofs. The bricks were often supplied by the collieries' own brickworks. Both through cottages and back-to-backs were built, often to a two-up, two-down design. Throughout the north Midlands, Yorkshire and County Durham the late nineteenth-century brick-built terraces of miners' housing are characteristic components of the present-day landscape of the coalfield areas.

Although the quality of miners' cottages was criticised in the later nineteenth century, they were often quite superior to the housing of other industrial and many agricultural workers. Clearly in the Great Northern Coalfield they were sufficiently desirable for their provision to be an inducement for labourers to work in the pits. Much of the criticism of miners' living conditions seems to be aimed not so much at the housing itself as at the inadequate servicing of the settlements. Furthermore, the provision of housing often did not meet the demand, resulting in subletting and overcrowding (Brown 1995, 303).

The industrial expansion of the later eighteenth and nineteenth centuries caused many rural communities to expand and new rural industrial settlements to appear. Some of these had elements of community planning and rows of workers' housing sponsored by industrialists. In some instances, however, the industrialists sought to create entirely new 'model' settlements, either as villages or as suburbs. There seem to have been two fundamental philosophies motivating the development of these communities: a genuine desire to avoid the problems of the industrialised urban areas – overcrowding, crime, rowdiness and poor health – and an appreciation of the advantages in terms of social control and dependence that such paternalism could bring. By raising the moral standards of their labourers employers hoped to create docile and productive workforces (Gauldie 1974, 61). As is suggested by the names of some these settlements, such as Edward Akroyd's Akroydon and Titus Salt's Saltaire, they were also intended as monuments to the personalities of their creators.

These model communities were built in the shadow of the factories the housed workforce was meant to serve. One of the earliest was Josiah Wedgwood's settlement of Etruria, built in Staffordshire after the establishment of his new ceramic works in 1771 (Raistrick 1972, 234). It is perhaps in central Scotland that the most significant of the early purpose-built factory communities were established. Here the growth of the textile industry required new immigrant

Model houses at Copley, near Halifax, Yorkshire, built for Edward Akroyd's workforce in the mid-nineteenth century.

workforces which could in part be supplied by work-seeking, homeless, evicted Highlanders (Gauldie 1974, 60). Supply and demand necessitated the creation of new housing. At Stanley, Perthshire, in the last decade of the eighteenth century a model village, consisting of terraces of two-storey housing built in stone or brick, was created to house the workforce of the two mills built by 1790 (RCAHMS 1986, 84). Contemporary with this development was the more famous settlement of New Lanark, Lanarkshire. Originally built by David Dale, who had previously created the village of Catrine, Ayrshire (Gauldie 1974, 60), it was bought out by a partnership including Dale's son-in law Robert Owen in 1799. At Catrine, Dale had built two-storey cottages, but at New Lanark he constructed two- or three-storey terraces, presumably in order to cater economically for a larger workforce. Although some writers considered Dale's housing to have been of poor quality (Tarn 1971, 30), compared to other contemporary industrial workers' housing and the housing of the rural poor, particularly in Scotland, it was of a reasonable standard. Owen developed Dale's housing so that by the 1820s New Lanark's accommodation consisted of three- or four-storey, stone-built tenement blocks, usually terraced into the hillside so that the lowermost floors were back-to-earth. Dwellings varied in size from one to four rooms and included in some cases cellars (RCAHMS 1986, 81–2). Evidence for inbuilt box beds have been found in most rooms, so there seems to have been little initial specialisation in room usage.

The mid-nineteenth century witnessed another spate of factory-based model village construction. In Yorkshire, Edward Akroyd built a village at Copley, near Halifax, between 1849 and 1853 (Caffyn 1983, 179). Although he was criticised a decade later in the influential journal *The Builder* for his reliance on back-to-backs (Tarn 1971, 32), Akroyd's houses were of an adequate standard in comparison to other contemporary industrial workers' housing. Built of stone with slate roofs and designed in an old English cottage style, the first houses had a living-room with two bedrooms, offering a combined floor space of about 36.5m², plus a cellar. These proved to be rather too expensive and the later houses were said to be in the 'common style of the country' and consisted of only a living room with a box bed, and a bedroom (Gauldie 1974, 61). Ten years later Akroyd was building another model settlement at Akroydon on the outskirts of Halifax, and it is clear from the evidence of the houses there that he was investing in housing of superior quality to that at Copley. At Akroydon the dwellings were either two-up, two-down or three-up, two-down, with cellars and with fireplaces in the bedrooms (RCHME 1985b, 59–61). Other near-contemporary model settlements with even better housing included Bromborough Pool on the Wirral, built in 1854 by Price's Patent Candle Company (Gauldie 1974, 62), and the most famous of all, Saltaire near Bradford, built between 1854 and 1872. Too much can be made of the altruism of these model community developers; although they were interested in the moral and social condition of their labour forces, the dwellings they built were generally no better than contemporary industrial workers' housing erected by speculative developers. As with other industrial workers' housing, there was a development away from vernacular-influenced two-celled structures, with little specialisation in space usage evident, towards multi-roomed and stylistically non-vernacular buildings with better sanitary provision and greater possible levels of comfort.

One final category of rural-based industrial workers' housing is that associated with impermanent settlements, created as a result of major construction and engineering projects such as canals, railways and reservoirs. These navvy camps are a distinctive feature of the nineteenth- and early twentieth-century archaeological record (Morris 1994). Impermanent dwellings had always been a feature of the lives of transient industrial workers. Charcoal-burners' huts erected in the woods, for example, were small temporary structures of wood and turf. Coal-miners who searched for suitable pit sites and undertook the initial shaft sinking were often housed in temporary structures, usually wooden huts similar to log cabins (Emery 1992, 148). Because of their temporary nature such structures do not survive, and earthwork survey and/or excavation is necessary to supplement the pictorial record.

In areas with a good supply of housing, navvies tended to be largely housed in rented accommodation, but in less populated areas they lived in hut settlements (Morris 1994, 573–4). In the early nineteenth century there were two basic forms of hut, the shant and the sod hut. The former was provided purpose-built by the contractor, and might be a stone- or brick-built one- or two-celled structure; the latter was erected by an employee and was made out of whatever materials were available (Morris 1994, 575). Associated with the Woodhead tunnel on the Sheffield to Manchester railway, the foundations of dry-stone dwellings have been recorded, including a six-unit single-storey terrace, which appears to be documented contractor-provided housing (Morris 1994, 575–6). This tradition of contractor-supplied and employee-erected houses continued into the later nineteenth century. At Ribblehead in north Yorkshire a group of navvy hutments, occupied between 1870 and 1875, was erected for the labourers on the Ribblehead viaduct, at Blea Moor tunnel and in the stone supply quarries at Littledale. The houses seem to have been either contractor-supplied prefabricated wooden huts of up to three rooms, with felt and tar roof coverings, or labourer-built squatter-type cabins with low dry-stone walls supporting a roof covered in turfs (Mitchell 1996, 28–9). The buildings were not intended to be 'permanent' (Cardwell et al. 1996, 11). With their exotic names, like Sebastopol, Jericho,

Salt Lake City and, more prosaically, Batty Green, contemporaries compared the appearance of these settlements to the frontier and mining towns of the New World (Mitchell 1996, 8). In their wild lawlessness and inhospitable situation they may also have duplicated similar social and environmental conditions.

Urban Housing before the Industrial Revolution

As in the countryside, the needs and aspirations of all socio-economic groups were represented in town housing. The most important distinction between urban and pre-industrial rural housing across all groups, however, is that town houses were largely not intended to be farmhouses (Brunskill 1997, 108). Their occupiers' primary reason for locating in towns was to engage in commerce and/or craft industries. These different requirements affected the design of town housing and the relationships between neighbouring buildings. This distinction between the urban and rural was already apparent in the Middle Ages. Medieval urban housing may have developed in tandem with the rural vernacular and had its roots in the countryside (Pantin 1963, 202), but the constraints and requirements of urban living frequently adapted the rural house types to fit. Open halls flanking a town street did occur where space allowed (Schofield 1997, 131), as did some parallel arrangements of halls set back from the street, fronted by a courtyard with, adjacent to the street, gates and ancillary buildings or even a gatehouse (Grenville 1997, 165). Often such buildings were gentry, rather than merchant, houses, for whom display was more important than street frontage, as at Plas Mawr, Conwy, north Wales, built in the late 1570s. Generally, however, particularly in the more successful towns, such building types were incompatible with the nature of the narrow, often subdivided, burgage plots that made up urban properties. At Totnes and York by the fifteenth century street frontage was characteristically no more than 20ft (6.1m) (Brunskill 1997, 108; Laithwaite 1984, 67). In situations where street frontage was severely restricted and at a premium for fronting a business, houses were designed to run along the length of the burgage plot and were built three or four storeys high (Brunskill 1997,

Jettied buildings in Shrewsbury.

108; Grenville 1997 165–7); floor space was maximised by the construction along the frontage of a stepped series of jetties.

An indication of the ground-floor plans of town houses, and their layouts in relation to property boundaries, during the early post-medieval period is provided by the detailed surveys of London districts compiled by Ralph Treswell in the late sixteenth and early seventeenth centuries (Schofield 1987). The houses of the most wealthy often corresponded to the courtyard plan. There was a variety of designs for middling-sized town houses, many of which had their origins in buildings originating in the late fourteenth century. They included houses with halls on the ground floor and up to five other ground-floor rooms, which might include a parlour, a kitchen, a buttery, a shop at the front of the property and a storeroom. More common was the house consisting of a two-room plan on three or more floors, with the hall situated on the first floor (Schofield 1987, 18). Examples of this type have been documented outside London, as for example in late sixteenth-century Manchester (Willan 1980, 108). Often such houses formed the street frontage to larger houses set in their own grounds (Schofield 1997, 131). The smallest houses depicted by Treswell in London in about 1600 were those with a single room per floor and only three storeys high (Schofield 1997, 132), though on principal streets they could be up to five-and-a-half storeys high (Schofield 1987, 15). Again these buildings often fronted the properties of larger houses which lay behind them (Schofield 1987, 15).

While it is very likely that single-room, single-storey houses would have been present in many later medieval towns (Brunskill 1997, 148), it has been suggested that they were disappearing from towns in the sixteenth century (Dyer 1981; Schofield 1997, 131), although the remains of one tentatively dated to the sixteenth century were excavated in Walsall. The smallest houses in the sixteenth and early seventeenth centuries in Kings Lynn, Norwich, Taunton and Exeter were also one-up, one-down houses (Schofield 1997, 132; Taylor 1974; Portman 1966). In the less-well-developed towns of the north and west of Britain, before the onset of industrialisation, such urban dwellings would have been common for the poorer town inhabitants into the eighteenth century. These early examples of the housing of the poorer urban dwellers are unlikely to survive today, having been either replaced or incorporated into other structures (Taylor 1974, 71). Single-cell houses continued to be built during the sixteenth and early seventeenth centuries. While new building in towns may not have been common in the sixteenth century, it did take place. The redevelopment of the St Bartholomew's fairground in London in about 1600 involved the replacement of 400 booths with about 175 houses, of which 80 per cent conformed to the single-cell ground floor plan (Leech 1996, 204–10). These dwellings were three storeys high with an attic and cellar, and were built, like many medieval town houses, in rows, in this case conforming to the previous layout of the booths.

Fire, rot and, in some cases, poor initial construction would all have contributed to the attrition rate of medieval houses, ensuring that replacement was required (Currie 1988, 2–3). The types and plans of town houses built, however, indicate that attrition through fashion may not have been a major factor at the time. For most people radical changes to building forms and plans appear not to have taken place before the later seventeenth century, a pattern also noted elsewhere in Europe (Schofield 1997, 141). Although late medieval house plans and types were retained in new domestic building into the early seventeenth century throughout Britain, changes in style, decoration and building materials were introduced. Thatched roofs were replaced with tiles, timber-frames were rendered or in some cases were encased in or infilled with brick, and new buildings were erected wholly in brick. The St Bartholomew's fair development, though primarily of timber-framed construction, is also the earliest evidence for large-scale brick building in London (Leech 1996, 224–6), and included back-to-back dwellings to maximise space (Leech 1996, 213, 226). Some new urban house layouts do seem to have evolved. Houses planned around a central staircase, an urban vernacular derivative of the lobby-entry house, initially flourished in London between 1660 and 1680 (Kelsall 1974, 88–91), but first appeared in London and other towns in south-east England from the late sixteenth century (Schofield 1984; Leech 1999b, 46). Even with the lack of new building, some of the processes of change in housing noted by Johnson in a rural context do appear to be present in the urban environment (Johnson 1993a). Since town houses were multi-storey from the later medieval period, in part at least as a response to space constraints, fireplaces, stairs and ceilings appeared early. For the ordinary inhabitants of most houses, changes seem to have been pragmatic responses to developments in the urban environment, rather than symbols of social evolution within the house; the use of tile and brick, for example, was encouraged because of their fireproof qualities, while jetties were discouraged because they encroached on the street space and reduced light (Schofield 1997, 140).

The unchanging medieval form and layout of the smaller houses – with a shop on the ground floor, hall on the second floor and bed chamber above – allowed for little change in lifestyle. A study of seventeenth-century town houses in Taunton indicates a similar separation between work space on the ground floor and domestic above, but gives little indication of any space specialisation within the domestic context (Taylor 1974, 75). Specialised room use, beyond a crude work/household divide, gender-specific spaces and social exclusion are not developments evidenced in the houses of the ordinary urban dwellers. Even so, studies in Norwich indicate that lifestyle was not wholly static. During the course of the sixteenth century more cesspits appear to have been provided per house, cellars became more common and there was an increase and diversification in material culture (Schofield 1997, 141). Yet overall it is difficult to escape Schofield's conclusion that between *c.* 1400 and *c.* 1600 (and perhaps as late as *c.* 1670), for at least the majority of urban dwellers, 'there were no violent changes in culture or thought as far as houses were concerned' (Schofield 1997, 142).

During the earlier post-medieval period a common theme in the development of town housing was the increased use of more durable and fireproof materials (Borsay 2000, 110; Crossley 1990, 91). The close proximity of large numbers of timber-framed buildings, infilled with wattle and daub and roofed with thatch, and sometimes with timber-built chimneys, inevitably risked conflagration, from both domestic fires and the large numbers of craft occupations using fire in their manufacturing processes. In some areas where there was plentiful and easily worked stone, medieval town houses were often masonry structures, though even then timber-framing could be used as a fashion statement, as in sixteenth-century Burford, Oxfordshire (Schofield 1997, 140). The majority of British towns in the sixteenth and early seventeenth centuries had a substantial timber component in their fabric. In Worcester the city council in the later sixteenth century was very aware of the fire risk to their largely timber-built town, and repeatedly prohibited timber chimneys and encouraged the replacement of thatched with tiled roofs (Hughes 1980, 282). Similar local authority prohibitions were put in place at Winchester in 1656 (Jones 1968, 146). The Great Fire of London in 1666 is the best known example of the effect of fire within a largely timber-built urban environment, but there were many other towns whose fabric was severely affected by fire damage. A study of towns in Wessex indicated the very common occurrence of major fires between 1650 and 1780 (Jones 1968, 141).

Throughout the kingdom towns were subjected to major fires: Wolverhampton in 1590, Berwick-upon-Tweed in 1659, Northampton in 1675, Warwick in 1694 and Blandford Forum in 1731. Some towns, like Stratford-upon-Avon and Beaminster, suffered severe fire damage on repeated occasions (Porter 1994, 13; Jones 1968, 143–4). Fire became a particular hazard during the Civil War when towns under attack were frequently set alight intentionally and sometimes by accident (Porter 1994).

The statistically verifiable reduced risk of fire in towns from the later eighteenth century has been in part attributed to improved firefighting technology (Jones 1968, 144), but it is primarily considered to be a consequence of the gradually increasing use of more fireproof materials. Although the risk of fire was appreciated from the sixteenth century, it was often not until a major fire had occurred in a town that inflammable materials, such as timber-frames and thatched roofs, were routinely avoided, starting with the replacement of the destroyed structures (Clifton-Taylor 1972, 224). The effect of this on the townscapes of Northampton and Warwick was noted by Defoe, who commented on their houses having been rebuilt in brick and stone following fire damage (Jones 1968, 145). In London, following the Great Fire, Building Acts limited the use of timber, and bricks and freestone became the principal building materials (Johnson 1991, 18). The regular nature of brick was well suited to building houses with classical pretensions. Generally, in the later seventeenth and early eighteenth centuries, rebuilding in the Midlands and in southern England was in brick, which was at the time both fashionable and becoming cheaper than stone (Clifton-Taylor 1972, 224). On occasion this happened in the north of England too, such as in Newcastle-upon-Tyne (Heslop and McCombie 1996, 167). For reasons of fashion it even made a sporadic appearance in the new town of Whitehaven, Cumberland, in the later seventeenth century (RCHME 1991). Brick, for reasons of fashion and fireproofing, was used in the renovation of many existing buildings in the late seventeenth century, as at the Cooperage, Newcastle-upon-Tyne (Heslop and Truman 1993).

In London the Great Fire has been described as an historical and archaeological turning point (Schofield 1993b, 211), but while it did hugely affect the appearance of England's capital its significance in the development of housing can be overstated (Reed 1983, 110). There is clear evidence from other urban centres that the late seventeenth and early eighteenth centuries saw a period of rapid and fundamental change in the nature of urban housing. Even without the fire major changes would have been likely in London's housing in the later seventeenth century. In Norwich a study of probate inventories, mainly of tradesmen and craftsmen, revealed a gradual increase in the specialisation of room use between 1580 and 1730, with internal reorganisation and subdivision being most frequent in the late seventeenth century (Priestley and Corfield 1982). Throughout England, at least, the late seventeenth century saw the widespread adoption of window glass, as glass-houses to manufacture it were erected across the country (Platt 1994, 149).

Fire damage and prevention, the effects of attrition and an expanding population all contributed to a need for new dwellings in later seventeenth- and early eighteenth-century towns, but beyond this was a desire for new buildings as a signifier of progress. Both in Britain and in the American colonies this process took place and is often termed Georgianisation (Glassie 1975; Deetz 1977). The middle classes adopted regularity, symmetry, restraint and dignity in their choice of new housing design. Architectural ornamentation and style were influenced by these developments, and even the choice of building materials was conditioned to an extent by such considerations. In 1801 Gloucester was praised for its civic improvements,

A late seventeenth-century, brick-built, middle-class town house, Newent, Gloucestershire. This is an early example of the use of brick in the county in the construction of a classical-style house.

including the refacing of timber buildings in brick and the removal of buildings which obstructed highways, but the civic authorities were castigated for not removing the many surviving jetties (Ayres 1998, 32). Georgianisation was a very middle-class phenomenon, reflecting values which came to the fore in the eighteenth century. Such traits were not frequently exhibited in the classically influenced palaces of the aristocracy, which were often excessive and overly fussy, nor were they clearly visible in the housing of the labouring classes, except where provided or controlled by entrepreneurs. Georgianisation was then a middle-class process which marked the housing of members of a group who shared values and aspirations; the stylistic adoptions were deliberate and intended to distinguish the house's occupants from those outside their social group (Woodforde 1978, 2). Corporate authorities also considered the adoption of classical architecture to be a sign of the progressiveness of their towns.

These values went beyond an aesthetic appreciation of restrained classicism. It has been argued that the middle classes, in the English-speaking world, shared a common materialist world view. This was developed in the context of capitalism (Leone and Potter 1988). As Matthew Johnson put it, 'in this perspective the reflection in material culture of Georgian principles is seen as an expression of a dominant ideology' (1996, 16). The rational approach to architecture, with its symmetry, balance and compartmentalisation, is seen as an expression of the middle-class desire for an ordered, well-structured and restrained society. In Bath classical architecture may even have been an expression of the religious beliefs of one of its principal architects, John Wood (Neale 1974, 269–73). The division of houses into separate rooms is an indication of a desire for privacy and the breaking down of communal ties and traditional social relationships, but it is also a sign of order with discrete functions – male/female, business/domestic, day/night – being contained and compartmentalised.

Johnson has argued that many of the changes identified by American scholars as part of the Georgianisation process, and seen almost as marking a distinction between 'medieval' and 'modern', were in actuality prefigured by changes in the seventeenth century if not earlier (1996, 177). With regard to domestic architecture, Johnson argues that Georgianisation was the culmination of a longer post-medieval process which saw the introduction of various forms of 'closed houses', finally culminating in the Georgian-style house. While Johnson's arguments seem reliable on the basis of much observed rural evidence, it must be questioned in regard to urban housing. From the late medieval period to the later seventeenth century urban domestic buildings remained relatively constant in design and function, mirroring other aspects of urban material culture. Despite archaeological evidence for increased material wealth among the merchant class, particularly in some towns in the fifteenth century, by the mid-sixteenth century the majority still lived in largely undivided small homes with few goods or chattels (Courtney 1996, 90–1). As late as the 1660s open halls continued to be a feature of many Bristol merchants' houses (Leech 1999a, 29). It is only from the mid-seventeenth century that growth in consumer goods begins a noticeable upward trend (Courtney 1996, 91). It is from then also that there appears to be a notable increase within the urban house of space subdivision and room specialisation. Service accommodation is removed to the rear of buildings, domestic and business space is increasingly distinguished, and the worlds of women and men become increasingly separated. Rather than prefiguring Georgianisation, however, these late seventeenth-century developments, particularly in London, represent the beginnings of it. The urban evidence suggests that the American distinction between 'medieval' and 'Georgian' seems reasonable and applicable to at least the English and Welsh urban scene, the only difference being that in some English towns the process of Georgianisation should be seen as commencing in the 1670s, rather than at the beginning of the eighteenth century.

Roger Leech has argued that distinguishing the urban architecture of the Georgian period from what preceded it, the traditional stance of the architectural historian, is problematic (1999a, 27). As already highlighted in a rural context, aspects of Georgian housing can be seen as developments from the vernacular tradition of the preceding three centuries (*see* Leech 1999b). Yet it is clear that town housing in the eighteenth century reflects an urban society which had changed significantly from that of the early seventeenth century, which seems to have had more in common with the fifteenth century. While Leech is correct to stress the need to review the architectural history of the sixteenth to eighteenth centuries as a continuum (1999a, 27–8), there is an observable distinct change between the nature of the Georgian town and its predecessors which is marked in the domestic architecture of at least the elite and middling classes. Such distinctions are not clear in the countryside. There, the effects of elite and middle-class ambitions and attitudes were more diffused. Conservatism more strongly balanced trends for modernity. Perhaps above all rural housing tended to reflect individual needs and identities only, whereas urban housing also reflected corporate and civic identities and values.

In towns the process of Georgianisation had particular effects beyond the adoption of certain architectural styles and choice of building materials. The advent of the double-pile house in the

A typical Georgian terrace in Clifton, Bristol, exhibiting architectural uniformity and conformity.

later seventeenth century had as significant an impact in towns as it did in the countryside (Brunskill 1997, 128), but towns spawned their own types of housing. In particular, houses in terraces, or later occasionally in crescents, appeared in towns throughout England and Wales. In London they were built following the Great Fire, with those built by Nicholas Barbon between 1670 and 1700 being among the earliest in the country (Brunskill 1997, 138). Urban houses had been built in rows since the medieval period, but terraces were distinct, even though partially derived, from the earlier rows. Often designed *en bloc*, they had shared architectural characteristics and continuous roof lines, displaying order and symmetry. Terraces encouraged other innovations such as the construction of chimney stacks against party walls. They facilitated the wholesale planning as a unit of entire streets and squares, encouraging the development of standardised and economic house designs. One effect of this was the development of the rear staircase plan and the consequent phasing out of the central staircase plan (Kelsall 1974, 88).

Various plans for terraced housing developed during the eighteenth century, but the narrow-fronted 'universal terrace house' is the most common. Brunskill describes it thus: 'the universal terrace-house plan provides two rooms on the ground floor, one at the front and a slightly narrower one at the rear. Alongside the front room is the entrance lobby; alongside the back room is the staircase rising in one long flight to the half-landing and then in a shorter return flight to the first floor, and so on up the full height of the house' (1997, 138–40). The significance of this plan for subsequent urban house design cannot be overstated. This house type and its variants marked a decisive break with the late medieval tradition that preceded it, and as such was symbolic of the new rational age and of the increased significance and power of the middle classes. These buildings allowed for a greater segregation of function and inhabitants within the house, servants' quarters, for example, being separated to the rear of the dwellings. For the middle-class owners and occupants of these houses it marked their rejection of local vernacular traditions as terraced housing was introduced via pattern books to many of the towns of England and Wales.

The building of standardised terraces was facilitated by the increased requirement for completely new developments, occasioned by population growth within towns, partly in response to economic stimuli and attrition of the existing building stock. However, throughout the eighteenth century the desire to replace the old with the new in towns was ever-present and is clearly evidenced in the works of the numerous local histories and travel and agricultural commentaries that were written during the century. Old vernacular-tradition, timber-built towns were not simply considered to be hazardous but regarded with distaste and embarrassment. If they could not be completely rebuilt they would be hidden behind classical façades. Well-regarded genteel towns were those with new brick and ashlared stone structures, such as Bath, regularly laid out, neat, homogeneous and restrained (Borsay 2000, 106). Much of the growth of London in the eighteenth century consisted of housing of this type. *The Times* in 1803 advertised a genteel commodious house in Islington, three storeys from the cellar with four rooms to a floor (Reed 1983, 126). By then this was typical of the middle-class housing to be found in many towns and was to influence the way in which this now influential political class would view and seek to change the houses of the poor and labouring classes during the nineteenth and twentieth centuries.

A further factor influencing new building in some towns in the late seventeenth and earlier eighteenth centuries was industrial growth. One of the earliest industrialised towns with surviving purpose-built industrial workers' housing was Frome in Somerset. In the later seventeenth century, as a consequence of prosperity resulting from woollen cloth manufacture, Frome experienced a rapid increase in population to such an extent that in the 1720s Defoe compared its growth to that of Manchester (RCHME 1981, 1). Fortuitously for the survival of the buildings erected in that period, its prosperity did not last out the eighteenth century. Much of Frome's housing expansion was contained in a greenfield site now known as the Trinity area, which was developed between about 1660 and 1725 (RCHME 1981, 3–7). The houses were built of local stone in rubble courses, windows were one- to four-light mullions for the smaller houses, with four-light mullion and transomed windows for the larger ones. The latter also had symmetrically designed façades with classical pretensions, though the rest of the dwellings were clearly vernacular in tradition. Constructed initially in rows of houses of varying designs but later in relatively uniform terraces, the dwellings complied to a restricted set of basic plans. The most common consisted of either a single room on the ground floor with one or two chambers above, or a hall and parlour on the ground floor with chambers above (RCHME 1981, 10–15). Those with a single-cell ground-floor plan could have a ground-floor space as tiny as 13m². Similar houses were built elsewhere, including nearby in Shepton Mallet (RCHME 1981, 17), though not necessarily for industrial workers.

A contemporary urban development was Whitehaven on the Cumberland coast, but unlike Frome its houses were designed with pretensions beyond the vernacular tradition. A new harbour town planned by Sir John Lowther to meet the needs of his family's coal and salt interests, it was laid out on a grid pattern in the 1660s (RCHME 1991, 1–2, 26–7; Platt 1994, 146). Influenced by the principles of polite architecture, Whitehaven's surviving houses of late seventeenth- and early eighteenth-century date superficially do not belong to the prevailing local vernacular. Well-

Late seventeenth-century clothiers' and weavers' houses, Frome, Somerset.

proportioned and relatively symmetrical, the houses were intended to be built in rows to a uniform style, appropriate to a town designed for regularity and conformity (Platt 1994, 146–8). Yet a closer examination reveals that the houses of the late seventeenth and early eighteenth century were generally rooted in the local vernacular tradition. Windows were usually two- or three-light mullions. Stone newel stairs, set in rounded projecting stair turrets, accessed the two- or three-storey structures (RCHME 1991, 71), just as in farmhouses of the Cumberland countryside. Individualism among the householders spoiled the intended uniformity of the rows. A third of the houses built in Whitehaven before 1740 were of a single-cell ground-floor plan, like those in Frome, though few now survive, and they were typical of the houses built for the urban poor in the seventeenth century throughout England (RCHME 1991, 85). Although their plans were similar, being a functional response to limited space, the use of materials and detailing would have distinguished all these houses, giving them distinct local styles. Indeed, it was not until the later eighteenth century that Whitehaven's housing lost its local character (RCHME 1991, 109).

To an extent the development of housing in Scottish pre-industrial towns seems to reflect the situation in England and Wales, but the effect of nineteenth-century rebuilding has removed most of the upstanding archaeological evidence. One development dating to the sixteenth century in towns such as Edinburgh and Dundee was the appearance of flats within multi-storey buildings, with a single stair accessing the floors from top to bottom (Brunskill 1997, 234; Schofield 1997, 139). Here then seems to be the origin of the tenement building which was to prove to be such an enduring feature of Scottish urban housing in the eighteenth and nineteenth centuries. The building of tenements was encouraged by a lack of space within cramped urban areas in tandem with the Scottish practice of land purchase, which consisted of a lump sum payment and a feu, or ground rent paid in perpetuity. The feu could sometimes be offset against another lump sum payment calculated usually at a value of twenty-one years' feu (Reed 1983, 118). As a result, land was expensive to rent and so, to maximise the return on an investment, as many dwelling units as possible were placed on any given area of ground, thus encouraging the development of high-rise tenements. Unlike most other forms of urban housing, tenement dwellings shared external entrances and circulation routes, stimulating communal and class unity. A similar effect may have been created by the development of lower-class courtyard housing, in response to space restrictions in the eighteenth century. The yard was a communal space, and all court dwellers had to enter the domestic world of the court via a shared alley linking it to the public world.

During the later eighteenth century the constrictive nature of the larger Scottish towns was a cause of much concern. In line with developments in England new areas were added to existing towns to accommodate development (Reed 1983, 120–2), and new houses were built in elegant neo-classical Georgian style, though often these buildings continued to be subdivided into flats rather than being single-family dwellings (Brunskill 1997, 234). By the later eighteenth century suburbs intended for less wealthy families were also created; in Glasgow from 1795 the Gorbals were progressively divided up and feued, and tenement blocks were erected (Reed 1983, 118). Developments witnessed at towns such as Whitehaven seem to have occurred a century later in Scotland. In Galloway town development and the improvement of urban housing took place in the late eighteenth century as a consequence of increased regional prosperity rising from agricultural improvement, combined with attempts to establish industrial towns. At Kirkcudbright the town council in 1790 authorised a plan by Lord Daer to feu land for development (Marsden 1997). The council imposed controls over the development, stipulating that the houses had to be at least two storeys high, reflecting the tradition in smaller Scottish towns of continuing to build rural-style single-storey structures well into the nineteenth century. They also required slate roofs and demanded that houses should be built to a 'reasonable' plan (Marsden 1997, 91). Even when aristocratic developers were not restricted by a town council they still attempted to impose minimum standards. At Gatehouse of Fleet single-storey houses were only to be allowed in the rear streets, and the results of this prohibition can be clearly seen in the fabric of the town today (Marsden 1997, 94–5).

Back street in Gatehouse of Fleet, Kirkcudbrightshire, with single-storey houses.

Elite and 'Middle-class' Urban Housing in the Nineteenth Century

Less has been written by historians about the urban housing of the wealthier classes in the nineteenth century than about that of the working classes, and the subject has been almost totally ignored by archaeologists. During the nineteenth century the middle classes expanded greatly to encompass engineers, civil servants, accountants and the like (Newton 1977, 20). By the end of the century grocers, shopkeepers, teachers, junior office managers and many others formed the lower middle class, differentiated as much by aspiration as wealth from some skilled labourers. The nineteenth century witnessed a massive increase in the size of many towns and it was in those growing towns that new middle-class and elite housing was erected.

New housing seems to have been primarily erected to meet the new demand and generally not as a replacement for earlier buildings. The surviving middle-class housing of earlier periods was, given adequate maintenance, both structurally sound and capable of meeting the requirements of urban living. In developing urban areas eighteenth-century middle-class housing was abandoned in favour of new housing. It was not directly replaced, however; rather, old areas were abandoned in favour of new ones, as the moneyed classes left the town centres for new planned developments on the periphery. The housing left behind might be completely redeveloped as commercial or industrial premises or as more dense working-class housing, depending on the demand for town centre sites, or buildings might be retained but transformed from single-tenant middle-class housing to multiple-tenancy working-class housing. Generally, eighteenth-century middle-class housing does not seem to have been replaced on the same site by nineteenth-century middle-class housing. Although individual buildings were on occasion partially modernised to reflect new architectural tastes, the costs of rebuilding a house of this type were likely to be high in comparison to the cost of building from scratch on a virgin site.

The fashionable district was more important than the fashionable house as the middle classes sought to put distance between themselves and the increasingly polluted urban centres (Beresford 1988). The eighteenth century witnessed the blossoming of class-exclusive housing developments, facilitated by building terraces of similar house types and fuelled by the growing middle class's need to define itself as belonging to a distinct group. In the early nineteenth century well-designed areas of middle-class and elite housing were seen as matters of monumental civic pride, often sponsored by an aristocratic developer, such as the Earl of Moray, who was responsible for the exclusive residential development of Moray Place in Edinburgh (Reed 1983, 124).

The architectural style of these buildings owed little to vernacular traditions. They were professionally designed by architects taking their inspiration from style guides and pattern books. Stone could often be moved over great distances for the most exclusive and expensive developments, so that even the materials used in construction need owe nothing to the locality within which a building was erected. The same was true of decorative brickwork (Lucas 1998a). The houses were intended for display both individually and as a group. Individual display was focused on the street entrance, which in the early century featured entrances that were often pillared and pedimented, as can be seen in Regency developments in Clifton (Bristol) and Cheltenham. Later architectural styles were less restrained than the classicism exhibited by much Regency architecture. Gothic and Renaissance styles were often more flamboyant in decorative motifs. Technical innovation and expansion in the brick industry led to the mass production of brick mouldings, facilitating the availability of cheap, elaborate ornamental architectural effects in first Gothic and Tudor styles, and later in Italianate, Byzantine and other revivalist styles (Lucas 1998a). Indeed, the popularity of the most highly decorated architectural styles was undoubtedly facilitated by the availability of decorative brickwork.

The plethora of architectural styles that began to be used in the mid-nineteenth century broke the classical unity of many areas of middle-class housing in British towns. In some towns, such as Glasgow, classical influences held sway until the end of the century, reflecting the conservative tastes of the local middle classes, but creating a distinctive townscape in the West End (Simpson 1977, 77–8). Typically for Glasgow much of this middle-class dwelling space was formed of apartments within tenement blocks, and such buildings from the late eighteenth century were often fine, classically inspired structures (Worsdall 1979, 72–4). In the mid-nineteenth century Grecian-style crescents and terraces were constructed, which on close examination prove to be rows not of individual houses but of tenements (Worsdall 1979, 88–90). Other mid-nineteenth-century middle-class housing in the city was formed of villas. The villa was very different from the eighteenth-century town house. They were detached or semi-detached properties built away from the squalor of the urban centres, often in areas made accessible by the railways. This was the situation in Manchester, where middle-class villa developments grew in satellite towns such as Altrincham and Sale (Nevell 1997, 111). Unlike the buildings in the Georgian and Regency terraces, villas were individualistic, displaying a variety of styles and plans. Perhaps this individualism is a symptom both of a greater competitiveness among the upper middle classes and of a greater confidence. The need to define themselves as a group was past and replaced by a desire to distinguish themselves from their peers and to segregate themselves further from the masses in an effort to maximise their privacy. For the lower middle classes conformity and a need for group identity may have continued to strongly influence their choice of houses, and the terraced house remained their principal form of urban housing in the late Victorian period.

By the end of the nineteenth century urban middle-class terraced housing had developed a number of plan variants which can be recognised from one town to another where there are concentrations of Victorian housing. Particularly good examples are contained in the neighbouring Welsh ports of Cardiff and Barry (Thomas 1984, 338–9). Lower-middle-class housing consisted of an entrance hall leading to a stair well. To the side of the hall at the front of the building was a parlour, while a living-room to the side of the stairs gave access to a scullery contained within a two-storey annex. The stairs provided access to a landing, off which was a front master-bedroom stretching the full width of the house, a bedroom to the side of the landing and a rear bedroom above the scullery. The remainder of the property was occupied by a paved yard with an earth closet against the rear wall.

Middle-class housing intended for wealthier families was built to a similar plan but with additional rooms. On the ground floor there was a breakfast-room, behind which lay the scullery. These two rooms were contained in an annex above which on the first floor were a bedroom and a plumbed-in bathroom with separate water closet. Further bedrooms were situated on the second floor, which were often attic rooms contained within the roof space. These rooms usually housed the live-in domestic servants essential to the running of a late nineteenth-century household of such size and status. The external property space was occupied by a small yard and garden. Built in stone, brick or a combination of the two, architecturally these middle-class homes were generally Gothic in style with bay windows, decorative dormers and steeply pitched roofs with ornamental ridges. Internally they had decorative plasterwork on the ceilings. They were discrete homes, highly privatised and segregated, with each room, other than the scullery, sealed off from all others. All rooms were entered by a single entrance, except for the living-room in the smaller house or breakfast-room in the larger example; this was the only room that came close to having a communal function for the household, but it was tucked away in an ill-lit, secluded corner of the house well away from the front door and access to the wider world. Rooms had specialised functions. Status differences, gender roles and familial relationships were defined and constrained by these physical spaces and their organisation. These same spatial influences were repeated nationally, as the exact building pattern was, with minor variations, replicated from town to town. Within such homes the twentieth-century British, urban, middle-class worldview was born and moulded.

Urban-based Industrial Workers' Housing in the Late Eighteenth and Early Nineteenth Centuries

The economic growth that resulted in the creation of industrial and trading towns such as Frome and Whitehaven in about 1700 was insignificant in comparison to the urban expansion which followed in the wake of the Industrial Revolution. Increasing economic activity in the later eighteenth century, particularly in the textile and other industrial districts, led to the development of industrial workers' housing in urban locations. The labouring classes had always been present within the towns and had not been affected by the Georgianisation of their dwellings. Attrition had taken its toll of earlier buildings, however, and new structures continued to be erected by and for the poor. The nature of these seems to have varied regionally in relation to local vernacular traditions, but unfortunately the evidence for their nature is often lacking.

Lancaster is a town whose character appears to be primarily Georgian, a consequence of eighteenth-century prosperity resulting from transatlantic trade, including slaves, followed by mid-nineteenth-century stagnation (White 1993, 1–3). Its nineteenth-century circumstances distinguish it from nearby Preston, which had a similar eighteenth-century history and developed into a noted genteel town, but subsequent nineteenth-century industrialisation and the consequent development of new housing has removed most of the evidence of Preston's Georgian past. However, despite the survival of the Georgian middle-class housing in Lancaster, which gives the town its character, there is little surviving which exemplifies the houses of the contemporary poor. Documentary and pictorial sources indicate that they were living, in part, in older unreplaced houses, including some with thatched roofs, or in small cottages infilling the rear of plots and yards (White 1993, 17–18). In Whitehaven such houses consisted of back houses, built along the sides of passages or lining the rear plots of street-frontage houses (RCHME 1991, 60–1). Some of the earliest examples of such housing there dated to the late seventeenth century, usually built singly or in pairs, but most are later and by the late eighteenth century they were being built in rows or entire courts filling any available space. This was common in many towns at the end of the eighteenth century where restrictions on space had forced the development of open spaces behind the street frontages. Often such buildings were blind-backed, being built as lean-tos utilising pre-existing walls.

As the industrialised towns expanded outside their earlier municipal areas, new houses were laid out in courts and terraces. Economical of space, particularly with back-to-back houses, and symbolic of good order, the working-class terraced house seems to have had a number of influences. Rows of similarly designed labourers' cottages were constructed in the eighteenth century in industrialising

Workers' small terraced cottages at Whitehaven, Cumberland, built to fit into available space within the existing eighteenth-century urban plan.

rural areas, often in partial response to topographical constraints. In urban areas rows of similarly designed houses, for artisans, had been built since the early seventeenth century, and these buildings had their roots in medieval rows (Leech 1999b, 49). The excavated seventeenth-century houses at the Aldgate (London) were two-room plan houses built in short rows (Thompson *et al.* 1984), and one-room plan examples have been found throughout London (Leech 1999b, 47). The primary influence, however, on the development of the working-class terraced house, in long rows of identically designed houses, is likely to be the eighteenth-century urban middle-class Georgian terrace. Nevertheless it is impossible to ignore the vernacular traditions influencing these developments. Perhaps between 85 and 90 per cent of the houses of England and Wales, by about 1910, were built in rows, mostly of nineteenth-century terraced type (Muthesius 1982, 1).

In many growing industrial towns in about 1800 back-to-back accommodation was the most common form of terraced housing developed for urban workers. Maurice Beresford in particular has argued that the popularity of back-to-backs in towns in Yorkshire is linked to local vernacular developments in housing, rather than being a response to a need to supply cheap housing (1971, 119). In other areas with equally low wages back-to-backs did not appear; they did not occur generally in the industrial areas of London, for example, despite first being built there in the seventeenth century (Leech 1999b, 46). They were built both by speculative developers intent on profit and by co-operative housing clubs financed by the intended occupiers of the houses (RCHME 1985b, 41). Rather than a cheap housing option, they seem to have initially appeared in many towns around 1800 as a high-density housing option evolved from local developing vernacular traditions.

By the mid-nineteenth century back-to-back houses had been built in their tens of thousands in many industrial urban centres, such as Birmingham, Leeds, Manchester and Nottingham (Beresford 1988, Chapman 1971, Roberts 1986). Manchester alone had ten thousand by the 1890s – and this was following the prohibition of their construction and the demolition of many early examples. Standing examples, usually in terraces, reveal that they were common in Oldham, Rochdale, Keighley and many of the other Pennine textile towns. It must be emphasised that they were not the only house type used for labourers' housing, however, and even in northern England they were not uniformly common. In Blackburn, for example, the two-up, two-down through house was the most common form by the Victorian period (Daunton 1983, 49). Back-to-backs came to be condemned from the mid-nineteenth century as undesirable homes, but they were not necessarily regarded as synonymous with poverty in about 1800. They seem to have been a popular form of housing. Provision of back-to-back accommodation by employers was capable of attracting workers. One-up, or two-up, two-down house plans, often with floor space amounting to between 20 m² and 40 m², were attractive to many workers used to late eighteenth-century rural housing conditions. Research in towns such as Leeds, Manchester and Sheffield has indicated that in the earlier nineteenth century back-to-backs were often inhabited by skilled artisans, clerks and even policemen.

Below many back-to-backs were cellars. These were let as separate, usually one-room, dwellings. There was no internal stair connection to the house above, and in Leeds and other towns they were reckoned as separate homes in the 1801 census (Beresford 1988, 210). In the early nineteenth century Liverpool in particular became notorious for its cellar dwellings (Treble 1971). In late eighteenth-century Manchester three-storey houses were erected with cellars. The attic was often a loomshop, as the factory-based weaving shed had not developed at this time, and the cellar was let as a separate occupancy (Roberts 1986, 54). Cellar dwellings were accessed by a separate doorway, either to the side of or below the main entrance to the house above, and were reached by a flight of descending steps from the street frontage. Some cellar dwellings are likely to have been converted loomshops. In Lancashire the dampness of cellars was utilised in domestic handloom weaving. In Preston and Stockport, Cheshire, it has been argued that cellars were built in the late eighteenth century for handloom weaving (N. Morgan 1993; Coutie 1992). With the decline of urban-based domestic weaving in the face of factory-based competition in the nineteenth century these cellars were available for conversion to separate dwellings. In the Old Mount area of Ancoats, Manchester, handloom weavers were both living and working in the cellars beneath the back-to-backs as late as the 1860s (Hayton 1998, 75).

For contemporary social commentators, cellar dwellings were considered to be the worst kind of urban housing occupied by the poor (Gauldie 1974, 95; Hayton 1998, 69). As with some of the meanest forms of rural labourer housing, cellar dwellings came to be associated in particular with the Irish immigrants who helped to swell the urban populations of towns like Glasgow, Liverpool and Manchester in the early nineteenth century. Undoubtedly many of the documentary descriptions and pictorial representations do portray an apparently unsavoury existence and a high degree of squalor. In many, the poverty of the inhabitants is vividly demonstrated by the lack of material possessions; bedding is on the floor, chairs and tables are largely absent and crockery and other utensils are minimal (Hayton 1998, 70–1). All this at a time when the access of the poor to material possessions was greatly increasing. Such representations may be misleading, however, as they were drawn to illustrate a point, and it is unfortunate that to date no such dwellings have been archaeologically excavated.

In the north-west of England the poverty of cellar dwellers, particularly the Irish, was remarked upon in part because of racist attitudes. Friedrich Engels' view was that the lifestyles of these immigrants was largely responsible for their domestic circumstances (Hayton 1998). The cellar dweller was seen as bestial, the cellar itself representing literally the lowest and, in its troglodytic associations, most primitive form of dwelling. Yet recent writers have highlighted its advantages in comparison with other forms of contemporary labourers' housing. With floor spaces often around

12m², they were certainly small living areas even in comparison with the living spaces of the most badly housed rural poor, but at least they had private entrances, unlike lodgers or flat dwellers (Gauldie 1974, 95; Roberts 1986, 55). Some cellar dwellings were better lit, more spacious and well drained, and with the advantage of creating private family space they may well have provided more favoured accommodation than some alternative urban living spaces.

Urban Housing, Public Health and Decency

In the first half of the nineteenth century the increasing focus on factory production within urban areas, coupled with the lack of public transport facilities, forced labourers to crowd into areas close to their places of work. Thus enormous pressure was placed on housing stock within restricted areas. Rents were often high and space limited. Hence cellars formed homes, and back-to-backs were built in blocks behind street frontages (Lloyd-Jones and Lewis 1993, 33–4). In some instances factory owners provided housing, as was common practice in many of the new factory towns like St Helens (Jackson 1979). In older established towns, like Wigan and Manchester, speculative builders or building clubs often provided the bulk of the housing (Jackson 1979; Lloyd-Jones and Lewis 1993). The housing was usually basic, built in terraces or short rows around courtyards, often no more than two storeys with a room on each floor (Muthesius 1982, 106). Very little of this housing survives today, and much of it was demolished in the later nineteenth or earlier twentieth century. This was not necessarily because the houses were so poorly built, though some, particularly in London, undoubtedly were (Wohl 1971), but because the houses were replaced by others that were considered more appropriate. Unlike the housing of the middle classes and the elite, the motivation for building replacement seems not to have come from within the group of people who were to live in the buildings but was rather an imposition from without. Through a series of campaigns and legislation aimed at housing improvement, new multi-roomed houses were provided for the poor in the later nineteenth century.

Generally, it was not in the interests of speculative builders or industrialists to build non-durable houses (RCHME 1985b, 41). Durable but undesirable, many courts of back-to-backs were demolished in the later nineteenth and early twentieth centuries. In Manchester the earliest-known surviving examples date to 1791, but most early examples have long since been demolished or were converted to through houses during the course of the nineteenth century (Roberts 1986, 54–5). This was typical of so much urban housing provided for the poor in the early to mid-nineteenth century. At St Helens between 1843 and 1846, fifty small, one-storey terraced cottages were built at Moss Bank. These were demolished in 1902, not because they were insubstantially built but because they had few facilities and by the early twentieth century they were considered to be inadequate for the perceived needs of urban living (Jackson 1979, 131 and photograph 3). This is an historically documented case of the primary reason for the replacement of the houses of the poor in the post-medieval period: a perceived lack of adequacy for purpose within the developing class-related social context of domestic living.

In Chester, just such a perceived inadequate domestic abode, a probable one-up, one-down house, has been recently excavated (Matthews 1999). The investigation focused on a courtyard development known as Herbert's Yard, the northern side of which was occupied by terraced cottages erected before the 1850s and demolished as part of a slum clearance programme in 1939 (Matthews 1999, 162–3). The houses were brick-built with slate roofs and consisted of a single cell on each of the presumed two floors. Room specialisation would have been minimal. Sanitary facilities were

Mid-nineteenth-century back-to-backs at Sowerby Bridge, Yorkshire. Built in a classical style, they were intended for skilled workers and artisans.

communal. One of the most interesting discoveries concerned a series of forges attached to one of the houses dating to the early twentieth century. These were small scale, suitable for small tool manufacture or repair. The excavation results raise two interesting points. Firstly, they indicate that for the poorest urban dwellers by the end of the nineteenth century the world of work was still not necessarily distinct from the domestic world. Secondly, the small size of the working spaces within the forges indicate that they must have been operated by children, despite the legislation passed in the nineteenth century against the exploitation of child labour (Matthews 1999, 165–6).

It was the middle classes who brought about the clearance of undesirable working-class urban housing. They wrote pamphlets, they campaigned against 'slums', they enacted legislation at national and municipal levels aimed at 'improving' the housing of the poor. Their motivations for doing so were both altruistic and selfish, philanthropic and profit-led. The middle classes had by the early nineteenth century decided that the centres of the industrialising towns were not fit places for them to live. By the 1830s studies in towns like Manchester were beginning to demonstrate that the urban poor had higher mortality rates than much of the rest of the population and were at greater risk from contagious diseases (Roberts 1986, 56). Reports and inquiries combined with actual epidemics led to a raised awareness among the middle-class electorate about the housing conditions of the poor they had left behind in the urban centres. Overcrowding, poor building standards and a lack of sanitation were all causes for concern (Gauldie 1974, 131). As a consequence, in 1842 a government-sponsored investigation was published, the *Sanitary Report on the Labouring Population*, and this was followed by legislation later in the 1840s: the Towns Improvement Clauses Acts and the first national Public Health Act

(Gauldie 1974, 131–3). At a local level, too, studies were initiated and legislative action taken; in Manchester the Police Acts of 1844 banned the building of houses without yards and privies (Roberts 1986, 57). In Halifax in 1850–1 William Ranger's report on the town's sanitary conditions recommended among other provisions the end of cellar dwellings, of which there were 485 in 1851, a growth of 52 per cent in just six years (Webster 1998, 75–6).

It was not only the health issue that concerned the middle classes, as the moral well-being and civil obedience of the working classes were also of concern. The new urban areas were home to previously unknown concentrations of the poor, and the fear of the unruly crowd was prevalent among the ruling classes. Indeed civil unrest and public health could be linked. 'The extraordinary coincidence of outbursts of rebellion in Europe with outbreaks of cholera made the public fear the germ of sedition as much as the germ of disease' (Gauldie 1974, 136). The 1851 census revealed how few of the urban poor attended church (Gauldie 1974, 137). This was a vivid distinction between the middle and working classes because by the mid-nineteenth century organised religion was an important element in defining the urban middle class (Gunn 1996, 23). The lack of religious instruction and the overcrowded living conditions of many of the poor, with insufficient rooms to allow for separate male and female bedrooms, were seen as causes of promiscuity, illegitimacy and incest (Gauldie 1974, 137). Above all, there was a gulf between the customs and values of the poor and those of the middle classes. Decent housing, modelled on middle-class houses and exemplifying the perceived virtues of middle-class living, was seen as one of the main ways in which the crowd could be placated and controlled.

The concern over the housing of the urban poor gave rise to the model dwelling movement. This was a largely philanthropic movement founded on the belief that good housing improved the occupants. Others argued that it was the attitudes of the occupants that caused buildings to become slums. One such was Octavia Hill, who firmly believed in the ethos of self-help. She considered that the poor should learn to live decently within the housing they already occupied (Tarn 1971, 24). The general view of the middle classes seems to have been that the poor were the antithesis of themselves; rather than provident, sober, sexually restrained and Christian, they were improvident, intemperate, promiscuous heathens (Gunn 1996, 34–5). To many, the urban labouring classes largely comprised the 'undeserving poor'. Nevertheless, self-interest in the preservation of their own standards and values ensured that the middle classes undertook to 'civilise' the poor. Multi-roomed terraced housing for the working classes is as much a physical expression of this undertaking as are the churches, chapels and missions that spread throughout the urban areas in the late nineteenth century.

Cellar dwellings, back-to-earth underdwellings and back-to-back houses in particular were the most criticised forms of working-class housing and those against which most prohibitions were made. Even so, while in some towns like Manchester local legislation discouraged back-to-back building in the later nineteenth century, in towns like Leeds it continued to be a preferred house design (Caffyn 1983, 179). The unique defect of all blind-back housing was the lack of through ventilation (Beresford 1971, 98). While undoubtedly not the healthiest of environments, they were considered particularly unhealthy because of a lack of understanding about the spread of disease. There was a widely held misconception in the earlier nineteenth century that contagion resulted from bad air, usually referred to as a miasma (Gauldie 1974, 135–6). In back-to-back houses the poor environment caused by damp as a consequence of the lack of ventilation was exacerbated by the density of occupation allowed by the building design. Back-to-backs also lacked rear yards for ash pits and privies, and where they were built in enclosed courts even the positioning of communal facilities at the end of the terrace was impractical (Roberts 1986, 55). However, it was the overcrowding rather than the intrinsic nature of the housing that was the real problem. Despite the contemporary condemnations of house types such as back-to-backs and cellar dwellings and of the people who lived within them, it was neither the people nor the buildings that were the cause of poor health. The culprits were, as in the Durham mining villages, the overcrowding, the lack of adequate drainage and sanitation, and the lack of clean water.

The Public Health Act of 1875 is regarded as the turning-point in house building regulation. This permitted all sanitary authorities to make bye-laws which would control building standards and design (Daunton 1983, 7). From then until the First World War fairly standardised housing was built throughout British towns, and the dwellings erected at this time are usually known as bye-law houses. The majority were similar to those houses described in Barry and Cardiff. Built in long terraces of identical dwellings with the gable end to the street and rooms laid out one behind another, the resultant houses were typically gloomy but efficient in their use of land. They symbolise the imposition of middle-class values on to the labouring classes. The terraced house was not the only house design for bye-law houses; tenements continued to be built in Scotland and occasionally elsewhere. The gradual increase in room numbers within the English labourer's terraced cottage in the nineteenth century led to a growth in room specialisation; space was less differentiated in a tenement flat (Daunton 1983, 54; Morris 1981). In particular there was lack of distinction between bedrooms and living rooms, with the latter having a bed recess. These differences and the shared nature of the facilities in a tenement made for a different experience of urban domestic life between Scottish tenement dwellers and those living in English and Welsh terraced cottages (Daunton 1983, 54). In Newcastle-upon-Tyne and its neighbouring towns of Gateshead and South Shields terraced apartments known as Tyneside flats were built. These were essentially two-storey dwellings with separate accommodation on each floor, each reached by independent street doors. The later nineteenth-century versions had a parlour, kitchen, scullery and bedrooms (Daunton 1983, 39–41). In London from the mid-nineteenth century improvement societies and charitable trusts built apartment blocks containing purpose-built flats with a living room and bedrooms, but often sharing communal facilities (A. Cox 1996). With such houses the poor at last had dwellings in which the developing social trends evident in elite and middle-class housing could be enacted.

The growth of a more literate proletariat and empowering legislation affecting urban suffrage in 1867 and the householder franchise in 1884 all contributed to a perceived need to embroil the working classes in middle-class values and belief systems. One of the reasons for increased church building in the later nineteenth century, as well as the philanthropic endowment of working men's educational institutions, was the fear of a growing ungodly, urban and powerful working class (Green 1993). Throughout the nineteenth century, however, despite middle-class efforts to shape their lifestyles and viewpoint through, among other things, the provision of 'appropriate' housing, the material culture of the urban labourers indicates that they were perpetuating traditional lifestyles which had originated in the countryside. This aspect of the nineteenth-century development of the lifestyles of the labouring classes has been previously commentated on by social historians (Burnett 1974). For the poorest, by the end of the nineteenth century work was still not entirely separated from the family and the home. Middle-class concepts of private space and respectability were not universally accepted or practised. Values of shared and communal living were carried forward into the twentieth century but were soon eroded.

CHAPTER FOUR

LANDSCAPE ARCHAEOLOGY

ARCHAEOLOGY AND THE POST-MEDIEVAL LANDSCAPE

The usefulness of the term landscape archaeology as a subject divider is debatable. After all, the entirety of the immovable archaeological record can be taken to form the landscape. In this sense *all* archaeology, including artefacts stratified within deposits, is landscape archaeology. Within modern archaeological fieldwork, however, a clearer, more focused view of what constitutes landscape archaeology has developed. Artefacts once removed from a buried archaeological context or existing as still-functioning cultural items are portable and not part of the landscape, though they may inform its interpretation. Buildings, in terms of their character and appearance, rightly or wrongly, tend to be treated as a separate, almost artefactual, entity, though their distribution and relationships to external space are clearly integral to the understanding of landscape (Pearson 1998). Thus landscape archaeology has come to be represented by the study of distributions and connections rather than of individual items, and settlements rather than buildings, as well as field systems, land use and management. Nevertheless, concerns have frequently been expressed in the past decade over the lack of a coherent body of theory for landscape archaeology (Darvill *et al.* 1993) and over how the landscape may be meaningfully defined as part of an archaeological investigation (Tolan-Smith 1997). In general, however, landscape archaeology has moved on from the essentially descriptive, though nevertheless valuable, approach of the local historian W.G. Hoskins (1955), to encompass a more critical and analytical framework derived from social archaeology.

Landscape archaeology has become not only a broader context within which to place archaeological sites and monuments but also a mechanism for analysing the social structuring of the environment (Hodder 1987). It is recognised that the past environment was perceived in various ways dependent on the social situation of the viewer, and that this in turn influenced shared values and understandings (Schama 1995; Darvill 1998, 10; and see Cosgrove and Daniels 1988). The perception, experience and utilisation of the environment were dependent on the contemporary understanding of the significance of the spaces within which people worked, moved and lived; their demarcation, their links and their ownership. More recently, the utilisation of the natural environment, its interaction with human influences in the landscape (McGlade 1995) and the way natural features may have been imbued with meaning and gave context to people's lives in the past have been developed as an approach in prehistoric archaeology (Tilley 1994; Bradley 1999). This approach at attempting to understand the experience of landscape in the past has been little used for the post-medieval period, but it is worthy of consideration (Williamson 1997), particularly for a period when concepts of national identity and sense of place attributed to the physical environment are documented in surviving literature (Cosgrove and Daniels 1988; Newman 1999).

For the most part there has been a lack of a specifically archaeological approach to the post-medieval landscape, and thus it can be questioned what has distinguished post-medieval landscape archaeology from landscape history or historical geography. Clearly many of the methodologies, techniques and sources are shared (Newman 2000). Yet the archaeologist can provide a unique perspective. Using detailed techniques such as excavation, palaeoenvironmental analysis, survey and fabric analysis, in conjunction with topology, distribution analysis and documentary research, archaeologists can gain an unrivalled in-depth picture of past landscapes. More importantly, standard archaeological approaches to landscapes can reveal insights into the lives of post-medieval people at the experiential level. Recent work by the University of Manchester Archaeological Unit demonstrates this. Investigating the historical archaeology of the lordships of Ashton and Longdendale between 1642 and 1870, they were able to show that people's experience and perception of their environment must have radically altered as a consequence of changes to the landscape (Nevell and Walker 1999). These changes, evidenced today as categories of archaeological site, clearly reveal that for many the period 1760–1840 was one of perceived revolutionary change in the physical environment, both directly affecting and reflecting, as well as being symbolic of, changes in lifestyle (Nevell and Walker 1999, 11–14).

If there can be a specifically archaeological agenda to the study of post-medieval landscapes, it must lie in the interpretation of the physical remains of the past environment to provide insights into past human experience. Humans create cultural landscapes, an articulation between the man-made and the natural world. Historians and geographers using documents can explain the economic and social dynamics behind developing cultural landscapes, and this data must be used by archaeologists, but it is the interpretation of the experience of the physical remains, set within their historical context, that the archaeologist has to offer. Such an approach is not exclusive to archaeologists (*see* Schama 1995), but they are uniquely placed to exploit it.

Even archaeologists, particularly some prehistorians, have dismissed an archaeological approach to the post-medieval landscape. Indeed, a recent summary of the development of post-medieval archaeology hardly mentions the landscape approach to historical archaeology, so dominated has it been by the study of artefacts and the consideration of buildings in isolation (Courtney 1999). The excellent set of essays on aspects of British historical archaeology, *The Familiar Past?*, completely ignores agrarian and industrial landscapes (Tarlow and West 1999). Yet at no time in the past, throughout most of Britain, did the landscape change as radically as it has in the post-medieval period, particularly between about 1750 and 1850. Moreover, in relative terms landscape archaeologists have paid more attention to the post-medieval period than have archaeologists concentrating on other avenues of research (Williamson 1997, 92). As has been recently pointed out, the 'historic' landscape, and the archaeological record it contains, is primarily a product of the post-medieval period (Newman 1999, 395; Williamson 1998, 7). A landscape approach to the historical archaeology of Britain is both essential and central to the understanding of the post-medieval period.

DESIGNED LANDSCAPES AND PLEASURE-GROUNDS

The creation of image, so important to the rural land-owning elite, could not be achieved by the architectural splendour of a house alone. The buildings had to be set within complementary grounds. The size of these grounds isolated the house and any immediately associated buildings from the local pattern of settlement and agriculture. This and the designed nature of the grounds, concentrating on the ornamental rather than the productive aspects of the landscape, divorced the country house and its domain from its surrounding environment. It created an impression of exclusivity and dominance, over both nature and social inferiors. In Scotland the fields, ornamental gardens and plantations surrounding a country house were known as a policy (Whyte and Whyte 1991, 128). They created in most parts of Scotland some of the few islands of enclosures within a sea of open land given over to peasant agriculture, thus further distinguishing their owners from the majority. In England during the post-medieval period the effect of the creation of elite ornamental landscapes was so profound that by the early twentieth century such landscapes had come to be equated with the English countryside. While landscaped parks and other ornamental grounds never represented more than a tiny percentage of rural land-use, the perception was that they typified the English rural landscape. The Liberal politician Charles Masterman in 1909, while unfavourably contrasting the 'elite' landscapes of England with the 'peasant' landscapes of the continent, was able to state that 'the typical English countryside is that of great avenues leading to residences which lack no comfort, broad parks, stretches of private land, sparsely cultivated, but convenient for hunting, shooting, and a kind of stately splendour' (Mandler 1997, 163). This view was an exaggeration, intended as part of a political critique, and came at the end of a period of agricultural depression and depopulation, but it is nevertheless indicative of how deeply elite-created ornamental landscapes affected (and still affect) the perception of the English countryside in particular.

This perception – that the English countryside was primarily an ornamental one designed for elite pleasure – has influenced the development of landscape studies. For many landscape academics and professionals in the late twentieth century, the study of landscape in Britain was synonymous with the study of designed landscapes. This view has been superseded in no small part as a consequence of the involvement of historical geographers and archaeologists in the study of post-medieval landscapes. One consequence of this involvement has been the growth of the use of archaeological research methods for investigating the past forms and sequential development of ornamental grounds, especially gardens and to a lesser extent parks. While excavations were undertaken on post-medieval gardens before the 1970s, as at Aberglasney, Carmarthenshire (Briggs 1999), it was work at Kirby Hall, Northamptonshire (Dix *et al.* 1995), and Painshill Park, Surrey (Howes 1991), that established post-medieval garden archaeology. The literature has since become extensive and is growing rapidly (Pattison 1998; Everson and Williamson 1998). It is not the intention to review this topic here in any detail, but merely to examine some of the more provoking developments in designed landscape research. Much of the work undertaken, however, has been progressed with a view to site management or restoration; as a consequence the quality of analysis and interpretation derived from some garden archaeology projects can be disappointingly low.

The archaeological study of gardens takes two main forms: the survey of existing and relict features and buildings, and excavation to reveal buried features relating to the past structure of the pleasure-grounds, and to recover where possible palaeoecological evidence of past planting regimes. The latter approach tends to be applied to gardens only, the more extensive landscape of parks being explored primarily through surface analysis. Between the sixteenth and eighteenth centuries it is estimated that about five thousand formal gardens were established by members of the aristocracy or gentry. The archaeological significance of these sites lies both in their representation of changing fashions in style and in their reflection of the affiliations and preoccupations of their owners (Everson and Williamson 1998, 146).

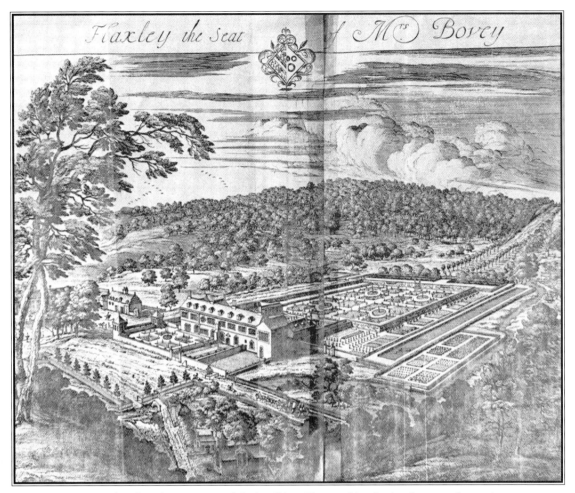

Johannes Kip's early eighteenth-century print of Flaxley Abbey, Gloucestershire, showing the converted monastic buildings and a Dutch water garden.

The Dissolution gave an impetus to the laying out of formal gardens and influenced their form, since many of the new country houses were former monasteries (Bowden 1999, 148). An appreciation of the geometrical layout of many monasteries, based around the cloister, became mixed with a taste for Italian art and architecture (Briggs 1997, 90), possibly transmitted via France (Woodhouse 1999, 11). The possession of a formal garden was an important mark of distinction in Tudor England, and, along with clothes, was perhaps the most obvious way of displaying one's taste, sensibilities and fashion sense. It was also quite deliberately a place where a range of messages could be imparted. The symbolism in Elizabethan gardens was quite overt, as it was in all Tudor art, much of it connected with the queen herself. Flowers, groves and gardens were symbolically associated with Gloriana (Woodhouse 1999, 25). Robert Dudley, Earl of Leicester, laid out a new pleasure-ground at Kenilworth Castle in 1575, in advance of the visit of Elizabeth I. In the course of doing this, a medieval defensive ditch was infilled before the site was levelled up to create the garden (Morley *et al.* 1995): an indication of the changes in the importance and meanings the elite attached to their residences and grounds.

The plans and aspects of sixteenth- and seventeenth-century gardens can only be captured through a combination of a study of plans and illustrations, and a study of the surviving earthworks of those that were abandoned, as for example those at Raglan Castle, Monmouthshire (Whittle 1989). In Wales the regularity of Renaissance landscape design continued to dominate the layout of gardens into the eighteenth century (Briggs 1997, 91). The majority of the gentry continued with the older forms of geometric formal gardens until the later eighteenth century (Everson and Williamson 1998, 151). By the early eighteenth century, however, the great estate owners in England were developing pleasure-grounds of less rigid design than seen previously. New layouts incorporating irregular plantings and serpentine paths sought to provide a less geometric and apparently less contrived landscape effect. The division of the garden from the park became less precise, as did that of the park from the surrounding landscape. Thus vistas were opened up and, to achieve this, new features such as the ha-ha were adopted, enabling animals to be excluded from the garden without the view being interrupted by a visible boundary (Everson and Williamson 1998, 151).

One of the most important archaeological explorations of an eighteenth-century garden has been at Castle Bromwich, near Birmingham (Currie and Locock 1993). The detailed work carried out there not only allowed for the reconstruction of the eighteenth-century gardens, but also enabled an attempt at spatial analysis to gain further insights into the way the gardens may have functioned. The conclusions were that the gardens appear to have been implemented not in relation to a formal design, but rather adapted to circumstances by local craftsmen and estate tenants (Locock 1994, 244). Similar conclusions have been reached elsewhere, as at Lyme Park, Cheshire, where a design by Giacomo Leoni seems to have acted as a guide, but was interpreted on the ground to suit available resources, existing topography and the needs of the park's users (LUAU 1996b). At Castle Bromwich, however, a unity of design can be envisaged. The gardens were balanced rather than symmetrical, and it was open, with no clear distinction between pleasure-grounds and productive plots, or screening of them (Locock 1994, 246–7). This is indicative of the way in which productive gardens were viewed in the eighteenth century, since to many in the eighteenth century the areas set aside for household or commercial supply were pleasurable to behold. This seems to be a continuation of ideas which would have been very familiar in the Tudor period, when the combination of pleasure and profit, as represented by the orchard, was at the heart of garden design (Roberts 1999). This contrasts with the views of the nineteenth century. The analysis of the Castle Bromwich gardens has also revealed how access and movement may have been controlled and social intercourse negotiated.

To an extent the investment in landscaped pleasure-grounds in the late eighteenth and nineteenth centuries is indicative of the wealth being accrued by the elite through both agricultural improvement and industrial investment. They are indicators of aspiration. Indeed, it has been speculated that the park at Colomendy Hall, Flintshire, may have been established as a mechanism for boosting its owners' status at a time when they were childless and contemplating the extinction of their lineage (Baker and Jones 1996, 43).

The Appropriation of Earlier Material Culture

The owners of landscape parks appropriated and consumed the material culture of earlier times. They acquired movable items when on the 'Grand Tour', or more locally from other parts of their estate, and they incorporated existing historical features into their designed landscapes. Mottes, as at Downton in Wiltshire, were incorporated into pleasure-grounds as mounts, along with natural eminences and specially created mounds. The mount was a particular prestige feature of seventeenth- and eighteenth-century gardens (Baker and Jones 1996, 42). At Lyme Park, Anglo-Scandinavian cross-shafts were removed from a local churchyard (LUAU 1996b). Classical sculptures were acquired to be placed within the neo-classical temples and summer-houses erected in the grounds. At Badger Dingle in Shropshire a Hellenistic head was found during operations to recover architectural masonry to assist in the rebuilding of a ruined eighteenth-century neo-classical park building (Higgs *et al.* 1996). Its casual discard reveals the lack of value placed upon the object. It seems to have been a themed ornament, neglected when the building fell into disuse. The appropriation of antiquities and the material culture of the Middle Ages was undertaken to exemplify taste, education and discernment; to establish group identities, and family and class affiliations; and as a mechanism of establishing often bogus histories. The arrogation of past symbols of authority in the landscape in particular helped to link insecure elite newcomers to an established elite past.

CHANGING THE AGRARIAN LANDSCAPE

The post-medieval landscape was structured by a clearly understood (in contemporary terms) series of overlapping bounded land divisions containing differing and changing meanings, constraints, rights and obligations. In this sense the landscape was both formally structured and dynamic. The land associated with a particular community was defined as the township or vill (Tolan-Smith 1997, 3). This often coincided with a tithing. One or more townships formed a parish. These land divisions gave a focus for shared community experiences; they formed the basis of local taxation and a framework for civil responsibilities and obligations. Overlapping with these divisions was the manor, which might equate with a township or might span a number of townships, or form only a part of one. These divisions were often physically represented in the landscape by boundaries, field systems and local communications networks. They aided the development of distinctiveness and a sense of place, providing a context at a local level within which power relationships were negotiated and different constituencies competed.

One of the major theoretical influences on recent post-medieval archaeological thought has been closure theory. First developed by Max Weber, the theory proposes that social groups will define themselves through the acquisition and protection of rights. Group interests are maintained by excluding non-group members from access to resources (Nevell and Walker 1999). Matthew Johnson views social space, in the countryside and in the house, as increasingly divided and bounded during the fourteenth to eighteenth centuries, in accordance with individual interests (1993a; 1996). These developments are related to the increasing influence of market forces. With regard to cultural landscapes it can be seen that a process of closure has relevance since the landscape is organised by members of society 'to facilitate the activities and movements of some individuals, while concurrently constraining others' (Rotman and Nassaney 1997, 42). As Richard Muir has written: 'the landscape is property, partitioned by transactions shaped by formerly prevailing systems of class and power'; this context places restrictions on an individual as their 'freedom to move within this landscape will be constrained by ownership and status' (1998, 6). These differences between individuals leading to inclusion or exclusion mean that different groups will have had differing experiences and perceptions of the landscapes they inhabited and moved through. The changes wrought in the landscape by developments in agriculture in the post-medieval period can be readily appreciated as fitting this model.

Consolidation and Enclosure

The single greatest landscape change which took place in parts of the British countryside in the post-medieval period was enclosure: the process whereby a relatively open and unbounded landscape was converted into a series of bounded parcels. Enclosure did not simply change open fields cultivated in common into small private closes; though it did do this, its impact was much wider than that. It also brought massive areas of uncultivated open land into permanent or semi-permanent cultivation, regularised areas of squatter settlements and privatised most of the landscape. Its effects were not uniform, however, varying with the nature of the pre-existing landscape, and neither can enclosure be a period-limited process. Enclosures, in a purely physical sense, have been made in the British landscape since at least the Bronze Age. Their presence in the landscape has waxed and waned in tune with changes in agricultural practice and social organisation. It is, and always has been, an ongoing process in constant conflict with forces acting against enclosure. The enclosure process in the post-medieval period, however, does have specific significances and meanings relevant to its social context, and produced a huge increase in the boundedness of the British landscape.

The impact of enclosure was subject to regional variations. In the English Midlands, where regular open common field systems were extensive in the sixteenth century, the impact of enclosure was enormous. In Scotland, too, the landscape was very open in the sixteenth century and in the Shetland Islands remained so until the mid-nineteenth century (Knox 1985). Elsewhere, however, the countryside was already highly enclosed by the sixteenth century: in Cornwall, parts of west Wales and the south-east of England small fields possibly of late prehistoric origin dominated the landscape. In other districts a more mixed pattern of landscape was typical. In the Welsh borders and the south Wales lowlands large regular open fields were found adjacent to areas of enclosures interspersed with multiple small irregular fields farmed in common. The field pattern of such areas often varied from township to township (*see* Campbell 1981). In addition, throughout England and Wales there were large islands of open uncultivated land formed of upland moor and lowland moss.

The term common field applies to any bounded area over which common rights of pasturage were applied after the harvest; in this way the land received natural manuring before being ploughed or, in the case of meadow, before the next year's grass growth. Hence, as Dahlman (1986) has argued, there was a balance in the system between the need for arable and the need for manure to maintain productivity. The common fields were usually internally divided into strips by baulks, and not by hedges or walls, so when the commonable animals were let in they had unhindered access throughout the field. Not all common fields were open fields, however, for occasionally they were divided into enclosed strips, the enclosed form possibly, but not necessarily, evolving from the open form. The term open field is a vague one (Butlin 1961, 102), but in essence it refers to any field which is undivided by physical barriers, but with more than one landholder within it. Such a field was not necessarily commonable. A field could be divided between landholders without having any common grazing rights over it, so that each parcel was legally treated as if it were a separate enclosure.

By the mid-sixteenth century the former area of open fields farmed in common had clearly been reduced, particularly in those areas where the existing common fields were relatively small, and thus had few landholders and tended to be widely scattered within an existing arrangement of ancient enclosed fields. The process of enclosure continued so that by the end of the eighteenth century only vestiges of the common open field system remained in England and Wales. These were the areas that were then enclosed, along with the remaining open wastes, by Act of Parliament in the later eighteenth and early nineteenth centuries. Contemporary with this final phase of enclosure in England and Wales, the process of agricultural 'improvement' was active in Scotland, leading to a sudden and massive increase in enclosure there. It is important to appreciate, however, that the process never completely removed some of the earlier forms of agricultural practice. Elements of these earlier systems survive at Braunton (Devon), the Isle of Axeholme (north Lincolnshire), Laxton (Northamptonshire), North Ronaldsay (Orkney) and Rhosili (Glamorgan) and as Lammas meadows scattered throughout the country but with a particular concentration in Herefordshire and Worcestershire (Brian 1993, 65)

Any consideration of the process of enclosure needs to take account of both the diversity and the resilience of the pre-existing agricultural systems. Farming in unenclosed fields was the norm throughout much of Britain until the later eighteenth century, despite hundreds of years of demand and pressure for enclosure. Much of what is described as medieval may have originated then, but in its present form, as earthworks or fossilised boundaries, it often dates to the eighteenth century. The most frequently observed archaeological feature associated with open common field farming is aratrally curved ridge and furrow, the reversed 'S' curve being caused by the movement needed to turn a plough team. Ridge and furrow can be caused by a number of processes besides common field agriculture. For example, straight ridge and furrow was used for tree-growing in orchards (Newman 1983), and narrow rig for drainage in non-common fields, as in the nineteenth century in the northern English uplands and perhaps earlier in the sixteenth and seventeenth centuries on Dartmoor. Ridge and furrow can also be created by hand digging, as is the case in the Hebrides, where it was formed by the hand digging of lazy beds. It has been argued that the purpose of most ridge and furrow was for drainage (Kerridge 1951), and certainly this appears to be the case in Scotland, but even elsewhere drainage was clearly one of its purposes (Cook 1994, 58). Even so, it is still generally accepted that sinuous curved ridge and furrow was the result of arable common field farming. Yet even this interpretation is open to question as it has been shown that such ridge and furrow is sometimes found in common meadows, as at Lydney in west Gloucestershire, as well as on former arable land (Newman 1988, 27–8). Nevertheless, and in spite of these caveats, the aratral curved ridge and furrow found particularly in English Midland counties like Leicestershire and Northamptonshire is indicative of the former existence of open common fields and a testament to their durability.

The questions of why enclosure happened and why previous systems of agricultural organisation were replaced are of course tied into the question of why some open common field systems proved so durable. The many arguments relating to the reasons for and social significance of enclosure have been recently summarised by Johnson (1996, 59–68). In most of these discussions there is a linkage between improvement and enclosure, and an assumption that enclosure led to better farming methods and greater yields (see Dahlman 1986). This view has been challenged and it has been explicitly stated that enclosure was not responsible for improved productivity (Allen 1992, 17). Indeed, this progressive view of enclosure fails to take account of the evidence for the existence of enclosures at earlier periods, before the occurrence of open fields. Since enclosures have come and gone through time, their occurrence must be related to factors other than the purely economic. Nevertheless, such a conclusion does not exclude, as a factor in their adoption, the perception of enclosures being important for improvement, and this view was current from the sixteenth century (Frazer 1999, 84). Certainly this was a view

Former ridge and furrow within the common meadow of Lydney, Gloucestershire. The aratral curves of the ridges are clearly shown under flooded conditions.

underlying much parliamentary enclosure in England and Wales and field reorganisation in Scotland in the late eighteenth and early nineteenth centuries, irrespective of whether or not there was a scientific basis for it. Indeed, the linking of enclosure with improvement in the minds of contemporary landlords was important to its spread and adoption. It could be seen as a physical expression of their willingness to improve land and output. As such it can be interpreted as a 'legitimating device' emphasising a landowner's fitness to be a member of the ruling classes (Williamson 2000, 72).

The motivations behind enclosure, viewed from a broad historical perspective, are many, varied and complex; however, when examined at the level of the local and particular, they can be surprisingly simple, often related to local factors of social organisation and geography. Enclosure was not a movement or a cohesive process, though it was assisted by central government abandoning an anti-enclosure stance in the 1630s (Dyer *et al.* 2000, 88), but as more land became enclosed it did achieve a momentum that resulted in the Enclosure Acts. Even so, between the fourteenth and the mid-nineteenth century, albeit with local variations in timing and scale, enclosed private field systems replaced open commonable ones throughout Britain. This resulted in the replacement of communal shared rights with private, individual rights. In the landscape enclosure created new boundaries which not only physically but also symbolically cut and replaced older systems of land control and authority (Johnson 1996, 75). It produced an individualised and private farming landscape, no longer regulated by the customs of local communities (Williamson and Bellamy 1987, 192), but rather governed by the changing needs of the market. It was a landscape that allowed for greater flexibility and creativity – but it was also less secure.

Motivation alone, no matter what lay behind it, was insufficient to achieve enclosure of common fields: the existing field systems had to be receptive to the pressure to enclose. As

Yelling pointed out, the survival of common fields into the eighteenth century depended on 'the prior existence of a particular form of common field organisation' (1982, 414). However, there is no monocausal explanation for why such common field organisation decayed or persisted; rather a variety of factors was influential, depending on the locality. A study of common field enclosure in west Gloucestershire demonstrates this clearly. This is an area sometimes considered to have lacked many open common fields, but detailed documentary research and fieldwork indicates that all townships had them in the medieval period. The region can be divided into two broad districts, one where the enclosure of the common open fields was well under way, and completed in some townships, before 1600, and the other where they survived until the end of the eighteenth century (Newman 1988).

The early enclosed district lay adjacent to or within the medieval bounds of the Forest of Dean. It was mainly higher, less fertile land with large tracts of commonable rough pasture and woodland pasture. Manorial organisation appears to have been weak, with many manors held *in absentia* by the seventeenth century (Newman 1988, 26). There were many opportunities for non-agricultural employment in both rural-based extractive and manufacturing industries. A combination of these factors seems to have influenced the enclosure of the open common fields throughout this district. In the late enclosed district, the fields' histories varied from township to township, their persistence usually dependent on their degree of regularity and complexity, which was influenced by factors such as manorial history, local environmental conditions and the nature of the settlement pattern (Newman 1988, 51).

In general the smaller the common field and the fewer the landholders, the easier it was to extinguish common rights, consolidate holdings and achieve enclosure. Early enclosure tended to be made in a piecemeal manner and by agreement among the landholders, often following a period of holding consolidation. Landscape evidence for this process can be seen in fields which in form fossilise the earlier strips. Particularly good examples occur in Cumberland, where drystone-walled strip fields close to the settlement indicate the former strips of an infield, and in parts of south Wales, as at Pop Hill, near Dinas Powis, Glamorgan (Reed 1986, 93). Enclosure by agreement could be far less collaborative than the description might suggest. At Whixall Moss in Shropshire enclosure in 1704 was opposed by a minority of the commoners who threw open the enclosures after they were made (Leah *et al.* 1998, 21). A study of Castleton in Derbyshire has shown that the smaller and poorer landholders, faced with the loss of customary common rights, had little choice but to agree to enclosing strips within the open field in order to retain somewhere to husband their animals (Frazer 1999). The enclosure of the common waste in Castleton by the end of the seventeenth century was undertaken by a coalition of the gentry and yeomanry. It is argued that by their ability, through literacy, to use written material culture, they were able to both legitimise their sponsored process of enclosure and to disadvantage the probably illiterate husbandmen and smallholders (Frazer 1999, 89). Resistance to this process has been inferred from an enclosure survey of 1691, where planned strip-like enclosures are shown on the common pasture allocated for the smallholders. These were never implemented and it appears that the smallholders continued to stint their stock in accordance with customary practices (Frazer 1999, 94).

In the later eighteenth and early nineteenth centuries most of the remaining common field systems and huge areas of upland pasture were enclosed under Act of Parliament. In all, 25 per cent of the surface area of England was affected and 11 per cent of Wales (Chapman 1987). This process had considerable and frequently discussed landscape impacts (Reed 1983, 65–71;

Post-medieval hedged and drystone-walled enclosures of former common upland in south Wales. Large areas of upland were enclosed in this way during the later eighteenth and nineteenth centuries.

Williamson and Bellamy 1987, 107–9). It led to wholesale replanning of boundaries, and sometimes roads, along rigid geometrical precepts, and the creation of new farmsteads set among the enclosed fields. Much of the straight hawthorn hedging of large parts of England, particularly in the Midland counties, owes its origin to the preference of the enclosure commissioners for this type of boundary (Chapman 1993, 51). Like the contemporary agrarian improvements in Scotland, these enclosures appear imposed on the landscape, and they were often imposed on the landholders. Parliamentary enclosure could be enacted where agreement was obtained from the holders of four-fifths of the holdings, and thus the power to enclose was not vested in the majority of the proprietors but in the major landholders.

The Scottish agrarian landscape appears to have been distinct from that encountered in England or Wales during the sixteenth to eighteenth centuries. There were few enclosures; it was remarkably treeless, particularly in the Lowlands; and in general it was less intensively exploited than elsewhere in Britain. Our evidence is derived from commentators, however, and although they are remarkably consistent in their descriptions from the sixteenth to the eighteenth centuries, many were English and predisposed to characterise Scotland as backward and unchanging (Whyte and Whyte 1991, 52–4). Nevertheless enclosures were very few in comparison to England. Arable farming was organised on an infield and outfield system, similar to that encountered in northern England. The infield was usually much smaller than the outfield, and was permanently and intensively cultivated. In the countryside around Edinburgh there was a greater intensity of cultivation, with a much higher percentage of land under permanent arable (Whyte and Whyte 1991, 57), presumably in order to supply grain to the capital, which remained Scotland's largest town until the later eighteenth century. Generally, neither the infield nor the outfield had permanent internal boundaries, and they were divided from the open rough pasture by a head dyke (Whyte and Whyte 1991, 55). There were regional and intra-regional local variations to the system. The policies of the great estates contained enclosures surrounding the mansion and home farm. In the Hebrides internal dykes do occur which may have been either former boundary dykes before expansion or in some cases markers for stock routes (Dodgshon 1993, 386). In the Loch Tayside area of Perthshire pre-improvement boundaries survive, which are indicative of both permanent dykes between townships and low, semi-permanent dykes formed by field clearance within the infield (Smout 1996). Similar field boundary patterns have been noted in Nithsdale, overlain by post-improvement enclosures (Smout 1996, 54).

As in England's open fields, landholding in the infield and outfields was generally fragmented and intermixed (Whyte 1995, 141), a system of allocating land known in Scotland as runrig. Under this system the two fields were farmed broadly in common, with common grazing rights and communal control of cropping (Dodgshon 1993, 385). The system has recently been considered to be a late medieval introduction into the landscape of the Hebrides at least, and it is possible that a similar late origin can be attributed to it elsewhere in Scotland (Dodgshon 1993, 396). As in English and Welsh open fields, the surface of the runrig allocated fields was corrugated with aratrally curved ridge and furrow, though in Scotland the link between this type of plough-formed earthwork and drainage seems more certain than elsewhere. Most Scottish ridge and furrow occurs on sloping land with the ridges aligned downslope to facilitate drainage. The ridges fitted in with the pattern of strips allocated under the runrig system and the fossilised remains of these can be seen in a still surviving unenclosed open field on North Ronaldsay, Orkney (Whyte and Whyte 1991, 61–3).

The very different agricultural context of most of Scotland in comparison to England meant that the process of enclosure was generally very different, though as in England it was often demanded by the wealthy and led, to an extent, to the exclusion of the poor. Some early examples of enclosure appear to reflect practices in England, resulting in strip fields fossilising the layout of the runrig, as in parts of Ayrshire (Reed 1983, 76). The earliest examples of a movement for enclosure come from Galloway in the early eighteenth century. Closer than other parts of Scotland to major English markets for beef, landlords in Galloway enclosed large areas as parks for fattening cattle. This must have had an effect on those who had previously cultivated the land, though much of the land involved was home farm demesne, and consequently these enclosures inspired riotous gatherings to throw down the enclosure walls in 1724 and 1725 (Whyte and Whyte 1991, 130). Elsewhere, during the early eighteenth century, Anglophile agricultural reformers, like John Cockburn of Ormiston in East Lothian, began to organise their estates along English lines, and enclosure was one of the features of the improvements introduced by them. By the mid-eighteenth century Cockburn's estates had a network of rectilinear enclosed fields, very distinct in appearance from the open lands which surrounded them (Whyte and Whyte 1991, 131–2).

The majority of enclosures in Scotland, however, occurred after *c.* 1760. Unlike England and Wales, where by the later eighteenth century the enclosure of the remaining open fields required a separate Act of Parliament for each parish, the process of enclosure in Scotland could be achieved for the most part by a decision on behalf of the landlord (Whyte and Whyte 1991, 135). Holdings in multiple-tenancy fermtouns could be consolidated and amalgamated by refusing to renew the existing leases when they fell due. In some parts of Scotland this process of amalgamation had been under way from the seventeenth century, creating ever larger holdings and fewer tenants in the fermtouns (Whyte and Whyte 1991, 135–6). As fermtouns were replaced by single-tenanted farms in the Lowlands and southern Highlands, and the dispersed strips of the runrig were converted into consolidated holdings, so the previously open landscape became bounded by enclosures. In the Western Isles and northern and western Highlands, the crofting system was introduced. Small, straight-edged, strip-like allotments were attached to each croft to provide a subsistence food supply, though this was rarely regarded by the tenants as sufficient. Even in the twentieth century the crofters had not forgotten their former land rights, or the extent of their dispossession (Withers 1990, 47). Nevertheless, the walled small fields of the crofters became one of the dominant landscape features of the northern and western areas of Scotland. Outside the crofting areas, larger enclosures were formed; like contemporary parliamentary enclosures in England, these were generally regular and rectilinear, clearly showing the influence of the land surveyor. In some cases the layouts of whole farms were rationalised, for example on the Lanarkshire estates of the Duke of Hamilton, where the farms in existence in the later eighteenth century had their irregular-shaped territories reorganised along rational lines (Richens 1997). Patterns drawn on a map were imposed on the landscape, often with little regard to traditional or natural boundaries. These new boundaries were formed of quickset hedges in the southern uplands, but even there the drystone wall was common and elsewhere was the most common field delineator (Whyte and Whyte 1991, 137). Drystone walls were particularly favoured as they provided a mechanism for disposing of the stones collected from the enclosed fields when they were improved for cultivation. This form of land management has an ancient history going back to the earliest days of cultivation. In Scotland, during the improvement period, it sometimes resulted in the construction of massive linear mounds such as the Consumption Dyke, near Aberdeen, a pile of stones some 800m long and up to 8m wide (Reed 1983, 76–7).

With the exception of new farmsteads, enclosures are the most archaeologically identifiable feature of Scottish agrarian change in the late eighteenth century, but a whole range of less visible improvements in agricultural practice accompanied them (Devine 1994, 165). These are sufficient for one recent author to regard them as revolutionary (Devine 1994), in contrast to others who have characterised the late eighteenth century agrarian changes as a culmination of long-term patterns of change (Whittington 1983; Lynch 1991). It would appear that the change in the fabric of the Scottish agrarian landscape was sufficiently dramatic in the later eighteenth and early nineteenth centuries to be considered revolutionary at the experiential level. Devine's (1994) detailed examination of four lowland counties certainly indicates this for lowland Scotland, an area generally considered to be less radically altered by improvement than the Highlands. Clearly, while sixteenth- to early eighteenth-century Scottish agricultural practice was not static (Whyte 1999; Whyte 1995), the pace of change from the late eighteenth century was far more rapid than that previously experienced. This has been attributed to a coalition of factors in the late eighteenth century. The desire of the landlords for more revenue had been a constant factor in estate management from the medieval period, but in the later eighteenth century it was assisted in its ends by a growing group of tenants who were able to operate commercially, as a consequence of previous holding amalgamations (Devine 1994, 165–6). The opportunities to exploit these holdings appropriately occurred with the acquisition of sufficient capital to invest in improvements and the development of cash markets to sustain profitability.

Reclaiming Wetlands

From at least the Roman period onwards there is archaeological and documentary evidence of land reclamation, particularly with regard to draining and converting wetlands into productive agricultural land. During the sixteenth and seventeenth centuries in eastern and southern England

The reclaimed Arnside Moss in south Westmorland. This was one of the many wetlands drained and converted to agriculture in north-west England in the eighteenth and nineteenth centuries.

reclamations were attempted on previously unknown scales (Crossley 1990, 15). Two obstacles faced the reclaimer: opposition from interests in the wetlands other than those of the potential farmers, and the high cost of reclamation works. For that reason the major reclamation projects were usually sponsored by elite landowners such as the Earl of Suffolk, who drained land around Weymouth (Aston and Bettey 1998, 128). In eastern England in the seventeenth century these reclamations were the first land improvements to develop regular, rectilinear fieldscapes, a development assisted by the flatness of the land, but perhaps also indicative of the employment of professional engineers (*see* Taylor 1975, 128–32). The Severn Estuary is an area that has a history of flood defence and drainage schemes stretching back to the Roman period. These continued on into the post-medieval period with small reclamations often matching other areas lost to the sea (Rippon 1997, 247). Between 1606, the year of disastrous floods along the estuary littoral, and 1660 there were major drainage schemes on the peat moors of Somerset, as for example at Sedgemoor (Williams 1970, 95–102). For the first time wind pumps were used – the usual response in the seventeenth century where gravity drainage was insufficient (Cook 1994, 55). The resultant reclaimed landscapes are characterised by highly regular patterns of fields, reflecting the systematic approach to reclamation (Rippon 1997, 247). Between 1660 and 1770, however, there was little further reclamation, but in the last thirty years of the eighteenth century a series of Enclosure Acts facilitated the reclamation of the remaining inland moors (Williams 1970, 110).

Major reclamation projects in the north of Britain lagged behind those in the south, presumably indicative of the relative differences in economic power before the eighteenth century. Lancashire was bedevilled with raised mires to such an extent that communications and economic development were hampered by them (Newman 1996). Early post-medieval reclamation was limited to the moss margins and was a slow, piecemeal process, often as a result of peat-cutting (Middleton *et al.* 1995, 208). It was not until the eighteenth century that major reclamations, including entire wetlands, took place. Lytham Moss, near Blackpool, was reclaimed at its north-western end between 1786 and 1844. The field and road pattern consists of a patchwork of small irregular fields and kinked lanes varying in width, suggestive of piecemeal enclosure along tracks extended in sections into the moss, and in part defined by the development of the fields (Middleton *et al.* 1995, 102). In the south and east the pattern is different. There the fields are rectilinear and regular, aligned off straight roads, and from part of a wider, grid-like landscape extending beyond the former moss. This is the result of a single estate-sponsored reclamation and enclosure initiative in the early 1840s and the consequent employment of professional land surveyors. The work was undertaken by the Clifton family of Lytham Hall, who carried out widespread reclamations in the south of the Fylde during the earlier nineteenth century, in order to make their estate a 'showpiece of agricultural improvement' (Rogers 1981, 31). Their efforts appear to have been more concerned with gaining social prestige and political influence than with sound economics, for in common with many of Lancashire's great estates, the investment in land purchase and improvement was seldom recovered in increased rents (Middleton *et al.* 1995, 104). An emphasis on wider estate improvement as a prestige activity is typical of the estate land management of the later eighteenth and nineteenth centuries, and characterises much of the elite improvement activity in Scotland.

In many areas of Scotland the river valleys in particular were poorly drained. Runrig farming had been adapted for sloping ground, but the heavy, often peaty, soils of the valley bottoms remained undrained into the eighteenth century. Here and on the moorland margins reclamation was undertaken. In many instances reclamation was encouraged by landlords but undertaken by smallholders, who were given remission of rent to offset the costs of land improvement. On the Blairdrummond estate in the Forth valley mosslands, the initial fieldscape created by these smallholders was one of long strips running away from the access road adjacent to which the steading was established, similar to coastal crofting patterns. With time the smallholders were bought out and the strip-like crofts amalgamated and turned into large enclosures (Whyte and Whyte 1991, 134). Some reclamations were overly ambitious. On the Sutherland estate reclamations of peat bog were attempted in the late nineteenth century by cutting trenches using steam-ploughs. Farms were established, but the expense of keeping the land drained outweighed the income and by 1914 all the reclaimed land was reverting and the farms built in the 1870s were abandoned (Wade Martins 1998, 51).

Watermeadows

One of the most visually distinctive new features of the post-medieval agrarian landscape was the watermeadow. This was a system of irrigation which enabled a field to be seasonally flooded, protecting it from winter frosts and producing an early spring crop of grass. These were found to be particularly valuable in the sheep-rearing districts (Bettey 2000, 42). The earliest occurred in Herefordshire in the sixteenth century as catchwork systems which allowed water to run down a slope from a leat back to the parent watercourse (Cook 1994, 61). The more typical valley bottom system, consisting of parallel ditches feeding water across the field from the leat to the stream via sluices, was developed in the early seventeenth century and was introduced widely into the chalkland valleys of Wiltshire, Dorset and Hampshire (Aston and Bettey 1998, 128–9). At Burleston, Dorset, a system considered to originate in the seventeenth century was still in use in 1992 (PMA 1993, 271). The encouragement of the Earl of Pembroke led to the construction of watermeadows throughout his estates in Wiltshire, on the rivers Avon, Ebble, Nadder and Wylye, and at least one system remained operational on his estates within the Avon valley until

Former watermeadows on the outskirts of Salisbury. They were part of an extensive system of watermeadows stretching along the river valleys that drain the chalklands of south Wiltshire.

the 1990s. The introduction of watermeadows was an expensive undertaking so their adoption was usually under manorial direction (Aston and Bettey 1998, 129; Cook 1994, 64), and their spread may have been limited until periods of increased profitability.

Watermeadows are recorded in west Gloucestershire in the early eighteenth century (Newman 1988, 82), and were being laid elsewhere in the Midlands and East Anglia as well. Contemporaneously, they had also spread to parts of Scotland (Whyte 1995, 141). In the 1850s there were 45,000 hectares of watermeadows in southern England (Cook 1994, 64), greatly increasing the pasture productivity of the country. Most went out of use in the late nineteenth century, as a consequence of the agricultural depression (Bettey 2000, 42).

Woodlands

As has recently been pointed out, while not a conventional archaeological monument, a woodland can be seen as a 'a distinct archaeological entity' (Bowden 1999, 135). Woodlands, and the nature of the trees within them, are evidence of past land-use management, and are particularly significant for changes in land-use in the post-medieval period. Their history and interpretation, however, has been dealt with superbly by Oliver Rackham in a series of books (1976; 1980; 1986), and it is not the intention here to re-cover this territory in detail. Nevertheless, woodlands also contain a variety of archaeological sites that are distinct to their environment, relating to features associated with woodland management and with woodland-based industries (Bowden 1999, 135).

For many years historians were inclined to argue that the post-medieval period witnessed a decline in tree cover and a reduction in woodland. This was attributed to the excessive wood consumption of fuel-hungry industries, particularly the charcoal blast-furnaces. Evidence for timber shortages varies from the Crown's attempts to preserve timber for naval use, to the increasing costs of timber, the decline in the use of timber for building, and the importation of timber from the Baltic and the Americas. All of this can be generally explained by a rising demand for woodland products rather than a wood shortage. This rise in demand ensured that woodlands remained valuable resources and were not, therefore, generally grubbed up and turned over to agriculture or some other form of land-use. It was not in the interests of woodland owners to allow their woodlands to be ruined or their wood supplies exhausted. Increasingly in the sixteenth and seventeenth centuries privately owned woodlands were turned over to coppice production, to ensure efficient wood regeneration and to supply the variety of products required by the market. Timber increased in cost because mature trees became scarcer in many woodlands as they were converted to coppice; timber represented a longer-term investment than coppice, which provided a quicker and – if well managed – regular income. The government developed plantations for timber in the Crown woodlands because the navy was expanding and the mature trees necessary for shipbuilding were no longer being produced in the private woodlands. Timber was used less in building because stone became more popular, particularly in towns, as a consequence of reduced fire risk and fashion.

To allow regeneration by preventing animals browsing it was necessary to enclose coppices and thus subdivide woodlands into compartments. These enclosures were also embanked, usually topped with a post-and-rail fence. Coppicing was a hugely important form of land-use. The products of coppices were many and varied, and included besoms, hoops, staves and tops for barrels, wattle panels for internal walling, hurdles for fencing, and fuel for a number of woodland-dependent industries, principally the charcoal blast-furnace industry. Coppicing affected the distribution of tree species. Ash was one of the most common trees in the private woodlands around the Crown-owned Forest of Dean in west Gloucestershire, yet it was absent from within the Forest itself (Newman 1988, 266), and the explanation for this was concerned with land-use, not with land condition. The maintained enclosures in the Forest of Dean in the seventeenth and eighteenth centuries were plantations intended for ship timber. The preferred tree was oak, though beech was also used. Outside the plantations, enclosure for coppice was either absent or generally ineffective, because coppice enclosures were leased from the Crown on insecure, short-term arrangements which encouraged the lessee to take as much wood as possible, but discouraged investment in enclosures for future regrowth. Without enclosure, highly edible trees, such as ash, were browsed to extinction. By contrast, in the well-fenced private coppices, ash was protected by browser exclusion, and deliberately encouraged as a species because of the ease with which it coppices and its product versatility. In the Forest none of these products, such as broom handles, poles and barrel hoops, was made after 1668 (Newman 1988, 281).

The most common woodland industry was charcoal burning. This produced fuel for a number of industries, but perhaps most notably for the charcoal blast-furnace industry. The remains of charcoal burning are prevalent in many woodlands but particularly in regions associated with the charcoal blast furnace, as for example the Furness area of Lancashire. Roughly circular shallow depressions usually mark the location of former pitsteads, and small, roughly circular, oval or rectangular earthworks signify the presence of charcoal burners' or other seasonal woodland workers' huts. Often these huts were turf- or plank-walled so that the only structural remains will be the tumbled remnants of a stone chimney (Bowden 1999, 137).

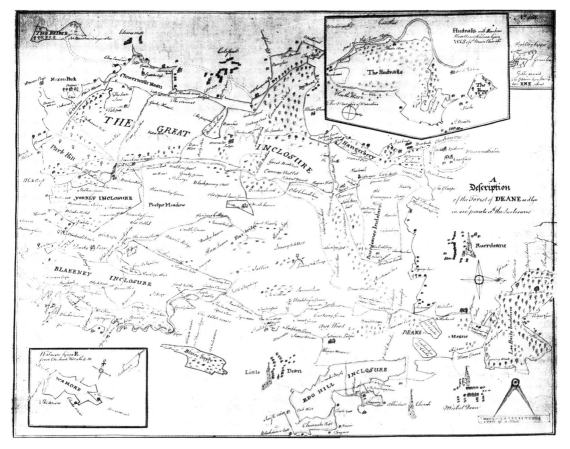

Late seventeenth-century map of the Forest of Dean, showing the enclosures made for coppices. (© Public Record Office)

Many new, often small, woods were created in the post-medieval period, mostly as cover for game. Woodlands were bounded entities, usually defined by a bank with an external ditch. Post-medieval newly planted woodlands, like post-medieval field enclosures, tend to be more regularly shaped than earlier ones, and the banks are smaller (Bowden 1999, 135). Plantations were established for a variety of reasons, including their value as ornamental additions to the landscape. The majority of small coverts, however, were probably established for hunting purposes. After a decline in the popularity of hunting among fashionable society in the seventeenth century, as evidenced to an extent by the decline of the deer park, it achieved a renaissance from the late seventeenth century (Thirsk 1985, 366). In particular, during the eighteenth century fox hunting on horseback increased in popularity as a leisure pursuit among the landed classes. Unlike many other hunting pursuits, this was not largely confined to marginal land but actively encouraged on champion farm land. There were regional variations in its popularity, but in those districts where it was particularly prevalent, as in the Cotswolds, Wiltshire and Leicestershire, coverts to encourage foxes became an important feature of the landscape (Hoskins 1955, 196), along with the removal of standard trees from hedgerows to facilitate the movement of the hunt (Dyer *et al.* 2000, 93). In the nineteenth century further coverts were laid out as cover for the increasingly popular elite pastime of pheasant shooting. Many great estates from southern Scotland to Sussex improved their woodland for pheasants by planting thick shrubs around their perimeters to reduce draughts (Vandervell and Coles 1980, 36, 110). The rhododendron probably made its first appearance in many woodlands as a consequence.

The planting of woodlands for elite sporting pursuits, and their development as parts of the elite pleasure-grounds that were the landscape parks, must have contributed to the perceived link between woodlands and elite resource use that was established with the popular conception of the medieval royal forest. These new types of woodland were also areas of exclusion, both physically and legally. It is unsurprising then that much radical thought linked trees and woodlands in Britain, France and America to oppression and political dominance (Daniels 1988, 52–9).

Game and the Landscape

The elite consumption of game had a wider impact on the landscape than just the occurrence of coverts. Hunting in the eighteenth century became associated with elite lifestyles as never before, and was one of the principal mechanisms by which the elite defined themselves. This association is reflected particularly in oil painting. In contrast to the seventeenth century, when nobility and martial prowess tended to be associated, the eighteenth-century commissioned portrait of a landowner was likely to show an association with field sports. Landscape paintings, too, often portrayed a hunting scene (*see* Vandervell and Coles 1980). Not only was fowling with a gun, and other game shooting, a gentleman's pastime, but the acquisition and eating of game were also indicative of status. Substantial land resources were also devoted to trapping, to sustain the elite's taste for game. As in the medieval period the hunting and trapping of game was a land-use activity largely confined to agriculturally marginal zones, such as wetlands, uplands and wood pasture areas.

The duck decoy consisted of a stretch of open water up to three acres in size, with a number of curving and narrowing channels (pipes) extending from it. These pipes were covered with nets and the wildfowl were lured into them. The design was introduced from the Netherlands in the seventeenth century. One of the earliest recorded is Sir William Wodehouse's decoy at Waxham in Norfolk, established before 1620 (Williamson 1997, 101). Numerous decoys were constructed on West Country estates in the seventeenth century, with that at Abbotsbury – now a famous swannery – being established by 1655 (Aston and Bettey 1998, 131). More than forty decoys were made in the Somerset wetlands during the seventeenth century (Aston and Bettey 1998, 133), with similar structures established in the Gwent levels on the other side of the Severn Estuary. Duck decoys were built for the lords who owned rights to Martin Mere in south Lancashire, with the Scarisbricks having a decoy at Wet Holsome by the early eighteenth century (Coney 1992, 59). Most decoys appear to have been built following the Restoration. There may be a number of reasons for this. Along with other forms of what Williamson has called intermediate exploitation, such as rabbit warrens and dovecotes, which were monopolised by the manorial lords and their social superiors, duck decoys represented a form of agricultural diversification (Williamson 1997, 102). Agriculture was in something of a depression between 1650 and 1750, as population growth slackened, and these activities represented an economic way of exploiting more marginal land (Thirsk 1985, 366–8). However, it is quite likely that the growth in numbers of features like duck decoys was delayed until the Restoration because during the Civil War and the Interregnum they were seen as symbols of status and privilege (Williamson

A grouse butt of probable nineteenth-century origin on the moors of the Forest of Bowland.

1997, 102–3). Thus the proliferation of such features, and the renewed interest in hunting from the late seventeenth century, can be seen as a reassertion of traditional symbols of elite taste following a period of enforced retrenchment (Williamson 1997, 106).

The grouse, another high-status bird, was, like the pheasant, shot for sport. Grouse shooting is recorded in the eighteenth century, but for most the inhospitable upland moors which the bird inhabited were too difficult to reach on anything other than an occasional basis. The commercial exploitation of the moors for grouse shooting became possible with the mid-nineteenth-century expansion of the railways (Vandervell and Coles 1980, 114). Around the same time the techniques of moorland management to increase grouse stocks were improved, with the introduction of controlled regular heather burning. The main archaeological artefact of grouse shooting is the grouse butt, a cone-like pit, revetted with either wood or stone, in which the gun took position. Grouse butts were in use in Yorkshire by the 1860s (Vandervell and Coles 1980, 116), and late nineteenth-century examples occur in Scotland, north Wales and throughout the Pennines. Shooting lodges were also established in upland areas in the nineteenth century to provide shelter during grouse shoots. Vast areas of upland became dedicated to grouse shooting, heather moorland was encouraged, and public access was curtailed as a consequence.

Grouse shooting was one of the ways in which the great estates in Scotland opened themselves up to elite sportsmen. They also offered salmon fishing and deer stalking. The commercial exploitation of estates for field sports grew in Scotland in the nineteenth century as a form of estate diversification. On the Sutherland estates extra income was sought through letting for deer as early as the 1850s (Wade Martins 1998, 37), but deer became much more important in the Highlands generally with the collapse of wool and meat prices in the 1880s.

By the end of the nineteenth century many of the sheep farms created at the beginning of the century had been abandoned and the buildings converted to gamekeepers' houses. The popularity of deer stalking in part resulted from the patronage of Queen Victoria and her family. Victoria's love of the sporting life of the elite in the Highlands was depicted in paintings by Edwin Landseer, and helped to mythologise nineteenth-century Scotland and its landscape (Pringle 1988; Newman 1999, 395), forming the basis for the twentieth-century Scottish tourist industry. Victoria's hunting interests allowed the portrayal of a tamed, pastoral and pacified Highlands, willingly and loyally given over to the pleasure pursuits of the ruler. This was an image made possible by the huge changes that had taken place within the Scottish landscape. The Highland Clearances allowed the exploitation of the landscape for hunting and had also broken the 'disloyal' resistance to the 'English' Crown of traditional Highland society (Pringle 1988, 153).

The development of the landscape for the exploitation and hunting of wildfowl and game, as well as for fox hunting, was an elite initiative to support and symbolise elite lifestyles. The landscape features thus created carry messages of privilege, oppression, exclusion and identity myths. Even today public access is strictly limited on the upland grouse moors, and the preservation of the perceived privilege of being able to hunt with dogs on horseback is considered a key countryside policy for rural traditionalists.

RURAL SETTLEMENT

The Medieval Settlement Pattern

One of the most significant examples of the consumption of medieval culture in the post-medieval period is in the great continuity of use of medieval rural settlements in England and Wales. While a few settlements in industrialising areas became urbanised or were absorbed into conurbations, as in the vicinity of London, and a small percentage of others were abandoned or shrank beyond immediate recognition, the vast majority of rural settlements in existence in 1550 remained so in 1900. Moreover, they retained their distinctive character, identity and layout. The street layout, the pattern of buildings and, in some cases, their fabric remain. In many instances medieval village crosses were retained, where they had not been destroyed by puritan zealots; the remnants of at least twenty-two exist in County Durham (Rimmington 1999, 44). Many were restored during the post-medieval period with the cross head often replaced by a less religious symbol, like a ball or pyramid. Such retention of the physical aspects of medieval culture is to an extent indicative of the conservatism inherent in the lifestyles of the rural inhabitants.

The situation in Scotland was strikingly different. The late eighteenth-century 'improvement' of the Scottish countryside radically altered the rural settlement pattern. Only in the Lothians did an earlier settlement pattern survive, and here it was very reminiscent of that of north-east England, consisting of planned villages laid out in rows or around a green (Whyte and Whyte 1991, 9). Elsewhere the pattern established in the Middle Ages was swept away, although in areas of mixed settlement pattern, such as the southern Scottish Lowlands, the dispersed farmstead and nucleated burghs survived. For example, as in northern England, many of the dispersed farmsteads of Eskdale in Dumfries can be demonstrated to have existed by the fourteenth century (Corser 1993, 15; Corser 1982).

The reconstructed fermtoun at Auchindrain, Argyll. (© Lancaster University Archaeological Unit)

Settlement Change in Scotland

The settlement pattern over much of Scotland between the sixteenth and eighteenth centuries was dominated by the fermtouns and kirktouns (or clachans). These were small, open, unplanned nucleations, usually loosely scattered along a series of paths or lanes. Boundaries were not well defined in the way that the croft of an English or Welsh village was defined, and the layout changed quite rapidly through time as old, relatively impermanent dwellings and outbuildings were replaced. The fermtoun was primarily a shared farm worked by several tenants and labourers (Whyte and Whyte 1991, 4–5). Kirktouns, or clachans in the Highlands, were similar but were often larger and had a wider function as they possessed a church. Fermtouns were spread throughout most of Scotland, though in the Lowlands in particular by the sixteenth century they formed part of a mixed settlement pattern which included English-style nucleated settlements and dispersed farms. The remains of such settlement patterns are encountered in both Dumfriesshire and Perthshire, for example (Corser 1993). There is some indication that by the post-medieval period in the Lowlands fermtouns were likely to be on the fringes of more marginal land – at least this is where their remains survive, although it is difficult to date them without excavation. Where this has been done, however, as at Lour, near Peebles, clay pipes indicated occupation into the seventeenth and eighteenth centuries (Whyte and Whyte 1991, 24). Even in the Highlands and islands, however, the settlement pattern prior to the Clearances was more complex than just that described for the loosely grouped fermtoun. Recent work on Islay, for example, suggests a range of settlement types probably related to tenure, and including settlements focused on a laird's residence, planned and unplanned settlements without a lordly focus, and dispersed settlement (Caldwell *et al.* 2000, 65).

Population growth through the sixteenth to eighteenth centuries stimulated rural settlement expansion in Scotland. Townships split and new fermtouns were established. Often these were occupying and reclaiming more marginal land, as reflected in the incorporation into their place-names of terms like bog or moss (Whyte 1995, 133). The shielings of the fermtouns were also converted for permanent habitation by tenants, and such developments are a notable feature of the Glen Strathfarrer district. New shielings were established on ever more marginal land throughout the post-medieval period up until the mid-eighteenth century (Bil 1990). The new shielings infringed on the deer forests at the expense of the game (Whyte and Whyte 1991, 18–19), and consequently such settlement activity was frequently forbidden in the tenants' charters of lease (Whyte 1995, 134).

While agricultural improvement removed the shared tenancies throughout Scotland, there is little historical evidence to suggest widespread forcible eviction and settlement desertion in the Lowlands (Devine 1994, 118–19), though this view is not shared by all historians. Although the number of tenants on lowland estates declined in the face of holding amalgamation, this does not appear to have been particularly rapid (Devine 1994, 115). Rather than a mass and enforced process of population clearance, as some authorities have inferred (Gray 1974), the process seems similar to the rationalisation that occurred in England and Wales in the later seventeenth and early eighteenth centuries. One victim of this process may have been the farm of Over Newtown in Upper Clydesdale, shown by excavation to have been occupied between at least the late sixteenth century and the mid-eighteenth century, though the artefact assemblage indicates some occupation of part of the site into the nineteenth (Dunwell *et al.* 1995). There were winners and losers among the tenantry, but the reduction in the numbers engaged in farming activities may have been no more significant or forced than that experienced in south Wales in the eighteenth and nineteenth centuries (Newman and Wilkinson 1996, 229–30). This appears to be in stark contrast to the Highlands, where mass depopulations were enforced (Devine 1994, 119).

The archaeological evidence appears to bear out the differences between Lowland and Highland rural depopulations. The upstanding and best preserved remains occur generally in the Highlands (Corser 1993, 23). This is in part a factor of differential preservation, with cultivation often being entirely abandoned in the Highlands, initially in favour of sheep rearing, which in turn was superseded by deer reserves, both forms of land-use likely to preserve remains. In contrast, cultivation continued in the Lowlands, and often the fermtouns developed into single farmsteads. This is similar to the situation in parts of the northern English uplands, where vaccaries, small multiple-occupation settlements, are often invisible because they are occupied by later single-family farmsteads. Moreover, the Lowland fermtouns have a longer history of abandonment and a more intensive post-abandonment land-use (Corser 1993, 23). Although these factors help to attribute differences in deserted settlement distribution in the Lowlands and Highlands to differential preservation, they also emphasise the different nature of the landscapes created by rationalisation. In the Lowlands the township areas continued to be cultivated, the place-names often preserved by the new dispersed farmsteads, and the processes of farm amalgamation can be seen to have been more gradual.

The Highlands of Scotland, courtesy of the Clearances, are littered with deserted settlement remains, very few of which have been excavated, so their material culture is not well understood (Dixon 1993, 24). Typically they consist of houses, barns and drying kilns surrounded by the earthwork remains of their field system, forming a degree of past landscape preservation difficult to match elsewhere in north-western Europe for extent and complexity (Hingley and Foster 1994, 8). Some remains clearly relate to pre-Clearance desertions, as for example at Ardtornish Castle in northern Argyll, where the remains of settlement appear to have been deserted following the abandonment of the castle by the MacDonalds in the later seventeenth century

(Stell 1993, 13). The desertion of these settlements, along with the abandonment of castles, symbolises in the landscape the changes that were taking place in Highland society in the seventeenth and eighteenth centuries. In the southern and eastern Highlands, as in the Lowlands, change was gradual through the seventeenth to nineteenth centuries. Holdings were amalgamated and fermtouns replaced by individual consolidated farms. In the north and west, however, change was later and more dramatic, with entire glens cleared of their traditional communities to make way for commercial sheep farms during the period 1770–1820 (Whyte and Whyte 1991, 26). The traditional medieval forms of lordship and lifestyles were being transformed, finally being swept away by 'improvement' and the Clearances.

It is obvious that change was taking place in traditional Highland society during the sixteenth to eighteenth centuries, just as it was in the Scottish Lowlands. Yet no other area of Britain experienced the depth of rural change that occurred in the Highlands and island communities of Scotland during the later eighteenth and nineteenth centuries. While change, particularly in such a perceived 'backward' society, was inevitable, it is inconceivable that the transformation of the Highlands would have been so dramatic without the unique political circumstances that surrounded them in the eighteenth and early nineteenth centuries. Following the Act of Union of 1707 the Highlands would have seemed like a foreign country within Britain (Symonds 1999). The inhabitants spoke Gaelic, their society was organised on a clan basis aimed at providing clan chiefs rapidly with a body of fighting men, and the farming system and housing conditions appeared primitive. In addition, the financial return on the estates was meagre in comparison to those achievable elsewhere in Britain. Until the late seventeenth century the military emphasis of the clan structure led to attempts to maintain the maximum number of people possible within a clan territory (Whyte and Whyte 1991, 154). Consequently the Highland farming system was under stress by the eighteenth century, as expanding populations had in some cases advanced arable cultivation to the point where there was too little winter feed to sustain sufficient stock in order to manure the arable (Dodgshon 1998). Moreover, with a diminished need for fighting men to sustain their positions, the aristocracy had little need for the services offered as rent. At the same time their requirement for money increased as they attempted to support increasingly expensive lifestyles typical of the British aristocracy elsewhere (Whyte and Whyte 1991, 156). In summary, Highland society was a military threat to Hanoverian security, an affront to progressive, rational Georgian society, and inadequately productive for the needs of its elite.

In response to these issues Highland society, and thus its landscape, was changed during the eighteenth century by government policy, but above all by the increasing commercialisation of the estates (Whyte and Whyte 1991, 156). The introduction of cattle ranching and later sheep farming gave a better return from the estates and removed the need for the fermtouns. On the Sutherland estates improvement began in the 1790s, ushering in almost a century of constant rural change. The farmsteads that replaced the fermtouns were large, mechanised industrial farms, laid out to the most up-to-date concepts of farmstead design, with purpose-built structures grouped around a central yard, and the stones stamped with the name of the estate (Wade Martins 1998). On South Uist and elsewhere in the Outer Hebrides commercialisation resulted in the retention of the population in crowded crofting communities to service the islands' economy through kelp gathering (Symonds 1999, 104). For the most part it was not in the interests of the improving landlords to entirely remove the population if they could be profitably employed. Thus the evicted fermtoun populations were accommodated elsewhere on the estates, in coastal and loch-side locations; here, housed in blackhouses, they could derive a living from fishing and kelping (Whyte and Whyte 1991, 170). Between 1800 and 1820 the settlement pattern and fieldscape of the northern and western parts of Scotland were transformed through this system. A blackhouse excavated at a crofting settlement at Airigh Mhuillin on South Uist revealed occupation between *c.* 1790 and 1830, during the peak years of crofting in connection with kelp gathering. The finds assemblage was dominated by cheaper ceramics, and specialised products such as teapots and sugar bowls were absent (Symonds 1999, 115–16), demonstrating a degree of poverty and a lack of opportunity.

In the Outer Hebrides the crofting system did not involve the widespread displacement of populations. Instead, existing settlement and field patterns were remodelled. The smallholdings of the runrig system were replaced by crofts. This involved the implementation of regularised holdings into a 'rigidly geometric pattern' (Whyte and Whyte 1991, 173). At Waternish in Skye survey work has revealed the complexity of the pre-Clearance landscape and the tremendous difference wrought by late eighteenth-century improvement. The ridges of lazy beds and the haphazard sprawl of fermtouns survive as highly visible earthworks. The latter starkly contrasted with the rectangular crofts, extending at right angles from the linear settlements spread along access roads (Dixon 1993, 25–6). Not only were new patterns of landscape introduced but new concepts of building and farmstead design were imposed as well. In contrast to the single-storey, dry-stone-walled, thatched longhouses of the fermtouns, and also very different from the blackhouses of the crofts, the new farms were built of mortared stone, with two storeys, chimneys and many glazed windows. They were comparatively large, imposing and alien (Symonds 1999). So although the Clearances in the Outer Hebrides did not lead to the removal of the populations, the effect on the landscape – and thus on the perception and psychology of its inhabitants – was dramatic. This may help to explain why, despite often quite enlightened landlords reducing old holdings slowly and attempting to ensure a variety of alternative employments, there was considerable tenant opposition to the changes. Later in the nineteenth century the collapse of the kelp industry and the failure of the potato crop among other factors led to even more rationalisation among the islands, leading to evictions and consequent emigration (Symonds 1999, 109).

Settlement Desertion and Shrinkage in England and Wales

In England and Wales the settlement pattern was far more stable than in Scotland. Aside from the effects of industrialisation and urbanisation, the rural settlement pattern elsewhere in Britain did not experience radical change in the post-medieval period. As had always happened, new settlements developed and older established settlements shrank or were completely deserted. Often this desertion is far more subtle than the abandonment of a nucleated village, which left behind traces in readily identifiable earthworks; rather, it involved the gradual thinning of dispersed farmsteads within townships, as holdings were amalgamated. The sixteenth century was at the end of a period that had seen huge numbers of nucleated settlements fail: perhaps twenty thousand hamlets and two thousand villages in England alone were deserted or shrank greatly during the late fourteenth to sixteenth centuries (Dyer 1997, 72). While this process slowed after the sixteenth century, it did continue, despite a background of a generally rising population.

Two principal factors seem to have affected settlement survival in the post-medieval period: estate rationalisation and the attractions of the new growing industrial settlements. In Cumberland and Westmorland for example, traditionally considered to be a rural area, the population seems to have reflected national trends in growth from the sixteenth century and increased by perhaps 25 per cent during the course of the eighteenth century. Yet many rural parishes suffered population decline, particularly in the late seventeenth to mid-eighteenth centuries, and this seems to have been a result primarily of intra-regional migration to growing towns like Kendal, Whitehaven and Workington (Evans and Beckett 1984, 6–7). While small hamlets could disappear quite quickly as a result of these factors, larger settlements, unless subject to manorial-initiated desertions, tended to have a lengthy period of croft abandonment. At Wawne to the north of Hull in Yorkshire the village reached its zenith in the fourteenth century. Excavations show that it underwent gradual decline and desertion in the early post-medieval period, with some late medieval structures being abandoned as recently as the eighteenth century (Hayfield 1984, 50). The village was never completely deserted and since the Second World War has expanded again. The post-medieval decline of Wawne is most likely to be related to the amalgamation of holdings. This process is often linked to enclosure, and in many instances, particularly in the English Midlands, this was a factor, but it was not as universal as might appear from some of the literature (Taylor 1983, 204–5). In west Gloucestershire particularly dramatic examples of estate rationalisation can be inferred from documentary, cartographic and earthwork evidence to account for the fate of two very different settlements, Highmeadow and Ruddle. In neither case was open field enclosure a factor in decline.

Highmeadow was a settlement of medieval origin which in 1608 formed a linear nucleation consisting of one capital messuage and fifteen other inhabited crofts. In 1613 the settlement was part of the manorial estate passed from the Bell family to the Hall family. In the later seventeenth century Benedict Hall built a mansion there, replacing the old capital messuage. During the seventeenth century references to Highmeadow as a settlement cease and the name becomes associated with the mansion only, although a print of *c*. 1720 shows that associated with a farmstead and a cottage. By 1792 only the farmstead and the mansion remained, the latter being demolished in the nineteenth century. It seems that the desertion of Highmeadow related to the

The earthwork remains of Highmeadow House, Gloucestershire.

creation of the mansion and a reorganisation of the estate around the home farm (Newman 1988, 355); presumably the former tenants moved to local settlements like the nearby expanding town of Coleford (Hart 1983). Ruddle, unlike Highmeadow, was in 1618 a small township with a dispersed settlement pattern. Consisting of fourteen farms scattered throughout the township and four messuages together in a small settlement focus, by 1763 fewer than a third of these sites were still occupied and eight properties were described as 'where a messuage lately stood' (Newman 1988, 358). Estate rationalisation resulting in the amalgamation of farms into larger units caused both depopulation and the shrinkage of settlement within the township, a process that continued into the twentieth century.

Dispersed settlement patterns formed in upland areas by seasonally occupied shieling sites were greatly affected by desertion during the post-medieval period. The remains of seasonally occupied sites in the uplands of England, Scotland and Wales are notoriously difficult to date (Fox 1996), not only because when excavated they can be finds-poor, but also because in structure they often change little over many centuries, within a regional context. In Wales the construction of isolated buildings 9–10m long in association with a small enclosure continued throughout the Middle Ages into the early modern period. These *hafodau*, used for tending cattle, were replaced in the eighteenth century by *lluestau* for sheep farming, but the chronologies of occupation are not well understood, and even the terminologies for site characterisation and description need to be established and refined (Yates 1996). The remains of both are widely scattered throughout the Welsh uplands, but their desertion is indicative of no more than changing farming practices, as they were never representative of permanent settlement. In England, too, sites similar in appearance, and with similar archaeological issues of definition and dating, occur throughout the northern uplands (*see* McDonnel 1988). In all areas, including in Scotland, the system was in retreat by the late eighteenth century.

In Scotland the shieling system may have been largely abandoned with the changes in agricultural practices which gathered pace in the eighteenth and nineteenth centuries in upland areas, but it should not be seen as a primitive, inflexible subsistence system. It is known that in Scotland, in the sixteenth to eighteenth centuries, it had an important role in the development of commercial cattle rearing for export to England. Parallels have been made with the *seter* system in Norway, and the part it played in the development of a moneyed economy there in the seventeenth and eighteenth centuries (Cheape 1996, 18), but in Britain it is likely that shielings formed part of a commercial farming economy, particularly on monastic estates, by the late medieval period (Hair and Newman 1999).

In some areas the settlement effects of estate amalgamation and changing farming practices were exacerbated in the eighteenth and nineteenth centuries by the attraction for the rural poor of nearby industrialising settlements and growing towns. At Llanmaes in the Vale of Glamorgan, south Wales, a group of buildings was excavated that belonged to a late seventeenth-century expansion of the village along one side of the village green (Newman and Wilkinson 1996). Seemingly the cottages of husbandmen or similar, they had been deserted by the end of the eighteenth century as a result of a general depopulation within the Llanmaes area, attributed by contemporaries both to farm amalgamations and to emigration to the 'manufacturing districts' (Newman and Wilkinson 1996, 229–30). A similar cause can be attributed to desertions elsewhere. In the West Riding of Yorkshire the earthworks forming the remains of the shrunken settlement of Stock have been considered to be medieval in date (Newman 1996, 118), but recent documentary research has shown that the site did not experience any significant contraction until the nineteenth century at the earliest (J. Darlington pers. comm.). Stock is situated close to Barnoldswick, a growing textile town in the nineteenth century. As Stock shrank so Barnoldswick grew, and it is tempting to link the two phenomena.

New Farmsteads

At the same time that many small established farms were driven out of existence through amalgamation and estate rationalisation, new farms were established in recently enclosed areas, particularly in areas of land reclamation. Enclosure and settlement dispersion tended to go together, as land held in discrete, enclosed and usually compact blocks was best farmed from within that block. The lack of communal involvement in land management also tended to work against the need for nucleated settlements. The assarting of the 'waste' and the establishment of new dispersed farmsteads were familiar processes in the Middle Ages, but from the sixteenth century onwards the conversion of zones of intermediate land-use into areas of productive farmland progressed at an unprecedented rate. Aided by ambitious great estate-sponsored drainage schemes, and changes in the legal status of some land through processes such as disafforestation, large areas of previously unoccupied upland and wetland were opened up for settlement and thus more intensive exploitation.

The draining of the Fens is one of the best known examples of settlement following reclamation, and resulted in 'a remarkable expansion of dispersed settlement' (Taylor 1983, 207). From the 1650s into the nineteenth century isolated farmsteads were established throughout the reclaimed Fens. Some of these farms failed, but overall a new landscape of dispersed settlement was created. Indeed, wetland reclamation was a major influence in changing the settlement pattern, introducing permanent settlement to areas where no previous settlements existed (Taylor 2000, 167). In Lancashire and Yorkshire the disafforestation in 1507 of many upland areas, primarily used for rough grazing under the medieval vaccary system, led to a complex process of land colonisation. The vaccaries themselves grew into villages and hamlets in many instances, especially in the Forests of Pendle and Rossendale (Porter 1980, 29–38). However, new isolated farmsteads were established as the old farms expanded during the sixteenth century and then divided through sub-letting (LUAU 1997b, 26). The established communities of southern Bowland, an area colonised and partially enclosed during the medieval period, approached the landowner, the Crown, to enclose the large areas of open common grazing along the boundaries of their townships. While the division of the commons was initiated in the 1550s, it was not completed until 1630 (Porter 1978, 13). Among the areas enclosed was an area of moorland (totalling some 2,400 acres) known as the Champion. Between its enclosure in 1622 and the later seventeenth century, twenty-three new farmsteads were built there (Porter 1980, 33–4), most of which still survive. In today's landscape the dispersed farmsteads, relatively regular, straight-sided fields, and the straight character of some of the surviving public rights of way seem to presage – at a smaller, more intimate scale – the landscapes that would be created a century or so later through parliamentary enclosure.

Areas of open upland rough grazing occurred in southern England, too. Exmoor was such an area until enclosure following an Act of Parliament of 1815. Of the 10,117ha enclosed, 6,070ha were sold by the Crown to John Knight as one estate (Millward and Robinson 1977, 94). It was bounded by a 46km perimeter wall, and after 1841 fifteen separate, primarily livestock, farms were established within its circuit (Millward and Robinson 1977, 94). The farmsteads appear to

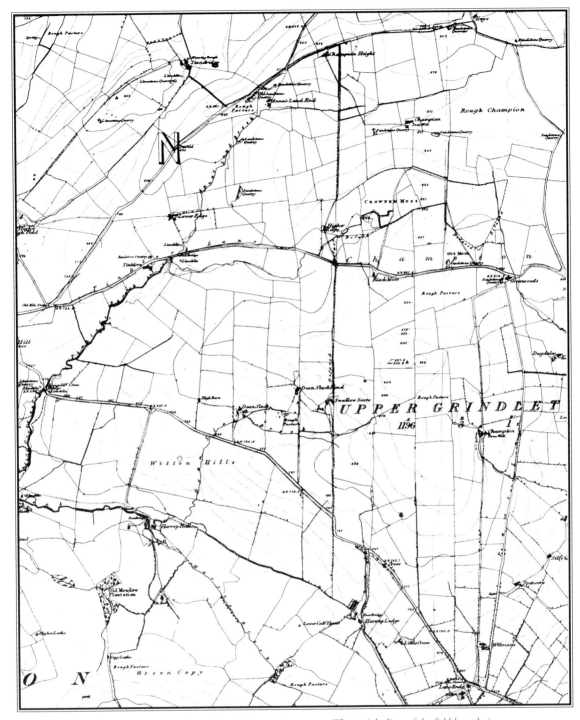

The Champion, as shown on the first edition Ordnance Survey map. The straight lines of the field boundaries characterise the area from the surrounding landscape. (© Lancashire County Council)

have been carefully sited to protect them from the elements (Harvey 1989, 48). Built to typical nineteenth-century yard plans, they have proved durable. As late as 1989 ten of them survived as farms; only three had been abandoned and two of those were as a result of being requisitioned by the Army for training during the Second World War (Harvey 1989, 52). Such a fate on a wider scale befell the farmsteads of the Salisbury Plain reclamation. In southern central England, in the chalkland districts, areas of common pasture abounded in the sixteenth and seventeenth centuries as much as they did in northern England. Following enclosure at the end of the eighteenth and early nineteenth centuries the chalk downlands of Salisbury Plain were gradually colonised. Within the central portion of what is now the Ministry of Defence's Salisbury Plain Training Area, thirty-two farmsteads and twenty field barns were established, mostly after 1850, following the Tithe Commutation Act (Brown 1999, 121). The open sheep pastures were converted to enclosed mixed farms with significant land under arable cultivation. Soon after the establishment of these farms, however, the late nineteenth-century agricultural depression occurred and much of the land was turned back to sheep pasture. The position remained critical for these farmers until the end of the century, creating an advantageous situation for the War Department to purchase the land and convert it into a military training area (Brown 1999, 126–7). As a consequence the hegemony of enclosure and dispersed farmsteads was brief, and Salisbury Plain reverted to an open, relatively unsettled landscape.

The changes wrought by reclamation, and by parliamentary enclosure in particular, altered the perception of the major differences in the settlement geography of England. From Dorset to Yorkshire, where nucleated villages and open fields had dominated the landscape until the late eighteenth century, new isolated farmsteads appeared among the straight-sided fields laid out by the enclosure commissioners (Prince 1989, 26–7). New farms, incorporating the latest principles of farmstead design, were set among discrete blocks of fields in a regular and rational landscape (Prince 1989, 27). The post-enclosure farms of the Midlands districts are characterised by names redolent of Hanoverian triumphalism, such as Quebec or Trafalgar (Hoskins 1955, 204–7). Such planned landscapes, adding dispersed elements to previously highly nucleated settlement patterns, are well known and frequently discussed, but they are only one aspect of the evolving post-medieval settlement pattern of England and Wales. An equally significant addition was occurring primarily away from the champion districts. In the more complex landscapes of the so-called woodland districts of areas like the Weald and the Welsh borders, new settlements grew through encroachment.

Encroachment and Squatting Settlements

The antithesis of the new farmsteads, in both process and result, was the genesis of squatter settlements generally within areas of common pasture. Rather than estate-sponsored settlement expansions, these were originated in the main by the poor and landless, though often with the complicit support of the manorial lord. They are the most dramatic landscape symbol of resistance to the post-medieval estate-driven rationalisation of the agrarian landscape. Irregular, unplanned and sometimes sprawling, and confined both to the margins of cultivation and to the edges of townships, they represent a physical manifestation of successful strategies of resistance to social exclusion.

Squatter settlements occurred where cleared land was available to be encroached. This was most commonly provided by areas of common grazing, usually developed from areas of

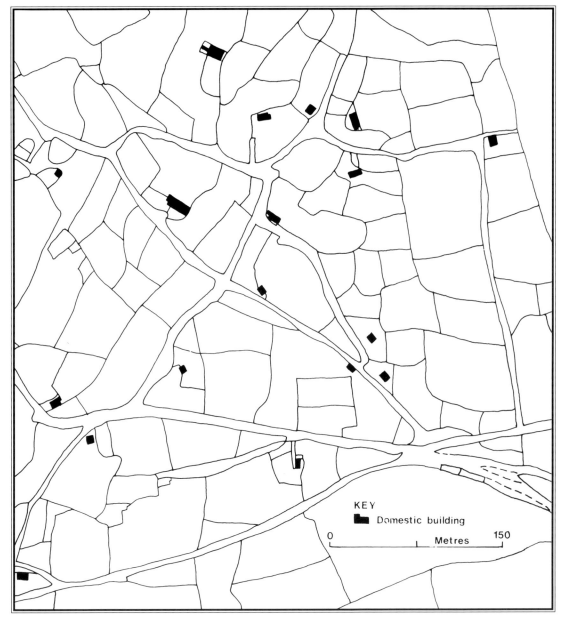

Part of St Briavel's Common squatter settlement in Gloucestershire, c. 1840. The settlement is characterised by the dispersed nature of its buildings, the small enclosures and the 'spider's web' network of roads.

woodland pasture, where the trees had disappeared because of constant browsing without enclosure to allow regrowth. Smaller squatter settlements also developed on smaller common areas of rough grazing and even along road verges. In Wales in the sixteenth century large areas of open rough grazing were held under the system known as *cytir*. This left land unenclosed to be shared by the co-heirs of a holding, thus ensuring that partible inheritance did not reduce grazing land beyond the point of viability. In 1542 English legislation abolished partible inheritance and at the same time the great estate holders began to treat *cytir* land as if it were common land (Reed 1986, 94). Faced with the disfranchisement of their land rights, tenants in Wales enclosed the open land, paying their English lords a composition for what they regarded as an encroachment. By this means much of the open pasture land of Wales was enclosed and settled with cottages during the sixteenth and seventeenth centuries, and the traditional, long-established Welsh relationships of landholding, tenancy and stewardship were radically altered (Reed 1986, 95).

Many squatter settlements were short-lived and suppressed by the local manorial lords, but some squatters appear to have been tolerated. The common waste, over which rights of common pasturage and other varying rights applied, was held by the lord of the manor. Thus, while he held the soil and the mineral rights, he did not have exclusive use of it, sharing it with the commoners. By levying an annual fine on the squatters for encroachment, the manorial lord in effect increased his rentable land at the expense of the commoners but at little expense to himself, while providing a means toward a more profitable exploitation of an under-utilised resource. Moreover, where the local manorial lord was engaged in the industrial exploitation of his manor, the squatters provided an available workforce (Newman 1988, 368). In the disafforested Crown lands of the Pennines this was also true, with the Crown effectively legalising the occupation of encroachments through nominal fines in its manorial courts (Porter 1980, 30).

Not all former forest areas experienced an influx of squatters. Bowland, for example, on the Lancashire/Yorkshire border, in general did not. The reason for this appears to be a lack of opportunity; for post-medieval smallholders to survive, employment other than subsistence farming had to be available, but in Bowland it generally was not (Turner 1987, 198). Conversely, Yorkshire forests like Knaresborough were areas with a dual economy, combining farming and industry (Turner 1987). In Bowland the lack of industrial development in the sixteenth to eighteenth centuries prevented the emergence of squatter settlements (LUAU 1997b, 26).

One region where the optimum conditions for the development of squatter settlements applied was the south Herefordshire/west Gloucestershire border, where a string of settlements developed along and across township, parish and even county boundaries. The region offered plenty of common wastes, and from the sixteenth century there were opportunities for employment in woodland, iron and extractive industries. The early seventeenth-century traveller and commentator John Norden noted that in Gloucestershire there were 'very many cottages raised upon the forests' (Porter 1978, 1). Indeed, the Forest of Dean especially was very attractive to squatters in the seventeenth and eighteenth centuries as it offered numerous industrial opportunities to supplement the often poverty-stricken existence of the smallholder (Newman 1988, 372). As well as employment in industry, money could be earned from fruit growing. Orchards were an important agricultural feature of the region, and an orchard, once mature, allowed for the pasturage of sheep or pigs within its confines. The products of these mainly apple orchards were sent to a public cider mill. Orchards for cider production were the best way for most smallholders to maximise the profitability of a small amount of land (Newman 1983, 212). So successful was this strategy that William Marshall, the late eighteenth-century agricultural commentator, stated in relation to this region's cider production, 'that cottagers from encroachments made upon commons and larger wastes (paying, perhaps, the Lord of the manor a small quitrent) throw in collectively, no inconsiderable quantity of liquor' (Newman 1983, 211).

Squatter settlements developed from a series of individual encroachments by a process of accretion. Large squatter settlements consisted of a haphazard spread of small enclosures and houses, with roads, often unhedged, forming a spider's web pattern in the gaps between the encroachments. Since squatter settlements lacked legal status, their existence was always precarious until common rights were extinguished and their position regularised. At Horton Heath, Dorset, the remains of a group of paddocks and buildings represent a squatter settlement established by the mid-seventeenth century but deserted by the mid-eighteenth (Taylor 1983, 207). The enclosure by Act of Parliament of the commons upon which the encroached holdings remained regularised them into legal tenancies. Legitimacy was often celebrated by investment in the smallholder's house, an act recorded by datestones.

Encroachment settlements were a result of rising post-medieval rural populations in the sixteenth to eighteenth centuries, combined with estate rationalisation, together producing a landless group attracted to certain areas by the availability of uncultivated, open land and the possibility of by-employment. This led in some areas, like the central Pennines and west Gloucestershire, to the development of a new rural settlement pattern of smallholders. The inhabitants of these settlements had developed new strategies for dealing with their exclusion from traditional forms of landholding and subsistence, and for engaging in an increasingly commercialised society. The busy, haphazard and unbounded settlement landscapes created by post-medieval squatting reflect these strategies. The squatters intensively exploited their resources and broke through the boundaries and constraints of traditional rural society.

Estate Villages

Changes in inheritance law in the mid-seventeenth century, and a healthy market for agricultural produce for much of the later seventeenth and eighteenth centuries, encouraged the development by the elite of great landed estates (Williamson and Bellamy 1987, 122–3). Hand in hand with the improvements they made to increase agricultural productivity went the development of lavish landscaped parks. Both processes led to the removal of existing settlements and their re-creation in what the estate owner deemed to be more suitable locations. Often, as at Rufford in Lancashire, the earthworks of the abandoned original settlement were left within the park (Newman 1996). At Milton Abbas in Dorset in the mid-eighteenth century the Earl of Dorchester removed the old village from its position at the gates of the former Benedictine monastery, built a mansion on the monastic ruins, and relocated the village over a kilometre away from its original site (Hoskins 1955, 172). The new settlement was constructed as a model village, with labourers' cottages built as semi-detached two-storey, thatched pairs. Similarly, at Harewood House near Leeds the old village was removed from within the landscape park, though the church remained, and was repositioned outside the main gate (Taylor 1983, 209). These new settlements, as at Harewood, were often built in an estate style, as a clear mark of ownership, and formed part of a pattern of alterations imposed on the landscape. At Harewood these included making the highway from Collingham, the current A659, into a straight, avenue-like approach and diverting other roads around the park. The remodelling of the landscape and of tenants' lives in this way is one of the clearest indications of the almost absolute power of some of the great estate owners, a power particularly evident in Scotland in the later eighteenth century.

In Scotland the planned post-medieval village erected under the guidance of a great landowner was even more common than in England and Wales. The village of Bothans in East Lothian was demolished at the end of the seventeenth century to make way for the Marquis of Tweeddale's park at Yester House; the old village was replaced by the planned estate settlement of Gifford

(Whyte and Whyte 1991, 21). Other than in the far north and west of Scotland, where surplus population was accommodated through crofting, the removal of fermtouns through estate improvement created a body of homeless ex-agricultural labourers and smallholders. While many of these emigrated either to the Americas or to the industrialising urban growth areas like Glasgow, sufficient remained to populate new settlements (Reed 1983, 79). Thus the new estate villages can be seen both as an attempt to increase estate wealth and as an exercise in benevolence by landlords towards those they had dispossessed. Most of these settlements were established with an emphasis on rural industries, particularly textile manufacture, and were often in part designed to act as local market centres (Whyte and Whyte 1991, 147). They formed part of the improvement process which included the laying out of new ports and towns on the same rational principles of regularity. The villages contained the same classically proportioned and neatly arranged stone houses, often architect-designed. Overall, in the later eighteenth and nineteenth centuries, around 350 new towns and villages were created in Scotland (Reed 1983, 79).

The estate villages were not entirely a feature of late eighteenth-century 'improvement', however. Estate villages of similar rational design had been laid out previously, such as Gifford in the late seventeenth century. Moreover, Scottish landlords had a tradition of laying out new planned settlements in an effort to stimulate economic activity (Whyte and Whyte 1991, 145). From the Middle Ages they had created burghs of barony – which were attempts at establishing trading centres. Some of them were, or grew into, towns, such as Alloa or Dunfermline, but many others remained small rural nucleations (Smith Pryde 1965). The establishment of such settlements was particularly common in the sixteenth and seventeenth centuries, but continued

The village square at Newcastleton in the Scottish borders. This was one of a number of planned settlements developed in Scotland in the eighteenth century and intended to be sustained by textile weaving.

on through the eighteenth and into the nineteenth (Smith Pryde 1965). In legal status the burghs of barony differed from the estate villages, but in appearance they were often very similar, and whatever the initial intention they performed a similar local function. They are indicative of a deep-seated desire among the Scottish landlords to impose a regulated and regular settlement structure in Scotland in order to better enrich themselves. In both burghs and estate villages this could result in better housing provision and even in improved opportunities for the inhabitants, but they were still an imposed settlement form – and in the case of the estate villages one which the lord's tenants had little choice but to accept.

The estate villages tended to be laid out on a regular, geometric street plan, and the larger examples incorporated central squares of considerable size, as at Newcastleton, a textile-weaving estate village established by the Duke of Buccleuch in Liddesdale, southern Scotland (Whyte and Whyte 1991, 145). In their form they are clearly 'Enlightenment' settlements, and contain messages both of paternalistic benevolence towards the poor and of economic exploitation and social control. The nucleated nature of the estate village was generally an alien form of settlement in Scotland and is indicative of the triumph of English culture as embraced by an Anglophile landed elite. Some of the villages, such as John Cockburn's Ormiston, were deliberately modelled on English villages (Whyte and Whyte 1991, 148), although the regular layout of most is very distinct from the traditional English village evolved over many centuries. Like many alien plantations, the estate village system failed to flourish; though most settlements have survived to the present day, many have not expanded beyond their original layout. The rural industries that formed their economic base were quickly overtaken by the development of the industrialising towns and their market functions were made redundant by the railways (Reed 1983, 79–80).

Specialist Settlements

A further addition to the rural settlement scene in the eighteenth century was the industrial village. These occurred throughout the north of England, in the West Country, in Scotland and in south Wales. Some of the earliest were in west Gloucestershire, developing in and around the Forest of Dean during the seventeenth century at Soudley, Lydbrook and Redbrook. These were linear settlements following, and constrained by, the valleys of the watercourses that powered the mills which the settlements served. A range of industrial rural settlements arose throughout the country during the eighteenth and nineteenth centuries; some were planned and others unplanned, but all developed in relation to local industrial enterprises. Some, like Abbeydale, near Sheffield, were purpose-built labourers' cottages incorporated into the fabric of an industrial complex, in this case a mid-eighteenth-century scythe works. At Styal, Cheshire, a 'model village' was built in the 1780s close to the textile mill which employed its inhabitants (Taylor 1983, 220). Others, like Denholme, near Halifax, were polyfocal settlements of unplanned clusters of dwellings around coal pits and mills (Porter 1980, 63), in this instance primarily developing in the early nineteenth century.

The opportunities offered by industrialisation, and particularly by textile manufacture in the north of England, in the eighteenth century encouraged the development of other types of specialist settlement. The Moravians, a Protestant sect, established a community at Fulneck, near Leeds, in the 1740s. Following patterns of settlement foundation already established in central Europe, they built a community sustained by a mixed economy of farming and textile production (Stead 1999). The patronage of Count Zinzendorf of Saxony was important to the

Moravians' success and is reflected in their Congregation House, erected in 1744 in the style (externally) of a German schloss (Stead 1999, 14), even though the community's members were primarily Yorkshire dissenters. Tenement blocks for single brethren and sisters were erected in a restrained classical style. Later single- and two-storey cottages were built behind the principal settlement buildings, and workshops were sited away from the main settlement (Stead 1999, 16). Although initially planned in accordance with the religious community's views and needs, in the later eighteenth century Fulneck evolved in a similar fashion to other Pennine industrial villages. Nevertheless, it remained sufficiently distinctive to be described by James Dugdale in 1819 as 'in form a village unequalled in its appearance of comfort and tranquillity . . . the appearance of Fulneck is such as indicates the civil, industrious and sober character of its inhabitants' (Stead 1999, 105). Fulneck was followed by other Moravian settlements, such as Fairfield, now incorporated within the Droylesden district of Manchester but still forming a discrete and distinctive group of buildings.

URBANISM

By contemporary European standards England was not an urbanised society in the early sixteenth century. The English were not considered to like urban life, and to a late fifteenth-century Italian only London, Bristol and York were considered to have any importance as towns (Dobson 1977). In contrast, it has been estimated that in the later sixteenth century there were about 750 settlements in England that could be considered as functioning towns (Everitt 1979), but in terms of size most of these were tiny, with populations of well under a thousand inhabitants. Aside from London, no British towns were large by western European standards (Clark and Slack 1976, 10). In the early sixteenth century London was by far the largest city, being five times the size of Norwich, its nearest rival (Clay 1984, 197). If England was unurbanised, Scotland and Wales were much more so, the urban centres of both being relatively small in number, and more significantly very small in size. By the end of the nineteenth century Britain was the most urbanised country in Europe: London was the capital of a global empire and the largest city in Europe, Glasgow was the second city of the empire and Cardiff was the world's premier coal-exporting port. This change was enormous: it was the single greatest alteration in the physical fabric of Britain. For the lower Thames Valley, the English Midlands, northern England, south Wales and the central belt of Scotland the landscape was dramatically altered. Consequently, the material cultural experience of living in these places in the nineteenth century was hugely different from the sixteenth century, even for those inhabitants in the surrounding, still rural, areas. Outside these areas, however, the changes wrought by urban growth were less marked, and in the furthest reaches of the Highlands and islands of Scotland perhaps hardly noticeable. A recent distribution map depicting civic buildings in Scotland reveals the total lack of urban development outside the south and eastern seaboard before the mid-nineteenth century (RCAHMS 1996, x).

Historians have been very active in considering the economic function and development of towns and cities in post-medieval Britain (Briggs 1963; Clark and Slack 1972; 1976; Corfield 1982; 1987) and historical geographers have examined the physical spread of individual towns (Beresford 1988). Archaeologists have until recently been less inclined to examine the evidence for development and change. Despite the pioneering work of Ivor Noël Hume in London after the Second World War (1978), the urban archaeological units established in the 1960s and 1970s concentrated for the most part on the archaeology of earlier periods. Often the post-medieval deposits were ignored, with the occasional notable exception of artefact assemblages (Courtney forthcoming). This situation continued well into the 1980s (Davey 1987, 70), and is vividly demonstrated in Martin Carver's otherwise still excellent summary of urban archaeology, *Underneath English Towns* (1987), which for the most part ignored the post-medieval period. As late as 1990 a scarcity of excavated data was perceived for the sixteenth to eighteenth centuries, let alone for the nineteenth century (Crossley 1990, 75).

The lack of excavation data was and is partly attributable to a lack of collection and research. Most of the major urban excavation campaigns from the 1960s to the 1980s were established because the towns in which they were located already had known important Roman and/or medieval remains. In towns such as Winchester, it was the remains of those periods that were targeted. In London the most fully published post-medieval site to date, the seventeenth-century row of houses at Aldgate (Thompson *et al.* 1984; Egan 1999, 62), was investigated as a by-product of an investigation into a Roman cemetery. The scarcity of post-medieval excavation data has also been attributed to the nature of such deposits. Their vulnerability, particularly to cellaring, is frequently cited, but this oversimplifies the issue and ignores the equal vulnerability in most towns of medieval and Roman deposits to such deeply penetrating intrusions (Crossley 1990, 75; Whyte 1999, 265, 276). Nevertheless, sixteenth- and seventeenth-century deposits, along with earlier ones, are often destroyed along street frontages by later cellaring, as demonstrated by a series of excavations in Prescott, Lancashire (Philpott 1988, 33).

Post-medieval urban archaeology is disadvantaged stratigraphically in comparison to the archaeology of earlier periods. It is closer to the surface and more likely to be damaged by relatively superficial ground disturbance; indeed, it should be remembered that much of the post-medieval urban archaeological resource, in terms of buildings, is not buried but still standing and extant. From the later fourteenth century the build-up of soil layers, characteristic of medieval towns, ceases as rubbish was removed from properties to the town dump, and in many instances the intensity of occupation within the towns was reduced (Carver 1987, 69; Schofield and Vince 1994, 212–13). In London residue evidence suggests that fourteenth- to seventeenth-century cess pits were emptied and reused, the composted materials presumably being removed off site (Malcolm 1997, 51). The revetting of the Thames riverbank with a stone wall in the sixteenth century stopped further expansion of the city into the river by preventing further rubbish dumping in the Thames. Alternatives for rubbish disposal were sought, and the Moorfields area in Islington, the site of abandoned clay pits, appears to have been used as an unofficial city dump (Malcolm 1997, 42). While rubbish disposal in pits and the build-up of soil layers recommences in some towns in the seventeenth century (Carver 1987, 69), the Tudor period is, as a consequence of the lack of soil accretion, often archaeologically difficult to identify by excavation, as noted at investigations in Hastings (Rudling and Barber 1993).

From the 1980s concern for the resource increased, and was expressed in reviews of the post-medieval archaeological potential in some of the provincial towns which had received the most intensive archaeological study (Atkin 1987; Ayres 1991). These, however, serve to highlight the relative lack of published excavated data, as opposed to information derived from standing structures and topographic analyses. In the 1990s post-medieval urban archaeology began to reach maturity in Britain. The targeting of exploratory archaeological investigations in accordance with planning needs, rather than with archaeological research agendas, led to a flood of new work in the 1990s. Much of this came from small towns which had previously received relatively little archaeological attention. This is particularly important, as implications for urban life cannot be reliably made for the many small provincial market towns from observations in Bristol, Norwich or particularly London. Often with populations of fewer than a thousand in the sixteenth century, these provincial market towns cannot compare with London, an international entrepôt with a population 10,000 per cent larger. Unfortunately, the lack of archaeological prioritisation has prevented resources being targeted at those sites which would yield the greatest information, through a combination of good archaeological survival and a full range of documentary records (Crossley 1990, 77). Moreover, aside from brief notes in *Post-Medieval Archaeology*, little of this new work has been published to date. These notes, and the unpublished 'grey literature' lodged in Sites and Monuments Records, are data-rich, but poor in terms of analysis and integrated interpretation. Nevertheless, the new data that have come through in the past decade have tended to indicate that for all the characteristic difficulties exhibited by the post-medieval urban archaeological resource the lack of previous information owed more to a want of looking than to a deficit of opportunity.

Of greatest import has been the extension of archaeological investigation to the many towns that had previously lain uninvestigated. The best post-medieval urban archaeological investigations before the 1990s, as at Moulsham Street, Chelmsford (Cunningham and Drury 1985), were in towns where they were almost the accidental by-product of archaeological interests focused elsewhere. Even in the 1990s it was notable that some of the best work was done in Chester, where archaeological investigations have long been routine within the planning framework because of the town's Roman and medieval deposits. Hence, the only analysed and published investigation of a nineteenth-century domestic court is there (Matthews 1999) and not nearby in St Helens or Wigan. In towns perceived to have only a relatively recent history the investigation of the modern and familiar is usually not considered to merit archaeological conditions attached to planning permissions. Within these towns, swathes of worthwhile archaeology are removed every year without record. Even in cities with considerable time depth, the pressure to complete projects ahead of development still means that the most recent deposits tend to be sacrificed, even if those of sixteenth- and seventeenth-century date are now routinely investigated (Egan 1999, 62). It is to be hoped that the recognition of the importance of later post-medieval archaeology, through extensive county-based urban surveys, and indicated by the new English Heritage focus on heritage-led urban regeneration, will redress this situation.

No matter how inadequate the planning system continues to be in relation to more modern archaeological deposits, the fact remains that in the 1990s much important new work was undertaken in towns such as Stirling and Dumbarton in Scotland, Monmouth in south Wales, and Hereford, Plymouth and Romsey in England, as well as in the great cities such as Bristol and London. This work has proved invaluable, particularly through artefactual study, in revealing the lives of those whom documentary history often ignores: the poor, children and foreigners (Egan 1996; Gaimster 1994; Matthews 1999). Much work remains to be done in these areas, particularly in investigating the suburbs of the poor, which expanded in the post-medieval period (Courtney forthcoming). Situated away from the historic urban cores, and thus not containing either earlier urban deposits or elite post-medieval structures, these areas have not been targeted for examination. A further difficulty continues to be encountered in marrying up back-plot deposits of pit groups and ancillary structures with street frontage structures (Crossley 1990, 76–7).

Moving away from property-specific investigations, the landscape archaeological approach to towns, studying the relationship between and within groups of structures and the spaces between them, has also shed new light on the post-medieval history of urbanism (Leech 1999a). The development of market places, civic and corporate edifices, domestic gardens, and even the distribution of public toilets and their effect on focusing movement and congregation among the urban mass (Leech 1999a, 21) have all attracted archaeological attention.

Town Defences

Fortifications in the form of town walls, often linked to castles, were one of the most obvious physical legacies of the Middle Ages. Indicative of the medieval role played by some towns, they are also a direct link with a feudal past, and even a Roman one. Indeed, in sixteenth- and seventeenth-century towns where Roman town walls had survived to form the basis for medieval defensive circuits, as at York and Chester, the internal layout was defined by the plan of the Roman fortifications (Reed 1986, 180). The defences were physical definitions of urban limits and thus a potential restriction on future growth. Relatively few examples of defensive circuits survive today (Kenyon 1990, 183), and some towns had lost their medieval defences by the sixteenth century. For the most part this was due to neglect and mode of construction rather than to deliberate removal in the course of urban expansion. In common with most other towns in south Wales, Newport in Monmouthshire developed little after the Middle Ages until rapid coal-based industrialisation in the nineteenth century, yet in the 1530s Leland noted only three gates surviving and no defensive circuit. This suggests that the ramparts had been earth- and timber-based rather than stone-built and had disappeared during the course of the later Middle Ages (Soulsby 1983, 204). Elsewhere, as at Leicester, the robbing of masonry defences was a problem from the fifteenth century. In the 1490s there was municipal concern for encroachments upon the

The surviving medieval town gate at Chepstow, which was restored in the nineteenth century.

wall, but a hundred years later such concerns had apparently disappeared. The Corporation was leasing properties along the defensive circuit, and other properties were allowed to be built over the ditch (Buckley and Lucas 1987). Clearly, in Leicester interest in the maintenance of the defences had ceased by the end of the sixteenth century, and not even the Civil War seems to have revived interest in maintaining the medieval urban fortifications here (Courtney and Courtney 1992).

During the later seventeenth and eighteenth centuries most towns with defensive circuits expanded beyond them, obliterating the defences as they grew. Kenyon (1990) has argued that this was primarily an eighteenth- and nineteenth-century development, but the town panoramas drawn by the Buck brothers show that the removal of medieval defences was already well under way by

Part of the defensive circuit of Berwick-upon-Tweed, consisting of earthen ramparts and angle bastions intended both to provide gun platforms and to resist enemy artillery bombardment.

the early/mid-eighteenth century (Hyde 1994). However, even in London, where the city sprawled across its medieval walls in the seventeenth century, some fragments survived into the nineteenth century (Harrington 1992, 27). Towns where good medieval defences survive tend to be those that were least successful and developed little in the post-medieval period, such as the north Wales town of Conwy. Other towns with well-preserved and primarily post-medieval defences are those that continued to have a military importance, like Berwick-upon-Tweed.

The defences of Berwick-upon-Tweed are extraordinary. Its coastal location on the Anglo-Scottish border and its development as a garrison town from the eighteenth century meant that its defensive circuit remained in use for far longer than those of most other towns. The earliest phases of the existing defences date to the thirteenth century, but they were successively remodelled, redesigned and added to in order to adapt to developments in military technology (Grove 1999, 3). New defences erected in the Elizabethan period enclosed a much smaller area than that encompassed by the original fortifications, indicative of a contraction of activity after the thirteenth century. Certainly by the late sixteenth century the castle, which remained outside the circuit of the Elizabethan defences, was abandoned. Excavated evidence of fourteenth- to sixteenth-century levelling deposits in the Brucegate area is also indicative of the abandonment of parts of the medieval town (Rushton 2000, 9). The need to take account of artillery led to the reduction of the medieval town walls in the sixteenth century and the construction of angular, projecting gun platforms (bastions). One of these, the Windmill bastion, remained in use into the twentieth century; adapted in 1859 as a coastal defence battery, it was later reused for anti-aircraft guns (Grove 1999, 13). Similar continued emphasis on town defences was apparent at other militarily important towns, such as the naval base of Portsmouth.

Gateway forming part of the Civil War defences of Bristol.

Most of the major towns in England underwent some form of fortification during the Civil War, involving either the adaptation of earlier defences or the creation of new ones, as at Newark-on-Trent, where outlying 'star' fortlets survive as impressive earthworks (RCHME 1964). Widespread adaptation is significant for demonstrating that mid-seventeenth-century towns were little changed in size and layout from the late Middle Ages. Even so, in some instances, as at Gloucester, suburbs, often of medieval origin, were demolished in order to shorten the Civil War defensive circuit. Even Bristol, the most successful provincial town of the sixteenth and seventeenth centuries, was able to have its defences restored and added to. At Gloucester evidence for Civil War ditches has been found during excavations at the medieval south and outer north gates of the city (Atkin and Howes 1993, 23–4), and other excavated evidence has been interpreted as a bastion ditch (Atkin and Howes 1993, 26).

After the Civil War, most towns lost their military significance, and with growing urban expansion town defences were frequently swept aside, or allowed to decay, often forming convenient sources of building stone for new buildings. The pace and timing of such changes varied from town to town. Medieval Norwich consisted of a huge walled area, and though the city thrived in the sixteenth and seventeenth centuries there was little need to expand outside the walls (Ayres 1991, 7). Throughout much of the eighteenth century the city authorities continued to invest in the maintenance of the medieval defences, with substantial repairs in 1727. By the 1780s, however, there were calls for their demolition. They were considered 'a nuisance, that smells rank in the nose of modern improvement' (Ayres 1991, 11). As a consequence much of the defensive circuit and all twelve gates, the most in any English city, were removed. At Gloucester the heavily fortified Westgate survived into the nineteenth century, until the bridge that crossed the River Severn from it was replaced. In Brecon, south Wales, the defences were considered in good repair in 1698. The circuit of the walls was still visible in about 1800, but the gatehouses had been removed in 1775 because they were a hindrance to traffic (Locock 1996, 76). Nearby, Abergavenny in Monmouthshire, which grew little until the nineteenth century, was described as a 'faire waulled town' by Leland in the 1530s. It still retained much of its medieval stone defensive circuit into the later eighteenth century, though in a ruinous condition, the remains being removed in the nineteenth century. Lack of maintenance here, and elsewhere, may have necessitated demolition (Soulsby 1983, 66–7). Where they survived, though in a modified form, it was often in the leisure towns like Chester and York, where their tourist potential was realised in the late eighteenth century.

The effect of medieval town defences on the expansion of urban areas is debatable. Even in the Middle Ages towns had expanded beyond their defensive circuits. In some towns the defences may have provided a psychological barrier to development at times of weak growth, but when pressure for development mounted they do not appear to have constrained it. Town defences were incorporated into buildings and used as convenient sources of building stone. Certainly, before the late eighteenth century they do not appear to have been treated with any particular respect for their heritage value, and even then they were more often considered hazards to traffic. Frequently they may have been regarded as unwanted reminders of an old-fashioned and outmoded lifestyle and a turbulent past. However, the growth of towns was more likely to be inhibited by the land ownership of the elite than by physical barriers constraining urban expansion. At Reigate, Surrey, a large open space close to the medieval town core remained undeveloped into the twentieth century as a consequence of the eighteenth-century creation of the country estate of Reigate Lodge, which prevented suburban expansion to the east of Reigate castle (PMA 1998, 166).

Towns and Cities in the Sixteenth and Seventeenth Centuries

Not only was Britain considered to be relatively unurbanised in the early sixteenth century, but what towns it had were often considered to be decaying (Clark and Slack 1976, 12). In the reign of Henry VIII statutes were issued for the improvement of many towns, and the description of those causing concern have been often quoted. Nottingham, Shrewsbury, Ludlow, Bridgnorth, Queenborough and Gloucester were all described as having been in 'greate ruyne and decaye' for some time (Dobson 1977, 1). Towns are considered by historians to be in 'crisis', though the sixteenth and seventeenth centuries are also seen as a period of 'transition' (Clark and Slack 1972; 1976). Indeed, the later medieval period and much of the sixteenth and seventeenth centuries can be seen as a cohesive period for urban history, in which the early modern 'city' is considered to change little (Friedrichs 1995, 9; Leech 1999b, 49). Certainly this view seems to be reflected in urban domestic architecture, at least until *c.* 1660 (Schofield 1997). If the physical nature of the British urban scene in the sixteenth and seventeenth centuries reflected stagnation and decay, how does this square with evidence of growth in some towns, of increased commercial activity and commodity availability, globalisation and changing urban lifestyles?

The documentary record indicates that while some towns in the sixteenth and early seventeenth centuries expanded, both physically and economically, others, like Southampton and

Salisbury, declined. The legacy of economic disruption and declining population caused by disease and warfare in the fourteenth and fifteenth centuries, and changing patterns of trade and declining staple industries contributed to urban stagnation. In addition, the Dissolution of the Monasteries adversely affected some towns like Abingdon and St Albans (Glennie 1990, 214). Towns in south Wales had not recovered from the turbulent regional conditions from the fourteenth century, and Chepstow, for example, was considered greatly decayed in the early sixteenth century. Excavations and cartographic evidence indicate that the walled town contained much vacant space in the seventeenth century, utilised only for gardening and in one instance for quarrying (Locock 1995, 67). In Scotland, despite landowner attempts to stimulate new town formation and development during the sixteenth and seventeenth centuries, few were very successful, and in some cases, as at Preston, Kirkcudbrightshire, the settlement was eventually abandoned altogether (Whyte and Whyte 1991, 23). In contrast, a few towns, particularly in England, such as Great Yarmouth, benefited from increases in regional prosperity. During the late medieval and early post-medieval period London is considered to have undergone great socio-economic and cultural changes as a result of rapid population growth and the consequent physical expansion of the city. This was associated with incoming immigrant groups and the development of global trade (Giorgi 1997, 197). By 1700 rapid urban development associated with manufacturing and trade was commencing in some towns, such as Liverpool, Manchester and Birmingham. In general the proportion of the population sharing in the urban experience had increased. It has been estimated that less than 6 per cent of the population lived in towns with more than 3,200 inhabitants in 1377, but that by 1700 15 per cent lived in towns with a population exceeding 5,000 (Clark and Slack 1976, 11–12).

Leaving aside buildings, much of the published evidence of archaeological investigation of early post-medieval towns still comes from London. One aspect of the apparent intensification of urban occupation in sixteenth- and seventeenth-century London appears to have been the development of gardens, presumably as private tranquil green spaces, though gardens had been a feature of the city from the late medieval period (Schofield 1999, 74). Bedding trenches of sixteenth-century date have been excavated in a number of towns, such as Usk, Monmouthshire, and may be indicative of the importation of continental intensive gardening techniques (Courtney pers. comm.). Excavations at Battle Bridge Lane, Southwark, have produced sixteenth-century ceramic watering pots and fragments of box leaves suggestive of hedge clippings (Schofield 1999, 83). Gardens were developed, and leased without houses, outside the city walls as recreational spaces. Several are known to have had bowling alleys and appear to have formed part of an extra-mural leisure landscape which included the early theatres. In the Moorfields area in Islington public tree-lined walks were also laid out by 1620 (Schofield 1999, 84). Relatively little is known archaeologically about the plants grown in these early gardens, as it is difficult to distinguish plant remains grown in situ from those taken to a site (Schofield 1999, 74).

Plant remains are most frequently used as evidence for food consumption. A review of the archaeobotanical evidence for foodstuffs in London from the fourteenth to the eighteenth century indicated a broad continuity of food consumption patterns during this period, though the sample was generally biased towards higher-status sites (Giorgi 1997). The variable survival rates of the archaeobotanical remains also bias the sample towards fruit, and there is little evidence for foodstuffs known to be staples from the documentary record, such as cereals and pulses (Giorgi 1997, 209). The principal variation between the later medieval and post-medieval periods is in the increase of exotic species, indicative of increased global trade. These include seeds of marrow and pumpkins, soon after the earliest settlements in North America, brazil nuts, palm nuts and coconuts from sixteenth- and seventeenth-century deposits, pepper from the sixteenth century and allspice from the eighteenth century. The last two did not appear archaeologically until well over a century after their first documented importation into Europe (Giorgi 1997, 207–9; Giorgi 1999, 345). The excavation of an area used for rubbish dumping at Moorfields, and presumably representative of Londoners as a whole and not class exclusive, revealed some exotic but not unusual varieties like figs. In general, however, it produced an archaeobotanical and animal bone assemblage similar to a later medieval period assemblage – 90 per cent of the animal species were cattle, sheep/goat or pig (Malcolm 1997, 49–52). The animal bones did reveal that rubbish disposal was rapid and thorough, since the bones were ungnawed (Malcolm 1997, 52).

There is some evidence from London to suggest the intensification of the food processing industry. In England beer was first brewed using hops towards the end of the Middle Ages, but hops are found only infrequently in urban deposits, as in Norwich, before the sixteenth century (Greig 1988, 115), and in London hardly at all (Giorgi 1999, 343). In contrast large quantities of waterlogged hop seeds and bracts are found in some cut features in London dating from the sixteenth to the eighteenth century (Giorgi 1997, 207). This is probably indicative of brewing activity. From the early sixteenth century the field-scale cultivation of hops for use in brewing developed in Kent, and the production and consumption of beer expanded rapidly from then.

Changes in lifestyle and consumption among Londoners in the sixteenth and seventeenth centuries and the effects of globalisation are also hinted at by artefacts. These vary from ivory combs, ubiquitous from the early 1600s, testifying to links with Africa and India (Egan 1999, 63). In east London finds assemblages sometimes give an impression of expanding global commercial interests, including exotic items such as Iberian and Caribbean coins, Gulf of Mexico coral and ceramics designed for sugar processing (Egan 1999, 68). London might well be expected to exhibit evidence for global contacts through the consumption of exotic foodstuffs and imported goods, but it is questionable how much these consumption patterns should be expected in other less cosmopolitan and particularly inland towns.

Norwich, the second city to London in the sixteenth century, has produced evidence for plentiful imported goods, and in the context of non-wealthy assemblages they have been taken as signifiers of immigrants from the Low Countries (Margeson 1993). Outside such provincial capitals there is less evidence for imports within the artefactual assemblages of small, inland, urban centres. At Romsey in Hampshire, for example, despite the town's nearness to Southampton and its close links to the cloth trade there, imported pottery that was common in Southampton in the fifteenth and sixteenth centuries does not generally reach the town (Newman 1992, 103). As a consequence of high transportation costs, only the highest-value items travelled great distances inland (Platt 1976, 78).

It is also unlikely that the noted patterns of consumption were ubiquitous across all classes within any town. Even the use of tobacco, as evidenced by clay pipes, must have been partly linked to social groups in the sixteenth century. Insufficient numbers of these earliest pipes are found to suggest common use, and tobacco smoking may have remained a fashionable pursuit confined to the more wealthy and cosmopolitan during the sixteenth century (Oswald 1975, 5). More work on sites occupied by the poor may reveal palaeoenvironmental and artefactual evidence indicative of less change in lifestyles than is suggested by assemblages from more high-status sites. Sadly, the archaeological work which might answer questions relating to social and

Post-medieval hearth for a dyeing vat in Romsey, Hampshire. Such hearths remained identical in design from the fourteenth to the seventeenth century and provide an example of the continuity of much urban material culture during that period. (© C. Newman)

geographical variation in consumption patterns has only recently begun to be undertaken, and too little has been published. What does seem clear, however, is that even in London, and with a bias toward higher-status sites, the sixteenth and earlier seventeenth centuries did not, on the basis of archaeologically detectable material culture, witness huge changes in urban lifestyles in comparison to the later medieval period.

There is evidence for intensification of land-use in some large towns, as at Oxford, Bristol (Crossley 1990, 79) and Norwich (Atkin *et al.* 1985), and in some smaller towns. At Winchester Street, Andover, in Hampshire, plots that had been abandoned in the later Middle Ages were redeveloped (PMA 1985, 164), and at Perth in Scotland backlands previously used as gardens were improved (PMA 1998, 170), but in most cases provincial towns exhibit few signs of intensification of land-use until the later seventeenth century. The differences in development pressures evident in London and in the English provincial towns are vividly demonstrated by the diverging histories of the redevelopment of the former monastic sites. In London these were quickly adapted for new purposes, but elsewhere demolition and adaptation took many years, some sites not being totally built over for centuries (Crossley 1990, 80). At Warrington, for example, following the demolition of the church perhaps as late as the mid-seventeenth century, the site of the Austin Friars was used as a burial ground, before experiencing some domestic building, but it was not totally redeveloped until the erection of a candle factory in the nineteenth century (R. Heawood pers. comm.). Some new forms or uses of buildings appeared within the urban environment in the period 1550–1660, which now constitute additions to urban monument types. From the later sixteenth century playhouses appeared in London, though the first public playhouse seems to have been built by the Corporation of Great Yarmouth in 1538/9 (Wilson 1995, 27). With new fashions for imported beverages, coffee- and tea-houses appeared. Overall, however, change and addition to the urban fabric was limited and not radical. There was considerable continuity in use of medieval structures as well as a more general aggregation of medieval material culture (Giles 1999, 87–8).

With the exception of London, it would seem that the experience of living in the urban environment in British towns in 1660 would have been similar to that of the fifteenth century. There was little dramatic growth in any town other than London, despite a doubling in size between 1520 and 1660 of the national population (Glennie 1990, 200). London thus became even more dominant and extraordinary than it had been previously, physically more than doubling the

Post-medieval burial within the ruins of a former friary at Warrington. (© Lancaster University Archaeological Unit)

size of its urbanised area during the seventeenth century and swallowing Westminster within it (Clay 1984, 197–213). By 1700 London had a population of over half a million and was nineteen times larger than Norwich (Clay 1984, 197). Indeed, the very success of London must have been partially responsible for the lack of growth in other major towns, particularly in the south of England. In contrast, smaller towns within its immediate trading hinterland, or within a day's journey of the capital and on the main approach roads to it, seem to have prospered in London's slipstream (Crossley 1990, 87–9).

Urban Expansion During the Long Eighteenth Century

From about 1660 urban growth began to accelerate in Britain in towns other than London. Towns that were either entirely new or had never before been important began to expand (Glennie 1990, 214). There were a number of influencing factors, not the least of which was government policy. Parliamentary Improvement Acts were passed to regulate construction, street widths, water supply and the provision of gardens (Glennie 1990, 217). More directly effective in stimulating urban growth, however, was the establishment in the seventeenth century of permanent naval bases. Plymouth was a medieval port but it expanded during the seventeenth century as a consequence of naval activities. Portsmouth, like Plymouth, had major investment channelled into it in the late seventeenth century with the establishment of barracks and new fortifications (Douet 1998, 9). As a consequence of naval involvement, it expanded rapidly, was incorporated by Charles I and came to surpass Southampton as the principal town of the region. At Chatham a wholly new town was created as a consequence of the naval dockyard. First established in 1613, the town (still described as a village on the Buck print of 1738) had developed to service the dockyard by the early eighteenth century.

These three southern towns victualled, maintained and housed the Navy, which in turn enabled Britain to develop a trading empire and encouraged the development of ports. Of particular importance was the Atlantic trade, which increased as settlement in the colonies and in the Caribbean expanded. The importance of the slave trade has often in the past been ignored or coyly played down by archaeologists and economic historians dealing with urban development (*see* Ashmore 1982, 24). The ports of the Atlantic coast were also well placed for trade with Ireland, south-west France, the Iberian peninsula and west Africa (Bettey 1983), the latter two areas both central to the development of the slave trade. These factors enabled Bristol, and to a lesser extent the ports of the south-west peninsula like Exeter, to maintain their importance when other ports in southern England were adversely affected by London. Indeed, some ports, such as Dartmouth, exhibit clear signs of growth from the fifteenth century through to the eighteenth century. Excavations there have revealed an intensification of use, as exhibited by river frontage reclamation and the development of quays, warehouses and dwellings (PMA 1996, 259). By the end of the seventeenth century Bristol was second only to London as a port and, unusually for a provincial town, was already expanding beyond its medieval limits (Bettey 1983, 73).

Bristol entered the slave trade in the last decade of the seventeenth century, following the Royal Africa Company's loss of its exclusive licence to trade in slaves (Thomas 1997, 204–5). So successful was it that in the 1730s Bristol overtook London as Britain's main slave port (Thomas 1997, 245; Morgan 1993), though its hegemony was brief, as it was surpassed by Liverpool later in the eighteenth century. By the 1730s Bristol had also overtaken Norwich as England's second city (Reed 1983, 10). The city attracted new inhabitants to work in its burgeoning industries, and new areas of workers' housing were laid out (Leech 1999a, 25). Bristol's merchants displayed their wealth not only in their classically styled houses but by developing exclusive residential areas away from the commercial quayside. Queen Square, started in 1700, was the first large square built in any English city outside London (Leech 1999b, 44). During the eighteenth century Clifton was developed as a middle-class suburb (Bettey 1983, 73–4). Indeed, the indulgence in consumer activities engaged in by Bristol's mercantile class has been criticised as contributing to the city's failure to outcompete rivals like Liverpool later in the eighteenth century (Morgan 1993, 222; Leech 1999b, 44).

Liverpool's rise from a small port of medieval origin began with the Irish trade. A plan of 1644 shows the town as little bigger than its original medieval grid plan layout (Philpott 1988, 34), and the 1662 hearth tax records list only 190 houses. By 1670 the port was beginning to trade with North America and the West Indies, leading to the construction of a sugar refinery in 1670–3 (Philpott 1988, 40); slaving began in the 1690s (Thomas 1997, 246–7), stimulating the expansion of the town. From *c.* 1640 to 1710 the pool from which the town took its name was progressively infilled with rubbish until it was completely reclaimed (Davey and McNeil 1980, 27–9). New

The classical architecture of nineteenth-century civic buildings in Liverpool emphasised the city's imperial role and provided a sense of municipal identity and achievement.

streets were laid out by the principal landowners, the town expanded over the townfield and wealthy merchants endowed it with grand buildings befitting its status (Philpott 1988, 38). By 1753 its 222 streets were, along with its commercial buildings, considered to be matters of civic pride (Northcote Parkinson 1952, 109). New corporate, charitable and religious buildings changed the topology of the town. When St George's Church was built in 1726 much of the old market area was levelled, removing with it features such as stocks and whipping posts (Davey and McNeil 1980; Philpott 1988, 40). Physically, the associations with the old economic and civil order were removed, and in their place new classically inspired structures displayed the town's new international status. Here, as in the other expanding towns of the late seventeenth and early eighteenth centuries, classical architecture was used to express corporate sensibilities, as it was seen as a means to gain municipal as well as individual influence (Bourdieu 1984). Even in the mid-nineteenth century the imperial messages imparted by classical architecture were adopted by municipal authorities to mark a sense of civic identity and achievement (Morris 2000, 198). They were signifiers of dominance and internationalism, and thus it was no accident that these messages were communicated by the civic architecture of towns like Liverpool and Leeds.

Appropriately for an important trading centre like Liverpool, its largest buildings in the eighteenth century were warehouses, including some thirteen storeys high. Prophetically, in 1726 Defoe referred to Liverpool as the 'Bristol' of its region. By the 1760s Liverpool had overtaken Bristol as the principal slaving port, and in 1806, with some justification, could claim to be the second most important city in the British Empire (Thomas 1997, 246). Liverpool's economy

Eighteenth-century warehouses in Lancaster. Many have been converted into office blocks or apartments.

depended upon, and its most prominent citizens all had connections with, the slave trade, and architecturally it acknowledged this by the façade of the Exchange, which bears reliefs of negro heads (Thomas 1997, 248).

Other smaller ports on Britain's western seaboard also benefited from the Atlantic trade, including slaving, among them Bideford and Barnstaple in the south-west, and Chester and Lancaster in north-west England. By the mid-eighteenth century Glasgow had also begun to benefit from this trade, becoming the second most significant tobacco-importing port after London. Where towns reached their zenith of prosperity in the eighteenth century as a consequence of the Atlantic trade, the fabric of the towns reflects this. Thus both Bideford and Lancaster contain numerous fine examples of Georgian architecture. In Lancaster the prosperity derived from overseas trade, and the town's rise to the fourth most important slaving port in Britain between 1750 and 1775 (Thomas 1997, 264–5; Schofield 1985, 74), transformed the town's fabric from timber and thatch to stone in the course of a single century (White 2000, 1). This physically reflected the conversion of a provincial backwater into a substantial urban centre with international links. The merchant wealth that underpinned the renewal of Lancaster's urban fabric was heavily dependent on the plantation economies of the Caribbean and American colonies (Dalziel 1993, 95), which in turn were reliant on the enslavement of Africans. The Georgian heritage of Lancaster, like Liverpool, is redolent of human suffering as well as mercantile success.

Away from the Atlantic coast urban expansion was less marked. Outside London, the urban area of Newcastle-upon-Tyne and Gateshead was the principal growth area on the east coast in the later seventeenth and early eighteenth centuries. Their prosperity was based on the export of coal from the Great Northern Coalfield for domestic consumption to towns further south, particularly London. On the east side of the country, with coal seams close to the coast and embarkation points, the Tyne and Wear ports were ideally placed to benefit from the consumption needs of London, and to a far lesser degree other towns like King's Lynn and Ipswich (Pawson 1979, 133–4). As a consequence in 1750 the Newcastle/Gateshead urban area maintained its position, gained by the mid-seventeenth century, of being the fourth largest in England (Corfield 1982, 15; Carter 1990, 405).

Some provincial towns were growing on the back of increasing global trade in the later seventeenth century, and even those that were less prosperous and expansionist were experiencing changes in their fabric on a scale unprecedented in the previous two centuries. Studies of inventories have indicated new departures in urban house design for the middle classes (Dyer 1981, 217), which are clearly reflected in the physical fabric of many towns. Allied to the new middle-class and corporate fashion for classical architecture, and houses with multiple specialised rooms, were new concepts of urban space. In particular, the middle-class merchants at the heart of the swelling urban prosperity sought to create spaces in which private social status could be displayed and negotiated (Glennie 1990, 217), and through which civic status could be exemplified. As argued in relation to Bristol, the social geography of many of these towns was transformed from what it had been in the later Middle Ages (Sacks 1991, 331–62; Leech 1999a, 31). The centres of power and patronage had been totally altered. The monasteries and friaries had gone, the constrictive limitations of the medieval towns were broken and the inter-mixture of rich and poor was being replaced by a more class-structured environment. Civic architecture was expanded to facilitate ceremonial activities, which helped to develop class identity and corporate pride (Borsay 1984, 237). Assembly rooms were erected as exclusive indoor arenas for the urban elite (Borsay 2000, 111). Squares of elite housing, enclosing spaces adapted as socially exclusive gardens, were built as protected havens of calm and politeness away from the rude bustle of the commercial urban heartland (Borsay 1989; Neale 1974, 273). Around these, walks allowed for interaction, discourse and display (Ellis 2000, 10). The importance of the promenade as a mechanism for interaction between members of polite society was immense. In Chester, as was quite commonly the case elsewhere in Europe (Stobart 1998, 9), the medieval city walls were utilised for this function. The city corporation 'improved' the walls to facilitate a perambulation of the circuit by rebuilding sections and demolishing medieval towers (Carrington 1994, 102). In Scotland aristocratic dominance of the small towns led to wholesale urban remodelling along principles of regularity and polite architecture. At Inveraray the Duke of Argyll had the small port redesigned and shifted to form a pleasing view from his castle (Whyte and Whyte 1991, 158–9), and in its restrained and well-designed modern architecture it formed a testament to his taste, refinement and modernity. Through this town his British, rather than Highland, outlook could be expressed.

Just as the middle classes were breaking ranks with tradition in their use and design of houses, so in the growing mercantile towns the legacy of the Middle Ages was being swept away by expansion outside the medieval urban limits and changing use of space within them. The physical fabric of some towns became imbued with new meanings; they were global in outlook, colonialist, expansionist, supremacist, competitive and confident. They reflected the world view of the merchant and business classes that lived in them and made them operate effectively. The change in the nature of urbanism in the later seventeenth and early eighteenth centuries is just one symptom of changing middle-class lifestyles. The middle classes governed the towns, and it was their attitudes and consumption patterns that were reflected in the evolving urban fabric.

Documentary evidence indicates changes in the urban diet during the seventeenth century, as revealed in the growth of ownership of utensils associated with food preparation, cooking and eating (Shammas 1993; Weatherill 1993). Unfortunately, other than in London, there is a lack of detailed floral and faunal assemblage analysis to set alongside the artefactual evidence for food consumption (Pennell 1999, 44). This dearth of environmental archaeology in post-medieval research in general is demonstrated by a recent survey of environmental archaeology in Leicestershire (Monckton 1995), where a review of the late 1980s/early 1990s made no specific reference to analysis of post-medieval material, though it was acknowledged that evidence had been recovered 'from the early post-glacial to post-medieval times' (Monckton 1995, 38). Aside from implements associated with food, probate inventories detail new categories of furniture being used by middling families (Johnson 1996, 174), demonstrating an increase in the quality and variety of possessions (Courtney 1996).

Some artefact categories observably increase from excavations, such as clay tobacco pipes, which most commonly date to the late seventeenth and early eighteenth centuries. Their increase must in part relate to greater tobacco consumption as it declined in price and the duty on clay tobacco pipe production was removed (Jackson and Price 1974, 11–12). In Bristol the growth of the pipe industry is considered to be related to the town's role as a tobacco importer (Jackson and Price 1974, 12), and the close link between the industry and other ports engaged in the Atlantic trade, as for example Chester and Liverpool, is noticeable (Davey 1980). Lancaster developed as a furniture-making centre thanks to overseas trade. In Glasgow the descriptions of furniture and social habits of the merchant classes were indicative of their Atlantic trade: furnishings in rosewood and mahogany supported men engaged in ritualised drinking of rum punch and West Indian Madeira (Nenadic 1994, 146–9). Towns played a key role in the arbitration of taste and in changing patterns of consumption. It was in towns, particularly in ports of international significance, that people came across new ideas and new fashions were created (Weatherill 1988, 89; Leech 1999a, 24). Outside London in the later seventeenth and early eighteenth centuries, expanding towns helped to diffuse, fuel and define new trends in consumption, which in turn fuelled the commercial growth of these towns. Fashion and taste were forged in these new urban centres, and utilised both to compete and to make statements of belonging.

The urban poor would have noticed far less change in their lifestyles, but even for them Britain, particularly England, had become noticeably more urbanised by the early eighteenth century than it had been fifty years before. It was perhaps, after the Low Countries, the most urbanised region of Europe. Even so, life in Britain was still a largely rural experience for most people, whose encounters with urbanism remained dominated by their local market town. While many local market centres remained little changed in terms of size or even fabric in the period 1650–1750, their function was changing. No longer simply operating as local retail centres for local produce, they were increasingly becoming wholesale redistribution centres in response to changes in other urban centres, which were moving towards specialisation in manufacturing (Gräf 1994, 120). In Scotland, Edinburgh remained the first city and was probably the third largest in Britain after London and Bristol. Glasgow was growing rapidly, and Dundee, Perth and Aberdeen were all significant towns (Reed 1983, 9), but otherwise Scotland remained relatively

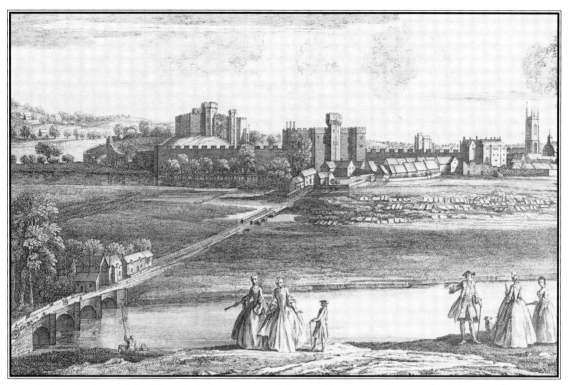

Buck brothers' print of Cardiff, 1748. It shows a town still dominated by its medieval castle and with few signs of post-medieval development.

unurbanised despite the efforts of Scottish landlords to establish new towns. Wales was even more so. In the Buck brothers' mid-eighteenth-century copper-engraved panoramas of towns, the Welsh towns depicted are all small and dominated by their medieval castles (Hyde 1994). The signs of change were present, however. Swansea, with its connections with Bristol, was already growing as a result of trade and manufacturing industry, and by 1800 it was becoming popular as a seaside resort.

The Growth of Manufacturing Towns in the Eighteenth and Nineteenth Centuries

Daniel Defoe used the term 'manufacturing towns' to describe those expanding and successful towns of his day, which were developing because of industrial specialisation (Corfield 1982, 23). They began to be noticeable in the later seventeenth century, as some towns began to distinguish themselves by their economic dependence on specialised production. The metalworking settlements of the English Midlands, such as Wolverhampton and Birmingham, were among the first to show accelerated growth (Glennie 1990, 218). Sheffield too showed early signs of growth based on manufacturing. By 1637 there were already nine corn mills and twenty-nine cutlers' works powered by water along the River Don, together with numerous bloomeries and coal mines in the vicinity (Scurfield 1986, 167). A century or so later there were more than a hundred (Scurfield 1986, 167; Trinder 1982, 25). The town which had only about 120 houses in 1637 had a population of 12,000 by 1750, and was described by Defoe in the early eighteenth century as populous and large. It was clearly already showing signs of unplanned growth and industrial pollution, since its streets were described as narrow and its houses as smoke-blackened (Scurfield 1986, 169; Trinder 1982, 25). The linking of industrial development and urban expansion became particularly marked between 1780 and 1850, as changing forms of labour organisation (the factory system) and technological change (steam power) lessened the advantages of a rural location for many forms of industry that had previously been based in the countryside (Morris 2000, 181).

These manufacturing towns changed the face of urbanism in Britain, dislocating what had previously been a relatively static provincial urban system. Suddenly there was considerable divergence between different provincial towns, even within a relatively restricted locality. In Leicestershire places like Hallaton remained small market centres, while Hinkley, which had been a similar town in the mid-seventeenth century, became a manufacturing centre. As a consequence, by the early nineteenth century Hinkley had become a relatively large town characterised by brick-built factories and terraced houses, whereas Hallaton remained a single street of one- or two-storey houses, many still with thatched roofs (Gräf 1994, 103). Similar comparisons can be made elsewhere. In Lancashire, for example, Preston and Chorley were physically and socially transformed by industrialisation in the earlier nineteenth century (Warnes 1970), while their less industrialised neighbour, Ormskirk, was little different in size and layout in 1846 from what it had been in 1609. The property boundaries were still those of the medieval town, with only some infilling at the rear of the burgage plots and no real expansion of the town outside its earlier limits (Philpott 1988, 44–7).

Some of the cloth-working areas were among the first to experience unprecedented urban growth in the late seventeenth and early eighteenth centuries. Frome in Somerset underwent a probable quadrupling of its population between 1660 and 1695, and continued to expand rapidly during the earlier eighteenth century (RCHME 1981, 1). As many other towns, development took place with the acquisition of blocks of land. At Frome, land to the west of the medieval town centre was divided into a number of enclosures, seemingly consolidated and enclosed from, and in part fossilising, the former common field strips (RCHME 1981, 4–5). Known as the Trinity area, its layout conformed broadly to the pre-existing field pattern, as blocks of buildings were erected in the separate enclosures between 1665 and 1725. After this period growth slowed, presumably as a consequence of the difficulties experienced by the West of England cloth trade throughout the remainder of the eighteenth century (De L. Mann 1971, 37–55). From then on most new housing was accommodated within existing domestic property boundaries (RCHME 1981, 9). Although the West Country wool trade experienced difficulties and was gradually out-competed by Yorkshire in particular, it generated considerable eighteenth-century prosperity which is reflected in the fabric of the principal wool towns. Quality Georgian clothiers' houses were built in Trowbridge, Calne, Shepton Mallet and Wincanton (Bettey 1980, 81), indicative of the contemporary economic success of these communities.

Unlike the development of Frome, in contemporary British colonies, where towns were established as new entities, a planned grid-iron system based on classical concepts of urban planning was widely used (Borsay 1989; Miller 1999). Such a system was rarely employed in Britain, as the urban areas were already established and wholesale building anew was seldom possible. Where possibilities for such urban planning were realised in the late seventeenth century, as at Whitehaven, individualism often acted against the guiding design principles of the town's founders. In Britain it was in the eighteenth century, with the laying out of new middle-class town areas, that the principles of baroque town planning came to be fully applied. In Leeds, a new area was laid out on the land of Richard Wilson, to be developed as a middle-class estate. Known as the West End, it was designed with a grid-iron pattern of streets and an array of squares (Beresford 1988, 132). This was probably the first attempt in a northern English city to establish a class-exclusive housing area. Elsewhere the most notable examples of this type of planning were the development of the Grosvenor estate in Mayfair, London, and the laying out of planned new towns for both Aberdeen and Edinburgh (Reed 1983, 111–22). Such planned areas, usually initiated by the wealthy elite landowners, represented a move away from the perception of urban areas as collections of individual parts to seeing them as integrated wholes (Borsay 1989, 80; Miller 1999, 73). They can also be interpreted as attempts by the traditional elite to control and define the growth and evolution of towns at a time when urban economic power was increasing – and so too, in the longer term, was the potential for political influence.

Of the three thousand new houses built in Leeds between 1767 and 1797 only a small percentage were erected in the West End. To the east of the town centre urban expansion was accommodated in the East End by the development of former farmyards, leading to scattered concentrations of houses in folds, slowly coalescing in a pattern that was unplanned and could not produce cohesive street frontages (Beresford 1988, 171). The layout of these lower-status expansions usually reflected the former field pattern, and the street development within the land blocks was often organic and haphazard. Where towns could not expand, or when growth was insufficient to warrant expansion, population increase in the seventeenth and eighteenth centuries was accommodated by the intensification of usage of existing plots. In Leeds, prior to 1767, despite a three-fold increase in population, no new streets of houses were built after the early seventeenth century (Beresford 1974, 282). In many towns, from the late seventeenth century, as the street frontages became fully developed, vacant space in yards and at the sides of tofts was filled in. Work yards and inn courtyards were developed. This resulted in courts of small dwellings set back from the street frontages. By the later eighteenth century, in those towns where expansion did occur outside the traditional town limits, the wealthy were abandoning the congested town centres for new suburban developments, and this allowed their former properties to be redeveloped and their backyards subdivided (RCHME 1985a, 8).

Increase in industrial activity led to increasing smoke pollution in the early nineteenth century. This, coupled with population growth, led to the West End in Leeds being abandoned by the middle classes and redeveloped for denser lower-status housing and industry (Beresford 1988, 272–303). A new West End was established, but this too was overwhelmed by industrial and working-class development, so that it in turn was replaced by the 1840s by the suburb of Headingley as the new residential refuge of the urban elite (Beresford 1988, 382). A similar history of development can be traced in other industrialising towns, such as Glasgow. Here, the population increased from 25,000 to 100,000 between 1750 and 1811 (Simpson 1977, 44), causing the old town centre to be shunned by the middle classes, affected as it was by pollution and the anti-social behaviour associated with poverty and overcrowding. The pollution problem was a definite health hazard, and not simply a nuisance. In Glasgow, as in northern towns like Widnes, alkali production fouled the air with hydrochloric acid (Clapp 1994, 24). The middle classes thus moved away from the city centre to new purpose-built terraces and squares in districts such as the Gorbals and Blythswood, both areas that by the 1840s had themselves become absorbed into the expanding industrial and working-class heart of the city (Simpson 1977, 45).

The middle classes moved increasingly further away from the manufacturing town centres, aided by developing transport facilities: first the turnpike roads, then more particularly the railways, and towards the end of the nineteenth century the electric trams. This culminated in the middle classes finally moving into settlements close to, but not fully part of, the expanding towns – in other words into the suburbs. For the middle classes in the nineteenth century the town centre was the public world of official institutions, but it was also populated by the problem poor, and thus the suburbs became their private and domestic world (Gunn 1996, 33), seemingly protected and insulated from the affairs of the factory workers. This physical separation intensified class distinctiveness and tension, and the concept of two peoples in one nation was born. In the early 1840s it was said of Manchester that the average inhabitant of the middle-class residential district of Ardwick, 'knows less about Ancoats than . . . about China, and feels more interested in the condition of New Zealand than of Little Ireland' (Cooke Taylor 1842, 164).

By the end of the eighteenth century a number of provincial towns had grown dramatically, and England was one of the most populous and urbanised countries in the world (Corfield 1982, 7–16). Scotland, though with far fewer significant towns, had nevertheless experienced a considerable drift in its population from rural to urban areas, so that Scottish society had become one of the most concentratedly urbanised in Europe (Whyte and Whyte 1991, 1). Far more Britons now shared the urban experience, creating the erroneous but pervasive impression among social commentators that half the country's population lived in towns. Even in towns where growth was more limited, their fabric had been renewed and had acquired new meanings and resonances. In rural regions like south-west Scotland new grid-plan designs, influenced by the layouts in Aberdeen and Edinburgh, were imposed on existing market towns at the same time as fashionable Georgian buildings were erected (Marsden 1997, 94–5). While the urban expansion which was to follow in the nineteenth century was even more dramatic, the urbanisation of much of Britain was already well under way by 1800, and the changes wrought in the urban system since 1650 were profound – perhaps even revolutionary.

While the seeds for rapid urbanisation had already been sown, the period after 1820 saw phenomenal urban expansion. Between 1821 and 1831 Birmingham grew by 41.5 per cent, Bradford by 65.6 per cent, Leeds by 47.3 per cent, Manchester by 44.9 per cent and Sheffield by 40.5 per cent (Briggs 1963, 86). Industrial growth in the nineteenth century led to the formation of new towns. In the Lancashire and Yorkshire textile districts the settlements surrounding the main industrial towns attracted mills and developed into communities of factory employees. They encroached upon each other until they formed continuous unplanned urban landscapes of terraced housing, physically and economically dominated by the huge mills they existed to serve (Fletcher 1996, 162). Valley-based settlements such as Bacup in Lancashire or Ebbw Vale in south Wales grew into new towns. The growth of such towns spurred the acquisition in the late nineteenth century of urban facilities such as libraries, reading rooms, institutions, public baths and civic halls, as well as a plethora of religious buildings. Elsewhere purpose-built industrial settlements, and ports to serve them, were established, such as Barrow, Fleetwood and Nelson in Lancashire and Barry in south Wales. The growth of these new mushroom towns was facilitated by the railways, which provided access to markets and the means to import the people and materials necessary for rapid expansion.

The physical conditions of these manufacturing towns were often appalling and excited much contemporary comment. Manchester in particular was noted for its pollution – of both water and air – and terrible living conditions. The main rivers that supplied the power for its mills, like

Gilfach Goch: an example of nineteenth-century urbanisation resulting from mineral extraction in south Wales.

the Irwell and Medlock, were described as black foetid sewers (Aspin 1972). Heavily industrialised, overcrowded and lacking adequate (or any) sanitation, drainage and a decent water supply, they were fouled and pestilential. The problems were particularly bad in towns that were unable to expand beyond their medieval limits, leading to a highly concentrated population in the town centre. In Nottingham, for example, this led to the creation of some of the worst urban living conditions in Britain (Chapman 1971; Reed 1983, 118). In Lancashire the manufacturing towns were characterised 'by an exceptionally high density of population crammed into hovels, courts and tiny cottages, in conditions of degrading squalor and with terrifyingly high mortality rates' (Crosby 1998, 92). As Reed (1983, 127) pointed out, however, towns had always been insanitary and unhealthy. What was new in the early nineteenth century was the level of overcrowding and degree of industrial pollution within the town centres. This was globally unprecedented; such conditions had never been experienced anywhere else before, and thus society was entirely unprepared for the consequences. Unruly crowds of uneducated, disenfranchised poor, rapidly spreading contagious diseases and highly polluted environments all had the potential to be politically dangerous, and could certainly be damaging to the economic well-being of the towns and their middle-class elites.

Archaeologically, the effect of late eighteenth- and early nineteenth-century urban conditions on town inhabitants is becoming more apparent through work carried out on urban burials. At Christ Church, Spitalfields in London, a thousand interments were recovered from the crypt, all dating to the eighteenth and early nineteenth centuries (Cox 1996). The church's graveyard contains a further 67,000 burials (Cox 1998, 112). The burials tended to be those of better-off artisans, including, in the eighteenth century, Huguenot immigrants. The wealthier individuals seem to have had a high-cholesterol, low-fibre diet, indicative of a generous meat content, while the poorer people ate little meat and consequently probably had a healthier diet (Cox 1996). Even so, infantile rickets was common. Interestingly the analysed burials from a Quaker cemetery at Kingston-upon-Thames, dating to 1664–1814, show a low prevalence of rickets, though this may be a consequence of the poor preservation of the skeletons of many of the infants (Start and Kirk 1998).

At St Bride's Church, Fleet Street, London, excavations revealed 227 persons buried in coffins bearing plates giving the name, age and date of death of the individual (Scheuer 1998, 101). Using documentary sources, attempts were made to compare the recovered crypt burials with other burials both in the crypt and in the outside cemetery. It was considered that the burials in the crypt were of a higher social status than those in the outside cemetery. The peak age of death for crypt interments was 60–9 years, whereas in the outside cemetery the number of child, juvenile and young adult deaths was so high that few people survived into old age (Scheuer 1998, 103). The age-of-death profile for the Spitalfields crypt burials is similar to that at St Bride's (Cox 1996). Where cause of death could be defined the most common was respiratory disease, particularly tuberculosis (Scheuer 1998, 107–8), also a feature of the Spitalfields burials. This disease is identifiable within the skeletal record, unlike many others, and the large number of sufferers is indicative of the problems of overcrowding within urban areas. This conclusion may be borne out by the lack of evidence for tuberculosis among the Quaker community at Kingston-upon-Thames (Start and Kirk 1998, 174), where the environment during the eighteenth century would have been much healthier than that of congested early nineteenth-century London.

The realisation among the urban elite that, no matter how far they removed themselves from them, the labouring classes' problems of crime and disease still had the potential to affect them eventually led to attempts to improve the living conditions for the poor. In towns throughout Britain the problems of drainage, sanitation and bad housing were tackled. Following the 1866 Glasgow Improvements Act, 88 acres in the centre of Glasgow were improved: old houses were demolished, new streets laid out, alleys widened and two polluted streams covered over (Kaufman 1907, 44). Huge changes were also wrought in the major manufacturing towns from the mid-nineteenth century by the coming of the railways. Their arrival in the town centres led to sudden and large-scale redevelopment. In Blackburn the entire town centre was remodelled (LUAU 2000b), and in London thousands of people were rehoused as a consequence of the building of the main-line stations (Gauldie 1974).

By the end of the nineteenth century the growth of the manufacturing towns ensured there were more urban dwellers than rural ones. The majority of these were labourers. To the rural visitor the larger towns offered a far starker contrast with life in the countryside than ever before. They were more crowded, noisier, busier, dirtier; their buildings were different and a range of large structures competed for architectural dominance. The great manufacturing towns were international in outlook and connections, and brought the produce of the world to the attention of the consumer. They included in their fabric symbols of corporate pride, such as the town halls of many of the northern textile towns, and well-designed and apportioned residential squares and crescents, as in Glasgow. They also encompassed squalid, overcrowded, badly built, high-density, low-status housing. To some people Leeds, like other great manufacturing towns, could be an unpleasant place, full of squalor; to others it was wondrous, its commercial successes exemplified in grand buildings, which indeed had been erected with a concern for appearance and image (Briggs 1963; Friedman 1996b).

The impact of the manufacturing towns on the existing urban system has been queried by some scholars (De Vries 1984). While acknowledging that the manufacturing towns of the nineteenth century were a novel and influential phenomenon, it has been argued that they modified rather than transformed the system (De Vries 1984, 254). The urban growth experienced throughout nineteenth-century Europe was seen as being rooted in an essentially medieval urban system. While this thesis may hold fast for some parts of Europe, it is not true of the British situation. Starting in the late seventeenth century and culminating at the end of the nineteenth century, the medieval/early modern urban system of Britain was transformed. Although London remained the principal city, its dominance was reduced. The urban hierarchy was radically altered and the regional pattern of urbanism wholly changed. This contrast between Britain and Europe has been explained as the result of industrialisation. In Britain, manufacturing towns for the most part grew ahead of the transport systems that developed to serve them, particularly the railways. In Europe in most instances industrialisation on the British scale followed the arrival of the railways (Carter 1990, 416). Hence industry created new and unique towns in Britain, whereas in Europe it was absorbed into an existing urban system.

Despite the phenomenal success of the British manufacturing towns in terms of physical growth and attracting inhabitants, they did not attain the prosperity of some other towns. Throughout the eighteenth and earlier nineteenth centuries the greatest concentrations of wealth were to be found in the commercial and financial centres like Bristol, Liverpool and London, and, more significantly perhaps, in the fashionable resorts (Dodgshon 1990, 275). These were the towns where consumption was at its most conspicuous and where a wholly new form of urban function and settlement type developed.

Resort Towns

The consumption needs of the urban elites in the great manufacturing and commercial centres led to the development of 'leisure' towns. Leisure, consumption and urban improvement were closely linked (Stobart 1998, 5). The resort towns were generated within a complex urban system (*see* Stobart 1996), one in which some towns had multiple roles. London, for example, was the capital city, a commercial and manufacturing centre as well as a fashionable resort (Reed 1983, 110). The roles of towns could alter through time, and this might be reflected in the development of their fabric. Preston in Lancashire, for example, was a county town and social centre in the eighteenth century (Phillips and Smith 1994, 113), and took on many of the characteristics of a genteel leisure town. In the early nineteenth century, however, it began to develop as a centre of textile production, and the needs of the new manufacturing town led to the replacement of much of the earlier urban fabric, occasioning documented destruction of medieval and early post-medieval archaeological deposits.

Like Preston, other older urban market centres of medieval origin, such as Chester, Shrewsbury (McInnes 1988), and York, were reinvented and began to develop as 'leisure' towns, leading to a renewal of their physical fabric. Many of these places were county towns and therefore were already the focal points of local society (Borsay 1989). These towns required facilities where the elite and middle classes could socialise and engage in favourite pastimes such as dancing, watching plays, gambling and generally 'being seen'. They thus acquired promenades, theatres and assembly rooms (Stobart 1998, 4), features shared with other towns but conspicuous in leisure towns by their numbers and size in relation to the urban area. One particular feature was the development of racecourses. Areas set aside for horse racing had been present on urban fringes since the late Middle Ages, but in the eighteenth century these developed into enclosed circuits equipped with grandstands. Many of the leisure towns and spa resorts possessed tracks, as at Bath, Chester, Cheltenham, York, Harrogate and Richmond, Yorkshire. There was also a particularly significant growth in the number of shops (Mitchell 1984), indicating that shopping itself was becoming a more important social activity. In Chester, as in Bath and Tunbridge Wells, the consumerism of the middle-class inhabitants and visitors led to the development of specialised shop buildings in the centre of the city along the main thoroughfares (Stobart 1998, 13). In Scotland this development has been noted in Arbroath, Dumbarton, Dundee and Inverness, where streetside buildings appear to have encroached on the forelands where goods were displayed. It is considered that in the seventeenth century these areas were overhung by the jetties of the upper storeys of the buildings, forming an arcade, as can still be seen in Elgin and Edinburgh (Perry 1999, 69). The inclusion of these display areas within buildings presumably meant that goods were now displayed behind shop windows.

Leisure towns were successful because they were fashionable and attracted an 'in-crowd'. For a resort like Bath this social group would have been of national, if not international, significance, while at others, such as Harrogate, the society was perhaps more of a regional or county significance. Where streets had developed into important fashionable social spaces for consumption and display, as in the case of the new shopping streets, there was an incentive to improve them. In Chester such areas underwent progressive improvement from the late seventeenth century to ensure that they were clean, well paved and adequately lit (Stobart 1998, 15–16), and thus overall were 'desirable places to be and to be seen in' (Stobart 1998, 19). Towns reliant on fashion for their prosperity had to have fashionable buildings, and their heydays are reflected in the date and character of their fabric. Some of the best examples of contemporary urban design and architecture occur in these fashionable resorts, as at Bath and Cheltenham. Frequented by influential members of society, these resort towns assisted the diffusion of ideas and tastes away from the cosmopolitan centres like Bristol and London and into the provinces. In particular they helped to inform, shape and sustain middle-class attitudes, lifestyles and thus consumption patterns (Glennie 1995).

One aspect of the changing fashions in elite consumption was the adoption from the late seventeenth century of the continental idea of drinking spring water as a health tonic (Whyte 1999, 277). Bath and Tunbridge Wells both began to develop as spas in the later seventeenth century, the former close to Bristol and the latter within a day's journey of London. The importance of spas is demonstrated by Bath, that quintessential Georgian town, which by 1801 was the ninth most populous town in England and Wales (Carter 1990, 406). Throughout the eighteenth century new spa towns emerged. Not all were as successful as Bath, Cheltenham or Leamington, and some, like Melksham in Wiltshire for example, never flourished and were out-competed by other, more favoured towns. One of Melksham's disadvantages was its proximity to Bath, and it remained a small provincial market town.

The birth of the seaside resort can be traced to the late seventeenth century. Unlike spa towns and other inland leisure towns, which were usually pre-existing urban centres, the seaside resorts were generally wholly new urban areas. As such they were very significant for the changing urban geography of the eighteenth and nineteenth centuries. The earliest seaside resort was Scarborough in Yorkshire (Whyte 1999, 279), where there were bathing machines in operation by the 1730s (Corfield 1982, 62). These were depicted on a Buck print of 1745, which also shows the elegant carriages of the well-to-do drawn up on the beach (Hyde 1994). Like the taking of spa water, bathing in the sea was advocated for health reasons (Corfield 1982, 62). During the eighteenth century it became increasingly popular among the wealthy classes, who

Engraving of Melksham, Wiltshire, in 1830. Melksham was a failed early nineteenth-century spa.

were the only ones who could afford to travel to the bathing spots. Despite the limited numbers of people able to indulge in sea bathing, their impact was sufficiently significant to encourage the development of a number of new towns. As with the spas, these were often linked closely to existing urban centres. Brighton and Margate both developed in the eighteenth century as a consequence of their proximity to London, and Lyme Regis grew as a seaside resort for the fashionable society of Bath (Bettey 1980, 122).

Brighton, unusually, was both a spa and a seaside resort. A humble fishing town of about 1,500 inhabitants in the early eighteenth century, Brighthelmston, as it was then known, grew rapidly (Corfield 1982, 62; Reed 1983, 10), initially as a consequence of the remarks of Dr Richard Russell, fashionable society's influential medical endorser of sea bathing. However, visiting the resort became a fashionable necessity for the socially aware from 1783, when it became favoured by the Prince of Wales. Brighthelmston's elevation to a fashionable status on a par with Bath resulted in a change of name, its development as one of the centres of the new Regency architectural style, its acquisition of monumental buildings such as the royal pavilion (a cathedral to elite pleasure-seeking, built between 1784 and 1820), a huge increase in population and the physical expansion of the urban area. In the second decade of the nineteenth century Brighton was the fastest growing town in England, outstripping all the manufacturing towns (Reed 1983, 214). By 1851 it was larger than Bath (Corfield 1982, 62). A few other resorts also achieved considerable growth in the eighteenth century. Melcombe (now part of Weymouth), on the Dorset coast, was patronised by the Duke of Gloucester in 1780, and soon afterwards he built a residence there (Bettey 1980, 122). From 1789 the Prince of Wales's father, King George III, regularly visited the town, leading to the adoption of the title Melcombe Regis. As with Brighton, Melcombe's late eighteenth-century popularity is reflected in the surviving fabric of the town (Bettey 1980, 122). The success of Brighton and Melcombe spurred speculators to try to develop new resorts. Sir Richard Hotham attempted to develop the Sussex coastal hamlet of Bognor into a resort called Hothampton, but was largely unsuccessful (Corfield 1982, 63), the settlement not developing into the resort of Bognor Regis until later in the nineteenth century.

During the nineteenth century London continued to spawn new seaside resorts like Southend, as did other urban centres. Southport developed as a seaside resort for the people of Liverpool and Manchester, while Bristol provided the stimulus for the growth of Clevedon and Weston-super-Mare. Both were no more than moderately sized villages in 1801 but were towns of about 2,000 and 4,600 inhabitants respectively fifty years later. The railways facilitated even greater expansion in the later nineteenth century (Bettey 1980, 123–4), before which time these seaside resorts were largely inaccessible to the majority of the population, greatly restricting their capacity for growth.

Just as elite/middle-class concepts of housing and other forms of consumption were taken up by the working classes in the later nineteenth century, so too were concepts of leisure. None was more completely adopted than the seaside holiday, and the impact of working-class consumers on the urban fabric development of some towns was profound. The working classes were enabled to participate in the pleasures of the seaside because of the availability of holidays (a product of the structured work environment of the factory), and the cheap and quick transport provided by the railways, which allowed affordable and short-duration breaks. The extension of the railway system in the later nineteenth century removed the dependence of the resorts on relatively local urban centres, and enabled mass tourism to begin. In particular the railways allowed access to the seaside for the burgeoning working-class populations of the industrial towns of northern England.

The town which, even today, is the symbol of mass tourism in Britain is Blackpool. In the early eighteenth century Blackpool was a tiny fishing hamlet containing thatched, cruck-framed cottages (LUAU 1998, 98). By 1754 a number of inns seem to have been established to accommodate people who went there to bathe (Smith 1959, 73). The resort initially seems to have evolved to serve Preston, but without a large accessible urban market, or a wealthy patron, its development was slow. By 1782 there were coach services from Manchester and Halifax, and the resort began to flourish as a small bathing place for the gentry and merchant classes of the Lancashire and Yorkshire manufacturing towns (Smith 1959, 77). Even so, it remained a mere small collection of inns and purpose-built hotels with no urban facilities and services. There were no more than fifty houses and just four hundred visitors at the height of the season (LUAU 1998, 98). Some major residences, such as Raikes Hall, had been built, but Blackpool did not receive the investment in middle-class residences associated with many other resorts, and it was still considered to be a village as late as 1837 (Smith 1959, 93). During this period Blackpool, like all seaside resorts, catered primarily for the elite, though as early as 1815 it attracted 'crowds of poor people from the manufacturing towns' (Smith 1959, 84). In 1827 it was said to be flooded with large numbers of cotton workers from the Lancashire textile towns (Smith 1959, 91).

By 1840 Blackpool had numerous hotels and lodging houses and all the trappings of a town: shops, places of worship and schools. The population numbered 1,304 (Smith 1959, 94). The opening of railways to Poulton-le-Fylde and Fleetwood, short coach rides distant from Blackpool, in the early 1840s, followed by a direct rail link in 1846, precipitated a boom in Blackpool's fortunes. As well as new accommodation, much of it designed for working-class families, the town erected attractions. Piers opened in 1863, 1868 and 1893. In addition, an electric tramway was opened in 1885 and the famous Tower was built in 1891, two years after the Eiffel Tower was erected in Paris. In 1894 the first golf course was laid out. Two years later the Ferris wheel known as the Great Wheel opened and the modern seaside resort was born (LUAU 1998, 98). By 1901 Blackpool had a population in excess of forty thousand and received three million visitors annually. Sadly the late nineteenth-century building boom removed most of the structures associated with Blackpool's early development. Many of the late nineteenth-century buildings were put up cheaply by speculative developers. Unlike Brighton, however, Blackpool was built for the mass market and its architecture reflects that; indeed, the familiarity of its brick-built terraces to its working-class visitors may have contributed to its popularity (Walton 1998, 68). In 1887 the *Morning Post* wrote that Blackpool had rediscovered the art of entertainment and offered 'more fun for less money than anywhere else' (Pevsner 1969, 68).

Resorts such as Bournemouth continued to grow along the southern English littoral during the later nineteenth century, aided by rail connections to London. Even so, the link between the seaside and the manufacturing districts of Britain is clearly revealed in the distribution of rapidly developing coastal towns in the later nineteenth century. There was a particular concentration along the Lancashire coast and a less marked but still significant one along the south Wales coast. Money earned in Bradford, Manchester and Merthyr Tydfil was spent on consumption in Blackpool, Morecambe, Barry Island and Porthcawl. The prosperity this pursuit of pleasure brought was not reflected by investment in grand buildings to edify these urban areas. Grand structures and the creation of a genteel ambience were unnecessary to the success of these resorts for they were pleasure towns of the masses, not leisure towns of the elite. While the working classes in the nineteenth century may have emulated the middle classes of the eighteenth century in taking seaside holidays, the nature of the monuments and the fabric of the working-class-dominated resorts indicates the considerable differences between working-class and middle-class consumption (Glennie 1995, 177).

The Growth of Suburbs

Urban areas did not simply expand by growing outwards from the existing town. A successful town affected the settlements around it, and these often began to grow, to provide services for the town and to take on urban characteristics. Sometimes entirely new settlements would develop to accommodate an out-of-town industry or service. Early seventeenth-century maps depict the beginnings of such suburban development (Crossley 1990, 82). London is the best example of suburban expansion: extra urban settlements grew, became suburbs and then were incorporated into the expanding city, though in many cases they retained their separate community identities. In the seventeenth century a series of suburbs developed to the east of the city behind the Thames wharves and a little further inland to the north: these were Wapping, Ratcliff, Stepney and Poplar. Evidence of early seventeenth-century timber-framed houses has been found along Poplar High Street (PMA 1973, 110; Crossley 1990, 82), and at Ratcliff and Limehouse the development of suburbanisation has been intensively studied (Phillpotts 1999, 65). In this latter area during the seventeenth century pasture lands which had been reclaimed from the Thames marshes were infilled with houses and gardens (Phillpotts 1999, 73). Initially settlement was facilitated by the digging of ditches called common sewers. Excavations have shown these to have been revetted with planks (Phillpotts 1999, 70). Much of the area was initially given over to gardens and orchards before being developed for housing.

These east London suburbs were part of a ribbon development along the northern bank of the Thames which, during the seventeenth century, extended the built-up area from the city to Greenwich (Phillpotts 1999, 73). In the eighteenth century development moved inland, away from the Thames. The hamlet of Mile End Old Town was favoured as an out-of-town location for courtiers in the seventeenth century, and it boasted a number of grand houses as a consequence, as well as the buildings necessary for the support services required by these illustrious inhabitants. Indeed, the settlement has been described as a pleasure resort and retirement village (Watson 1993, 237). As a consequence it had grown appreciably, leading to the enclosure and development of land which had previously formed part of Mile End Green. Still a distinct settlement in 1703, by the mid-eighteenth century it had been virtually absorbed into Stepney (Watson 1993). Similar fates befell other settlements in the London orbit. Dalston, a hamlet near Hackney, became popular in the mid-eighteenth century through the patronage of George II, whose mistress resided there (Tyler 1996, 159). It grew substantially in the late eighteenth and early nineteenth centuries, though remaining an independent settlement in 1831, but by 1873 it had been completely subsumed within Hackney (Tyler 1996, 159–60). The desire of the elite and middle classes to live away from the bustle of the town in rurally located but urbanly connected settlements continued, and a number of London communities owe their origins to this fashion. The migration of the middle classes away from urban centres continued into the nineteenth century, aided in particular by the railways, which allowed rapid transit over considerable distances between home and workplace.

Suburbs also grew as part of the expansion of industrial towns, particularly where manufacturing plants were established near towns, allowing the formation of industrial settlements. The nineteenth-century history of the urban development of the south Wales port and manufacturing town of Swansea is illustrative of this (www. swanseahistoryweb.org.uk). New urban-like residential developments grew on the outskirts of Swansea at places like Landore, a residential area developed between 1830 and 1870 to serve the Vivian family's copper works. By the 1840s a new suburb was developing at Greenhill, between the town and the industrial developments of Hafod and Landore. This was a concentration of cheap, low-quality housing, now redeveloped, heavily settled by Irish immigrants. Later in the nineteenth century further suburbs developed, and by the end of that century these were being planned by the municipal authorities; for example, the Mount Pleasant estate was a development of byelaw housing on a gridiron street plan. Interestingly, the influence of the middle-class town burghers was very clear in this development. In an effort to ensure decent living among its primarily working-class inhabitants, the estate was designed without provision for public houses.

Urban Utilities

One of the consequences of the intensification of urban living and the growth of towns was an intolerable increase of pressure on the existing urban services. In particular, the problems of waste disposal and the disposal of the urban dead both reached crisis point by the middle of the nineteenth century. Fear of contagion forced urban authorities to address both these problems.

Excavation at the back of burgage plots frequently produces evidence of wells cutting through abandoned cesspits. Given the intensity of land-use through time, such occurrences were inevitable where drinking water was retrieved from ground water and rubbish disposal was in pits. Streams were used as sewers from earliest times, and even in a relatively undeveloped small

A post-medieval well cutting through a cess-pit at Worcester.

provincial town like Romsey, in Hampshire, one of its principal watercourses was known by the sixteenth century as the Shitlake. Middens accumulated in streets before being removed by ad hoc scavengers, and the resultant state of some streets is reflected in their names, as in Foul Vennel in Dunfermline and Shitt Wynd in Glasgow (Harrison 1999, 68). By the seventeenth century local ordinances were being applied in many towns to deal with waste disposal, including organised scavenging, though often, as in Leeds as late as the 1840s, the town corporation had no power to remove accumulations of waste (Beresford 1988). In Stirling in Scotland, however, as early as 1616 the burgh council ordered the removal of middens from streets (Harrison 1999, 67). Where such orders were made they usually formed part of attempts to upgrade the streets for safe passage and to improve their appearance, as in the case of Chester's late seventeenth-century shopping streets (Stobart 1998, 15–16). The clearance of middens was linked to other street improvements like cobbling and paving, which were also carried out to facilitate movement and reduce dirt. By the late seventeenth century numerous towns throughout Britain, particularly leisure towns like Preston, had their streets paved. The link between filth and disease had not been conclusively established in the seventeenth century, so the cleanliness or otherwise of the streets was a matter of civic pride, not public health. Even so, epidemic outbreaks, particularly of bubonic plague, could be tenuously linked with filth in the minds of contemporary authorities and could precipitate efforts to improve the cleanliness of towns (Harrison 1999, 74).

The removal of cess from within urban households was a continuing problem from the medieval period. Often stored in chamber pots, the contents were either placed in pits at the back of the property or increasingly, from the sixteenth century, were removed from the streets by scavengers. The lack of archaeologically identified waste pits in Salisbury, for example, is usually attributed to an organised system of night soil disposal, although this may have consisted of no more than emptying pot contents into the flowing water-filled 'canals' which ran through the streets. The modern method of human waste disposal – the water closet – appears to have been invented in the sixteenth century. Its application, however, was limited until the arrival of piped water and an adequate sewage system (Clapp 1994, 28). Excavations at Tron Kirk, Edinburgh, uncovered a late sixteenth-/early seventeenth-century sewer, and a timber-lined sewage conduit of seventeenth- or eighteenth-century date was excavated at Canterbury (Crossley 1990, 96). Individual sewers do not make a system, however, and even in major towns appropriate piped water and underground sewage conduits were seldom widely available until the nineteenth century. Although Edinburgh had piped water in 1675, Glasgow did not acquire it until 1807 (Harrison 1999, 73–4), and London's trunk sewers were not completed until 1864 (Clapp 1994, 28). Even when they were available, water closets were not universally favoured. In Manchester the building of water closets was discouraged in the 1860s and 1870s, and in Leeds in the 1860s there were three times as many privies with cesspits as there were water closets (Clapp 1994, 28). By the end of the nineteenth century the disposal of human waste was still not resolved in all urban areas by the development of sewer systems. Even in a new town like Barry in south Wales, an architect-designed, four-bedroomed, middle-class house of 1891 was not served by a water closet but had an ash closet privy in the back yard, from which waste was collected by scavengers (Thomas 1984, 338).

Scavengers were increasingly employed by the town authorities to remove night soil from cesspits from the seventeenth century (Johnson 1991, 20), although often they lacked the authority to remove middens. In many towns the removal of middens was enforced, as in Stirling in 1678 (Harrison 1999, 70), or, as at Prescott in Lancashire, their use was licensed. New homes within towns were built with cesspit privies in the eighteenth century, from which scavengers or nightstallmen could remove the matter directly. Post-medieval cesspits were built to be repeatedly emptied, and are consequently often found to be brick- or barrel-lined. By the mid-nineteenth century ash or earth closets were being advocated, as these deodorised the waste matter (Sheail 1996, 194). Alternatively ash pits were used; these were wooden boxes into which ash, domestic refuse and night soil might be deposited (Clapp 1994, 28). Again the material was carted, removed by scavengers and sold as manure. By the mid-nineteenth century, however, concerns over public health, prompted by epidemics, and the costs of hauling the increasing quantity of waste were forcing the authorities to consider other methods (Sheail 1996, 194).

In many cases towns resorted to disposing of their waste through the river systems. Until the early twentieth-century development of chemical sewage treatment, the only treatment effluent received before discharge was physical, by the use of sieves and settling tanks. Raw sewage was thus increasingly discharged from towns into rivers, which caused concern about pollution and a perceived inefficient use of resources. Consequently sewage farming was advocated so that the effluent could be purified by crops. In Edinburgh by the mid-nineteenth century the use of urban waste as rural manure had been developed by having a third of the town's filth drain into a stream known as the Foul Burn, the flow of which was diverted outside the town to fertilise 300 acres of meadow (Sheail 1996, 191). Sewage farming did not catch on in Britain, however. Farmers were not convinced by it and the prevailing Victorian attitude was one of disgust and a desire to rid themselves of filth as rapidly as possible (Sheail 1996, 203–10). While health was a prime concern in the disposal of human excrement and household waste by the nineteenth century, it was still mixed with concepts of civic respectability. Urban cleansing had throughout the post-medieval period been equated with decency and morality. Attempts to cleanse towns were often linked with the removal of vagrants and other perceived degenerates (Harrison 1999, 74), such as prostitutes, along with the excrement, though in an era of rampant venereal disease the linking of immorality and pestilence was understandable. The abhorrence of filth among the urban elites in the nineteenth century evolved from these views but also included developing concepts of civilised living and national superiority. Thus in 1872 Dr Augustus Voelker of the Royal Agricultural College, Cirencester, felt unable to advocate the traditional practice of using carted nightsoil as a fertiliser. While conceding the agricultural benefits of nightsoil, and its esteemed use in other countries, he considered the collection of nightsoil by scavengers to be incompatible with contemporary British 'notions of cleanliness, decency, comfort and health' (Sheail 1996, 194).

People were not the only waste producers, for the towns were full of animals, too. The flood of rural peasants into nineteenth-century towns, particularly the Highlanders in Scottish towns and the Irish practically everywhere, brought rural outlooks and lifestyles into the towns. Familiar with keeping animals in longhouse-type arrangements, such immigrants often kept animals, especially pigs, in their urban dwellings. In Leeds in 1866 the resident sanitary inspector considered that the three most significant sanitary problems for the town were, in order, ash pits, pigs and inadequate drainage (Clapp 1994, 29). Cows were also kept in feeding stalls in order to provide the towns with fresh milk. Above all, horses were the main form of haulage transport within urban areas, even after the coming of the railways and the electric tram. There may have been as many as 300,000 horses in London in the late nineteenth century, 50,000 of which in 1900 were pulling London buses (Child 1997, 5). Abandoned drinking fountains and troughs for horses still survive within some town centres, many associated with public houses, a testament to their importance for nineteenth-century intra-urban haulage. The consequence of all these animals is that long after middens of human excreta had been banished from town centres, stables and cow byres continued to produce problematic middens into the late nineteenth century (Harrison 1999, 70).

The wells and watercourses that provided urban water supplies were often highly polluted by the nineteenth century, and it is not surprising that epidemic diseases were rife in congested urban areas. Piped fresh water had to be obtained from uncontaminated supplies if it was to provide the answer to the health problems caused by polluted ground water within built-up areas. The solution lay in the construction of out-of-town reservoirs. One of the greatest landscape impacts of nineteenth-century urbanisation in the central Pennines, for example, is the creation of reservoirs on the fringes of the urban areas (Hassan 1985). Towns like Manchester, Blackburn, Leeds and Halifax were fortunate that the wet climate and elevation of the Pennines provided excellent water-gathering grounds. As the towns grew, however, the consumption needs of their populations outstripped the capacity of these relatively small reservoirs, and larger ones further afield had to be built. Manchester's needs were finally met by water from the Lake District, culminating in the conversion of Haweswater Lake into a reservoir in 1929. Supplying the conurbations with water resulted in the late nineteenth and early twentieth centuries in some of the greatest engineering schemes ever undertaken in Britain. The acquisition of land by the water boards and the architectural impact of their dams and pumping stations were symbolic of the spread of the power and influence of the great towns, as well as being expressions of urban civic pride within rural contexts.

Entwistle Reservoir, Turton Moor, Lancashire. This reservoir was built before 1844 and was modified by the Bolton Waterworks in 1884. It is one of many similar artificial lakes created in the central Pennines to supply water to the rapidly expanding local urban populations.

Another consequence of the rising urban population was an ever-quickening congestion within existing church and chapel cemeteries, so that insufficient time was allowed for decomposition before a grave had to be disturbed. Even the cemetery of High Street Congregational Chapel in Lancaster, opened in 1773, was full by 1837, with 575 burials in 200 plots (J. Price pers. comm.). By the 1830s overcrowded cemeteries were considered a public health issue. The solution was to remove burial from small churchyards within towns and to open large non-denominational municipal burial grounds. The first cemetery company to be established and to set up a burial ground unattached to a church was the Rusholme Road cemetery in Manchester in 1820. This was intended for dissenters, but in practice it, and the similar cemeteries that quickly followed it, allowed use by all denominations (Rugg 1998, 46). In 1832 the 77-acre Kensall Green Cemetery in London was licensed by Act of Parliament (Reeve 1998, 214). So successful was it that it became a fashionable place to be interred, and in 1843 George III's son Augustus Frederick, Duke of Sussex, was buried there. Britain's major urban areas all established similar burial grounds, opening what became magnificently monument-endowed cemeteries, such as that at Jesmond, Newcastle-upon-Tyne. Unlike the crowded, and often unkempt, church graveyards, municipal cemeteries tended to be attractively landscaped and well maintained (Rugg 1998). They were designed with a view to taste and restraint, and amenity value, as examples of civic pride and markers in inter-town rivalry (Rugg 1998, 50–1). A well-landscaped municipal cemetery came to be seen as essential for any successful and civilised town. By the mid-nineteenth century even relatively small towns were acquiring them. The establishment of a municipal cemetery at Tewkesbury in Gloucestershire led to the development of a substantial part of Gastons Field, the site of the Battle of Tewkesbury in 1471, and a considerable southward extension of the urban area.

The provision of sewage systems and piped water, the development of water closets, cobbled or tarmac streets, and the supply of gas and electricity, in addition to other distinctly urban utilities like municipal cemeteries and rapid transit systems, were issues of civic pride as well as public necessity. They further sharply distinguished urban from rural life in a way that was inconceivable in the eighteenth century, let alone in the sixteenth. Town service provision helped to create a distinctly urban environment and lifestyle.

COMMUNICATIONS

Many of the archaeologically recognisable changes in the landscape were only possible because of improvements in communications. Much has been written on the transport revolution, and especially on the economic impact of canals and railways. It is not the intention to repeat this material here but rather to assess the impact of changing communications on the landscape and to assess their relevance as material culture. In particular, their function as linear routeways has led to the development of corridors of interrelated archaeological remains, both directly and indirectly dependent in their origins on the existence of the routeway. Moreover, an awareness of their roles as facilitators of movement through the landscape and as contributors to the experience of the landscape is essential to an understanding of the processes of change in the post-medieval period. The study of routeways as corridors of associated material culture has been pioneered in the USA, with Schelereth's study of US40 in Indiana a notable example (1985). In Britain Hughes's work on the Montgomeryshire Canal (1988) and the Brecon Forest Tramroad (1990) are both studies of the unifying effect of routeways and their wider impact on the development of the landscape.

One of the major characteristics of British industrialisation was improvement in transportation, without which industrialisation could not have progressed in the way it did. So important were the developments in transportation that took place in the period 1750–1850 that the engineers who pioneered much of the work have remained household names. The significance to contemporaries was immense, too. In the early nineteenth century first the canal and then the railway became some of the most popular subjects for paintings and prints (Rees 1980). A German visitor to Manchester Grammar School in 1844 remarked that the favourite subjects for desk graffiti were canals and railways, with barges and locomotives on them (Trinder 1982, 129). The railways in particular were popularly seen as spreading improvement and civilisation, terms used by Charles Dickens in describing the impact of the Camden Town cutting (Rees 1980, 10).

Roads

Much has been written on the appalling state of post-medieval roads. Throughout Britain from the sixteenth to the eighteenth century most roads outside towns did not have made surfaces, hence erosion over time formed holloways. In dry weather and with little wheeled traffic this was not a problem, but where these conditions were not met roads often became impassable. Post-medieval roads faced two main problems: increasing traffic and an inadequate system for ensuring maintenance. The suppression of the monasteries hastened the demise of an already collapsing system of road maintenance as an obligation of land-holding (Rackham 1986, 270). In 1555 parishes were obliged by statute to adopt the burden and cost of road maintenance for those roads which passed through their territory; a similar Act was passed in Scotland in 1669 (Whyte and Whyte 1991, 178). In areas where the traffic was local this system was both fair and potentially workable, but in parishes crossed by routes approaching major towns it was neither (Reed 1983, 156). Another difficulty for this system was caused in woodland districts, particularly where the woods were Crown-owned; here, timber haulage was both highly destructive of surfaces and all-too-often of little local economic benefit.

The problem of road transport worsened during the seventeenth century, though with regional variations. Particular difficulties were experienced in Hertfordshire along the route of the Great North Road; not only was long-distance traffic heavy, as it was the principal northern route into London, but the clay nature of the local subsoil caused drainage difficulties and lacked suitable hardcore for repairs (Reed 1983, 156). Scotland seems to have had few roads before the eighteenth century, and the rugged character of much of its countryside encouraged the use of packhorses as opposed to wagons (Reed 1983, 167). As in England, outside towns, few roads had properly made surfaces (Whyte and Whyte 1991, 178). Parishes everywhere lacked not only the expertise to maintain roads adequately but also the incentive to invest. Rackham (1986, 272) pointed out that this was physically manifested by the lack of bridges built in the period 1540–1740 in comparison with the later medieval period. Economically, the effect was potentially crippling, with the cost of road transport rising in real terms by 250 per cent between 1540 and 1690 (Rackham 1986, 272). By the end of the seventeenth century many of the most important and busiest routes were slow, dangerous and frequently impassable.

A variety of responses to this situation developed during the seventeenth and early eighteenth centuries. In some areas responsibility for road maintenance fell to the Crown, where its activities were hampered by their execrable condition. In the Forest of Dean, for example, the Crown was faced with a major difficulty in transporting timber to the Severn estuary for transhipment to the naval dockyards. Not only did timber haulage cause great damage to the road surfaces, but as a royal forest the Forest of Dean was extra-parochial, so no mechanism existed for road maintenance. The roads became so poor that by 1662 the Navy's ability to haul timber from the Forest's woodlands was compromised (Newman 1988, 324). As a consequence the Crown began to finance road repair out of wood sales. A new road, known as the Timber Route, was built between the Forest and the small ports of Purton and Gatcombe. By 1761 the Crown was paying an annual sum for repair of the roads used for hauling timber, and between then and 1786 it spent over £11,000 on road maintenance in the Forest of Dean (Newman 1988, 325–6). Since the roads used for timber haulage ran through townships that were outside the Forest and included within a parochial system, the Crown found itself paying for parish roads, too. One of the consequences was that the highway between the market towns of Mitcheldean and Monmouth was, by the 1780s, one of the best maintained roads in the kingdom (Newman 1988, 326).

In Scotland the Crown had other incentives for making or improving roads. The efficient movement of troops between the forts and into the Highlands was seen as an important part of the pacification process that had begun after the Jacobite rising of 1715 (Reed 1983, 167). In a programme of works that echoes the efforts of the Roman army some 1,600 years earlier, the roads and forts became symbols of military dominance. A further echo of the efforts of the legions during this period was the construction of the Military Road between Carlisle and Newcastle-upon-Tyne, approximately along the line of Hadrian's Wall. These new military routes were generally straight, wherever possible. They tended to follow higher ground to assist drainage, and consequently often have gradients that were unacceptable for wagons or coach traffic (Reed 1983, 167). As with the Roman roads, however, they were primarily intended to carry troops on foot. Between 1724 and 1736 General Wade, the commander in charge of the road-building programme, had caused to be built 400km of new roads in Scotland, along with forty major bridges (Whyte and Whyte 1991, 192). Following the rebellion of 1745, a further 1,200km of military roads were built. In addition to their direct impact on the landscape, these roads must have acted as a vector for change in the Scottish Highlands, which had for so long been comparatively isolated from cultural developments elsewhere in Britain. As in the Roman Empire and elsewhere in contemporary European empires, native settlements must have been affected by the presence and accessibility of an occupying army and its distinct culture. At the Spey valley settlement of Easter Raitts excavations have revealed an eighteenth-century building seemingly dedicated to housing animals, an apparently unique example for the period in the Highlands (Lelong and Wood 2000, 47), and perhaps a consequence of animal husbandry specialisation made possible by the nearby presence of a Wade military road.

While they were not always engineered to a particularly high standard, and had some overly steep gradients, later road engineers usually maintained the routes (Whyte and Whyte 1991, 192). The continued use of the military roads has meant that few stretches survive in their original state. Where they have been abandoned they have on occasion been so comprehensively forgotten that their earthwork remains have been mistaken for former Roman roads. A stretch of supposed Roman road, aligned with the present A811 near Stirling, had a section excavated across it. This revealed the substantial foundations of a road of more recent origin, probably a stretch of the Dumbarton to Stirling military road built between 1771 and 1780 (Page and Page 1995). There was little sign that the road had ever undergone heavy usage, and it is possible that it was not in use for very long (Page and Page 1995, 105).

While the Crown had both the incentive and the resources to engage in adequate road construction in some areas, few others did, other than some of the great estate owners within and around the confines of their parks. Elsewhere, outside towns, there was a lack of expertise, finance and incentive. Those charged with responsibility for maintenance of many major routes (the parishioners) were not directly related to those who gained most benefit from it (the road users). Following an appeal to Parliament in 1663 by the Hertfordshire and Cambridgeshire parishes affected by the Great North Road, the first Turnpike Act was passed, allowing for the establishment of three toll-gates (Reed 1983, 156). After a slow start turnpike roads spread throughout Britain during the eighteenth century, and by 1770 there was a particularly dense network established in a chain running from north Somerset through the southern Welsh borders, the west Midlands and into Derbyshire (Pawson 1977). The turnpike system radically changed the nature of road funding, placing the burden on the road user rather than on the inhabitants of the place through which the road passed. It also introduced a range of new features into the landscape, including toll-houses, toll-gates and regular mileposts. The turnpikes were managed by Trusts, and different Trusts favoured different styles in toll-house architecture or in milepost design, to the extent that some can be said to have created a brand image. Despite all these changes, however, the lack of trained road engineers, the piecemeal and limited nature of the turnpike administration of the road network, and the increasing traffic meant that for the most part the improvements to road conditions were patchy and often minimal (Ransom 1984, 22–3). A county-wide Trust for Aberdeenshire under an act of 1795 built a turnpike road from Aberdeen to Inverurie (Day 1999, 46). Although a new road, it was plagued with maintenance

Barrowford toll-house, near Nelson, Lancashire.

problems and remained in a poor condition until the 1830s, when it was rebuilt (Day 1999, 52–3).

Central government involvement in the building of roads in Scotland continued even after the general adoption of turnpike roads throughout that kingdom. The problems of access to the Highlands and some of the other remoter parts of Scotland remained and were seen as an impediment to good government, 'improvement' and the spread of 'English' civilisation. Not only were new roads in Scotland seen as an aid to improving agriculture but they were also regarded as morally uplifting (LUAU 1999, 64). In 1803 Parliament established the Commission for Making Roads and Building Bridges in the Highlands of Scotland (Ransom 1984, 95). The engineer placed in charge of the programme of works was Thomas Telford. Of his work in Scotland it was stated that, 'before Telford . . . they [the Highlanders] did not know how to work, having never been accustomed to labour continuously and systematically' (Smiles 1874, 205). The principal road engineer of the early nineteenth century, Telford introduced a more rigorous and scientific approach to road and bridge construction. During the course of his career he helped to establish the profession of civil engineering and pioneered modern concepts of project management and quality assurance. He was not, though, an innovator in his road construction techniques. Aside from his bridges, the methods and technologies employed were traditional and developed from those of some of the better turnpike engineers, men like John Metcalf in Yorkshire (Ransom 1984, 23), who, like the military engineers, used solid foundations to help produce a better surface.

As well as carrying out government-sponsored work in Scotland, Telford was commissioned first to survey and later to design and build a new road from Shrewsbury to Holyhead, the modern A5 (Ransom 1984, 97). Built between 1819 and 1831, the Holyhead road and the contemporaneously built road from Chester along the north Wales coast, via Conwy, are remarkable testaments to the skill and motivation of Telford and his sponsors. The roads are linear archaeological zones consisting of a range of monuments, including the Menai Straits and Conwy suspension bridges, toll-houses, weigh-bridges, embayments (depots), cuttings, embankments and wayside inns (LUAU 1999). The accuracy with which the design plans for the Holyhead road are matched by features on the ground reveals the ability of the surveyors and the efficacy of the design. The construction of the bridges and the high-quality identical milestones

– stone blocks with recessed iron plates – reveals a concern with elegance that transcends the functional and was clearly aimed at impressing the traveller. The milestones, sunburst-design toll-gates and the toll-houses themselves show a degree of Telfordian branding, aimed perhaps at creating an image of regularity, control and efficiency – an image at odds with the rugged, seemingly untamed, landscape through which the road passed.

The Holyhead road had been commissioned to hasten the safe passage of travellers between Ireland and London, particularly MPs, following the Act of Union between Britain and Ireland in 1800 (Ransom 1984, 97). Its effects beyond meeting this purpose were limited. While the road did take some freight traffic from the developing trade of the Penrhyn estate slate quarries, most slate exports went by rail to the coast for transport by sea, at least until the appearance of a direct rail link with England in the mid-nineteenth century (Trinder 1999, 60). Other than stimulating output of some coal mines on Anglesey, the road had very little effect on the

A milestone on Telford's Holyhead road through north Wales. (© Lancaster University Archaeological Unit)

industrialisation and trade of north Wales, particularly in comparison to the impact of the Ellesmere Canal and later railways (Trinder 1999, 59). However, the establishment of good-quality inns and hotels along the route, to cater for the Ireland trade, did enable the later growth of settlements such as Capel Curig and Betws-y-Coed as tourist resorts (Trinder 1999, 59). The importance of well-disposed inns during the days of long-distance coach travel is indicated by some of the milestones. These post distances to places that are now apparently insignificant but which were once the sites of coaching inns, as at Cernioge Mawr (LUAU 1999, 38). The Holyhead road milestones were originally designed to be read easily by passing coachmen, and thus stood 1.25m above the surrounding ground surface, but they have been gradually buried by successive road resurfacing and now usually stand no more than 0.5m above the ground.

During the course of the nineteenth century the innovations in design and construction employed by Telford and McAdam were introduced to all the major road routes throughout Britain. Even so, roads were eclipsed as major long-distance transport carriers during the nineteenth century by other transport networks such as canals and especially railways. Consequently, by 1850 it was reported that Telford's Holyhead road had grass growing on it because of lack of traffic, and thus could no longer be considered of such national significance as to warrant the expenditure of public money on its maintenance (Trinder 1999, 60). Despite improvements in construction, the limitations in speed and capacity of horse-drawn wheeled vehicles held back the development of roads for rapid mass transport until the twentieth century.

Part of the Mamhilad road, Monmouthshire. The pitched-stone surface and kerbing can be seen to the right and beyond the rubble from the collapsed revetment wall.

River Navigations, Canals, Tramroads and Wagonways

At the same time as new and better roads were being built, alternative transport systems were being developed that were more suited to handling heavy freight traffic. Waterways and railways carrying horse-drawn wagons were the preferred options by the later eighteenth century for the carriage of heavy goods. Unsurprisingly, much of the investment in these transport systems came from industrialists. They had considerable incentive to improve transport facilities, and as well as tramroads and canals they even invested in roads, as for example at Mamhilad in Monmouthshire, where a pitch-stone road was built to assist packhorse traffic. For the most part, however, the need to transport heavy goods could not be met by road transport. The management and modification of rivers for navigation had been under way for centuries, but by the seventeenth century the gated pound lock had been introduced (Rolt 1985, 29). More efficient in water retention than the older flash locks, the pound lock allowed for greater control of water levels. As more river navigations were undertaken in the eighteenth century, so ever longer sections of artificial cuts were used to bypass difficult river sections (Ransom 1984, 36). It was an obvious progression from such cuts to wholly artificial waterways. The first canal was the Duke of Bridgewater's, built in 1759–61 to link his mines at Worsley with Manchester (Ransom 1984, 36).

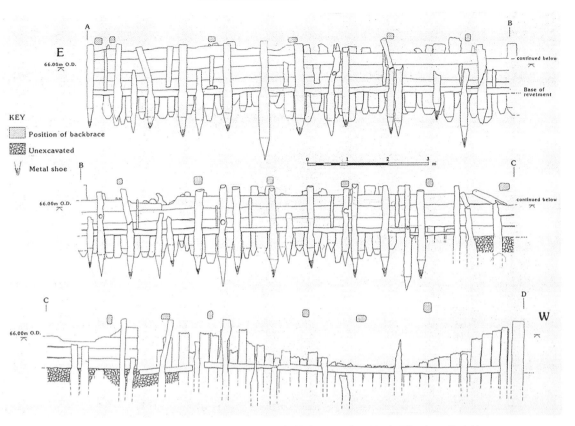

KEY

☐ Position of backbrace

▨ Unexcavated

⩔ Metal shoe

Section of the late eighteenth-century revetment of the turf-sided lock at Monkey Marsh, Thatcham, Berkshire.
(© Wessex Archaeology)

From early in the eighteenth century dock facilities were introduced at both coastal and estuarine locations, in an effort to improve harbours badly affected by tides. By 1715 Liverpool was the first port outside London to have built artificial docks (Philpott 1988, 38). These were so successful that within a hundred years small docks were being built to stimulate trade even in isolated rural locations, as at Bullo Pill on the River Severn. The construction of docks often went hand-in-hand with the building of river navigations or canals. A particularly good example of this process is the building of the Berkeley–Gloucester canal and Gloucester docks. The Berkeley–Gloucester canal was built to bypass an awkward section of the River Severn which had stunted Gloucester's development as an inland port. In the sixteenth century the arrival of a 30-ton barque at Gloucester was a noteworthy occurrence, and by the eighteenth century the Severn below Gloucester was considered impassable for sea-going vessels (Newman 1988, 337). The opening of the canal, however, led to the building of docks at Gloucester between 1793 and 1799, with on-going development throughout the early nineteenth century. The dock basins were the focus for multi-storey warehouses, at the time the largest structures in Gloucester after the cathedral.

Similarly, in the heart of Manchester, at Castlefield, docks were built in 1764 at the junction of the rivers Irwell and Medlock to serve as a terminus to the Duke of Bridgewater's canal. Further docks linked to canals were added there and at Piccadilly in the early nineteenth century (Ashmore 1982, 107). As in Gloucester, the docks saw the construction of large warehouses, while the canals were also foci for development. In the expanding conurbations like Birmingham and Manchester they provided nineteenth-century alternatives to the river valleys for the locating of mills and factories. They provided distinctive corridors of development, even in rural situations, forming linear archaeological zones. Stephen Hughes's study of the Montgomeryshire Canal in mid-Wales (1988) revealed an enormous number of monuments generated by the presence of the canal. These range from canal features such as basins, wharves, locks, bridges and aqueducts, to directly associated structures like lock-keepers' houses, weigh-bridges, wharf workers' houses, stables and offices, and also include features relating to activities supported by the canal such as settlements, inns, maltings, mills and lime-kilns.

While the impact on the landscape of canals and navigations was often radical, the techniques employed in their construction were, as in contemporary road construction, often highly traditional. Excavation of some of the locks forming part of the Kennet Navigation, and later part of the Kennet and Avon Canal, has revealed that timber tie beams were used in the late eighteenth century to brace and anchor post and plank revetments forming the lock sides (Harding and Newman 1997, 46; Harding 1995). Exactly the same techniques were recorded locally in use for riverside frontages at Reading in the mid-eighteenth century (Harding and Newman 1997, 46), and are reminiscent of medieval water frontage revetment-bracing techniques. Moreover, the turf-sided locks used on the Kennet Navigation were a form of water impounding which dated to the sixteenth century (Rolt 1985, 31–2). Not only were the techniques used in the construction of waterways well established, but the boats which sailed upon them were built using traditional methods (Crossley 1990, 121). During the eighteenth and nineteenth centuries several local variants of flat-bottomed, usually double-ended, clinker-built boats were developed for use on rivers and later canals, including the Mersey flat and the Severn trow. Examples have been excavated from around Britain, for example, at West Mersea in Essex (Dean 1985), in the River Usk above Caerleon (Parry and McGrail 1989) and at Lydney on the River Severn (Barker 1992). All of these boats are traditional in their modes of construction.

An undoubted innovation in transport, however, was the use of rails. Various forms of railways developed in the later eighteenth century (Ransom 1984, 51–3), usually to facilitate local short-distance haulage of heavy materials like minerals to the nearest coastal port, navigable river or canal. They were essentially a response to the problems of rutting caused by heavy wagons on roads. The problem was overcome by placing the wagons on rails. Initially made of wood, but soon replaced by iron, the rails were designed to fit the gauge of a wagon's wheels. Wagon wheels were either flanged to fit the rails, as in later and modern railways, or they were unflanged and ran along L-section rails known as plateways or tramways (Ransom 1984, 52). These were spiked to stone blocks to hold them in place, and other than earthworks such blocks are usually all that survives of a tramway. As a transport system it spread rapidly in the later eighteenth and early nineteenth centuries in all areas of heavy industry, particularly in mining districts where versions of the system were used underground as well. Despite the advent of the steam locomotive, horse-drawn tramways remained a feature of some industrial areas into the twentieth century.

The remains of tramroads are particularly common in south Wales. Here the early nineteenth-century enthusiasm for them in a rapidly industrialising area caused many lines to be built. Their survival is indicative of the early abandonment of industry in many districts outside the core mining valleys, though even there important remains survive, such as parts of the route of the

The Tredunnoc boat, River Usk, Monmouthshire. This was a flat-bottomed, clinker-built river boat.

Penydarren tramroad which once linked the ironworks of Merthyr Tydfil with the Glamorganshire Canal at Abercynon. The most intensive archaeological study of a tramroad system was also undertaken in south Wales, with the examination of the Brecon Forest tramroads. It was originally begun in the early 1820s as a scheme to supply lime to John Christie's estate farms in the recently enclosed Fforest Fawr, but the need for coal on the estate and attempts at industrial exploitation within the estate led to extensions and integration into the wider south Welsh industrial transport network (Hughes 1990, 11–23). As a consequence, rural mid-Wales was opened up as a hinterland for the industrial south. Between the 1820s and 1840s this system of tramroads hugely influenced the development of the landscape, facilitating improvements, introducing industry into previously unindustrialised areas, sustaining new industrial communities like Onllwyn (Hughes 1990, 88–9) and creating corridors of development in previously little-exploited areas. Ultimately, outside the northern Swansea valley, the tramroad network ran through an area of limited economic potential, and this underlay both the eventual failure and abandonment of the tramroads and their long-term survival.

Railways

The transformation of a system of short-haul transport for heavy goods, particularly minerals, into a long-distance rapid freight and passenger carrier system was brought about primarily by the steam locomotive. Steam power was initially applied to tramroads on inclined planes, where

Nineteenth-century terraced houses in Carnforth, Lancashire, built in response to the development of a railway junction at Carnforth.

wagons were hauled up on chains powered by static steam engines, as used on the Lancaster Canal tramroad at Avenham near Preston in 1803–4 (Ransom 1984, 60). Similar systems were later used to haul tourist trams, as on Southport pier. The story of the development and spread of railways and steam locomotion from these early beginnings has been frequently told and need not be repeated (Trinder 1982). Even so, the importance and extent of their impact is such that it is worth a brief review. Their spread in a single generation between 1825 and 1850 was truly revolutionary, and their effect on society and the landscape in mainland Britain was extraordinary. They facilitated the improvement and development of areas previously relatively impervious to radical change. They consummated the development of the consumer society, making any goods from anywhere available quite readily in most areas of the country. Rail travel enabled mass tourism to develop, with the resultant development of more, and more populist, resort towns. Industrial location became less dependent on physical geography. This, and the engineering needs of the railways themselves, spawned new urban development, as at Carnforth in Lancashire, Crewe in Cheshire and Swindon in Wiltshire (Armstrong 2000, 217).

Rarely a commercially viable venture in themselves, their effect on the viability of many industrial ventures, their real importance in bringing rapid change and their symbolic significance as mechanisms of improvement, and thus of modernity, ensured continued investment in their development in the nineteenth century The gradual loss of all these perceived benefits in the twentieth century, with the continued difficulties of running a commercially viable railway, led to a collapse in investment and the loss of much of the railway network. Rather than being functioning elements of an integrated public transport system, much of the railway network is now archaeology, like all other redundant physical remnants of the past.

LANDSCAPES OF COMMEMORATION AND BELONGING

Religion and religious beliefs were at the heart of many social changes in post-medieval Britain. The Reformation, the Civil War, the rise of nonconformity and Victorian social attitudes are a few examples of the range of core issues in sixteenth- to nineteenth-century history, for which the appreciation of developing religious beliefs is central. Religious belief informed and defined individual outlooks and actions. Moreover, even the non-believer was governed by institutionalised religion in the performance of the most basic tasks of life: birth, marriage and death. Thus the registration and acceptance into the community of the new-born, the establishment of sexual and family alliances and the disposal and commemoration of the dead were all affected by religion. In turn apparently religious practices inevitably became influenced by concepts of community identity, social group affiliation, celebration and memory. Yet until very recently archaeologists have paid little attention to post-medieval remains associated with religion (Mytum *et al.* 1994, 111). Religious belief is dealt with in only eight pages on 'church archaeology' in Crossley's 1990 review of the subject, and is considered only obliquely in Johnson's *An Archaeology of Capitalism* (1996). Tarlow and West's more recent *The Familiar Past?* (1999) reflects some of the work carried out from the mid-1990s, particularly by scholars from the University of York. Even so, the two recently published volumes of essays on aspects of post-medieval archaeology (Gaimster and Stamper 1997; Egan and Michael 1999) are both notable for their exclusion of religion as a theme. Before the 1990s there was little archaeological work aimed at post-medieval religious buildings (*see* Chapter 2), and until very recently, in Britain at least, even less archaeological consideration of the memorials and monuments within the landscape, and the organisation and development of the spaces within which they are set (Mytum *et al.* 1994).

Churchyard burials can be archaeologically studied in two principal ways, through excavation of the interred remains and by the analysis of the surface features relating to the interments (Mytum *et al.* 1994, 111). The former approach is fraught with difficulties. While the lack of post-medieval skeletal analysis to set alongside that of earlier remains is frequently bemoaned, most archaeologists accept that with such recent burials their disinterment and scientific analysis can be a sensitive and emotional issue. Indeed, given the archaeological evidence for a fear of grave-robbing and subsequent dissection (Cox 1998, 123–4), archaeologists must be sensitive to past as well as contemporary views. Frequently, only small samples are recovered that would lack any statistical viability if an attempt was made to map patterns within the burial community. In such circumstances it is difficult to justify the scientific analysis of the skeletal material in the face of pressure to respectfully re-inter the bodies with the minimum of delay and interference to the remains (*see* Reeve 1998 and Cox 1998). Moreover, such material is often encountered in small-scale projects funded by cash-strapped church authorities. Without a very good academic argument, funding for analysis in such circumstances is unlikely to be forthcoming. Consequently, most worthwhile research into the skeletal remains of post-medieval interments has come from large urban assemblages, most notably that from Spitalfields, London (Cox 1996). More viable in terms of available resources and prevailing sensitivities is an archaeological approach to surface features and monuments. The archaeological study of post-medieval churchyards and their funerary monuments was demonstrated by James Deetz as being an effective mechanism for exploring the past. He related stylistic changes in gravestones in New England to changes in the society that produced them (Deetz 1977, 64–90). In Britain research into cemeteries has recently adopted similar approaches for analysing its burial monuments.

Burial Memorials

Memorials are particularly appropriate subjects for archaeological study: they are easily dated, have architectural variety and detail, contain text structured by fashion and contemporary attitudes, and occur in sufficient numbers to give some statistical validity to comparative interpretations (Tarlow 1999, 185) Above all, they contain messages defining the deceased, and those who buried them, in terms of their social affiliations and group identities. Unfortunately such research is geographically limited to those areas where appropriate memorials survive; often this is in areas using easily worked but durable stone such as slate. Headstones and other memorials in areas using easily eroded sandstones, for example, have usually been 'tidied up' during the twentieth century and the older, more eroded and illegible memorials removed.

Sarah Tarlow's work on Scottish memorials has identified changes in memorial style symbolic of changes in social attitudes to death. Late sixteenth- and seventeenth-century headstones in Britain and America often contain, to modern eyes, macabre epitaphs and symbols emphasising mortality and the inevitable decay of the human body, which is contrasted with the reborn spirit. Similar iconography, such as decaying corpses and a skeletal depiction of death, were used on sixteenth-century monumental brasses, and are part of a tradition stretching back into the Middle Ages (Norris 1992). Death in the seventeenth century was a necessity to ensure eternal life; it was a relief from the legacy of sin and mortal decay. The tombs themselves are styled as portals to suggest that they are the gateways to the afterlife (Tarlow 1999, 185). These earlier tombs also contain much emphasis on the status and position of the deceased in life. By the later eighteenth century and through the nineteenth century the headstones and their iconography portray a very different view of death. References to the corruption of the body are no longer present. Instead death is often portrayed as a form of sleep; 'here lies' is replaced with 'in loving memory'. Texts are no longer moralising but affectionate (Tarlow 1999, 189). For couples, death is seen as a brief separation before reunion. The deceased are identified in terms of a network of relationships, rather than by status, and these networks, which aided the definition of the individual in life, are no longer separated from the body in death. These changes are part of more general changes in attitude to the treatment of death, which indicate a greater stress on the individual (Gittings 1984), a process that was under way from the Middle Ages (Johnson 1996, 205). This process was aided by the development of wage labour and the consequent breakdown of traditional familial and social hierarchies, which allowed for more freedom in the choice of marriage partner. Marriage for romantic love rather than family alliance may have been an influence in the adoption of more sentimental and less status-defining memorials (Tarlow 1998, 42–3). The greater freedom of choice given by the increased emphasis on the individual, as well as messages about death and other social attitudes, can be defined from gravestones. For some men, definition by their trade still appears to be important. The attitude to women as appendages of men is clearly revealed on many nineteenth-century gravestones, where only the woman's forename is used as an identifier and her role in life is defined by her marital relationship, as in 'the loving wife of'.

Late seventeenth- to late eighteenth-century headstones in Roxburgh churchyard, southern Scotland, showing a continuation of iconography despite changes in letter style and the nature of the inscription.

The changing nature of the headstones in the eighteenth century appears in some places, the Orkney Islands for example, to be accompanied by a boom in the numbers of gravestones (Tarlow 1998). In Scotland the seventeenth- and eighteenth-century prohibition on intra-mural burial appears to have been ignored by the Orcadians, and nearly all memorials were placed inside churches. Most of these, however, clearly related to the wealthier members of Orcadian society, and the memorials are often ornate and complex. From the late eighteenth century many more memorials appear in the churchyard, usually of a far more simple design and with limited content in comparison to the earlier intra-mural stones. Far more grave-markers are erected than can be attributed to differential preservation or increasing population from the late eighteenth century (Tarlow 1998, 36–7). The explanation appears to lie in social diffusion of the use of gravestones. In Orkney, as elsewhere in Britain, the practice of grave-marking appears to have spread to the middle classes, as indicated by the occupational status of those interred. Tarlow has argued that this cannot simply be seen in terms of elite emulation (1998, 39–40). The gravestones of these people are stylistically very different from the earlier elite ones; they are also locationally different and the motivation for erecting them are considered to be different. Rather than elite memorials to status and achievement, these are monuments to the personal feelings and sentiments of the bereaved for the deceased (Tarlow 1998, 42–3). Thus the expansion in grave-marker numbers is linked via social diffusion to changing perceptions of death. Middle-class

Late eighteenth-century headstone from Dymock, Gloucestershire. The blunt inscriptions and iconography of mortality of earlier headstones are replaced by a more decorous and sentimental style.

sensibilities in the eighteenth and nineteenth centuries inevitably repudiated the ornate and often grotesque monument styles of the seventeenth century on grounds of taste, but late eighteenth-century middle-class attitudes to death were also different in a way that characterised their contextual position.

Except for the elite, the status of individuals may not have been quite so overtly emphasised by grave memorials in the nineteenth century as it had been in the seventeenth century, but messages of social distinction were still conveyed through them. In Carmarthenshire and Pembrokeshire one particular form of grave-marker, the pedimented headstone, has been shown to be particularly characteristic of upper-middle-class burials in the 1830s to 1880s (Mytum 1999). Expensive to buy, and restrained and classical in style, it was both suitable in form to middle-class sensibilities, and not affordable by those without their purchasing power. Its use, with little variation, defined a particular social group in death. By the nineteenth century the companies running the municipal cemeteries were producing pattern books for headstone and tomb design, though a study of York cemetery has shown that dialogue between supplier and purchaser could result in variations to the standard designs (Buckham 1999). Clearly, grave-marker choice in the nineteenth century was regarded by many people as a highly personal issue, leading to consumer insistence on semi-bespoke solutions to their requirements, though within a generally acceptable range of styles.

A desire to distinguish the deceased from the surrounding interments could transcend denominational directives. Studies of Quaker cemeteries have shown that despite regulations governing Quaker burial, not all burials followed the laid-down procedures. Quaker tombstones tend to be simple slabs being the deceased's name and the date of death. This is given without naming either the day or the month but referencing them by number, thus Monday is the second day of the week and January the first month of the year (Stock 1998a, 131). Yet some gravestones do have named, rather than numbered, months. Some burials were marked during the period 1717 to 1850, when Quakers were not supposed to use gravestones, though it is not clear how many of those stones marking graves of that period were put in place retrospectively after 1850 (Stock 1998a, 139). Although for the most part there is little at the surface to distinguish social class within Quaker burial grounds, excavations have shown that below ground graves and coffin furniture are not always simple, and burial in walled graves and lead coffins does occur. At Bathford, near Bath, such graves were also aligned at 180 degrees from the other burials (Stock 1998b), implying some form of distinction; perhaps these were non-Quaker burials, which were allowed in Friends' burial grounds.

In their simplicity of memorials Quaker cemeteries clearly show a group identity and denominational distinctiveness, but there is emerging evidence to suggest that differences can be noted between other nonconformist sects and Anglicans (Mytum forthcoming). Where nonconformist groups had graveyards, they were not constrained by past use, unlike many Anglicans, as they did not have hundreds of years of burial history to contend with. Consequently, they tended to develop a more regimented landscape than Anglican graveyards (Mytum forthcoming). In north Pembrokeshire it has been noted that there is a linguistic difference between nonconformist and Anglican graveyards, the former more commonly having texts in Welsh on their memorials (Mytum 1994). This may in part be class-related, since English is generally more common earlier in the nineteenth century, when marked burials had still to be adopted by the lower classes. Thus nonconformist communities can be inferred as being predominately Welsh-speaking and probably less wealthy. Whether the memorials are in English or Welsh, both language groups followed similar fashions in dedication, the differences in fashion being reflected between burial grounds, and presumably therefore congregations, rather than between language groups (Mytum forthcoming). Again in Pembrokeshire, Mytum has noticed some differences in choice of monument type between nonconformists and Anglicans during the later nineteenth and early twentieth centuries. In particular, the use of tall columns, usually topped with an urn, was more common in nonconformist burial grounds, and even in Anglican cemeteries may be the consequence of nonconformist burials within them. Often nonconformist communities had no burial ground of their own and had no choice but to be buried in local Anglican cemeteries.

In towns, the lack of nonconformist burial grounds, and the resultant necessity to use Anglican graveyards, contributed to the mounting pressure for non-denominational cemeteries in the early 1800s. Indeed the link with nonconformity is one of the factors influencing the early distribution of municipal cemeteries, and helps to explain why urban growth and a lack of burial space were not always connected to the early development of such cemeteries (Rugg 1998, 45–6). The layouts of municipal cemeteries were defined by various forms of groupings. In Beckett Street cemetery in Leeds separate sections were allocated to Anglicans and nonconformists. There was also social division between those who could afford a private plot and those who were interred in collective graves. The latter were marked by single gravestones recording ten individuals, usually buried over a period of about a month (Beresford 1988, 448–9). Some cemeteries were opened with the intention of catering exclusively for the middle class and elite. Highgate cemetery in London was developed in a promenading area and its users were encouraged to build magnificent monuments (Rugg 1998, 50). Here and elsewhere, particularly in the municipal cemeteries of Scotland, like the Glasgow Necropolis, Egyptian-influenced monuments were erected. Many of these were the tombs of freemasons, a group who seem to have incorporated ancient Egyptian links into their mythology in the eighteenth century (Grant 1988, 240–3).

Religious Symbolism in the Landscape

Religious and cultural affiliation can be expressed through monuments in the landscape in a number of ways besides burial memorials. In County Durham, in the vicinity of Esh, the adherence to Roman Catholicism by the Smythe and other local families is shown in the landscape by a variety of surviving features constructed over a number of generations. Set high on the south front of the tenanted farm at Rowley is a stone block inscribed IHS/ES, with a cross on the bar of the H (Emery 1999b, 164). IHS is the abbreviation of the Greek spelling of Jesus and is a monogram noted in the houses of adherents to the Catholic faith in north-east Scotland from the sixteenth to the eighteenth century (Bryce and Roberts 1993). On Esh village green a cross was erected in 1687, as indicated by a date plaque. The erection of crosses, or at least of such an overtly religious one, in the seventeenth century was highly unusual, as to sponsor their construction was likely to attract censure (Rimmington 1999, 44–5). It is probably no coincidence that the cross was erected in the reign of the Catholic sympathiser James II. Nearby at Esh Laude a Roman Catholic church and presbytery were built in 1798–1800. At that time overt Catholicism still provoked violent opposition, and the structures were built to resemble a farm grouped around a central yard, in order not to attract attention. In the nineteenth century, following the Roman Catholic Relief Act of 1829, the need to hide one's religious affiliation was removed and the Smythe family provided the land for building the seminary of Ushaw College (Emery 1999b, 164). Only a mile or so from Esh, this seminary was designed by the Pugins, famous for their Catholic church architecture.

In Scotland, a number of elements of iconography associated with Catholicism, including the IHS monogram, were built into houses. The Arma Christi symbol linked its users to traditional late medieval beliefs in Scotland (Bryce and Roberts 1993, 365). The pierced hand of Christ which was part of this imagery was also used by supporters of the Pilgrimage of Grace in England in the sixteenth century, as on a spandrel at Rufford Hall in Lancashire (LUAU 1996c). At Rufford this symbol was an internal detail, hidden away and barely visible for fear of discovery, but in Scotland the imagery is often external and explicit. The use in 1671, for example, of the IHS monogram above a Latin inscription reading 'Jesus, your death on the cross draws forth my love' over the main entrance at Aboyne Castle is indicative of the Earl of Aboyne being sufficiently confident and secure in his position to be able to flaunt his religious affiliations (Bryce and Roberts 1993, 369). In north-east Scotland such imagery on clusters of elite buildings stamped the clear affirmation of adherence to the old faith on the landscape. Elsewhere, such overt symbols of Catholicism were too dangerous, even when hidden away as at Rufford, and more subtle displays of affiliation were used. At Rushton in Northamptonshire, Sir Thomas Tresham, who was imprisoned for his adherence to Rome, had a triangular lodge built in his park between 1594 and 1597. This unusual design is considered to be symbolic of the Trinity and thus was a covert expression of his faith (Johnson 1996, 148), as is another landscape garden feature, the heart-shaped pond at Shifnal Manor in Shropshire (Everson and Williamson 1998, 147).

CHAPTER FIVE

INDUSTRIAL ARCHAEOLOGY – MANUFACTURING A NEW SOCIETY

DAVID CRANSTONE

One of the over-arching themes in post-medieval archaeology is the development of 'industry' as a major element in the society and economy of Britain. Clearly this occurred within a broader social and economic context. Nevertheless, it is essential that any balanced study of historical archaeology engages directly with industry, industrialisation and the archaeology of production. It is ironic that the recent, and very healthy, upsurge of new work and ideas on a period whose later half is often referred to as the 'Industrial Revolution' has focused so strongly on the study of consumption, almost to the exclusion of production. For example, only two articles in *The Familiar Past?*, a recent review of the archaeologies of later historical Britain, touch directly on production (Gould 1999a, 142–3; Matthews 1999, 163–6, 168–9), and even these papers are directed primarily to other themes. Similarly, the recent review of later historical archaeology in both Britain and America, *Old and New Worlds* (Egan and Michael 1999), contains only one paper devoted primarily to industry (Cranstone 1999), although a paper dealing with the ceramic industry (Barker 1999) covers the relationships between production technology, demand and consumption. A recent collection of studies dealing with world historical archaeology (Funari *et al.* 1999) contains no papers primarily concerned with industry or production.

Within the British context, part of the problem relates to the existence of the separate specialism of 'Industrial Archaeology'. This developed from the 1950s onwards as an interest distinct from mainstream archaeology. 'Industrial Archaeology' remains torn between a period identity, and an identity as a study of industry regardless of period. In practice, industrial archaeology remains most comfortable within the overlap of these definitions, and has not developed into a comprehensive period discipline. For example, Trinder (1992, xviii) considers that 'the core of the discipline is the study of the physical remains of the large-scale mining, manufacturing and service enterprises that had their origins in the British Industrial Revolution of the eighteenth century', while Palmer and Neaverson (1998, 1) consider that 'the consensus now favours a definition of industrial archaeology as the systematic study of structures and artefacts as a means of enlarging our understanding of the industrial past'. Conversely, Clark (1999, 283) defines industrial archaeology as 'the archaeology of the late second millennium AD', though without fully rising to the challenge of this broader definition.

The topic identity has also focused on heavy or large-scale industry rather than on craft or domestic-scale production. This focus has normally been implicit, though Palmer and Neaverson (1998, 14–15) do hint at a definition where 'industrial archaeology' is confined to the study of production within the physical setting of the separate factory or works, and in the socio-political context of the capitalist system. This definition has not been rigidly applied in the editorial policy of *Industrial Archaeology Review*, which continues to include papers on, for instance, watermills originating within the feudal system and agricultural production at various scales, though coverage of craft and domestic-scale industry is very limited. A brief scrutiny of the *Review's* coverage in the 1990s indicates a strong focus on eighteenth- to twentieth-century heavy industry as well as on industrial housing, and with occasional forays into agriculture, topics covered elsewhere in this present volume. The current redefinition and development of 'historical archaeology' as a major subdivision of archaeology (Andren 1998; Funari *et al.* 1999) offers a clearer context within which 'Industrial Archaeology' can be placed; many of the features which Palmer and Neaverson (1998) consider to be distinctive of industrial archaeology as a 'discipline' can be placed within the context of Andren's synthesis, as a particular, if extreme, element of historical archaeology. In this present work, and in opposition to the view taken by Palmer and Neaverson, an attempt is made to re-integrate industrial archaeology, as the study of industrial-scale production, within its broader period context as part of post-medieval archaeology, itself part of the developing British and World sub-discipline of historical archaeology.

Production, whether industrial, craft or domestic in scale, is a process, and is normally carried out at least in part for pragmatic practical reasons, often crucial to the survival of the individual or society. The study of this process, with due weight to its practical importance, must always be an essential and major part of any balanced archaeological study of the post-medieval period. Such an approach is as essential and relevant as any consideration of more social and symbolic concerns. However, these approaches need to be integrated with an awareness of their place within the wider context of society and cultural change, and of broader processes such as the rise of capitalism and colonialism, and this awareness must give full weight to the potentials and constraints imposed by technology and industry on the wider fabric of society and vice versa. The archaeology of industrialisation is as much an 'archaeology of capitalism' as the social archaeology to which Johnson applied this label (Johnson 1996), and has at least as many, and as important, a set of insights to offer.

The challenge, surely, is to develop and use approaches that genuinely increase both our knowledge and our understanding of industrialisation and production in their own right, as well as integrating them into broader social and economic concerns. The archaeological study of production can provide genuinely new information on the properties of materials and on the physics, chemistry and metallurgy of past (and therefore potentially future) production technologies, and on the development of the natural environment and its reaction to human intervention, and these are worthy contributions to the ultimate goal of understanding both ourselves and the world that we inhabit.

At the same time, the very welcome refocusing of interests from data-gathering for its own sake to the 'big issues' must not obscure the continuing importance of good methodologies, including the traditional concern with recording of detail in excavation, building recording and landscape survey. This is of particular importance in industrial archaeology, where the sheer physical scale of many sites and the overwhelming amount of detailed information that they

Peg holes and the slight impression of the rail chair held by each pair of pegs, within the timber of an 1870s lead-dressing floor at Killhope lead mine, County Durham. This is the only evidence for the former existence of a narrow-gauge railway. (© D. Cranstone)

contain pose real problems for traditional archaeological approaches. While broad-brush and generalising surveys are clearly both important and pragmatically necessary, detail remains important for both the technological and the human elements of our study. For example, the careful recording of such features as wear-marks and heat-damage – accompanied in the latter case by scientific examination to determine temperature and chemical conditions – on the internal wall faces at Old Gang and Surrender smeltmills yielded important information on the processes carried out within the mills (Cranstone 1992a; Francis 1992), while nails and nail-holes may indicate the human use of space within the mills by the workforce, perhaps showing where coats were hung. The small-scale and ephemeral detail may, just as in earlier periods, form the only surviving field evidence of what were originally prominent and major features; for example, at Killhope lead mine, County Durham, the line of a narrow-gauge railway survived only as the pegholes by which it had been secured to the timber decking of the dressing floor (Cranstone 1989, 45–7).

Having placed the archaeology of production within its broader context, and reaffirmed the continuing importance of technology in its own right and of bottom-up detail, it is entirely appropriate to continue this review with a summarised examination of selected industries. These will be used to illuminate some of the issues that historical archaeology can and should explore in relation to industrialisation. The iron and steel industries will be discussed at some length, for three reasons: their scale and intrinsic importance throughout the period, both to society and to the process of industrialisation; the overall quality of both archaeological and historical research; and because, largely as a result of the first two factors, they illustrate many of the themes important to the study of industrialisation in post-medieval Britain. However, it is necessary to look briefly at several further industries in order to identify a broader range of the problems, solutions and inter-relations concerning the development of industrialisation and its archaeological study. The non-ferrous metals, another well-studied sector with abundant field remains, are summarised in order to highlight their differences from iron. Coal is briefly mentioned in order to highlight the continuing lack of study within an industry of such importance, especially in the later part of our period. Finally, salt and chemicals are discussed to focus attention on two related sectors with very different technologies to the 'classic' heavy industries on which industrial archaeology has concentrated. Nevertheless, though linked, they have very contrasting chronological trajectories. Of necessity, this is a highly selective review and excludes other important sectors, such as textiles, where others are far better qualified to comment.

IRON AND STEEL

The iron industry was one of the mainsprings of industrialisation, and has consistently received a high level of archaeological and historical attention, particularly as Abraham Darby's successful experiments with coke smelting at Coalbrookdale are seen as one of the foundations of the Industrial Revolution. Most attention has focused on smelting as opposed to either mining or ironworking. In addition, the introduction of innovations has received much more attention than the less-documented processes of development and spread of evolving technologies. The development of the charcoal-fuelled furnace and its associated finery forge have been discussed in detail by Crossley (Cleere and Crossley 1985; Crossley 1990), and the following discussion purposely concentrates on those areas of less interest to Crossley, and those where new information and ideas are now available, or are most needed. The post-medieval iron industry was very mobile geographically, owing to the varying relationships between the characteristics of the ore-bodies and the extractive technologies, smelting technologies, fuel sources and transport systems.

The Industry in the Sixteenth Century

In 1550 the small-scale hand- or foot-powered bloomery (Tylecote 1987, 179–201) may still have been in use in some areas. It required very little input in terms of fixed plant, large stocks or organised workforce, and produced wrought iron directly on a small scale. However, in the later Middle Ages it had been increasingly replaced by the water-powered bloomery. This required an appreciable investment in construction before the costs could be recouped from production, and thus represents a move towards centralisation and the development of industry as a specific and distinct activity. The range of late medieval and post-medieval bloomeries remains poorly understood, both in terms of the degree to which water power was used for blowing and/or hammering, and in terms of the range of smelting technologies and resultant hearth forms. The portmanteau term 'water-powered bloomery' may prove to obscure important differences between smelting and forging technologies linked only by the use of water power at one or more stages of the process. Sites such as Bishopdale, Yorkshire (Moorhouse 1995), represent considerable water-powered complexes, though the precise details of the technology are as yet unclear. Current work on the Rievaulx Abbey estates suggests that by about 1500 the high bloomery may have been in use at Timberholme (Vernon *et al.* 1998); this was a water-powered, high-shaft furnace, producing mainly blooms of iron for direct forging, but potentially capable of producing cast iron also. The relationship between ironmaking technology and tenurial factors (both land ownership and the source of capital for the ironworks) has not been systematically investigated; the literature suggests that 'water-powered bloomeries' do appear to be associated with monastic landholdings, whereas blast-furnaces do not, normally being set up by major secular landowners and the Crown (which had a strategic interest in the cast-iron cannon and shot that blast-furnaces could produce).

Since the high bloomery has previously been considered as an exclusively continental form, this raises the issue of the relationship between British and continental ironworking techniques at the start of the sixteenth century. It is now clear that the range of technologies used within Europe, and therefore available within the contact range of at least the wealthier ironmasters and operators, was extremely wide. As well as a range of bloomery technologies, small blast-furnaces, operated on a peasant ironmaster scale, were already in use in Sweden, Germany and Switzerland (Magnusson 1995). The extent to which these technologies were in use in Britain, but remain archaeologically unrecognised, is intriguing, as is the possibility that British ironmaking was an active contributor to the broader pool of European technologies. Conversely, if the traditional picture of British ironmaking as dominated by a very limited, almost standardised, range of bloomeries is correct, this contrast to the new continental picture is itself important.

The introduction of the blast-furnace may therefore have been a less abrupt and total change than previously supposed. The introduction is normally dated to 1496, when a works was set up at Newbridge, Sussex. References to a furnace, finery and hammer make it clear that this works consisted of a blast-furnace and a water-powered finery forge (Cleere and Crossley 1985, 111–13). There is also clear evidence for the migration of French ironworkers to the Weald from the 1490s onwards, and there seems little doubt that the large commercial-scale blast-furnace and finery forge, of a type developed in northern France and the Low Countries in the fifteenth century, was genuinely introduced at this point.

The Charcoal Blast-Furnace Industry

The blast-furnace was a large and complex structure, dependent on water-powered bellows. It differed drastically from all forms of bloomery in being a continuous process, its product being entirely in the form of molten cast iron which was run out into casting beds without interrupting the operation of the furnace. In fact, the furnace required continuous operation over periods of months, since cooling of the structure resulted in disruption to the internal chemistry, and cracking of the furnace lining. The use of the blast-furnace therefore imposed the need for investment not only in a large and complex structure, but in sufficiently large stocks of iron ore and charcoal, and sufficiently sophisticated and reliable water-power facilities to permit continuous operations for campaigns of several months, regardless of weather conditions. It also imposed a requirement for round-the-clock shiftwork by its operatives, with all the implications for the nature of employment and the impact of the industry on broader society. While the blast-furnace had a considerable impact on the scale of iron mining, it is not clear that this was reflected in the technology, which appears to have remained unsophisticated relative to contemporary metal- or coal-mining. The genuine 'bell-pit' remained common until the eighteenth century, although some so-called examples prove on underground examination to have given access to more extensive, though shallow, subterranean workings (Crossley 1990, 204–6).

The immediate product of the blast-furnace was molten pig iron, a high-carbon, hard, but very brittle alloy. Some of the iron was used directly in this form, being run directly from the furnace into casting pits for cannon, or ladled from the furnace forehearth for casting into moulds for gunshot or (increasingly from the later sixteenth century) for firebacks and other relatively small and simple cast goods. The separate iron foundry, remelting pig iron brought in from elsewhere, does not appear to have developed until the mid-seventeenth century, when references to urban iron foundries begin to appear; the archaeology of these early foundries remains virtually unstudied. However, the main demand continued to be for wrought iron. Pig iron from the forge was converted to wrought iron in the finery forge, the introduction of which therefore paralleled that of the blast-furnace. The normal finery consisted of a bellows-blown hearth at waist height, into which a pig of cast iron was progressively fed. The resultant bloom was then consolidated by forging under a water-powered hammer while still hot, and worked up into bars of wrought iron by a sequence of reheatings and forgings. This process was very much slower and more labour-intensive per ton than blast-furnace smelting, and imposed further demands for fixed plant, water-supplies and charcoal fuel, though coal was increasingly used in the chafery (reheating hearth) from the 1600s onwards in those forges located on or near the coalfields. It was also a highly skilled craft process.

The blast-furnace and finery forge 'package' was therefore in existence in Britain by the sixteenth century, though it was confined to the Weald (Cleere and Crossley 1985, 119–29). Elsewhere, the water-powered bloomery remained dominant. However, since both the contemporary documentary record and modern archaeological investigations are strongly biased towards the blast-furnace, the role of bloomery smelting in the sixteenth and seventeenth centuries is probably under-emphasised. The one area where these later bloomeries have received due attention is northern England, where seventeenth-century sites at Rockley Smithies, Yorkshire, and Muncaster Head, Cumberland, have been excavated (Crossley and Ashurst 1968; Tylecote and Cherry 1970). There is historical evidence that seventeenth-century bloomeries in Furness adopted much of the form and terminology of the finery forge (Awty and Phillips 1980), and here bloomery production continued into the early eighteenth century. It is ironic that the only conserved and displayed bloomery forge, at Stony Hazel (Bowden 2000, 73–6), was probably the last to be built and is of the finery-derived type, probably highly atypical of the overall range of water-powered bloomeries; the initial excavators' confusion over its nature is entirely understandable, though it has bedevilled the archaeology and archaeometallurgy of both bloomeries and fineries (Davies-Shiel 1970). This forge was in fact built as a bloomery in 1718, and was bought out and closed by the cartel of Furness blast-furnace ironmasters in 1725 (Cranstone 1986).

The charcoal-fuelled blast-furnace and finery forge, as developed in the Weald by 1540, remained essentially unaltered for two centuries, spreading to most iron-producing districts during the sixteenth century, and – except in Furness – totally replacing the bloomery during the seventeenth century. The vast majority of furnace sites from *c.* 1660 onwards are now known, and can be at least approximately dated (Riden 1993); regional and national trends in output can be estimated with some reliability (Riden 1994; King 1996). While individual regions showed considerable growth and decline during this period, overall national production remained remarkably constant at 19,000 to 25,000 tons.

The ownership of, and sources of capital for, the charcoal blast-furnace industry have not received much recent attention. King (1997) argues convincingly that the west Midlands industry was developed in the later sixteenth century by major magnates, making massive paper profits by use of their own uncosted woodlands. In the seventeenth century they were replaced by

Excavations at Stony Hazel bloomery forge, Lancashire, 1985. Sockets for the anvil and hammer bases can be seen in the centre of the picture, with the wheel pit beyond. (© D. Cranstone)

industrialist ironmasters, whose main running cost was the purchase of wood or charcoal from the magnate woodowners. The role of the Reformation in liberating capital for the early development of the landowner-dominated industry, and the initial sources of capital for the industrialist ironmasters require further investigation. A relative absence of surviving documentation for the earlier seventeenth century, as compared both with the earlier landowner industry and the later ironmaster partnerships, complicates this issue but may in itself be of significance.

There are hints even within the historical record that the picture of technological stability may be overstated; maximum annual output per furnace certainly increased considerably between the sixteenth and the eighteenth century. The archaeology of the charcoal blast-furnace received considerable attention in the 1970s and 1980s, and is well summarised, with references to the main site reports, by Crossley (1990, 156–65). Perhaps the main addition to the corpus of reports is Rockley Furnace, Yorkshire (Crossley 1995); this site also reflects the increased interest in the adoption of coke smelting (*see* below). The corpus does, however, concentrate on the sixteenth-century Wealden industry, and on the 'classic', large and well laid-out complexes of the eighteenth-century charcoal ironmasters' partnerships in the north and west. A full assessment of regional versus chronological variation, and intra-regional variation, cannot be undertaken. Technological factors such as improved construction, increasing efficiency of bellows, more durable refractories and increasing craft skill at furnace operation all appear to have been involved in the increase in production. There is a continuing need for archaeological and archaeometallurgical research on these aspects, in order to illuminate the bottom-up processes of developing craft skill and incremental development. Improvements in transport, organisation and capitalisation were also factors in this increase, and dialogue between the historical and archaeological evidence will, one hopes, become increasingly informed and sophisticated as 'historical archaeology' develops as a discipline.

The conserved and displayed site evidence for the charcoal blast-furnace concentrates on the three major eighteenth-century sites of Bonawe (Argyll), Duddon Bridge (Cumberland) and Dyfi Furnace (Cardiganshire). These all date from the 1730s to the 1750s, and were built by linked partnerships within a cartel of ironmasters supplying the west Midlands and outsourcing some of their pig production to regions with less competition for fuel and water-power. All three sites demonstrate sophisticated and well-planned complexes, laid out in terraces on sloping ground to aid process flow (Bowden 2000, 47–64). The large charcoal and ore storage barns are visually impressive, especially given their locations on the highest terrace of each works. The organisation of these works, as compared with the more cramped and haphazard layout of most earlier furnace complexes, undoubtedly gives some insight into the developing mindsets of industrialisation. Arguments for an element of symbolism or deliberate display are very tempting, especially in view of the timing of these works in a period where the charcoal iron industry and its ironmasters were under threat from the developing coke iron industry; however, such arguments would require fairly rigorous justification, in view of the clear functional benefit of large storage buildings and terraced layouts.

There has been very much less research on the finery forge, where the only major excavations remain those of Crossley at Ardingley and Chingley in the Weald (Cleere and Crossley 1985, 266–75), and there is no coherent corpus of archaeometallurgy on slags and other residues. In this situation, even basic issues of chronological and regional variation, let alone the issues of adaptations to varying qualities of pig iron or identifying the craft skills of individual forgemen, cannot yet be addressed. Forges were normally built and operated by the major ironmaster partnerships in conjunction with their furnaces, though their relatively limited capital and stock requirements did open this stage of the process to some extent to the 'small man'. Slitting and rolling mills have similarly received little recent attention.

The bulk of the iron produced was worked up from bars or rods into finished artefacts either by blacksmiths or by more specialised craftsmen such as nailors, in a workshop or semi-domestic context; in the west Midlands at least organised 'putting-out' systems, with similarities to the better-known systems of the textile industry, were developed and run by ironmongers (Rowlands 1975). Again, the smithies and workshops, and their operatives, of the sixteenth to the eighteenth century have received little attention relative to the blast-furnace and the major ironmaster.

A major exception to this picture of the manufacturing end of the industry is the Crowley organisation (Flinn 1962). Ambrose Crowley I was a west Midlands ironmonger, who was previously involved in the introduction of tinplating to Britain (Brown 1988, 42). In the 1680s and 1690s he developed a business centred in London, as the leading supplier of wrought-iron goods to the Navy. From 1691 to around 1717 he developed two massive integrated iron and steel works at Winlaton Mill and Swalwell in County Durham, using imported bar iron to produce nails, anchors and other goods on a huge scale. The works contained forges, slitting mills, plating forges, steel furnaces, grinding mills, anvil workshops and ranges of nailmakers' and filemakers' workshops, together with warehouses, offices and workers' housing. The survival of very extensive documentation and contemporary mapping, coupled with survival of the Winlaton Mill works and environs as well-preserved stratigraphy, offers a prime opportunity for archaeological research both on technology and production processes, and on the material

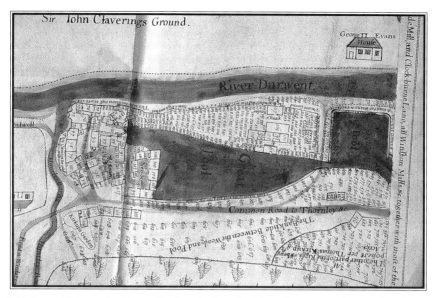

A plan of Winlaton Mill ironworks, County Durham, in the early eighteenth century. It shows workers' housing as well as industrial buildings. (© D. Cranstone)

culture of very closely definable social and occupational groups within the workforce. Comparison with the material culture of contemporaneous local non-Crowley nailmakers, forgemen and steelmakers would be possible and illuminating. The Crowley empire also included his headquarters in Greenwich, warehouses in Greenwich and London, and an extensive nail manufacturing business centred on Stourbridge. The whole operation was managed by four generations, including, from the 1740s to the 1780s, Theodosia Crowley. Female industrialists, by inheritance if not by achievement, were not unusual in the eighteenth-century Tyneside coal and iron industries (Bennett *et al.* 1990). The works in County Durham can be seen as the start of the continuing Tyneside traditions of heavy manufacturing for southern-based companies based on low local wage rates, and of heavy involvement in the armaments industry.

Steel Making

The early development of steelmaking as a separate activity also occurred within the sixteenth to early eighteenth centuries (Barraclough 1984a, 1–60). Steel, in the pre-Bessemer meaning of the term, is an alloy of iron with controlled amounts of carbon (0.5–1.5 per cent); it is very hard but forgeable. The forgeability of steel is, however, very sensitive to impurities such as sulphur and phosphorus, present in most British iron ores; while steel appears to have been successfully produced from some of these ores by the bloomery process, under blast furnace conditions the sulphur and phosphorus end up in the cast iron, and thence in the wrought iron produced by the finery, rendering it unsuitable for steelmaking. The early post-medieval production of steel in Britain is little-studied, though there is documentary evidence for a small number of specialist 'steel forges'. Some of these may have produced steel direct from iron ore, though there is evidence that the Robertsbridge forge, Sussex, operating from 1566 to 1572, used the finery process on specially smelted pig iron from low-phosphorus Glamorgan haematite (Barraclough 1984a, 28–9).

In the seventeenth century a new process, cementation, was introduced, which had been developed on the continent in the late sixteenth and early seventeenth centuries (Barraclough 1984a, 48–59). In this process, bars of high-quality wrought iron were packed with charcoal in a sealed refractory stone chest built into a furnace and heated for several days, allowing the carbon to diffuse into the bars and convert them to 'blister' steel, which could then be forged into end products. The furnace required a long-flame fuel to transfer the heat from a firegrate via flues round the chest, and reflecting (reverberating) down from the domed roof of the cementation chamber; since neither fuel nor fumes came into contact with the bars being converted, coal could be used. This innovation, along with analogous developments in the glass industry, can be seen as part of the first wave of coal use in heavy industry, in situations where contamination of the product could be avoided by separating the fuel from the product being heated.

Seventeenth-century cementation steelmaking is documented in various parts of England, notably the Forest of Dean, west Midlands and the Sheffield area, but the development of a workable technology, no doubt involving undocumented developments of both fixed plant and working methods, remains an untapped field for research. The 'package' was not, however, completed until the 1690s, when a group of German steelmakers were introduced to the Durham Derwent valley, producing 'shear steel' by careful grading of blister steel bars into 'billets' of similar composition, and repeated forging down into bars (Barraclough 1984a, 60–9). This industry may initially have been an attempt by a major partnership of ironmasters to develop an integrated iron and steel industry using low-phosphorus north Pennine ores, with the Hollow Blade Sword Company as end-users. If so, the smelting and finery forging end of the operation soon failed, and a self-contained specialist steel business developed, Newcastle and the Derwent Valley being the centre of British steel production until the 1760s. An eighteenth-century cementation furnace belonging to this network survives at Derwentcote, and has been excavated and displayed, though the associated shear steel forge and workers' housing remain unexcavated (Cranstone 1997).

Coke Smelting

The invention of coke smelting by Abraham Darby I in 1709 had the status of an origin myth among the first industrial archaeologists. Like most origin myths, however, re-examination reveals not a single-date event, but rather a more prolonged and subtle process. Attempts to substitute coal for charcoal in the blast furnace are recorded historically from the late sixteenth century onwards, but achieved no commercial success until the early eighteenth century. Explaining this has generated considerable controversy based on historical evidence and modern metallurgical knowledge (Rehder 1987; Ince 1989; 1991), but disappointingly little archaeological and archaeometallurgical research. It is now clear that the traditional explanation, that unusably 'red-short' (brittle at forging temperature) iron was produced because of the sulphur content of the coal, and that this problem was solved by the use of coke, is far from complete. In fact, the use of coke rather than charcoal fuel causes several changes in operating conditions; operating temperature rises (with implications for the stability and longevity of refractory linings), production rates fall owing to longer reaction times in the furnace; air consumption per ton of iron rises by 80 per cent; and the pig iron product contains more sulphur and silicon. The use of raw coal introduces further complications owing to its volatile content. The net result of these factors is that a large, well-designed charcoal furnace is close to the minimum size and blowing requirements of a coke furnace. It is therefore both surprising and interesting that at least one of the seventeenth-century experimenters, Dud Dudley, appears to have achieved at least partial technical success, producing up to 7 tons of pig per week in the 1620s (King 1997, 61–2). This iron may, however, have been unusable in the contemporary finery forge because of its sulphur content. There is a need for detailed archaeological and archaeometallurgical study of the remaining field evidence for early attempts at coke smelting to help illuminate the nature of the attempts made to resolve the technical problems of coke smelting.

The success achieved in 1709 may therefore have resulted partly from being in the right place at the right time. Whether by chance or judgement, Darby used a low-sulphur, low-silicon Shropshire coal, in a furnace designed for charcoal but which, by the incremental processes of development outlined above, had also attained the minimum parameters for coke smelting. However, Darby came from a background in the Bristol brass and copper industries, where the foundry trade was already well developed, and had patented the use of sand-moulding in the foundry for the production of thin-walled vessels. He may also have introduced the coal-fuelled reverberatory remelting furnace, recently developed in copper- and lead-smelting, to ironfounding, thereby both increasing the ability of the foundry to produce large castings in the absence of a blast furnace, and rendering the foundry independent of charcoal (Cox 1990, 129).

Darby's intention at Coalbrookdale was to develop a furnace-based ironfounding business, rather than enter the finery-forge wrought-iron trade. He thus, at a stroke, escaped the problems of converting sulphur-rich pig iron into usable wrought iron; indeed, the higher operating temperatures of the coke furnace, and the higher carbon and silicon content of the iron, produced a more fluid iron much better suited than charcoal iron to his sand-moulded foundry trade (Rehder 1987, 39–40). He also, presumably, escaped any determined opposition from the established ironmasters and landowners, since he did not threaten the established markets for charcoal and charcoal-pig; for landowners within the Coalbrookdale coalfield his arrival presumably afforded the opportunity for greatly enhanced income from coal and iron ore mining. Indeed, for the very considerable capital investments needed for his works, he was able to draw on the new money of the Bristol merchant class, derived in large measure from colonialism and the slave trade.

The immediate result of Darby's success was the development of a specialist coke-pig foundry sector of the industry, centred on the furnaces of Darby and his associates in Shropshire and north Wales, and of Isaac Cookson and partners in the north of England. Cookson built a coke furnace at Little Clifton, Cumberland, in 1721, supplying a foundry in Gateshead (Cranstone 1997, 20). This foundry sector supplied and doubtless stimulated a growing demand for cast-iron hollow wares such as cauldrons; the influence of this supply of cheap (relative to brass) cooking vessels on diet and food culture may merit research. Of greater importance to the development of industrialisation, however, was a close link to the development of the steam engine, for which thin-walled castings of machinable coke pig were virtually essential. The immediate take-off from the development of coke smelting was therefore in coal and non-ferrous metal mining, and in the development of a proto-engineering industry, rather than within the traditional iron industry.

The sea-change in the iron industry as a whole occurred around 1750, with a dramatic expansion of coke smelting and the adoption of coke pig as feedstock for the wrought iron forges. This had a huge impact on regional industrial developments, as the new technology spread widely, and new ironworks utilising it, such as that at Maryport, Cumberland, were established. In the case of Maryport, not only was a coke furnace erected, the largest in the world at the time, along with attendant innovative plant, such as pre-beehive-design coke ovens, but local coal production was stimulated and a new town and port developed (Miller forthcoming). The reasons behind this change have been hotly debated around the roles of technology or economics as motive forces, and the relative importance of the producer technologies of the furnace versus the consumer technologies of the forge (Ince 1991). At a technical level, the crucial innovation was the ability to convert coke pig to commercially viable wrought iron. The historical evidence indicates that Abraham Darby massively increased his production capacity in the early 1750s, the local forges started small-scale consumption and this was followed by a rapid and large-scale conversion of the forge sector to coke pig. This surely points to a producer-led initiative, and to a breakthrough in production technology by Darby that rendered his coke pig suitable for finery use. Clearly the documented events, often revealed by the chance, site-specific survival of evidence (Cranstone 1997, 24), are the tip of a far larger iceberg of development in both forge and furnace, and in working practice as well as in fixed plant. Much of this was not documented for reasons of commercial secrecy, and much may have depended on the experimentation and craft skills of non-literate furnace keepers and finers, whose voice can only come from archaeology. Analogy can be made with late nineteenth-century developments in the glass industry, where technological innovations were deliberately not recorded by families like Pilkingtons, in order to avoid industrial espionage (Heawood forthcoming b).

For the iron industry, the later eighteenth and early nineteenth centuries saw a period of rapid change in technology, organisation and scale of production. The availability of iron in unprecedented quantities and unprecedentedly low prices had widening implications for industrialisation and for society as a whole, as did the demands placed by the technology and organisation on the whole culture of the ironmaking districts. The adoption of coke smelting allowed, and indeed required, increases in the size of the blast-furnace, and removed dependence on limited and hard-to-transport supplies of charcoal. The use of blowing cylinders, which progressively replaced bellows from the 1750s (Ince 1989), allowed higher blowing rates and thus higher production, and the use of steam engines allowed further increases in blowing power. This eliminated dependence on water and on suitable locations for water power while, of course, increasing dependence on cheap supplies of coal. These changes were in themselves dependent on the earlier development of the coke-pig foundry sector. The result was a vast increase in production, and a massive concentration of the industry on to the coalfields. The average size of the individual works also increased, the new technology allowing the installation of banks of furnaces rather than the single furnace that had normally been dictated by the limitations of charcoal and water supply. For the same reasons, massive integrated works could now incorporate multiple furnaces, large foundries and multi-furnace forges on a single site. However, single-furnace works continued to be built, mainly by landowners or entry-level ironmasters. The charcoal-fuelled industry declined from around 1750 onwards. It had become virtually a niche speciality by 1800, producing high-quality pig for special purposes, and surviving where this niche was facilitated by the presence of haematite ores, as in Dean and Furness, or where a specific demand for charcoal iron existed, notably in south Wales for supplying the tinplate industry (Riden 1994).

Coke furnaces from this period have received a certain amount of archaeological attention, including both excavation and recording of standing structures, accompanied by varying levels of archaeometallurgical work. Excavations at Rockley, Yorkshire, revealed evidence for adaptations

Moira blast-furnace, Leicestershire. The blind arches on the furnace itself (to the left) form an unusual example of architectural design, on a structure type normally rigidly functional. The bridgehouse (centre) encases a three-arched internal bridge over workers' housing – an early example of houses 'underneath the arches'. (© D. Cranstone)

to coke-smelting in the late eighteenth century (Crossley 1995). The important Bersham works in north Wales was founded in 1717, but most of the structural and excavated evidence relates to its later eighteenth-century phases (Grenter 1992). Other investigated sites include, in south Wales, the Cefn Cribwr ironworks (Riden 1992), the Clydach ironworks, Monmouthshire (Wilson 1988), and the Moira furnace, Leicestershire (Cranstone 1985). All these sites are conserved and displayed, as is the much larger Blaenavon works; given the range and importance of technological developments during the period, however, they do not form anything like a comprehensive research base.

The Later Eighteenth- and Nineteenth-century Iron Industry

The forging sector of the iron industry went through, if anything, more fundamental changes in technology in the later eighteenth century than did the smelting sector, but no such corpus of excavated sites exists. In 1750, the finery forge was still the means of converting cast to wrought iron, and it remained a slow and labour-intensive batch process, relying on charcoal fuel and water-powered bellows. Blowing cylinders were only beginning to come into use; they are first documented as being installed at Backbarrow, Lancashire-over-Sands, in 1737, and were probably invented here by Isaac Wilkinson, who was then the 'potfounder' to Backbarrow Furnace (Cranstone 1991, 88). They were also used in the forge at Crowley's Swalwell works by the early 1740s. The traditional finery process must also have been adapted to some degree to cope with the different impurities and characteristics of coke pig, at the few forges that were already using it, but this important development is poorly documented.

With the take-off of coke smelting and the increase in pig production, the finery process became an acute bottleneck in the supply of iron. The 1750s to 1780s were, not surprisingly, marked by a floruit of innovation, and a great variety of processes (Mott 1983, 1–15). The new processes shared a reliance on coal fuel, and most therefore made use of the reverberatory furnace to separate the fuel from the iron and thereby avert contamination of the metal with sulphur. The archaeology of this period of experimentation has not been investigated, perhaps in part because the forge lacks the monumental character of the furnace, and is therefore less amenable to conservation and display. The best-known process was that of stamping and potting, which by the 1780s appears to have been steadily displacing fining as the main route to wrought iron. This period of variety and experimentation was terminated in the 1780s by the development of the puddling process (Mott 1983). Puddling was developed by Cort in Hampshire, but perfected by the Darbys in Shropshire and by Crawshay at Cyfarthfa in Glamorgan. For Crawshay and some other ironmasters the motivation was not wholly economic, puddling being seen as a means of de-skilling the workforce, and therefore breaking the considerable power of the finers (Evans 1993, 94–100). In this latter aim, however, it was not successful; like fining, puddling was a batch process, relatively slow and labour-intensive compared to the massive increases in production and productivity at the furnace, and dependent on a combination of great physical strength under arduous conditions with considerable craft skill. Puddlers soon attained, and used, a similar level of employee power to that formerly enjoyed by the finers.

The steel industry also displayed one major innovation in the mid-eighteenth century: the development of the crucible process (Barraclough 1984b). This was an extension from, rather than a replacement for, the cementation process, relying on blister steel as its raw material. It was a small-scale batch process involving a high level of craft skill, and heightened the distinction, in price, quality and production methods, between 'iron' (especially cast iron) and steel; iron was a bulk product whose sales depended primarily on price, whereas steel was a specialist product whose sales depended primarily on quality. Crucible steelmaking remained very strongly centred on Sheffield, where it was developed.

By the end of the eighteenth century both the iron and steel industries had been through a period of technological and organisational ferment, and had developed a new 'package' of technology. The further development of the industry through the first half of the nineteenth century was one of scale, organisation and incremental evolution of technology, rather than of fundamental innovation. Even so, the hot blast was introduced to the blast-furnace; as well as increasing productivity, this allowed a wider range of ores and coals to be used. The greatest implication was in Scotland, where the 'blackband' ores could be used for the first time, producing a massive expansion in the Scottish iron industry. Other developments in the blast-furnace were of size, construction – the increasing use of iron cladding rather than solid masonry construction – and refractory lining materials. The same applied to the forge, now totally dominated by the puddling process. Again, there was a shift from solid earthfast masonry construction to open-sided and increasingly iron-framed construction. These forms of construction were more flexible and, if not maintained, less permanent. Consequently, the iron industry, unlike textiles, did not establish monumental temples to industry. Thus the nineteenth-century industry has not left the legacy of conservable monuments associated with its sixteenth- to eighteenth-century predecessors. The relative lack of upstanding remains, and the increased survival of documentation, has combined to make the nineteenth-century industry seem less likely to produce worthy information via excavation.

From the 1850s the major development was that of Bessemer steelmaking, producing mild steel, a low-carbon alloy with very different physical properties from both wrought iron, on the one hand, and traditional carbon steel, on the other. In practice, it progressively replaced wrought iron while having little effect on the market for traditional steel; this went through its own evolution with the development of alloy steels (Barraclough 1984b, 124–53). The development of Bessemer steel is well documented historically (Barraclough 1984b, 113–23; Bodsworth 1998). Bessemer proceeded by a process of experimentation in Hertfordshire and London, commercial development nearly failed owing to the inability of the original Bessemer process to produce usable steel from phosphoric ores, and the massive take-off of the process depended on the development of refractory linings able to react with the phosphorus. While the plant of the Bessemer, and later, works was largely prefabricated and scrappable, archaeological evidence for the experimental stages, in the form of process residues as well as earthfast structural remains and their refractory linings, could be of great importance in the study of innovation.

The archaeology of the end product as opposed to the raw material aspect of the iron industry, encompassing both the engineering industry and the local smithy, has received little archaeological study. Some recent work has been undertaken on nineteenth-century urban foundries, as at St Helens, Lancashire (Hedley and Scott 1999). These enterprises are often poorly documented in relation to process and product, and seldom survive as upstanding structures. Even more poorly documented is the urban workshop. These may be encountered as part of the wider urban fabric discovered by chance within a rescue excavation context. An example of what can be revealed, from both the late and the small-scale ends of the spectrum, is the recent excavation of late nineteenth-century back-yard forges in Chester, an element of the iron industry virtually undocumented even at this period (Matthews 1999, 164–6).

NON-FERROUS METALS

There are a number of contrasts between the studies of the iron industry and those of non-ferrous metals. Studies of the latter have traditionally focused on mining; smelting has received less attention, and iron mining has been virtually ignored in the archaeological literature. This bias both obscures and reflects genuine differences in scale, on the one hand between the blast-furnace and the ore hearth or reverberatory smelter, and on the other between the bulk, shallow and easily won seams of most iron ores and the unpredictable, hard-rock-based and often deeply buried nature of most non-ferrous vein orebodies. It also reflects the destruction, in terms of visible landscape features, of much iron mining by later urbanisation and/or coal mining. In contrast, much non-ferrous metal mining was undertaken in areas that remained marginal and underdeveloped.

The main non-ferrous metals exploited in Britain have been lead, copper and tin; all three are found as ores, needing mining and ore-processing before smelting into metal. All occur in geographically specific and discrete orefields, mainly in the remoter upland regions. The lead orefields are mainly in the Pennines, the Peak District and several areas of mid- and north Wales, with smaller orefields in the Mendips, Shropshire and the Wanlockhead area of southern Scotland. Copper ores occur primarily in Devon and Cornwall, with important outlying deposits in Anglesey; Snowdonia and the Lake District form complex copper and lead orefields. There are other isolated orebodies in a rather wide range of geographical and geological situations across Scotland and northern and western England. Tin ores are wholly confined to south-west England, in a number of more-or-less discrete orefields on and around the granite massifs of this region. A number of other metals have been mined, of which arsenic (associated with copper and tin ores in south-west England, and to a lesser extent in Wales and the Lake District) and zinc (associated with lead in most of the lead orefields) were the most important.

The Technologies

At the start of our period the main extraction method for tin ore (cassiterite) was probably streaming. Unlike copper and lead ores, tin ore is both very heavy and also resistant to chemical and physical weathering, and is therefore naturally concentrated in secondary alluvial (river valley) and eluvial (hillwash) deposits. The various tin streaming processes used a combination of controlled steady flows of water (from leats) and manual labour to remove overburden and wash the ore, with drastic effects on the environments of the upland valleys and of the river valleys and estuaries into which the effluent ultimately passed. The massive areas of extractive landscape, often in association with contemporary settlement and agriculture, remain a major element in the landscape of Dartmoor, Bodmin Moor and the other granite uplands of the south-west (Austin *et al.* 1989; Gerrard 1987; 1996; 1997; 2000). Tin streaming continued until the twentieth century, though its economic importance progressively declined; its later technology has received little study, although it may be an important source for American alluvial mining methods.

A semi-comparable process for lead ore was hushing, the fundamental difference being that hushing used intermittent torrents of water on steep slopes, normally directed by artificial channels. Hushing appears to have used for prospecting, for exposing and mining of veins, and for washing wastes from mining and ore processing; it remains very under-studied in view of its landscape importance (Cranstone 1992b). Hushing was very typical of the Pennine orefields, though not of the Peak District, and is found in some Welsh mining areas, notably Cwmystwyth (Bick 1993, Part 6, 22–7). It is ostensibly absent in south-west England, though some 'beamworks' – sixteenth- to seventeenth-century opencuts for tin – on Dartmoor were served by water systems and may result from a fairly similar extractive process (Gerrard 2000). Chronologically, the peak of Pennine hushing seems to have been in the seventeenth and eighteenth centuries, though the technique has Roman antecedents and remained in use until the 1840s at least. The geographical and chronological distribution of hushing requires systematic study, with regard to tenurial and social factors and technological transfer (and its absence), as well as geological and hydrological controls.

Conventional mining for the three metals shows little variation between the metals being mined; the ores of all three occur predominantly as sub-vertical fissure fillings known as 'veins' in the Pennines, 'rakes' in Derbyshire and 'lodes' in the south-west. The technology and history are in general well published (Burt 1984; Kiernan 1989; Bick 1993). The overall development of mining technology may be summarised very briefly, in process-flow and chronological sequence. The simplest, though not necessarily the earliest, exploitation of an outcropping vein was by opencuts, and/or by closely spaced shafts, spoil being dumped to the side. Deeper orebodies were accessed either by shafts, sometimes angled to follow the 'hade' of the vein, or by horizontal tunnels known as adits or levels. The orebody was then 'stoped': slit out, working upwards or more rarely downwards from a level. In the sixteenth century rock was broken by pickwork, sometimes aided by firesetting; gunpowder-blasting, using holes drilled by a large chisel driven in by sledge-hammering, was introduced in the seventeenth century, but did not become widespread for another century.

Adit mines were self-draining to adit level, though the cost and time taken in driving a long adit, particularly before gunpowder-blasting, did not always make this a cheap or low-investment option. Shaft mines could be drained by hauling water in barrels up the shaft. Adit mines also allowed haulage, by carried basket, barrow or wooden railway; early shaft mines relied on manual haulage up the shafts, but otherwise winding was required. Mechanisation developed in some Crown mines, such as Bere Ferrers in Devon, by the late fifteenth century, using water-power, pumps and sophisticated surface leats (Claughton 1994), but otherwise the use of horse- and water-power, for both pumping and winding, did not become common until the seventeenth or even eighteenth century. The Newcomen pumping engine was rapidly adopted in the Cornish mines, but its impact was limited by very high fuel costs, so steam power did not take off until the development of the far more efficient Cornish engine at the end of the eighteenth century. The mosaic of regional mining traditions then coalesced into two main strands: a 'Cornish' style of mining characterised by shaft mines and steam-powered pumping and winding (Sharpe *et al.* 1991), and a 'Pennine' style characterised by long adits and water-power. Derbyshire followed a slightly different path, influenced both by geology, a hard-rock plateau with little surface water, and by tenurial factors – strong and persistent mining laws favoured the small partnership of working miners over the large company with the resources for long-term investment. Here, small shaft-mines persisted, often drained by long levels ('soughs') driven by specialist partnerships solely for the drainage of multiple small separate shaft mines. Compressed-air drilling and dynamite drilling were introduced from the 1860s onwards, but their widespread adoption was truncated, except in Cornwall, by the collapse of the industries.

The water-powered stamping mill was introduced for tin processing in the Middle Ages (Gerrard 1989), but remained rare in the lead industry. This reflected the higher value and more finely disseminated nature of tin ores, which had to be stamped to sand-size for efficient separation, whereas lead ores were generally in larger crystals, more efficiently concentrated at gravel-size by the jigger, and therefore normally crushed by hand until the development of the mechanised roller crusher in the 1790s. Mechanisation was generally introduced for ore preparation in the nineteenth century. It was overwhelmingly steam-powered in the Cornish tin industry, and predominantly water-powered in the Pennine lead industry, other regions using both power sources to varying degrees. In practice, both the equipment and the process-flow was more complex than this summary indicates, especially in the tin industry, which developed much more complex ore-processing technology in the late nineteenth century, while the lead and copper industries had their development curtailed through the collapse of the markets. Copper ore processing is much less well documented than lead or tin, both historically and archaeologically. It is often assumed to have been simpler, because of the low grade to which copper ore was dressed, but the field evidence at Coniston in the Lake District indicates that this was not always the case, and archaeological study is much needed.

Smelting shows greater variation between the metals, though unified by a general progression from water-powered and wood- or charcoal-fuelled smelting mills to coal-fuelled draught-blown reverberatory furnaces; as well as the change of fuel, this also represents a change from batch to continuous process. For tin, the water-powered blowing mill was already in use by the 1550s, though it later developed from a low hearth-like form into a taller shaft furnace. The reverberatory smelting mill was developed in the late seventeenth century, progressively replacing the blowing mill in the eighteenth century. However, a form of reverberatory wood- or furze-fuelled furnace was already in use by 1671 for calcining the ore to drive off arsenic; these furnaces remained in use, becoming mechanised in the nineteenth century, when they were also used for producing arsenic. They normally formed part of the process-flow of the ore-dressing floor rather than of the smelter. For lead, the wind-blown bole hill was dominant in 1550, being replaced by the ore hearth in the later sixteenth century. The reverberatory furnace was successfully developed around 1700, but never totally replaced the ore hearth, the relative economics depending on the local costs of good-quality coal versus wood and peat, the scale of operations and the availability of water-power sites. The resmelting of slags remained a blown process, normally by water power, though the steam engine was also used. The developing smelting technology allowed progressively finer-sized and lower-grade feedstock to be used, facilitating the development of the jigger in the sixteenth century and various types of buddle in the eighteenth and nineteenth centuries, and allowing the large-scale reprocessing of old dressing wastes and slags. Silver, a trace constituent of all British lead ores, was extracted from the smelted lead by cupellation, whereby the lead was oxidised to litharge in a reverberatory furnace, leaving the molten silver behind. More sophisticated processes, relying on the fractionation of silver content between molten and crystallising lead, and between molten lead and zinc, were developed in the mid- and late nineteenth century.

Copper smelting was normally a much more complex process, involving multiple roasting and smelting operations. In the sixteenth century the processes used by the German-dominated Mines Royal were water-powered (R. Smith 1994). Again, coal-fuelled reverberatory smelting was developed around 1700. Although initially strong in the Bristol area, the British industry became almost exclusively centred on the south Wales coalfield, owing to its very large consumption of fuel relative to ore, coupled with the economics of a two-way shipping of coal to the steam-powered mines of Cornwall and Devon, and ore to Wales on the return trip. The mines of Anglesey and the Lake District also had good sea links to south Wales, although they did not depend on Welsh coal. Contrary to the impression given in the historical record, a few small water-powered copper smeltmills survived in northern England. Their scale suggests that they are unlikely to have used the complex processes employed in south Wales, and their technology and its origins are poorly understood and in need of research.

The archaeology of copper mining, ore processing and smelting has received far less attention than that of lead and tin. A particular aspect, of wider importance, concerns the role of the Mines Royal company in the sixteenth century. This operation, set up under a royal monopoly and based in Keswick, is well served by surviving documents, and well studied; it involved a transfusion of German technology into the Cumbrian, and English, metal industries. However, the indigenous background into which this transfusion was made is virtually undocumented, and hence the assessment of the long-term importance, of the degree to which German mining and metallurgy were genuinely far in advance of English, and more broadly (it is generally assumed) of an important example of technological transfer, remains vulnerable to partiality in the documentary record.

A number of other metals have been smelted from British ores, and the field evidence, though rare, may be important for understanding the range and development of British metallurgy as a whole; antimony is an interesting example. Zinc was important for the manufacture of brass. Until the late eighteenth century this was made by cementation from copper metal and roasted calamine, zinc ore. Roasting was another very early development of the reverberatory process. A complex smelting process, using retorts and downward distillation, and perhaps ultimately of Indian origin, was developed by Champion in the eighteenth century, and was replaced by a more economic Belgian process in the nineteenth century, and only then did metallic zinc become widely used as the raw material in brass manufacture (Craddock 1990; Day and Tylecote 1991).

The Landscape

The obvious impacts of the non-ferrous metal industries can be seen in rural upland landscapes, most notably in the engine-house-dominated landscapes of Cornwall and the lead mines and hushes of the Pennines. The only major urban landscape generated primarily by non-ferrous metal manufacture was Swansea and Neath in south Wales, though the Camborne–Redruth area of Cornwall is an important smaller example. The actual impact of the industries was far wider than this, however; until the nineteenth century many miners were also farmers or at least smallholders, and mining and smelting should be regarded as integral parts of the post-medieval archaeology of the orefields, just as much as agriculture or settlement. While metal mining did in general become increasingly dominated by large companies during our period, this domination never became total. The small independent miner or miner/farmer survived into the twentieth century, selling the ore to larger smelting companies; almost domestic-scale mines and dressing floors survive in Cornwall, as well as the huge mechanised floors of the larger tin mines.

Similar arguments can be made for the importance of metals in the urban take-off of Bristol in the late seventeenth and early eighteenth centuries. With the development of reverberatory smelting, Bristol became an attractive location for the smelting of Cornish ores; the presence of zinc ores nearby in the Mendips combined with this to promote an important brass industry (Day and Tylecote 1991, 131–200). The influence of Bristol on the development of the Wye Valley led to the late seventeenth-century growth of a water-powered non-ferrous metals manufacturing-based settlement at Redbrook, south of Monmouth (Newman 1988). Bristol's developing slave trade also provided a ready market for, and was itself stimulated by, copper and brass production, with 'Guinea kettles' a major product. In general, the wealth produced from metal production found expression in urban development and rural stately homes well distanced from the producing areas, but the Bristol area was an exception. A notable example was, and is, the Warmley brass, copper and zinc works, whose water-power pond also functioned as the lake

Tin ore processing works dating to about 1900 at Polgooth, Cornwall. (© D. Cranstone)

Black Castle, Bristol, an industrialist's home built of cast slag blocks from the local copper smelter. (© D. Cranstone)

for the park of William Champion's adjacent stately home; within the park was a grotto encrusted with zinc slag, and in the lake a statue of Neptune girded with zinc slag (see Frontispiece).

Choice and Expression

In general, mines, dressing floors and smeltmills were very functional buildings and landscapes. However, engine houses, especially the later nineteenth-century horizontal examples, developed a distinctive style of round-arched openings and symmetrical gables which was not wholly functional in the sense of being the simplest and cheapest solution to the engineering problem. In south-west England the mine office was normally combined with the manager's house to form an architecturally polite 'counting house'. In contrast, the office at most Pennine lead mines was a simple, purely functional, vernacular building. The peat stores at many Yorkshire ore-hearth smeltmills were, however, designed and often deliberately imposing structures; that at Old Gang, though vernacular in form, was particularly impressive by its enormous length of over 100m. The rarity of formal architectural design, both of individual buildings and of overall site layouts, contrasts with, for example, the majority of textile mills. Although no systematic comparison has been done, it also appears to contrast with many continental mines and smelters, at least within the Francophone areas. An interesting sidelight on this difference, and on the relationship of material to documentary evidence, comes from comparing the illustrations of the Snailbeach and Stiperstones smeltmills at Pontesford, Shropshire, drawn by Moissenet in 1862 with the OS depiction and surviving field evidence; the quite cramped and irregular layouts of reality are portrayed as spacious and neatly rectilinear in the French illustration (Martell and Gill 1992, pls 2–5).

The influence of technology and economics on metal-industry sites was not as deterministic as the literature might suggest; choices were available, and can sometimes be read in the landscape.

For instance, in Gunnerside Gill, Yorkshire Dales, the Sir Francis Level was driven from 1864 onwards by a consortium of two companies (the Old Gang and AD Companies) to drain their separate workings on each side of the Gill, which formed the boundary between their leaseholds. Both companies drew their ore through the Level, but then processed it in separate dressing floors on their respective sides of the stream. The AD company constructed a state-of-the-art rectilinear mechanised dressing mill and floor, served by well-graded tracks. In contrast, the Old Gang Company, contemporarily and using virtually identical ore, constructed a manual dressing floor, only the crusher being mechanised; irregularly built and presumably designed by the mine's carpenters and masons, it was fitted to rather than imposed on the terrain, and was served only by footpaths and packhorse tracks (Cranstone forthcoming).

COAL

The purpose of including this brief section is to highlight the fact that, despite the enormous importance of the British coal industry for the Industrial Revolution, no new synthesis is yet possible to replace the limited coverage previously accorded by archaeologists (Crossley 1990, 204–8). Yet to omit all mention would be to perpetuate the under-study of an industry fundamental both to the Industrial Revolution and to continuing issues in British society; the influence of the past on the present, and of the resultant attitudes on the focus, or rather non-focus, of archaeological interest, is never clearer.

Three individual excavations have, however, greatly expanded our knowledge of the archaeology of the industry. At Coleorton, Leicestershire, extensive fieldwork during opencasting revealed sophisticated mining dating from the fifteenth to the seventeenth century (Hartley 1994). Access was by multiple shafts, though drainage was probably by a sough; underground working was by pillar-and-stall, at depths of up to 30m, with longwall working introduced in the 1620s. Anaerobic conditions allowed close dating by dendrochronology, and the recovery of an important collection of clothing and footwear, as well as miners' tools. At Wallsend, near Newcastle-upon-Tyne, excavations of the 'B' Pit have revealed an important complex of boiler bases and lever walls for Newcomen engines, air shafts, and surface air drifts, representing three main phases of activity between c. 1780 and 1840 (Oram et al. 1998). Also on the Tyneside coalfield, excavations at Lambton D Pit, Washington, concentrated on a very extensive wooden wagonway system, but also revealed the boiler bases for a pithead just beyond the limit of excavation (Ayris et al. 1998).

Current conservation-led field recording at Chatterley Whitfield Colliery, Stoke-on-Trent, shows the wealth of field remains to be expected at a large later nineteenth- to twentieth-century colliery site, together with the importance of fittings in and on the upstanding buildings, and of the above- and below-ground infrastructure of water pipes, steam pipes, cables and drains. While many buildings were purely functional in design, the 'grammar' of the circumstances where architectural politeness was introduced is interesting – in the nineteenth century it was limited to engine houses and the very early electrical power house of 1900–3, whereas in the 1930s it was reintroduced, in very fine Art Deco form, for the pithead baths and offices, and perhaps also for the contemporary access road (Cranstone and Hunwicks 2000).

Important studies have recently been completed of the history of the industry (Church 1986; Flinn 1994; Hatcher 1993) and of aspects of its physical character. An important study of wagonway systems has shown how they influenced the development of the Tyneside coal

The electrical powerhouse of 1900–3 at Chatterley Whitfield colliery, Stoke-on-Trent. This pioneering example of colliery electrification was discovered by fieldwork but ignored by the standard historical works on the subject. (© D. Cranstone)

industry (Bennett *et al.* 1990). A recent survey of the Somerset Coalfield is an important study, an example which should be widely followed (Gould 1999b). The thrust of recent work, however, has been on the twentieth century, under the impetus of rapid closure and site destruction; the two principal general surveys do, however, cover the pre-1900 features of the closing collieries (Gould and Ayris 1995; Thornes 1994).

SALT AND CHEMICALS

Salt and chemicals are two industries which became increasingly linked by the use of salt as a chemical raw material in the nineteenth century. At the start of our period, the two sources of salt were seawater and natural brine springs derived from underlying rock-salt beds, primarily concentrated in Cheshire and the Droitwich area of Worcestershire. Since seawater contains around 3 per cent salt, and saturated brine around 25 per cent, direct concentration of seawater into brine and then crystallisation into salt by boiling involved a more massive consumption of fuel than boiling out the salt from saturated brine. Brine springs were later supplemented, and eventually replaced, first by artificial brine-pits and wells tapping natural underground brine streams, and by mining of rock-salt, and later by controlled pumping of brine generated by artificially passing water through rock-salt beds. All these methods were, and in the latter two cases still are, confined to areas with substantial underlying rock-salt beds. The location of the rock-salt beds later in part influenced the location of aspects of the chemicals industry.

Coastal Salt Industry

In 1550 the coastal salt industry was in decline from a considerable medieval peak, owing to increasing competition from the inland industry and from imported 'Bay' salt, both reflecting improving transport and a move towards the agricultural enclosure of salt-marshes; climatic decline may also have been a factor. Three major technologies were in use to extract salt: solar evaporation, sleeching and direct boiling.

Solar evaporation was used mainly on the English south coast. It involved the concentration of seawater by natural summer evaporation, in large arrays of wide shallow rectangular pits known as 'pans'. These were situated on low ground just behind the coast, often protected by a sea wall. Most works appear to have been 'partial sunworks', where brine was concentrated by evaporation, but fuel was used for crystallisation by boiling; however, some 'total sunworks', where crystallisation was also performed by solar evaporation in earthwork 'pans' without the use of fuel, also existed.

In contrast, sleeching involved scraping-up salt-encrusted sand or silt from coastal flats between neap and spring high tide levels, and leaching out the salt with seawater to form a concentrated brine which was then boiled in 'salt cotes'; boiling was normally in lead pans, and wood, furze or peat fuel could be used, depending on availability. Sleeching had been the dominant medieval method throughout eastern England, and probably in the north-west, but was very much in decline by 1550, though it survived into the eighteenth century around Morecambe Bay and the Solway. All these are areas where the term salt cotes forms a distinctive place-name element. The main site indicator of sleeching, however, is the very extensive low mounds of clean waste silt, still often unrecognised as salt-making features. These form major elements of the Wash and Lincolnshire coastlands, both as flood-free bases for settlement and as a geomorphological factor in marine retreat (Grady 1998).

Direct boiling involved the simple boiling of brine for concentration and crystallisation, using cheap coal fuel; in practice iron rather than lead pans were necessary for the take-off of the process, lead being too easily melted by the heat of a coal fire. The process is generally considered to have been developed on Tyneside in the fifteenth century, but coal fuel was widely used in the Firth of Forth saltworks from the thirteenth century (Lewis et al. 1999, 5). The process may well be of Scottish origin, or have seen a more complex development along the eastern seaboards of both Scotland and England, possibly starting with the use of seacoal as fuel for the sleeching process. Direct boiling sites seem to have favoured rocky coastlines, rather than the flat coastlines preferred for the other processes, perhaps for the benefits of clean silt-free seawater. A site with such a situation and access to coal was Port Eynon in the Gower, south Wales. This appears to have functioned between the late sixteenth and mid-seventeenth centuries. Excavations revealed a stone-lined reservoir on the beach, from which seawater was drawn by a wooden pump for boiling in an unidentified panhouse (Wilkinson et al. 1998, 19).

Coastal saltmaking declined throughout the sixteenth and seventeenth centuries, becoming concentrated on coastal coalfields, notably on Tyneside, where the direct boiling process could use small 'pancoal', effectively a waste product from coal mining, since it had no market in the coal trade for domestic consumption. This in turn collapsed in the eighteenth century, consequent upon a variety of factors, including the continuing increase in competition from the inland saltworks, tax, and the development of the steam engine, which provided a competing use for 'pancoal'. While Scottish (Lewis et al. 1999) and Welsh (Wilkinson et al. 1998) direct boiling sites have been the subject of recent archaeological fieldwork, the English industry is virtually unstudied.

Coastal saltmaking *senso strictu*, however, was partly replaced by the growth of salt refining, whereby impure salt was dissolved in seawater, settled or filtered, and recrystallised to produce a pure white salt. The impure salt was initially imported 'Bay' salt (from solar works in France and Portugal, contaminated with sand and silt), or even occasionally Tyneside direct-boiling salt which was contaminated by dirty seawater and the soot of the coal fires. From the 1670s rock-salt from Cheshire and Ireland was increasingly used. Salt refineries were limited by Act of Parliament in 1732. The process can be seen as the lineal descendant of sleeching, differing in the

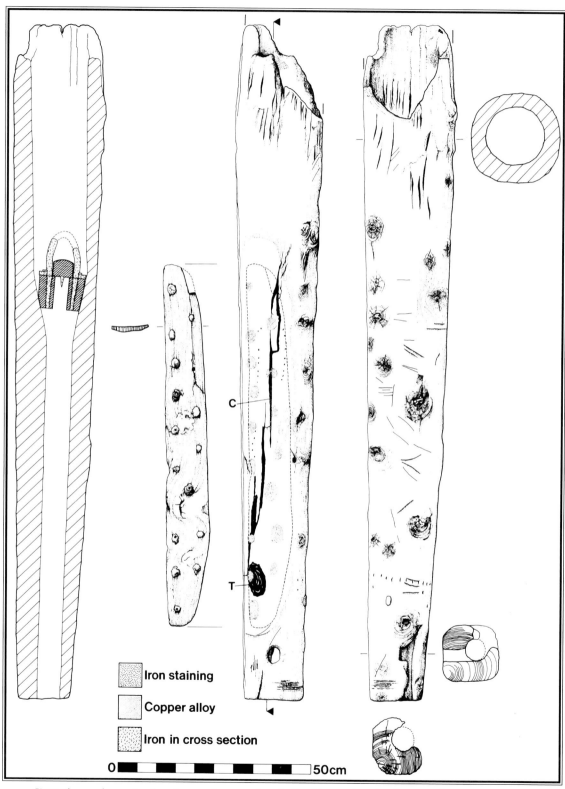

Iron staining

Copper alloy

Iron in cross section

0   50cm

Sixteenth- or early seventeenth-century wooden pump from the Port Eynon salt works, Gower, south Wales. (© Society for Post-Medieval Archaeology)

ratio of salt to impurity and in the use of coal fuel, while the crystallisation process appears to have been similar to that of the direct boiling and inland works. Refineries are not always clearly distinguished from direct boiling saltworks in the literature, which remains overwhelmingly historically orientated. The coastal salt industry largely disappeared after the removal of tariffs on imported salt in 1823 (Wilkinson *et al.* 1998, 18).

Inland Salt Industry

Inland saltmaking was concentrated at the major brine springs of Northwich, Middlewich and Nantwich in Cheshire and Droitwich in Worcestershire. It was controlled by borough monopolies, with complex rights and controls on production. The process is best understood at Droitwich, where the major Upwich brine-pit has been excavated (Hurst 1997). Here a pump was inserted into the brine well in the fifteenth century. Brine was passed into settling and storage tanks, and by the seventeenth century was boiled in pans over brick-built furnace structures.

The inland salt industry was revolutionised in the late seventeenth and eighteenth centuries by three developments. First, the borough monopolies of the old 'wich' towns were broken, allowing a flood of new saltworks to open, using brine springs and pumped artificial wells and shafts, and producing intense price competition. Secondly, rock-salt was discovered in 1670 near Northwich, and mining developed very rapidly. The mines were relatively simple, consisting of shafts giving access to pillar-and-stall workings, with winding normally by horse whim. Steam engines were used from the later eighteenth century, both for winding in the mines and for brine pumping. Thirdly, transport logistics and costs were revolutionised by canals to and through the saltfields, the Weaver Navigation of 1734 being the first. As well as the export of white salt, the canals facilitated the import of coal for the boiling process, and the export of rock-salt for refining.

There were few fundamental developments of technology during the nineteenth century; the coal-fuelled iron open-pan works remained almost universal, though a few attempts were made to use waste heat from other industries to heat salt pans. Transport improved further through the railways, and by the end of the century brine was being carried from Cheshire to the Mersey by pipeline, as feedstock for the burgeoning chemical industry. New saltfields were opened up, notably on Teesside, worked mainly by brine pumping from artificial wells and shafts.

The basic salt-making 'package', consisting of the boiling of brine in large coal-fuelled iron open pans, was therefore in place by the seventeenth century, and survived until the twentieth century. At the technological level the growth of the industry flowed from developments in the extraction of its raw material, and in transport technology. The industry also showed a strong centralisation on to the inland saltfields, where the salt towns were almost wholly dependent on it, contrasting markedly with the medieval industry where the salt towns were balanced by widespread coastal works. By the nineteenth century the industry was also notable for its environmental effects, owing to uncontrolled subsidence provoked by brine pumping and the flooding of old salt mines, themselves often pumped for brine. As well as the rural landscape, the salt towns themselves, and even the saltworks, were devastated by subsidence. Responses included the flimsy and expected short-life construction of many saltworks, with the surviving Lion Saltworks near Northwich being a prime example. In Northwich the threat of subsidence led to a reversion to timber-frame housing construction.

Given the symbolic importance of salt in the English language, it is surprising that the material expression of salt-making appears on present evidence to have been extremely functional throughout the period, with no obvious evidence of architectural elaboration, display or symbolism. However, the industry was highly price-competitive and with its simple old technology required little investment, so both the incentive and the resources to stimulate deviation from the functional may have been lacking.

Chemicals

In contrast to salt, with its long history and conservative technology, the chemical industries were late and innovative developers within the industrialisation of Britain. Yet they have received remarkably little attention from archaeologists. The earliest chemical industries, in the sense of specific sites and processes devoted to the manufacture of what we would now recognise as specific chemical products, were alum and copperas. Both developed in the late sixteenth century, their products being used as mordants and dyes in textile production. There are similarities in the processes and products; both are metal sulphates, and they may be conflated with each other in some sixteenth-century references. Alum production involved the quarrying of a pyrites-rich shale followed by slow calcining and leaching (Gould 1993; Marshall 1995). The resultant liquor was run by culverts into an 'alum house', where it was heated, cleared by precipitating out impurities, and concentrated by boiling in iron pans. Potash- or ammonia-rich liquors were then added, and after further precipitation and concentration the liquor was cooled, allowing the alum to crystallise. This complex industrial chemical process had been developed by the early seventeenth century, and remained in use until the mid-nineteenth century, when it was replaced by a far quicker process using hot sulphuric acid, and then incorporated into the broader

The alum house at Peak alum works, Ravenscar, Yorkshire. This eighteenth-century chemical works has been fully excavated and is preserved by the National Trust. (© D. Cranstone)

chemical industry. The industry centred almost exclusively on the North York Moors, where the shale quarries form a massive intervention in the landscape.

Copperas (hydrated iron sulphate) was produced by atmospheric oxidation of pyrites, in the form of nodules, followed or accompanied by prolonged leaching, boiling in pans, cooling and crystallisation. The process therefore had similarities to alum manufacture, and both in turn had some similarity to the direct boiling method of salt-making. Copperas-making occurred in various coastal areas of southern England, using pyrites nodules weathered-out from the cliffs, and in the northern coalfields, using pyritous Coal Measures shale and coal fuel. A coastal works at Whitstable (Kent) has recently been excavated (Allen 1999).

A broader inorganic chemical industry did not start to develop on any scale until the eighteenth century, with the manufacture of sulphuric acid, initially from copperas. This in turn allowed the take-off of alkali manufacture, used mainly for soap- and glass-making. The introduction of the LeBlanc process for alkali manufacture just after 1800 led to the production of cheap hydrochloric acid as a by-product. This in turn stimulated the mass production of chlorine-based bleaches for the textile industry, the acid reacting with salt (Cranstone and Rimmington 2000). The availability of coal and salt led to the development of chemical industries in north Cheshire, south Lancashire and Flintshire in the early nineteenth century. The proximity of the major cloth manufacturing areas stimulated the establishment of bleachworks along the rivers of the region. Bulk production of cheap acids also made possible the development of the chemical fertiliser industry in the mid-nineteenth century, with its implications for agriculture and the ability to feed the exploding urban industrial population.

Aside from alcoholic spirit production, the first organic chemical industry developed in the late eighteenth century, with the rise of tar and resin production by carbonisation and distillation of wood. This was rapidly eclipsed by the use of coal-tar, produced by coking of coal, initially as a by-product from gas production and coking for the iron industry. The first works was set up at Culross, Fife, in 1782. Distillation of coal-tar into a range of organic chemicals took off around 1850; these chemicals themselves formed starting points for the synthetic dyes, high explosives (Cocroft 2000) and pharmaceuticals industries. The rubber industry also developed in the nineteenth century, and production of synthetic textiles and plastics had begun by the end of the century, though their major impact was a twentieth-century phenomenon.

With the partial exception of alum, the chemical industries have received remarkably little archaeological attention, although they formed crucial building-blocks in the integrated industrial economy of the nineteenth century, particularly in relation to textiles manufacture and as a stimulus to coal production. Archaeological study of structural remains, stratigraphy, artefacts and process residues has the potential to produce major advances in our understanding of technological development, its relationship to developing scientific understanding, and the relationship of both to the normally undocumented processes of on-the-ground adaptation and developing materials and practice.

CONCLUSION

The above case studies illustrate part of the range of industries developing within post-medieval Britain, and of the present reality and future potential for their study within a broader context. A number of general issues are also illustrated. The first of these, as in all historical archaeology, is the role of material evidence and the dialogue between the material and documentary records.

Here the role of archaeology in recovering what was done on the ground, as opposed to what was said or planned, can be emphasised. In particular, while the historical record by its nature tends to emphasise the role of the invention and of the capitalist investor, the archaeology of industry can tell us much about the less glamorous processes of making the invention work. It can highlight practical modifications, structural adaptations and process residues that can reveal so much about actual performance and efficiency of the process, and of the dialogue between idea and practicality.

Secondly, compared to the topics discussed in other chapters, the archaeology of industry shows a surprisingly homogenous British picture, with little that is distinctively English, Scottish or Welsh. A note of caution is needed: the study of 'industrial archaeology' has been very much conservation- rather than academic-based, and hence strongly divided between the national agencies of the three components of 'Britain', rendering it hard to separate genuine differences and similarities in the archaeology from those in the research culture. Even so, it genuinely may be that industrialisation, developing largely after the Union of the Crowns, has been a major force for 'Britishness', and that this shows through in a relatively homogenous archaeology of industry. Ideas were circulated throughout Britain, as were familial interests, alliances and investments, and thus a uniformly British material culture of industrialisation may have been inevitable.

Related to this, the development of industry was a major cause of, as well as providing the practical mechanisms for, diffusion of ideas and movement of population, and thus was a force for the breakdown of local folk culture at every level, and the development of uniform national and eventually international culture, both material and social. This may prove a fruitful field of research, especially perhaps where artefact studies in association with documentary evidence can allow the material culture of industrial workers, sometimes of known non-local geographical origin, to be compared with contemporary and adjacent agricultural communities of more local origins.

Finally, the very existence of the industrial sites discussed in this chapter reflects the progressive separation of production from consumption through the post-medieval period. In monument terms these sites form a specific and distinct aspect of material culture. This is reflected in the traditional distinction between industrial and post-medieval archaeology, and in present society the political tensions in the Britain of the new millennium can be viewed in part as a continuing growth in the alienation between producer and consumer.

CHAPTER SIX

ARTEFACTS

CHRISTINE HOWARD-DAVIS

The years 1540–1900 witnessed great change and expansion in the material culture originating in the later medieval period (Crossley 1990, 1). Prolonged civil and economic turbulence had led to an increasingly fluid society, within which the traditional parameters that defined social status at all levels were challenged and realigned (Hinton 1990, 210). This phenomenon was illustrated in part by an increased reliance on the physical expression of social status through material goods and conspicuous display, as families that lacked the innate and implicit status of tradition sought to consolidate their upward path through society. Such was the desire for 'legitimisation' that, alongside large sums spent on building and the acquisition of goods, some turned to forgery and invention to add the solidity of an honourable past to their achievements. Not least among these was Henry VII, who 'constructed the programme of Tudor genealogy' (String 1996, 142) in order to further legitimate his claim to a throne won by the sword. At a more modest level, the head of the Andrewes family of Warwickshire, described in 1476 as a grazier or husbandman, applied for a grant of arms in the same year and, in support, blatantly manufactured a genealogy stretching back to the twelfth century (Alcock and Woodfield 1996, 66). Thus it was within an intensely competitive social context that the demand, and consequently the market, for an increasingly diverse and innovative range of goods was born and thrived. This challenged traditional technologies and established producers, ultimately forcing both technological and social change (Johnson 1996).

Early post-medieval socio-economic development can, at least in part, be characterised by an increased interest in, and proliferation of, material culture at all levels in society, except perhaps for the very poorest, where broadened expectation was not necessarily matched by any increased ability to purchase. This was a period when the number and range of artefact types, and the variation within them, increased dramatically. There was a marked increase in choice, variation of colour and form, even with artefacts used at a relatively low social scale. This change, however, was rapidly distorted by industrial-scale production – in part a response to increased demand – which fossilised the range of artefact forms through mechanical standardisation, guaranteeing a long-term repetition of form. Variety was only represented by value addition (more highly skilled craftsmanship) or value reduction (for example pottery seconds). Even so, mechanisation allowed for a far greater range of standard forms than hitherto, and through hand painting or finishing opportunities for individualisation remained.

The increased range of artefact types in the eighteenth and nineteenth centuries was phenomenal, as can be illustrated by any one of a number of trade catalogues that have survived, for instance that of Silber and Flemming *c.* 1883, which catalogues over five thousand contemporary items (Silber and Flemming 1991). Even the poorest social classes had increased expectations of a wider range of personal possessions, a desire reflected in the archaeological record on any long-lived settlement site. The remotest of all British islands, St Kilda, has yielded evidence to demonstrate that by the early nineteenth century even it had been absorbed into the world market 'in consumer goods' (N. Emery 2000, 162). For these reasons it is impossible to discuss the full range of post-medieval artefacts within the scope of this chapter. Instead the ensuing discussion will focus on the uses and meanings of artefacts as a material culture indicator within the study of later historical archaeology. Artefacts characterise the environment in which, and by which, individuals and groups with a common identity or purpose defined themselves. At St Kilda, for example, they also demonstrate the partial triumph of an industrialised, uniform British culture over local identity, which led to the eventual abandonment of the community (N. Emery 2000, 164).

POST-MEDIEVAL ARTEFACT STUDIES

In recent years the study of post-medieval artefacts has undergone a major change of perception with regard to its aims and goals. There is a move away from the listing, describing and dating of artefacts – though not an abandonment, for this process is invaluable in providing a repeatable baseline for interpretation. Recent work, much of it emerging from American schools of thought and investigation, has demonstrated that all archaeological remains, and most obviously artefacts, can be read at a number of levels (Orser 1996, 107–23; Johnson 1999b, 18). It has become legitimate to assume that not only do finds add to a description of the archaeological site from which they derive, but they have more widely applicable meanings (Gowlett 1997, 152). They can provide a fuller, if speculative, view of the life and aspirations of their producers, owners and users (Yensch 1993, 24).

Emphasis must be placed on artefacts such as ceramics, glass and metalwork, as it is these that survive with most frequency and in most quantity in the archaeological record, allowing conclusions to be drawn from a sample likely to be statistically valid. Some consideration of organic materials cannot be avoided, however, for even today they often comprise the most important and necessary everyday items, and in the form of clothing represent one of the most obvious and widely understood expressions of status and rank (Fair 1998, 63). Any artefact recovered from an archaeological context can be used for purposes of interpretation. At the most basic level, the mere presence of a man-made object provides evidence of human activity in the vicinity. Closely allied is consideration of the agencies and actors that might have brought the artefact to the site, whether human or natural, and whether directly involved with the production, function and purpose of the artefact, or incidental to it.

The most frequently required information from an artefact is an indication of date and its implication for the site or context of deposition. The forms of almost all objects have changed through time, although some change faster, some slower, and some so slowly that the process appears almost imperceptible. When that process can be reliably charted by the definition of a typological sequence, then almost any artefact can be used to provide a relative chronological baseline closely related to the stratigraphic succession of any archaeological site, and sometimes for a wider network of sites with common cultural origins. Unfortunately, typological studies have become something of a two-edged sword, tempting researchers to force artefacts into the 'strait-jacket' of strict chronological succession (Cumberpatch 1996, 58) in order to provide more refined dating. However, when such changes are reviewed in a broader approach they can be seen as illuminating physical, social and economic change in response to an evolving cultural context (Yensch 1993, 35). Because it is generally so durable and, certainly in the post-medieval period, subject to regular, if small, changes in design and decoration, pottery is frequently relied upon for dating, providing 'ceramic milestones' (Noël Hume 1968) for almost any archaeological site. More recently, however, this reliance has been called into question (Cumberpatch 1996, 55) as it is increasingly recognised that the dates furnished by pottery can be very fluid, especially in the medieval and early post-medieval periods, when they are only attributable to the nearest century or so. Sometimes an artefact or changing sequence of artefacts can be allocated to a particular date, for example a coin bearing a calendar date or a regnal year. Similarly, commemorative pottery vessels made to order to mark significant events such as marriages, births and elections were often inscribed and dated (Draper 1984, 21). It is possible to begin to tie such finds from a specific archaeological site to an absolute chronological sequence. It must be remembered, however, that such objects only provide a *terminus post quem* for the deposits from which they were recovered. Account must be taken of the 'heirloom factor' whereby groups or individuals might deliberately retain or acquire old or antique goods for their own purposes, a practice well known during the post-medieval period. In Britain the basic western European domestic toolkit has changed only slowly over the last two thousand years, and our own version really differs little in composition from that of the Romans.

The interpretation of the function of artefacts is coloured by the interpreter's motives (Li Bing-wu nd, 14). The resultant meaning attributed to an artefact may differ greatly from those attributed by the artefact's maker and user (Neustupný 1993, 84–96). Alongside this we must consider the cultural baggage which encumbers almost every object with which we share our own lives – effectively the meaning of an object both to an individual and to the cultural context within which it is created, acquired or used. Such meanings can be relatively simple and explicit; who in western European society would fail to apprehend the message of a skull and cross-bones on a power cable or on the outside of a bottle of poison? When, however, it is encountered carved upon a gravestone, its message is somewhat different; it is not warning of potential danger, but commenting upon the mortality of mankind as a reminder that death is ever present in life (Deetz 1977).

The messages conveyed by artefacts, however, can be rather more subtle or implicit as, for instance, with items such as sugar tongs or cigarette holders. Who, dropping a sugar lump into a cup of tea, considers its close association with the slave trade? Yet artefacts associated with the use of both sugar and tobacco, among other commodities, have their origins in a complex web of social and economic history originating with the discovery and exploitation of the New World. In various ways they reflect both the voluntary and enforced mass-movement of population and ideas that balanced trade and social interchange between the Old World and the New (Johnson 1996, 184). In addition, sugar tongs contain information concerning the interplay of status and social aspiration embodied in their use. Moreover, the tongs are associated with a range of artefacts required to produce, transport and modify sugar, as well as the equipment necessary to produce the tongs themselves. There is, then, a staggering quantity and depth of potential information represented in a single artefact.

Production

Perhaps the data easiest to win from the study of any particular artefact are those which detail the technology of its production (Gordon 1993, 74). A ceramic vessel, for instance, can be produced in a number of ways: by hand, thrown on a wheel driven by manpower or mechanical means, moulded, turned from a block, or cast (Hodges 1976, 19–42; Rice 1989, 113–66). The manner in which vessels are produced can also form a relatively direct chronological and technological progression, although in twentieth-century Britain the re-emergence of 'craft' pottery has revived the hand-thrown pottery industry with significant public interest in the individuality and 'character' of hand-thrown vessels.

In the most general terms, pottery production in the later medieval and early post-medieval periods was confined to wheel-thrown and cast vessels. The former can only be made in a relatively restricted range of simple, flat or rounded hollow forms, and decoration must be applied, usually in the form of coloured paints and glazes, or as plastic additions. In contrast, vessels formed by casting a thin slurry of clay into a mould can be produced in any shape required, and the body of vessels can be textured as well as receiving applied decoration. Wheel-thrown vessels are individual, each subtly different, even when the basic form and function is intended to be the same, while cast forms can be identical repeats. This technological progression can be seen in the changes in ceramic vessels between the relatively restricted range of hand-made forms of the later medieval period and the extravagance of the later eighteenth-century producers. This started slowly, often via expensive and fashionable imported vessels, in the late fifteenth and sixteenth centuries (Gaimster and Nenk, 1997, 174–6), leading to the proliferation in applied decoration seen in the later seventeenth- and early eighteenth-century home-produced wares, when colourful and highly ornate slip-trailed wares (both hand-made and moulded) became popular; the later eighteenth century witnessed the move to complex textures and a wide range of moulded and cast forms, and ceramic tablewares reached almost unrivalled heights of complexity and expense. Such extravagance is best seen in the novel fabrics and painted and enamelled porcelains of the Midlands producers such as Wedgwood, Royal Doulton and Spode.

Microscopic examination of the fabric of any ceramic vessel will afford clues as to the clay's origins (Orton *et al.* 1993, 132–49). This can enable the identification of some trading patterns. Again, changes can be seen through time; because transport was slow and probably fairly expensive for bulk goods, medieval potters usually used sources close to their potteries, even to the extent of moving their workshops as clay deposits were exhausted. Similarly, potteries were located close to supplies of fuel. In the post-medieval period, as potteries expanded to meet demand and became more dependent on investment in technology and equipment, their sites became fixed, and clay and fuel had to be brought to the workshops from further afield. Increased investment in raw material acquisition required increased turnover and greater profits. Thus markets further afield were sought, and the transport facilities used to import raw materials were also used to export the finished goods to more widespread markets (Barker 1999, 227). The highly localised pattern of distribution which characterised medieval pottery was replaced by a more dispersed pattern of wares. For example, late Cistercian wares, though much imitated and probably produced at a number of sites outside the production 'heartland' of Yorkshire, show a wide and remarkably consistent distribution of forms through a large part of northern England (Hinton 1990, 202). Contemporary southern products, such as 'Metropolitan' slipwares, are found as far north as Lancaster, Kendal and beyond, carried to Newcastle and the Northumbrian coast by sea (Crossley 1990, 251). Producers in central Scotland, although relying to a large extent on family members acting as travelling salespersons (pig-wives and muggers) and static shops to sell their wares (Caldwell and Dean 1992, 29), also invested heavily in shipping to

A range of mid-eighteenth-century pottery from the Wassail Place kiln, Swansea. The pottery includes plain and slip-decorated earthenwares, as well as two fragments of kiln waster (upper left) and is typical of the wares produced by small-scale potteries before their replacement by factory production, in this case Swansea's Cambrian Pottery. (© Glamorgan-Gwent Archaeological Trust)

transport their products to larger and more profitable markets. Central Scottish products, probably shipped from the Forth and Clyde estuaries, turn up as far afield as Panama (Caldwell and Dean 1992, 30–2). At about the same time, Glaswegian merchants were setting up and financing potteries in order to compete with London in the Delft trade to the Americas (Denholm 1982, 41).

The demand for novelty and innovation encouraged experimentation and the development of a wide range of fabrics. The high value and popularity of some imported ceramics led to copying of wares such as German stonewares, Dutch majolicas and, most interestingly, oriental stonewares and porcelains (Weatherill and Edwards 1971, 174–7). As some of these required specialised clays and other ingredients, it meant that clays were transported from yet greater distances, not least by ship from the china clay deposits of Cornwall to the Midlands potteries (Allan 1984, 126). Clay was transported from Poole in Dorset to London and Whitehaven (Wheatherill and Edwards 1971, 173), while Carrickfergus in Northern Ireland served potteries in Liverpool, Bristol and Glasgow (Denholm 1982, 40).

The desire to develop home sources of production for otherwise imported goods was also present in other contexts; although glass had been produced in England for several hundred years, the finest glass-wares were largely imported from the Venetian island of Murano. Venetian glassware, largely protected from imitation by restrictive trade arrangements, was not seriously imitated or challenged until 1674–6, when George Ravenscroft, at the behest of the Company of Glass Sellers, developed lead crystal (Bickerton 1984, 3). Interestingly, the composition of the new glass lent itself to more solid, thicker-walled vessels, rapidly introducing a new range of prestige drinking vessels (not least wine and ale glasses) more suited to English table habits than many of the over-ornate Venetian and *façon de Venise* forms available hitherto. Lead crystal glass was softer and therefore easier to engrave to a high standard of craftsmanship and was thus much sought-after by specialist Dutch glass engravers. In consequence large numbers of vessels were exported from major production centres such as Newcastle for finishing in the Netherlands, leading to occasional ironies such as fine Newcastle goblets engraved with depictions of the ships and monogram of the Dutch East India Company, a major trade rival of Britain's own East India Company.

Trade

The opening up of worldwide sea routes in the sixteenth century and the exploitation of overseas resources led to the beginnings of global trade. Although wood is rarely preserved within the archaeological record, surviving artefacts indicate that timber was traded extensively. It was imported from the Baltic, the Caribbean and the East Indies. Again, one can chart the complex cycle of the growth of demand fostering a specialist trade in artefacts and raw materials. Mahogany, for instance, traded as an adjunct to sugar from the West Indies, entered ports such as Lancaster during the eighteenth century in great quantities. It was thus cheap and easily available to local cabinet-makers. Able to produce high-quality furniture economically, local firms such as Gillow (later Waring & Gillow) exploited a climate interested in new, exotic products, and rose to a national pre-eminence. Their trade increased the demand for exotic woods, and continued the import of mahogany to Lancaster long after its sugar trade was eclipsed by other north-western ports, especially Liverpool. Sugar itself was imported into Britain only part-refined (as muscovado), before being refined by the processes of washing and claying (Brooks 1983, 8). The distinctive sugar cone moulds and syrup jars used in this process during the late seventeenth and early eighteenth centuries were reused again and again, often travelling large distances between the refineries of commercial rivals, or imported from Holland (Brooks 1983, 11). Spanish vessels were reused by the sugar-houses of England and Antwerp in the sixteenth and early seventeenth centuries. New tastes and increasing demand led to the importation of less exotic products than sugar. Even materials such as building stone (Wilson 1983, 104) and leather, where production often remained small-scale and highly localised as late as the early twentieth century, demand outstripped supply in general. From the late eighteenth century hides had to be imported from as far as away as South America, and consequently exotic raw materials for the tanning process, such as quebracho bark, to supplement local supplies of oak bark, were also imported in enormous quantities (Howard-Davis 1987, 240).

Taxation has long been an adjunct to trade and has on occasion been known to have a direct influence on the appearance of artefacts. It is well-known that tax on tobacco had a significant effect on the size of the bowls of tobacco pipes, which became smaller or larger as the price of tobacco fluctuated. As clay pipes were somewhat fragile and thus needed to be replaced frequently, even short-lived changes in, for instance, excise duties, can be seen swiftly reflected in the typological sequence (Oswald 1975). At a more subtle level, excise tax imposed on glass and earthenware in 1745 and levied by weight had a direct effect on the development of an elegant and technologically highly accomplished artefact form (Bickerton 1984, 13). This led to the development of teardrop and air-twist stems in order to reduce the weight of glass drinking vessels. The same excise levy led to the large-scale transference of English glass-production to

Ireland, where no excise was levied until 1825. With no tax restricting the weight of vessels, the Irish producers came to specialise in elaborate thick-walled cut glass vessels, as is still the case with Irish lead crystal.

The ability to recognise trade routes by linking production centres and sites where the finished objects were used and discarded has long been recognised as of significance in understanding the range of contacts between often quite far-flung or disparate groups. Perhaps some of the most extensively researched are the trading links between the North American colonies and Britain and the rest of Europe, especially France and Spain. The seventeenth- and eighteenth-century domestic assemblages recovered from sites such as Williamsburg in Virginia are virtually indistinguishable from those of comparable social status in Britain, with, for some time, a marked preference for imported goods, even though by 1635 earthenware vessels were produced in the New England colonies (Yensch 1991; Cooper 1981, 157–8). Ironically the lead powder needed to glaze them still had to be imported from Britain or, *in extremis*, cannibalised from the linings of tea-chests.

Less often discussed by archaeologists, but of lasting influence on British taste and domestic ceramics, is the Far Eastern trade, most directly with China through Canton (Cooper 1981, 55). Chinese blue and white porcelain rarely found its way to north-western Europe before 1600, despite its importation into Acapulco by the Spanish by 1573 as part of their Manila trade (van der Porten 1965, 6). Drake is known to have taken as a prize in 1579 four chests of porcelain, which appeared in South Devon by 1587 (on the *San Felipe*: Clifford 1912, 582). It has been suggested that this was possibly 'one of the earliest occasions when large quantities of porcelain were seen in northern Europe' (Allan 1984, 106); inevitably most of the consignment went to the Crown. Northern European interest in Chinese ceramics appears to have really taken off in Amsterdam in 1604, with the auction of a cargo of 100,000 porcelain items from a captured Portuguese carrack (Copeland 1988, 3). A fast-growing fashion for Chinese porcelain meant that it spread rapidly through the upper and middle echelons of society, and in Exeter in the 1620s 23 out of 104 surviving probate inventories list items of 'carricke or cheny' (Allan 1984, 107). However, there seem to have been problems with valuation, as if the value of such novel goods was not yet firmly established. Interestingly, this porcelain was always listed in the public living-rooms rather than in kitchens and butteries, clearly indicating its role as a display item, a suggestion reinforced by the early practice of mounting porcelain vessels in silver. The popularity of Chinese porcelain grew alongside that of the other great Eastern trade commodity, tea. As the fashion for tea-drinking grew, so did the taste for blue and white porcelain tea-wares which were imported with it. As this fashion spread downwards through society, so the scale of imports grew. By the early eighteenth century the huge amounts of porcelain coming into the country could no longer be handled through the 'China-men' of London, who had used the old network of contacts developed and employed by the Glass Sellers (Weatherill 1983, 27). While Chinese wares continued to be wholesaled in London, a new network of sales outlets developed across the country and specialist crockery shops began to appear; incidentally these gave a great boost to the developing English manufacturers, providing much-needed outlets for the growing Midlands producers. Numerous attempts were made to copy the blue and white designs of Chinese porcelain, initially in tin-glazed Delft wares. Porcelain with Chinese-influenced designs was made by Bow from 1747, and the demand for such pottery led ultimately to the invention of bone china by Josiah Spode, shortly before 1796.

Perhaps the most lasting effect of the trade was the development of underglaze transfer-printing which facilitated the industrial-scale production of blue and white earthenwares in the second half of the eighteenth century, and the widespread adoption of the ubiquitous willow pattern which still graces many a table today. It is undoubtedly of significance that the original tea house and its gardens depicted in this pattern is in Shanghai, a major trading port. Ironically, the increased demand for cheap chinoiserie led to a decline in the import market, as the lower end of the market was served by increased local production, forcing Chinese producers to change their products, tailoring traditional forms and designs to increase their appeal to individual western markets (Cooper 1981, 55), porcelain destined for the Middle Eastern market, for example, being of very different appearance from that for England (Haldane 1996, 86). Similarly, in the later eighteenth and early nineteenth centuries English blue and white china producers were making both Chinese-influenced and Americanised pottery specifically for the North American market. The decorative technique, allowing a rapidly changing sequence of designs to be printed on the same range of vessels, also led to an increasing use of quite ordinary table wares, reaching far down the social scale. Vessels of complex iconography and propaganda, especially, fostered a bucolic image of Britain in support of growing nationalism in the late eighteenth and nineteenth centuries (Brooks 1999, 52–3).

Information on trade from most archaeological sites is inevitably patchy, and although on occasion strong trends can be detected, especially in sites located at the furthest extent of trade routes, it is difficult to reconstruct changing trade patterns without reference to a number of sites. Ports such as London, Southampton and Exeter, where extensive archaeological investigation can be enhanced and complemented by detailed documentary records, offer the best picture of trade and its change and fluctuation, although it must be remembered that such ports have easier access to imported exotica than do other towns and cities. An examination of trading patterns in post-medieval Exeter revealed that between 1710 and 1720 some 95 per cent of Exeter's tile exports were made in the course of the sugar trade (Allan 1984). Pantiles were sent to the West Indies as ballast in out-going ships, but in 1722, when Exeter lost the sugar trade, the export of tiles collapsed. At approximately the same time Exeter was a significant port in the Dutch and German glass and pottery trade with the American colonies, with goods unloaded at Exeter, transported overland to the north Devon coast and re-exported. Although regarded as a cheaper route than sailing direct, goods apparently remained in bond for long periods before re-export, with one 1752 cargo to Carolina made up in three batches accumulated over the previous four years – a point of note for those using glass and pottery for dating.

Ships' manifests and the cargoes of wrecked ships can provide a clearer picture of the extent of trading enterprise than most archaeological sites. The *Nanking*, a Dutch East Indiaman wrecked en route from the East, was laden with at least 100,000 Chinese porcelain vessels destined for the tables of western Europe. A Portuguese trading junk wrecked off Vietnam *c.* 1690 gives a vivid picture of the range and quality of material transported over long distances at that time, and illustrates the differing trading needs of a relatively small coastal trader (Flecker 1992, 221–44). Alongside good quality porcelain – destined for the West, judging by the designs incorporating western buildings – there were large amounts of poor-quality vessels, simply stacked in the holds to serve as ballast. Small opportunist or personal trade items included 98 chatelaine sets, 52 pairs of tweezers, ink blocks, lacquer combs, etc., packed in small barrels and chests, as well as fruit and dried fish. These were presumably traded en route wherever and whenever the opportunity arose. The wreck of the *Maidstone*, sunk off the Ile de Noirmoutier in July 1747 while engaged in a blockade, also included substantial amounts of porcelain – probably the cargo of a ship taken as a prize (de Maisonneuve 1992, 22). Despite the porcelain aboard, the crew apparently preferred green- and brown-glazed earthenwares and stoneware, and the captain's and officers' stores showed their preference for pewter vessels. This, of course, may have been a pragmatic response to the avoidance of breakages in heavy seas.

The Household

The attribution of meaning to the acquisition and use of artefacts within households is equally fraught with difficulties of interpretation (Courtney 1997b, 99). Inevitably, the contents of any one household preserved within the archaeological record must to some degree reflect the status and social aspirations of the inhabitants. Anomalous and expensive items, imports or specially made objects, are often seen as an expression of status, based on the assumption that such things required wealth and social aspiration to encourage their acquisition. This is, perhaps, a slight over-simplification, as in some cases it can be established that the acquisition of old items, such as tapestries, was viewed as creating an air of long establishment. Documentary records show, for instance, that Cardinal Wolsey, something of a social upstart, scoured France for second-hand, unfashionable (and thus cheap) medieval tapestries to adorn his state apartments (Campbell 1996, 83). In fact he bought few contemporary bespoke works, and commissioned still fewer. None the less, his tapestry collection was unparalleled and was later acquired by Henry VIII at the time of Wolsey's fall from grace; he used it to much the same ends. Again, especially in the late sixteenth and early seventeenth centuries, an air of practical frugality was maintained by many of the wealthiest families. Bess of Hardwick, Countess of Shrewsbury, herself of uncertain origin but married to 'old' money, shows an interesting mix in her management of family affairs. She constantly recycled expensive textiles, using them again and again in ever smaller pieces. But in contrast she was profligate with her use of window glass in the new hall built at Hardwick. Undoubtedly this was facilitated by her ownership of a glassworks (Girouard 1994, 22). Again, the nature of the assemblage relates a complex web of factors, which defy a simple explanation and attribution of status on the basis of artefact category. It must be questioned as to whether a finds assemblage can ever be understood without a full appreciation of the physical and social context.

Until at least the later eighteenth century large households were often considerably more socially mixed than is the case today. Much of the domestic space was shared by all on a relatively egalitarian basis. Probate inventories show clearly that the owners' private rooms were rarely exclusive, with bedrooms especially often used as stores for agricultural equipment, linens and even cheese. It is not until the later eighteenth century that social and activity zoning can be clearly recognised, as servant and master, male and female, adult and child become increasingly socially polarised within the house (Priestley and Corfield 1982, 107). This can be most dramatically seen in the slave-owning societies of the West Indies and North America, where slaves were, on the whole, housed separately, often developing a separate cultural assemblage, combining influences from their own background and remembered origins with that of their masters, and often subtly modifying the use and significance of western artefacts introduced into their domestic assemblage. That examples of this have not been found in Britain is in part a consequence of the smaller numbers of black slaves present, but also of their greater integration as primarily household servants into a wider household culture (Gerzina 1995).

ETHNICITY, INTERACTION AND CULTURAL HEGEMONY

Recently, in North America and Australasia there has been an upsurge in interest in the archaeology of interaction between colonists and indigenous groups, or those forced into low-status communities, such as black slaves, aboriginal groups and transportees. Much work has been done in the attempt to establish the presence of these often archaeologically tenuous groups in archaeological assemblages by the recognition not only of culturally hybrid artefacts but also of atypical patterns of use and deposition. Many such investigations have centred on the recognition of slavery and, by extension, of ethnicity and gender within the archaeological record. This has proved difficult in the extreme for, despite the known widespread importation of black Africans into the southern states of North America, they had been effectively stripped of their material culture prior to their arrival, and were allowed access to only a limited range of new artefacts, purchased specifically, or cast off, by their (usually western European) owners.

In addition, it is all too often forgotten by modern analysts that such low-status groups rarely derive from a single background. There has never been a single black African culture, and slaves were taken from varying ethnic backgrounds, sometimes direct from their homelands, sometimes from Arab or other intermediaries, while still more were traded on from the Caribbean. In such circumstances the attempt to recover information on ethnic origins is difficult. In many cases the desire to produce or use familiar artefacts was deliberately and systematically suppressed by slave-owners, missionaries and social reformers, who were all well aware of the socio-political significance of objects.

Ferguson (1992, 3) has pointed out the shortcomings of some of the very active 'living' archaeology movements in the USA which draw heavily on reconstruction and reproduction of artefacts to chart the past, noting that the living museum at Williamsburg focuses almost exclusively on the material culture of its white settlers, despite the fact that over 50 per cent of the population of the early settlement was black, people perceived 'dimly or not at all'. The evolution of hybrid artefacts, especially Colono ware, from the mixture of cultural influences that met within American slavery, combining African and indigenous native American potting techniques with western European forms, can illustrate the complex web of interactions which resulted in the production of a particular class of artefact. The archaeological study and interpretation of Colono-type wares, for example, provides a vivid picture of social interaction and acculturation as a number of very different elements combined to produce a new artefact type. In this case it resembled indigenous predecessors but actually embodied influences originating from the material cultures of three continents brought together in a low-status and often disregarded set of artefacts.

A salutary warning to those attempting to determine low-status ethnic groups in a complex society can be seen in the way imported slaves merged into indigenous Zanzibar society between emancipation in 1897 and the 1930s. The slaves regarded themselves as native Zanzibaris and abandoned all material manifestation of both their original ethnic origins and their period of enslavement. Interestingly, the immigrant ruling class, Arabs from Oman, retained far more of the material paraphernalia of their ethnic origins, rigidly differentiating themselves from their Zanzibari subjects (Fair 1998, 71). The competitive upward mobility of females in the newly emancipated society was expressed by the adoption of colourful imported fabrics for clothing. Such was the race for status that many Zanzibari women were recorded as changing their clothing for a new pattern on a weekly basis, making fortunes for many merchants and provoking, shortly after the First World War, a fierce trade war between Britain, which produced the fabrics, and Holland, which block-printed the designs (Fair 1998, 71).

The two examples given above are relatively rare, yet they serve to illustrate the potential and pitfalls of using artefacts to recover information about minority ethno-social groups. As yet, few similar studies have been undertaken in Britain, although examination of the large number of burials from Christ Church, Spitalfields (Cox 1996), has led to some attempt to recognise immigrant groups, in this case Huguenots, from the archaeological record. Components of a set of specifically Jewish inscribed tin-glazed serving dishes were identified within a sealed late seventeenth-century group from London (Pearce 1998, 101), firmly associated with Jewish families known to have lived in the area. Nothing else within the finds assemblage, however, would have identified the ethnic origins of the household. Indeed, the precise affiliations of the owner remain ambiguous, as the inscription uses a script associated with the Ashkenazy sect, while documentary evidence points strongly to Sephardic Jews living on the site. Otherwise little attempt has been made, as yet, to chart the presence of other migrant groups in this country by examination of the archaeological record, despite the fact that in the recent past seasonally migrant groups, such as Scottish fishwives following the herring, or the influx of Irish and Welsh into the English textile towns in the nineteenth century, have been extensively considered by social historians.

The Material Culture of Food

British artefact studies have been more useful for recognising changes in social behaviour, particularly in relation to the preparation and serving of food. The introduction and dissemination of the use of cutlery, especially forks and spoons, throughout society marks a significant change in behaviour, reflecting the rise of interest in the individual. It was not until the Restoration that the provision of a personal place setting of knife, fork and spoon became standard, and it was not until the turn of the eighteenth century that place settings were laid for guests at the dining table. It is interesting that at this point table knives ceased to be an artefact expressing the wealth and status of the individual owner, who carried it to meals for his own use, but shifted to express that of the provider of the meal. With this change the emphasis of knife design also changed, from a concentration on uniqueness to the provision of large sets of identical cutlery. By the end of the eighteenth century table wares were stored in high-quality veneered mahogany boxes holding up to 120 pieces, which had themselves become items of display, made by the best furniture-makers of the time. Even today, a canteen of cutlery is often given on a significant occasion such as marriage; it is tacitly acknowledged as a display item, and reserved for special occasions rather than everyday use.

The changes in cutlery, the replacement of the bread or wooden trencher by ceramic plates, and the surprisingly late introduction of the soup bowl to the English table were all changes in the material culture of food, which filtered slowly down through society (Pennell 1999, 40). They represent facets of late medieval and early post-medieval social change. There was a move away from the communal production and consumption of food – cooking for the household – in the form of 'one-pot' meals and roasts, mirroring increased personal and spatial differentiation within the household (Yentsch 1991, 40; Johnson 1996, 174–7). The increasing range of tablewares emphasised the distinction between cooking and eating vessels, and facilitated the increasing desire to differentiate ingredients and move away from medieval styles of cooking. This may reflect a desire to try new introductions and improved varieties, for instance the potato and other foodstuffs from the New World occasionally found in the archaeological record (Giorgi 1997, 209). By being able to cook them separately (Yentsch 1991, 29), to serve and eat them separately, and thus to garnish them separately, this period led to an increased interest in sauces and in detailed recipes. Of course the introduction, as a result of trade and expansion, of tea, coffee and chocolate led to a completely new range of ceramic vessels. Indeed, it was during the seventeenth century that the 'polite' meal as we know it today was formalised (Drummond and Wilbraham 1939, 108), being separated into a succession of courses, differentiated by texture and taste. This led to the adoption of large and complex dinner services and place settings.

Alongside this can be seen the decline in the use of silver plate for dining in high-status households, killed finally by high taxation on silver in the late eighteenth century. Although little survives, relatively plain and utilitarian silver plate was common in well-to-do sixteenth- and seventeenth-century households, again representing conspicuous display, but in a rather more readily negotiable form than individualised (crested or monogrammed) china services. Documentary evidence, and a study of the few hoards of Elizabethan and slightly later silver, shows clearly that a silver service was regarded as an appropriate way to use bullion and thus quite literally to display personal wealth. The ornate range of miniature or toy plates in pewter surviving from this period presumably underlines their importance to well-off families (Egan 1996). Of course, the success of English privateers in harassing the Spanish silver fleets leaving the New World meant that significantly more silver was available in the sixteenth century. A service would be built up as personal circumstances allowed (Thornton and Cowell 1996, 152), and could readily be melted down as a source of finance. This accounts for its rarity today, as much early silver must have been melted down during the political turmoil of the seventeenth century. This piecemeal acquisition of plate meant that although families might have possessed a number of items, they did not necessarily match, and the notion of a silver service in which different components had distinct functions did not become fixed until the 1690s (Thornton and Cowell 1996, 163), a period which saw the introduction of a number of new forms, including saucers, sallet dishes and salvers. About this time, Pepys records the payment to himself of 'incentives' which he would collect in the form of silver plate, chosen in the presence of his patron on the premises of London silversmiths. Despite this pragmatism, however, silver tablewares still followed fashion, changing, as did ceramics, to accommodate and reflect the changing attitudes to food preparation and presentation.

Gender

The perception of social position, while easiest in high-status contexts, is not impossible in other echelons of society. By a combination of careful excavation and an appreciation of the iconography of simple objects, both status and gender can be established (Lydon 1993). The eighteenth century saw not only an increasing social polarisation in terms of living space, but also in terms of gender, with, even in quite lowly contexts, the man's role centred on public affairs and matters outside the house, while the woman's became increasingly domestic. Excavations at Lilyvale in Australia plotted the distribution of a large number of items associated with sewing, including thimbles, pins and needles, all deposited in the domestic context. Their distribution in rubbish deposits close to doors led to the conclusion that sewing was frequently undertaken on back doorsteps, where there was good light and fresh air. While this alone does not determine the gender of the sewers, the iconography of the decorated thimbles 'could literally be read for specific contemporary meaning' (Lydon 1993, 132). The likes of 'Reward for Industry', 'Forget me not', and 'I love you' illustrate the syncretism between sewing proficiency and devotion to 'hearth and home' as female attributes.

There are, however, surprisingly few obviously gender-specific artefacts in the modern British cultural assemblage. Some classes of artefact, such as jewellery, are gender-specific at some periods but not at others. Any number of Elizabethan portraits will demonstrate the general fondness of both sexes among the wealthy for display items such as jewellery (Murdoch 1991, 54). In succeeding centuries fashions and desires waxed and waned. Western society no longer entertains the notion of male and female types of artefact in the way that, for instance, Inuit men and women had different toolkits, reflecting a gender-specific differentiation of tasks (Hart Hansen *et al.* 1991, 125). Even so, there seems little doubt that in the past certain types, for instance kitchen equipment, were most closely gender specific, often personalised and frequently bequeathed to friends or female relatives (Pennell 1999, 42–3). Despite this there is a persistent stereotypical view that some objects and activities, for instance sewing and knitting, are female pastimes, and thus that artefacts/tools such as knitting needles might be gender-specific. This is not, however, the case, as the many male stocking-knitters of nineteenth-century Yorkshire would indicate.

Many archaeologists have attempted to determine gender in the archaeological record from the distribution of certain artefact types, sometimes with a measurable amount of success (Lydon 1993; Costin 1996) but often falling into the pitfall of stereotypical preconceptions of conventional 'feminine' attributes and roles. That certain artefacts are by their very nature gender-specific is perhaps most vividly illustrated by the condoms recovered from a Civil War midden deposit at Dudley Castle (Gaimster *et al.* 1996), but few such unambiguous objects survive within the archaeological record. There are, however, occasions in historical archaeology when certain artefacts can be firmly identified with one gender or another, as for instance the European cups and saucers given specifically to women as potlatch gifts in Nootka Sound, Canada, in the nineteenth and early twentieth centuries (Marshall and Maas 1997) and never destined for use, except as a display of status.

MESSAGES AND MEANINGS

Finally it must be noted that some artefacts can carry an implicit or explicit political or social status quite unassociated with their function and purpose. The compass, for instance, central to the maritime trading activities of eighteenth-century Britain, acquired at an early stage a veneer of religious symbolism that seems to have been understood throughout society. Many early compasses have an ornately decorated east point, indicating the direction of Jerusalem and Paradise (Fara 1997, 128–9). Compass needles became a widely understood metaphor for the 'constancy of human souls irresistibly drawn to the divine centre' (Fara 1997, 126), and for constancy and reliability in general. Thus the compass came to appear in numerous paintings as an expression of this virtue. Maps, globes, atlases 'and other tools of the geographic trade' (Schmidt 1997, 551), artefacts close to the expanding maritime heart of western Europe from the sixteenth century, likewise gained an explicit symbolism and became images of power and possession. As early as 1533 Holbein used them in this context in his portrait of *The Ambassadors*, depicting the representatives of the French embassy (Foister, Roy and Wyld 1997). Artefacts were also used to convey more explicit messages. From an early stage in their development clay tobacco pipes sometimes carried adverts in the form of the maker's name, but in the nineteenth century they blossomed into a veritable showcase of advertising, showing heraldic, social and political affiliation. To give but one example, a set of clay pipes appeared between 1807 and *c.* 1840, bearing a tableau commemorating the abolition of the slave trade (Oswald 1975, 108).

Hans Holbein's The Ambassadors, *which demonstrates the range of sixteenth-century courtly culture. Holbein used the objects symbolically to convey messages to the Renaissance observer. The distorted skull in the foreground, a sign of mortality, becomes undistorted when viewed from the correct angle. (© The National Gallery)*

The range and depth of information that can be deduced from excavated artefacts is immense. It is impossible at the end of the twentieth century for any one individual to comment in detail on post-medieval artefacts in the way that Noël Hume was able to list and discuss those of Colonial America only a few decades ago (1969). The number and complexity of artefact types expanded enormously during the eighteenth and nineteenth centuries in particular. It is hoped, however, that a closer examination of some of the less-well-known facets of artefact analysis and interpretation can demonstrate the wealth of information that might be gained from the presence of even a few broken pot sherds on an historical archaeological site.

BIBLIOGRAPHY

Adams, W.H. and Boling, S.J. 1989. 'Status and ceramics for planters and slaves on three Georgia coastal plantations', *Historical Archaeology* 23(1), 69–96

Airs, M. (ed.), 1994. *The Tudor and Jacobean Great House*, Oxford University Press

Airs, M. and Girouard, M. 1998. *The Tudor and Jacobean Country House*, Sutton Publishing

Alcock, N.W. 1983. 'The Great Rebuilding and its later stages', *Vernacular Architecture* 14, 45–7

Alcock, N.W. 1996. 'Innovation and conservatism: the development of Warwickshire houses in the late 17th and 18th centuries', *Birmingham and Warwickshire Archaeological Society Transactions* 100, 133–59

Alcock, N.W. and Woodfield, C.T.P. 1996. 'Social pretensions in architecture and ancestry, Hallhouse, Sawbridge, Warwickshire and the Andrewes', *Antiquaries Journal* 76, 51–72

Allan, J.P. 1984. *Medieval and Post-Medieval Finds from Exeter 1971–80*, Exeter Archaeological Report 3

Allen, R.C. 1992. *Enclosure and the Yeoman*, Clarendon Press

Allen, T. 1999. 'Copperas, the first major chemical industry in England', *Industrial Archaeology News* 108, 2–3

Andren, A. 1998. *Between Artifacts and Texts: Historical Archaeology in Global Perspective*, Plenum Press

Andrews, P. and Mepham, L. 1996. 'Medieval and post-medieval extra-mural settlement on the site of the Ashmolean Museum forecourt, Beaumont Street, Oxford', *Oxoniensia* 62, 179–223

Anon. 1922. *The Spires, Towers and Choirs of Southport*, Robt. Johnson & Co.

Apted, M.R. 1977. 'Social conditions at Tredegar House, Newport, in the 17th and 18th centuries', *Monmouthshire Antiquary* 3.2, 124–54

Apted, M.R. 1986. 'The building and other works of Patrick, 1st Earl of Strathmore, at Glamis, 1671–1695', *Antiquaries Journal* 66, 91–115

Armstrong, J. 2000. 'Transport', in Waller, P. (ed.), *The English Urban Landscape*, Oxford University Press, 209–32

Ashmore, O. 1982. *The Industrial Archaeology of North-West England*, Manchester University Press

Aspin, C. (ed.), 1972. *Manchester and the Textile Districts in 1849*, Helmshore Local History Society

Aston, M. and Bettey, J. 1998. 'The post-medieval rural landscape *c.* 1540–1700: the drive for profit and the desire for status', in Everson, P. and Williamson, T. (eds), *The Archaeology of Landscape*, Manchester University Press, 117–138

Atkin, M. 1987. 'Post-medieval archaeology in Gloucester: a review', *Post-Medieval Archaeology* 21, 1–124

Atkin, M., Carter, A. and Evans, D. (eds), 1985. *Excavations: Norwich 1971–78 Part II*, East Anglian Archaeology 26

Atkin, M. and Howes, R. 1993. 'The use of archaeology and documentary sources in identifying the Civil War defences of Gloucester', *Post-Medieval Archaeology* 27, 13–41

Austin, D. 1990. 'The "proper study" of medieval archaeology', in Austin, D. and Alcock, L. (eds), *From the Baltic to the Black Sea: studies in medieval archaeology*, Unwin Hyman, 9–49

Austin, D., Gerrard, S. and Greeves, T.A.P. 1989. 'Tin and agriculture in the Middle Ages and beyond: landscape archaeology in St Neot parish, Cornwall', *Cornish Archaeology* 28, 5–251

Awty, B.G. and Phillips, C.B. 1980. 'The Cumbrian Bloomery Forge in the Seventeenth Century and Forge Equipment in the Charcoal Iron Industry', *Transactions of the Newcomen Society* 77, 25–40

Ayres, B. 1991. 'Post-medieval archaeology in Norwich: a review', *Post-Medieval Archaeology* 25, 1–23

Ayres, J. 1998. *Building the Georgian City*, Yale University Press

Ayris, I.M., Nolan, J. and Durkin, A. 1998. 'The archaeological excavation of wooden wagonway remains at Lambton D Pit, Sunderland', *Industrial Archaeology Review* 20, 5–22

Baines, E. 1824. *History, Directory and Gazetteer of the County Palatine of Lancaster*, Wm. Wales & Co.

Baker, R. and Jones, R. 1996. 'The Park and Gardens of Colomendy Hall', *The Journal of the Flintshire Historical Society*, 34, 33–51

Banton, A.E. 1952. *Horningsham Chapel. The Story of England's Oldest Free Church*, Warminster, privately published

Barker, D. 1999. 'The ceramic revolution 1650–1850', in Egan, G. and Michael, R.L. (eds), *Old and New Worlds*, Oxbow Books, 226–34

Barker, R. 1992. 'A probable clinker-built Severn River trow at Lydney', *International Journal of Nautical Archaeology* 21.3, 205–8

Barley, M.W. 1961. *The English Farmhouse and Cottage*, Routledge & Kegan Paul

Barley, M.W. 1979. 'The Double Pile House', *Archaeological Journal* 136, 253–64

Barraclough, K.C. 1984a. *Blister steel: the birth of an industry*, The Metals Society

Barraclough, K.C. 1984b. *Crucible Steel: the growth of technology*, The Metals Society

Barrett, J. 1990. 'Archaeology in the age of uncertainty', *Scottish Archaeological Review* 7, 31–4

Barton, K.J. 1992. 'Ceramic changes in the Western European littoral at the end of the Middle Ages', in Gaimster, D. and Redknapp, M. (eds), *Everyday and Exotic Pottery from Europe, c. 650–1900. Studies in Honour of John G. Hurst*, Oxford, 246–55

BBC 1992. Head, *Blackadder II*, BBC Enterprises Ltd

Beaudry, M.C. (ed.), 1988. *Documentary Archaeology in the New World*, Cambridge University Press

Bennett, G., Clavering, E. and Rounding, A. 1990. *A Fighting Trade: rail transport in Tyne coal 1600–1800*, Portcullis Press

Beresford, M. 1971. 'The back-to-back house in Leeds 1787–1937', in Chapman, S.D. *The History of Working-class Housing. A Symposium*, David & Charles, 93–132

Beresford, M. 1974. 'The making of a townscape: Richard Paley in the east end of Leeds, 1771–1803', in Chalklin, C. and Havinden, M. (eds), *Rural Change and Urban Growth 1500-1800*, Longman

Beresford, M. 1988. *East end, West End: the Face of Leeds during Urbanisation, 1684–1842*, Thoresby Society, vols 60 and 61

Bettey, J.H. 1980. *The Landscape of Wessex*, Moonraker Press

Bettey, J.H. 1983. 'Some major influences on the post-medieval landscape of the Bristol region', *Landscape History* 5, 69–77

Bettey, J.H. 2000. 'Downlands', in Thirsk, J. (ed.), *The English Rural Landscape*, Oxford University Press, 27–49

Bick, D. 1993. *The Old Metal Mines of Mid-Wales*, Pound House

Bickerton, L.M. 1984. *English Drinking Glasses 1675–1825*, Shire

Bil, A. 1990. *The Shieling 1600–1840*, Edinburgh University Press

Blockley, K. 1997. 'Oxwich Castle, Gower: excavations by Dilwyn Jones, 1974–76', *Post-Medieval Archaeology* 31, 121–37

Bodsworth, C. (ed.), 1998. *Sir Henry Bessemer: Father of the Steel Industry*, Institute of Materials

Bold, J. 1999. '"A fix't intention for magnificence". The Royal Naval Hospital at Greenwich', *York Georgian Society Annual Report*, 33–5

Borsay, P. 1984. '"All the town's a stage": urban ritual and ceremony 1660–1800', in Clark, P. (ed.), *The Transformation of English Provincial Towns*, Hutchinson, 228–58

Borsay, P. 1989. *The English Urban Renaissance*, Clarendon Press

Borsay, P. 2000. 'Early modern urban landscapes 1540–1800', in Waller, P. (ed.), *The English Urban Landscape*, Oxford University Press, 99–124

Bourdieu, P. 1984. *Distinction: a Social Critique of the Judgement of Taste*, Yale University Press

Bowden, M. 1999. *Unravelling the Landscape. An Inquisitive Approach to Archaeology*, Tempus

Bowden, M. (ed.), 2000. *Furness Iron*, English Heritage

Bradley, R. 2000. *An Archaeology of Natural Places*, Routledge

Brandon, V. and Johnson, S. 1986. 'The Old Baptist Chapel, Goodshaw Chapel, Rawtenstall, Lancs.', *Antiquaries Journal* 66, 330–57

Brian, A. 1993. 'Lammas Meadows', *Landscape History* 15, 57–69

Briggs, A. 1963. (Penguin edn 1990). *Victorian Cities*, Penguin

Briggs, C.S. 1997. 'The fabric of parklands and gardens in the Tywi Valley and beyond', *The Camarthenshire Antiquary* 33, 88–105

Briggs, C.S. 1999. 'Aberglasney: the theory, history and archaeology of a post-medieval landscape', *Post-Medieval Archaeology* 33, 242–84

Brindle, S. and Kerr, B. 1997. *Windsor Revealed. New Light on the History of the Castle*, English Heritage

Brooks, A. 1999. 'Building Jerusalem. Transfer-printed finewares and the creation of British identity', in Tarlow, S. and West, S. (eds), *The Familiar Past?*, Routledge, 51–65

Brooks, C.M. 1983. 'Aspects of the sugar-refining industry from the 16th to 19th century', *Post-Medieval Archaeology* 17, 1–15

Brown, G. 1999. 'Post-enclosure farmsteads on Salisbury Plain: a preliminary discussion', in Pattison, P., Field, D. and Ainsworth, S. (eds), *Patterns of the Past*, Oxbow Books, 121–7

Brown, H.D. 1995. 'Colliery cottages 1830–1915. The Great Northern Coalfield', *Archaeologia Aeliana* 5th ser., 23, 291–305

Brown, P.J. 1988. 'Andrew Yarranton and the British Tinplate Industry', *Historical Metallurgy* 22/1, 42–8

Brunskill, R.W. 1971. *Illustrated Handbook of Vernacular Architecture*, Faber

Brunskill, R.W. 1977. 'Traditional domestic architecture of south-west Lancashire', *Folk Life* 15, 66–80

Brunskill, R.W. 1987. *Traditional Farm Buildings of Britain*, Victor Gollancz

Brunskill, R.W. 1997. *Houses and Cottages of Britain*, Victor Gollancz

Bryce, I.B.D. and Roberts, A. 1993. 'Post-Reformation catholic houses of north-east Scotland', *Proceedings of the Society of Antiquaries of Scotland* 123, 363–72

Buckham, S. 1999. '"The men that worked for England they have their graves at home." Consumerist issues within the production and purchase of gravestones in Victorian York', in Tarlow, S. and West, S. (eds), *The Familiar Past?*, Routledge, 199–214

Buckley, R. and Lucas, J. 1987. *Leicester Town Defences: Excavations 1958–1974*, Leicestershire Museums

Burnett, J. 1974. *The Annals of Labour: Autobiographies of British Working Class People, 1820–1920*, Indiana University Press

Burt, R. 1984. *The British Lead Mining Industry*, Dyllansow Truran

Butler, D. 1978. *Quaker Meeting Houses of the Lake District*, Friends Historical Society

Butlin, R. 1961. 'Some terms used in Agrarian History: a glossary', *Agricultural History Review* 9, 98–104

Caffyn, L. 1983. 'Housing in an industrial landscape: a study of workers' housing in West Yorkshire', *World Archaeology* 15(2), 173–83

Caldwell, D.H. and Dean, V.E. 1992. 'The pottery industry at Throsk, Stirlingshire, in the 17th and early 18th century', *Post-Medieval Archaeology* 26, 1–46

Caldwell, D.H. and Ewart, G. 1997. 'Excavations at Eyemouth, Berwickshire, in a mid 16th-century *trace italienne* fort, *Post-Medieval Archaeology* 31, 61–119

Caldwell, D.H., McWee, R. and Ruckley, N.A. 2000. 'Post-medieval settlement on Islay – some recent research', in Atkinson, J.A., Banks, I. and MacGregor, G. (eds), *Townships to Farmsteads. Rural Settlement Studies in Scotland, England and Wales*, BAR Brit Ser. 293, 58–68

Campbell, B.M.S. 1981. 'The regional uniqueness of English field systems: some evidence from eastern Norfolk', *Agricultural History Review* 29, 16–28

Campbell, T. 1996. 'Cardinal Wolsey's Tapestry Collection', *Antiquaries Journal* 76, 73–138

Campbell, W.A. 1971. *The Chemical Industry*, Longman

Campion, P. 1996. 'People process and the poverty-pew: a functional analysis of mundane buildings in the Nottinghamshire framework-knitting industry', *Antiquity* 70, 847–60

Cardwell, P., Ronan, D. and Simpson, R. 1996. 'An Archaeological Survey of the Ribblehead Navvy Settlements', Northern Archaeological Associates unpubl client report

Carrington, P. 1994. *Chester*, English Heritage/Batsford

Carruthers, A. 1993. 'Form and function in the Scottish Home, 1600–1950', *Review of Scottish Culture* 8, 29–34

Carter, H. 1990. 'Towns and urban systems 1730–1914', in Dodgshon, R.A. and Butlin, R.A. (eds), *An Historical Geography of England and Wales*, 2nd edn, Academic Press, 401–28

Carver, M. 1987. *Underneath English Towns*, Batsford

Cave, L.F. 1981. *The Smaller English House*, Robert Hale

Chalklin, C. 1999. 'County building in Leicestershire, 1680–1830', *The Georgian Group Journal* 9, 69–85

Chambers, B. 1992. *Men, Mines, and Minerals of the North Pennines*, Friends of Killhope

Champion, T.C. 1990. 'Medieval archaeology and the tyranny of the historical record', in Austin, D. and Alcock, L. (eds), *From the Baltic to the Black Sea: studies in medieval archaeology*, Unwin Hyman, 79–95

Chapman, J. 1987. 'The extent and nature of parliamentary enclosure', *Agricultural History Review* 35, 25–35

Chapman, J. 1993. 'Enclosure commissioners as landscape planners', *Landscape History* 15, 51–5

Chapman, S.D. 1971. 'Working-class housing in Nottingham during the Industrial Revolution', in Chapman, S.D. (ed.), *The History of Working Class Housing*, David & Charles, 133–63

Cheape, H. 1996. 'Shielings in the Highlands and Islands of Scotland: prehistory to the present', *Folk Life* 35, 8–24

Child, S. 1997. 'The horse in the city', *The Victorian Society Annual 1996*, 5–14

Church, R. 1986. *The History of the British Coal Industry. Vol. 3. 1830–1913: Victorian Pre-eminence*, Clarendon Press

Clapp, B.W. 1994. *An Environmental History of Britain since the Industrial Revolution*, Longman

Clark, C. 1995. 'Ticking boxes or telling stories? The archaeology of the industrial landscape', in Palmer, M. and Neaverson, P. (eds), *Managing the Industrial Heritage: its Identification, Recording and Management*, Leicester Archaeology Monographs 2, 45–8

Clark, K. 1999. 'The workshop of the world: The Industrial Revolution', in Hunter, J. and Ralston, I. (eds), *The Archaeology of Britain*, Routledge, 280–96

Clark, P. and Slack, P. (eds), 1972. *Crisis and Order in English Towns*, Routledge

Clark, P. and Slack, P. 1976. *English Towns in Transition 1500–1700*, Oxford University Press

Claughton, P. 1994. 'Silver-lead: technological choice in the Devon Mines', in Ford, T.D. and Willies, L. (eds), *Mining before Powder*, Peak District Mines Historical Society, 54–9

Clay, C.G.A. 1984. *Economic Expansion and Social change: England 1500–1700*, Cambridge University Press

Cleere, H. and Crossley, D. 1985. *The Iron Industry of the Weald*, Leicester University Press

Clemenson, H.A. 1982. *English Country Houses and Landed Estates*, St Martins Press

Clifford, E.T. 1912. 'Drake's treasure', *Transactions of the Devonshire Association* 41, 512–29

Clifton-Taylor, A. 1972. *The Pattern of English Building*, Faber & Faber

Coad, J. 1997. 'Defending the realm: the changing technology of warfare', in Gaimster, D. and Stamper, P. (eds), *The Age of Transition. The Archaeology of English Culture 1400–1600*, Oxbow Monograph 98, 157–69

Cocroft, W. 2000. *Dangerous Energy*, English Heritage

Colvin, H.M. 1982. *History of the Kings Works IV 1485–1660*, HMSO

Coney, A. 1992. 'Fish, fowl and fen: landscape and economy on seventeenth-century Martin Mere', *Landscape History* 14, 51–64

Cook, H.F. 1994. 'Field-scale water management in southern England to AD 1900', *Landscape History* 16, 53–66

Cooke, A.O. 1913. *The Forest of Dean*, Constable & Co.

Cooke Taylor, W. 1842. (3rd edn 1968) *Notes of a Tour in the Manufacturing Districts of Lancashire*, Frank Cass and Co.

Cooper, E. 1981. *The History of World Pottery*, British Museum Press

Cooper, N. 1997. 'The gentry house in the Age of Transition', in Gaimster, D. and Stamper, P. (eds), *The Age of Transition. The Archaeology of English Culture 1400–1600*, Oxbow Monograph 98, 115–26

Cooper, N. 1999. *Homes of the Gentry 1480–1680*, English Heritage/Yale University Press

Copeland, R. 1988. *Blue and White Transfer-Printed Pottery*, Shire

Corfield, P.J. 1982. *The Impact of English Towns 1700–1800*, Oxford University Press

Corfield, P.J. 1987. 'Small Towns, Large Implications: Social and Cultural Roles of Small Towns in Eighteenth-Century England and Wales', *British Journal for Eighteenth Century Studies* 10.2, 125–38

Corser, P. 1982. 'Platform buildings; medieval and later settlement in Eskdale, Dumfriesshire', *Scottish Archaeological Review* 1, 38–44

Corser, P. 1993. 'Pre-improvement settlement and cultivation remains in eastern Scotland', in Hingley, R. (ed.), *Medieval or Later Rural Settlement in Scotland*, Historic Scotland and Ancient Monuments Division Occasional Paper 1, 15–23

Cosgrove, D. and Daniels, S. 1988. *The Iconography of Landscape*, Cambridge University Press

Costin, C.L. 1996. 'Exploring the relationship between gender and craft in complex societies: methodological and theoretical issues of gender attribution', in Wright, R.P. (ed.), *Gender and Archaeology*, University of Pennsylvania Press

Coulson, C. 1979. 'Structural symbolism in medieval castle architecture', *Journal of the British Archaeological Association* 132, 73–90

Courtney, P. 1996. 'In small things forgotten: the Georgian world view, material culture and the consumer revolution', *Rural History* 7, 87–95

Courtney, P. 1997a. 'The tyranny of constructs: some thoughts on periodisation and culture change', in Gaimster, D. and Stamper, P. (eds), *The Age of Transition. The Archaeology of English Culture 1400–1600*, Oxbow Monograph 98, 9–23

Courtney, P. 1997b. 'Ceramics and the history of consumption: pitfalls and prospects', *Medieval Ceramics* 21, 95–108

Courtney, P. 1997c. 'Excavations by Dilwyn Jones, 1974–76', in Blockley, K., 'Oxwich Castle, Gower', *Post-Medieval Archaeology* 31, 133–5

Courtney, P. 1999. 'Different strokes for different folks: the transatlantic development of historical and post-medieval archaeology', in Egan, G. and Michael, R.L. (eds), *Old and New Worlds*, Oxbow Books, 1–9

Courtney, P. forthcoming. 'Social theory and post-medieval archaeology: a historical perspective', in Majewsji, T. and Orser, C. (eds), *The International Handbook of Historical Archaeology*, Plenum Press

Courtney, P. and Courtney, Y. 1992. 'A siege examined: the Civil War archaeology of Leicester', *Post-Medieval Archaeology* 26, 47–90

Coutie, H. 1992. 'How they lived on Hillgate. A survey of industrial housing in the Hillgate area of Stockport', *Transactions of the Lancashire and Cheshire Archaeological Society* 88, 31–56

Cox, A. 1996. '"An example to others": public housing in London 1840–1914', *Transactions of the London and Middlesex Archaeological Society* 46, 145–65

Cox, M. 1996. *Life and Death in Spitalfields 1700–1850*, Council for British Archaeology

Cox, M. 1998. 'Eschatology, burial practice and continuity: a retrospection from Christ Church, Spitalfields', in Cox, M. (ed.), *Grave Concerns: Death and Burial in England 1700 to 1850*, Council for British Archaeology, 112–25

Cox, N. 1990. 'Imagination and Innovation of an Industrial Pioneer: the first Abraham Darby', *Industrial Archaeology Review* 12/2, 127–44

Craddock, P. (ed.), 1990. *2000 Years of Zinc and Brass*, British Museum Occasional Paper no. 50

Cranstone, D. 1985. *The Moira furnace*, North West Leicestershire District Council

Cranstone, D. 1986. 'Stony Hazel Forge: the History', unpublished report to Lake District National Park Authority

Cranstone, D. 1989. 'The Archaeology of Washing Floors: Problems, Potentials, and Priorities', *Industrial Archaeology Review* 12/1, 40–9

Cranstone, D. 1991. 'Isaac Wilkinson at Backbarrow', *Historical Metallurgy* 25/2, 87–91

Cranstone, D. 1992a. 'Excavations at Old Gang Smeltmill', in Willies, L. and Cranstone, D. (eds), *Boles and Smeltmills*, Historical Metallurgy Society, 28–31

Cranstone, D. 1992b. 'To hush or not to hush: where, when and how?', in Chambers, B. (ed.), *Men, Mines and Minerals of the North Pennines*, Friends of Killhope, 41–8

Cranstone, D. 1997. *Derwentcote Steel Furnace; an industrial monument in County Durham*, Lancaster imprints

Cranstone, D. 1999. 'Cherishing the cradle of industry: protection of industrial monuments in England', in Egan, G. and Michael, R.L. (eds), *Old and New Worlds*, Oxbow Books, 203–7

Cranstone, D. forthcoming. 'Gunnerside Gill: process and mind-set in a Pennine lead mine', paper to North East England History Institute conference, September 2000

Cranstone, D. and Hunwicks, L. 2000. 'Chatterley Whitfield Conservation Plan: Archaeological Inputs', unpublished report to Donald Insall Associates and English Heritage

Cranstone, D. and Rimmington, N. 2000. Monuments Protection Programme: the Chemical Industries. Step I Report, unpublished report to English Heritage

Crosby, A. 1998. *A History of Lancashire*, Phillimore

Crossley, D. 1990. *Post-Medieval Archaeology in Britain*, Leicester University Press

Crossley, D.W. 1995. 'The blast furnace at Rockley, South Yorkshire', *Archaeological Journal* 152, 381–421

Crossley, D.W. and Ashurst, D. 1968. 'Excavations at Rockley Smithies, a water-powered bloomery of the 16th and 17th centuries', *Post-Medieval Archaeology* 2, 10–54

Cumberpatch, C. 1996. 'The medieval and post-medieval pottery', in Dunkley, J.A. and Cumberpatch, C., *Excavations at 16–20 Church Street, Bawtry, S. Yorkshire*, BAR 248, 55–137

Cunningham, C.M. and Drury, P.J. 1985. *Post-Medieval Sites and their Pottery: Moulsham Street, Chelmsford*, Council for British Archaeology

Curl, J.S. 1995. *Victorian Churches*, English Heritage/Batsford

Currie, C.K. and Locock, M. 1993. 'Excavations at Castle Bromwich Hall gardens, 1989–1991', *Post-Medieval Archaeology* 27, 111–99

Currie, C.R.J. 1988. 'Time and chance: modelling the attrition of old houses', *Vernacular Architecture* 19, 1–9

Currie, C.R.J. 1990. 'Time and chance: a reply to comments', *Vernacular Architecture* 21, 5–9

Dahlman, C.J. 1986. *The Open Field System and Beyond. A Property Rights Analysis of an Economic Institution*, Cambridge University Press

Dalziel, N. 1993. 'Trade and transition 1690–1815', in White, A. (ed.), *A History of Lancaster 1193–1993*, Keele University Press, 91–144

Daniels, S. 1988. 'The political iconography of woodland in later Georgian England', in Cosgrove, D. and Daniels, S. (eds), *The Iconography of Landscape*, Cambridge University Press, 43–82

Darvill, T. 1998. 'Landscapes: myth or reality', in Jones, M. and Rotherham, I.D. (eds), *Landscapes – Perception, Recognition and Management: reconciling the impossible?*, The Landscape Conservation Forum and Sheffield Hallam University, 9–18

Darvill, T., Gerrard, C. and Startin, B. 1993. 'Identifying and protecting historic landscapes', *Antiquity* 67, 563–74

Daunton, M.J. 1983. *House and Home in the Victorian City. Working-Class Housing 1850–1914*, Edward Arnold

Davey, P.J. (ed.), 1980. *The Archaeology of the Clay Tobacco Pipe III*, BAR Brit. Ser. 78

Davey, P.J. 1987. 'The post-medieval period', in Schofield, J. and Leach, R. (eds), *Urban Archaeology in Britain*, Council for British Archaeology, 69–80

Davey, P.J. and McNeil, R. 1980. 'Excavations in South Castle Street, Liverpool 1976 and 1977', *Journal of the Merseyside Archaeological Society* 4, 6–29

Davies-Shiel, M. 1970. 'Excavations at Stony Hazel, High Furnace [sic], Lake District 1968–1969: an interim report', *Historical Metallurgy*, 4/1, 28–32

Day, J. and Tylecote, R.F. (eds), 1991. *The Industrial Revolution in Metals*, Institute of Metals

Day, T. 1999. 'The construction and maintenance of the Aberdeen–Inverurie Turnpike Road, 1765–1866: a case study', *Review of Scottish Culture*, 46–56

De Lange, N. 1984. *Atlas of the Jewish World*, Guild Publishing

De L. Mann, J. 1971. (1987 edn) *The Cloth Industry of the West of England. From 1640 to 1880*, Alan Sutton

de Maisonneuve, B. 1992. 'Excavation of the *Maidstone*, a British man-of-war lost off Noirmoutier, in 1747', *International Journal of Nautical Archaeology* 21, 15–28

de Vries, J. 1984. *European Urbanization 1500–1800*, Harvard University Press

Dean, M. 1985. 'A boat recovered from the foreshore at West Mersea in Essex', *International Journal of Nautical Archaeology and Underwater Exploration* 14.3, 217–26

Deetz, J. 1977. *In Small things Forgotten: the Archaeology of Early American Life*, Anchor Press/Doubleday

Denholm, P.C. 1982. 'Mid-eighteenth-century tin-glazed earthenwares from the Delftfield Pottery, Glasgow: excavation at the Broomielaw 1975', *Post-Medieval Archaeology* 16, 39–84

Devine, T.M. 1994. *The Transformation of Rural Scotland. Social Change and the Agrarian Economy 1660–1815*, Edinburgh University Press

Dix, B., Soden, I. and Hylton, T. 1995. 'Kirby Hall and its gardens: excavations in 1987–1994', *Archaeological Journal* 152, 291–380

Dixon, P. 1979. 'Tower houses, pelehouses and Border society', *Archaeological Journal* 136, 240–52

Dixon, P. 1993. 'A review of the archaeology of rural medieval and post-medieval Scotland', in Hingley, R. (ed.), *Medieval or Later Rural Settlement in Scotland*, Historic Scotland and Ancient Monuments Division Occasional Paper 1, 24–35

Dixon, P. and Lott, B. 1993. 'The courtyard and the tower: contexts and symbols in the development of late medieval great houses', *Journal of the British Archaeological Association* 146, 93–101

Dobson, R.B. 1977. 'Urban decline in late Medieval England', *Transactions of the Royal Historical Society*, 5th ser. 27, 1–22

Dodgshon, R.A. 1990. 'The changing evaluation of space 1500–1914', in Dodgshon, R.A. and Butlin, R.A. (eds), *An Historical Geography of England and Wales*, 2nd edn, Academic Press, 255–83

Dodgshon, R.A. 1993. 'West Highland and Hebridean landscapes: have they a history without runrig?', *Journal of Historical Geography* 19, 383–98

Dodgshon, R.A. 1998. 'The evolution of highland townships during the medieval and early modern periods', *Landscape History* 20, 51–63

DoE. 1990. *Planning Policy Guidance Note 16: Archaeology and Planning*, HMSO

DoE and DNH. 1994. *Planning Policy Guidance Note 15: Planning and the Historic Environment*, HMSO

Douet, J. 1998. *British Barracks 1600–1914*, English Heritage

Draper, J. 1984. *Post-Medieval Pottery 1650–1800*, Shire

Driscoll, S. and Yeoman, P. 1997. *Excavations at Edinburgh Castle 1988–91*, Historic Scotland

Drummond, J.C. and Wilbraham, A. 1939. *The Englishman's Food. A History of Five Centuries of English Diet*, Jonathan Cape

Duffy, E. 1992. *The Stripping of the Altars. Traditional Religion in England c 1400–c 1580*, Yale University Press

Dunbar, J. 1996. 'The post-Reformation church in Scotland. The emergence of the reformed church in Scotland c. 1560–1700', in Blair, J. and Pyrah, C. (eds), *Church Archaeology. Research Directions for the Future*, Council for British Archaeology, 127–34

Dunwell, A., Armit, I. and Ralston, I. 1995. 'The post-medieval farmstead and field system of Over Newton at Crookedstane, Elvanfoot, Upper Clydesdale', *Post-Medieval Archaeology* 29, 61–75

Dyer, A. 1981. 'Urban housing: a documentary study of four Midland towns 1530–1700', *Post-Medieval Archaeology* 15, 207–18

Dyer, C. 1997. 'Peasants and farmers: rural settlements and landscapes in an age of transition', in Gaimster, D. and Stamper, P. (eds), *The Age of Transition. The Archaeology of English Culture 1400–1600*, Oxbow Monograph 98, 61–76

Dyer, C., Hey, D. and Thirsk, J. 2000. 'Lowland vales', in Thirsk. J. (ed.), *The English Rural Landscape*, Oxford University Press, 78–96

Egan, G. 1996. *Playthings from the Past. Lead Alloy Miniature Artefacts c. 1300–1800*, Jonathan Horne

Egan, G. 1999. 'London, axis of the Commonwealth? An archaeological review', in Egan, G. and Michael, R.L. (eds), *Old and New Worlds*, Oxbow Books, 61–71

Egan, G. and Michael, R.L. (eds), 1999. *Old and New Worlds*, Oxbow Books

Ellis, J. 2000. 'Georgian Town Gardens', *History Today*, January 2000, 38–45

Emery, A. 1996. *Greater Medieval Houses of England and Wales 1300–1500. Vol. 1 Northern England*, Cambridge University Press

Emery, A. 2000. *Greater Medieval Houses of England and Wales 1300–1500. Vol. 2 East Anglia, Central England and Wales*, Cambridge University Press

Emery, N. 1992. *The Coalminers of Durham*, Alan Sutton

Emery, N. 1999a. 'St Kilda: excavations in a 19th century Hebridean village', in Egan, G. and Michael, R.L. (eds), *Old and New Worlds*, Oxbow Books, 165–70

Emery, N. 1999b. 'The earthworks at Rowley Farm, County Durham', *Durham Archaeological Journal* 14–15, 161–71

Emery, N. 2000. 'The impact of the outside world on St Kilda: the artefact evidence', in Atkinson, J.A., Banks, I. and MacGregor, G. (eds), *Townships to Farmsteads. Rural Settlement Studies in Scotland, England and Wales*, BAR Brit. Ser. 293, 161–6

Evans, C. 1993. *'The Labyrinth of Flames': work and social conflict in early industrial Merthyr Tydfil*, University of Wales Press

Evans, D. 1999. 'The redoubts of Maker Heights, Cornwall, 1770–1859', *The Georgian Group Journal* 9, 44–67

Evans, E.J. and Beckett, J.V. 1984. 'Cumberland, Westmorland and Furness', in Thirsk, J. (ed.), *The Agrarian History of England and Wales. Vol. V.i 1640–1750: Regional Farming Systems*, Cambridge University Press, 3–29

Everitt, A. 1979. 'Country, county and town: patterns of regional evolution in England', *Transactions of the Royal Historical Society*, 5th ser., 29, 79–108

Everson, P. and Williamson, T. 1998. 'Gardens and designed landscapes', in Everson, P. and Williamson, T. (eds), *The Archaeology of Landscape*, Manchester University Press, 139–65

Ewart, G. 1980. 'Excavations at Stirling Castle 1977–78', *Post-Medieval Archaeology* 14, 23–51

Fair, L. 1998. 'Dressing up: clothing, class and gender in post-abolition Zanzibar', *Journal of African History* 39, 63–94

Fara, P. 1997. 'Navigational compasses as cultural artefacts', *British Journal for Eighteenth Century Studies* 20.2, 125–40

Farrer, W. and Brownbill, J. (eds), 1911. *The Victoria History of the County of Lancaster*, 5, Victoria County History

Fawcett, R. 1994. *Scottish Abbeys and Priories*, Batsford/Historic Scotland

Fenton, A. and Walker, B. 1981. *The Rural Architecture of Scotland*, John Donald Publishers Ltd

Ferguson, I. 1992. *Uncommon Ground. Archaeology and Early African America 1650–1800*, Smithsonian Institution Press

Flecker, M. 1992. 'Excavation of an oriental vessel of *c.* 1690 off Con Dao, Vietnam', *International Journal of Nautical Archaeology* 21, 221–44

Fletcher, M. 1996. 'Industrial archaeology', in Newman, R. (ed.), *The Archaeology of Lancashire*, Lancaster University Archaeological Unit

Flinn, M.W. 1962. *Men of Iron: the Crowleys in the Early Iron Industry*, Edinburgh University Press

Flinn, M.W. 1994. *The History of the British Coal Industry. Vol. 2. 1700–1830: The Industrial Revolution*, Clarendon Press

Foister, S., Roy, A. and Wyld, M. 1997. *Making and Meaning: Holbein's* Ambassadors, Yale University Press

Fox, H.A.S. 1996. 'Introduction: transhumance and seasonal settlement', in Fox, H.A.S. (ed.), *Seasonal Settlement*, Vaughan Paper 39, 1–23

Francis, A. 1992. 'Analysis of refractory material from Surrender Smeltmill', in Willies, L. and Cranstone, D. (eds), *Boles and Smeltmills*, Historical Metallurgy Society, 32–4

Frazer, B. 1999. 'Common recollections: resisting enclosure "by agreement" in seventeenth-century England', *International Journal of Historical Archaeology* 3.2, 75–100

Friedman, T. 1996a. 'The golden age of church architecture in Shropshire', *Transactions of the Shropshire Archaeological and Historical Society* 71, 83–134

Friedman, T. 1996b. *Church Architecture in Leeds 1700–1799*, Thoresby Society, 2nd ser., 7

Friedrichs, C.R. 1995. *The Early Modern City 1450–1750*, Longman

Funari, P.P.A., Hall, M. and Jones, S. (eds), 1999. *Historical Archaeology: Back from the Edge*, Routledge

Gaimster, D. 1994. 'The archaeology of post-medieval society, *c.* 1450–1750: material culture studies in Britain since the war', in Vyner, B. (ed.), *Building on the Past: papers celebrating 150 years of the Royal Archaeological Institute*, RAI, 283–312

Gaimster, D. and Nenk, B. 1997. 'English households in transition *c.* 1450–1550: the ceramic evidence', in Gaimster, D. and Stamper, P. (eds), *The Age of Transition. The Archaeology of English Culture 1400–1600*, Oxbow Monograph 98, 171–95

Gaimster, D. and Stamper, P. (eds), 1997. *The Age of Transition. The Archaeology of English Culture 1400–1600*, Oxbow Monograph 98

Gaimster, D., Boland, P., Linnane, S. and Cartwright, C, 1996. 'The archaeology of private life: the Dudley Castle condoms', *Post-Medieval Archaeology* 30, 129–42

Garnett, M.E. 1987. 'The great rebuilding and economic change in south Lonsdale 1600–1730', *Transactions of the Historic Society of Lancashire and Cheshire* 137, 55–73

Gauldie, E. 1974. *Cruel Habitations. A History of Working-Class Housing 1780–1918*, George Allen & Unwin

Gerrard, S. 1987. 'Streamworking in Medieval Cornwall', *Journal of the Trevithick Society* 14, 7–31

Gerrard, S. 1989. 'The Medieval and Early Modern Cornish Stamping Mill', *Industrial Archaeology Review* 12, 9–19

Gerrard, S. 1996. 'The Early South-West Tin Industry: an Archaeological View', in Newman, P. (ed.), *The Archaeology of Mining and Metallurgy in South-West Britain*, Historical Metallurgy Society, 67–83

Gerrard, S. 1997. *Dartmoor: landscapes through time*, Batsford/English Heritage

Gerrard, S. 2000. *The Early British Tin Industry*, Tempus

Gerzina, G. 1995. *Black England*, John Murray

Gilchrist, R. and Morris, R. 1996. 'Continuity, reaction and revival: church archaeology in England *c.* 1600–1880', in Blair, J. and Pyrah, C. (eds), *Church Archaeology. Research Directions for the Future*, Council for British Archaeology, 112–26

Giles, K. 1999. 'The "familiar" fraternity: the appropriation and consumption of guildhalls in early modern York', in Tarlow, S. and West, S. (eds), *The Familiar Past? Archaeologies of later historical Britain*, Routledge, 87–102

Giorgi, J. 1997. 'Diet in late medieval and early modern London: the archaeobotanical evidence', in Gaimster, D. and Stamper, P. (eds), *The Age of Transition. The Archaeology of English Culture 1400–1600*, Oxbow Monograph 98, 197–213

Giorgi, J. 1999. 'Archaeobotanical evidence from London on aspects of post-medieval urban economies', in Egan, G. and Michael, R. (eds), *Old and New Worlds*, Oxbow Books, 342–48

Girouard, M. 1978. *Life in the English Country House*, Yale University Press

Girouard, M. 1979. *Historic Houses of Britain*, Artus

Girouard, M. 1994. *Hardwick Hall, Derbyshire*, National Trust

Gittings, C. 1984. *Death, Burial and the Individual in Early Modern England*, Croom Helm

Gittings, C. 1992. 'Urban funerals in late medieval and Reformation England', in Bassett, S. (ed.), *Death in Towns. Urban Response to the Dying and the Dead 100–1600*, Leicester University Press

Glassie, H. 1975. *Folk Housing in Middle Virginia: a structural analysis of historic artifacts*, University of Tennessee Press

Glennie, P.D. 1990. 'Industry and towns 1500–1730', in Dodgshon, R.A. and Butlin, R.A. (eds), *An Historical Geography of England and Wales*, 2nd edn, Academic Press, 199–222

Glennie, P.D. 1995. 'Consumption within historical studies', in Miller, D. (ed.), *Acknowledging Consumption. A Review of New Studies*, Routledge, 164–203

Gordon, R.B. 1993. 'The interpretation of artifacts in the history of technology', in Lubar, S. and David Kingery, W. (eds), *History From Things. Essays on Material Culture*, Smithsonian Institution Press, 76–91

Gould, S. 1993. 'Monuments Protection Programme: the Alum Industry. Combined Steps 1–3 Report', unpubl report circulated by English Heritage

Gould, S. 1999a. 'Planning, development and social archaeology', in Tarlow, S. and West, S. (eds), *The Familiar Past? Archaeologies of later historical Britain*, Routledge, 140–54

Gould, S. 1999b. *The Somerset Coalfield*, Somerset Industrial Archaeological Society

Gould, S. and Ayris, A. 1995. *Colliery Landscapes*, English Heritage

Gowlett, J.A.J. 1997. 'High definition archaeology: threads through the past', *World Archaeology* 29.2, 152–71

Grady, D. 1998. 'Medieval and Post-Medieval Salt Extraction in North-East Lincolnshire', in Bewley, R.H. (ed.), *Lincolnshire's Archaeology from the Air*, Occasional Papers in Lincolnshire History and Archaeology

Gräf, H.T. 1994. 'Leicestershire small towns and pre-industrial urbanisation', *Transactions of the Leicestershire Archaeological and Historical Society* 68, 98–120

Grant, E. 1988. 'The sphinx in the north: Egyptian influences on landscape, architecture and interior design in eighteenth- and nineteenth-century Scotland', in Cosgrove, D. and Daniels, S. (eds), *The Iconography of Landscape*, Cambridge University Press, 236–53

Gray, M. 1974. 'Scottish emigration: the social impact of agrarian change in the rural lowlands, 1775–1875', *Perspectives of American History* 7, 95–174

Greatorex, C. 1995. 'An archaeological investigation of the Royal Military Canal, near Ham Street', *Archaeologia Cantiana* 115, 231–7

Green, S. 1996. 'The post-Reformation church in Scotland. Disruption, unification and the aftermath: the church in Scotland 1700–1990', in Blair, J. and Pyrah, C. (eds), *Church Archaeology. Research Directions for the Future*, Council for British Archaeology, 134–43

Green, S.J.D. 1993. 'The Church of England and the working classes in late Victorian and Edwardian Halifax', *Transactions of the Halifax Antiquarian Society*, New Ser. 1, 106–20

Greenhalgh, M. 1989. *The Survival of Roman Antiquities in the Middle Ages*, Duckworth

Greig, J. 1988. 'Plant resources', in Astill, G. and Grant, A. (eds), *The Countryside of Medieval England*, Blackwell, 108–27

Greig, M.K. 1993. 'Excavations at Craigievar Castle, Aberdeenshire', *Proceedings of the Society of Antiquaries of Scotland* 123, 381–93

Grenter, S. 1992. 'Bersham Ironworks Excavations: Interim Report', *Industrial Archaeology Review* 14/2, 177–92

Grenville, J. 1997. *Medieval Housing*, Leicester University Press

Griffiths, M. and Thomas, H.J. 1984. 'Evidence for the origins of the durable hall-house in Glamorgan: excavations at Cwmcidy, Barry, 1984', *Morgannwg* 28, 13–28

Grove, D. 1999. *Berwick Barracks and Fortifications*, English Heritage

Gunn, S. 1996. 'The ministry, the middle class and the civilizing mission in Manchester 1850–80', *Social History* 21.1, 22–36

Hague, D.B. 1973. *Old Beaupre Castle*, HMSO

Hair, N. and Newman, R. 1999. 'Excavation of medieval settlement remains at Crosedale in Howgill', *Transactions of the Cumberland & Westmorland Antiquarian and Archaeological Society* 99, 141–58

Haldane, C. 1996. 'Sadana Island shipwreck, Egypt: preliminary report', *International Journal of Nautical Archaeology* 25.2, 83–94

Hall, L. 1991. 'Yeoman or gentleman? Problems in defining social status in seventeenth- and eighteenth-century Gloucestershire', *Vernacular Architecture* 21, 2–19

Halley, R. 1869. *Lancashire: its Puritanism and Nonconformity*, vol. 1, Hodder & Stoughton

Harbottle, B. 1968. 'Excavations at the Carmelite Friary, Newcastle upon Tyne 1965–1967', *Archaeologia Aeliana* 5.9, 163–223

Harbottle, B. 1995. 'Prestwick Carr: its draining and enclosure', *Archaeologia Aeliana* 5.23, 1–15

Harding, P.A. 1995. 'An archaeological survey and watching brief at Garston Lock, Kennet and Avon Canal', *Industrial Archaeology Review* 17, 159–70

Harding, P.A. and Newman, R. 1997. 'The excavation of a turf-sided lock at Monkey Marsh, Thatcham, Berks', *Industrial Archaeology Review* 19, 31–48

Harrington, P. 1992. *Archaeology of the English Civil War*, Shire

Harris, J.R. 1988. *The British Iron Industry 1700–1850*, Macmillan

Harrison, B. and Hutton, B. 1984. *Vernacular Houses of North Yorkshire and Cleveland*, John Donald

Harrison, J.G. 1999. 'Public hygiene and drainage in Stirling and other early modern Scottish towns', *Review of Scottish Culture* 11, 67–77

Hart, C. 1971. *The Industrial History of Dean*, David & Charles

Hart, C. 1983. *Coleford. The History of a West Gloucestershire Forest Town*, Alan Sutton Publishing

Hart, C. 1995. *The Forest of Dean. New History 1550–1818*, Alan Sutton Publishing

Hart Hansen, J.P., Meldgaard, J. and Nordqvist, J. 1991. *The Greenland Mummies*, British Museum

Hartley, R.F. 1994. 'Tudor Miners of Coleorton, Leicestershire', in Ford, T.D. and Willies, L. (eds), *Mining before Powder* (Historical Metallurgy Society); Peak District Mines Historical Society Bulletin 12/3

Harvey, N. 1989. 'The farmsteads of the Exmoor reclamation', *Journal of the Historic Farm Buildings Group* 3, 45–57

Hassan, J.A. 1985. 'The growth and impact of the British water industry in the nineteenth century', *Economic History Review* 38, 531–47

Hatcher, J. 1993. *The History of the British Coal Industry. Vol. 1. Before 1700: Towards the Age of Coal*, Clarendon Press

Hayfield, C. 1984. 'Wawne, East Riding of Yorkshire: a case study in settlement morphology', *Landscape History* 6, 41–67

Hayfield, C. 1995. 'Farm servants' accommodation on the Yorkshire Wolds', *Folk Life* 33, 7–28

Hayton, S. 1998. 'The archetypal Irish cellar dweller', *Manchester Region History Review* 12, 66–77

Heawood, R. forthcoming a. *Old Abbey Farm, Risley, Warrington Borough. Building Survey and Excavation at a Medieval Moated Site*, Lancaster Imprints

Heawood, R. forthcoming b. *The 'Hotties'. Excavation and Building Survey at the Watson Street Cone House, St Helens, Merseyside*, Lancaster Imprints

Hedley, I. and Scott, I. 1999. 'The St Helens Iron Foundry', *Industrial Archaeology Review* 21, 53–9

Herring, P. and Thomas, N. 2nd edn 1990. *The Archaeology of Kit Hill*, Cornwall Archaeological Unit

Heslop, D.H. and McCombie, G. 1996. 'Alderman Fenwick's house: a late seventeenth-century house in Pilgrim Street, Newcastle', *Archaeologia Aeliana* 5th ser. 24, 129–69

Heslop, D.H. and Truman, L. 1993. 'The Cooperage, 32–34 The Close: a timber-framed building in Newcastle-upon-Tyne', *Archaeologia Aeliana* 5th ser. 21, 1–14

Hewett, C.A. 1973. 'The development of the post-medieval house', *Post-Medieval Archaeology* 7, 60–78

Higgs, P., Larson, J. and Wood, J. 1996. 'A Hellenistic head from the Badger Hall estate, Shropshire', *Journal of the British Archaeological Association* 149, 72–7

Hillier, W. and Hanson, J. 1984. *The Social Logic of Space*, Cambridge University Press

Hingley, R. and Foster, S. 1994. 'Medieval or later rural settlement in Scotland – defining, understanding and conserving an archaeological resource', *Medieval Settlement Research Group Annual Report* 9, 7–11

Hinton, D.A. 1990. *Archaeology, Economy, and Society*, Seaby

Hodder, I. 1987. *The Archaeology of Contextual Meanings*, Cambridge University Press

Hodder, I. 1991. 'To interpret is to act: the need for an interpretative archaeology', *Scottish Archaeological Review* 8, 8–13

Hodges, H. 1976. *Artifacts. An Introduction to Early Materials and Technology*, John Baker

Hoskins, W.G. 1953. 'The rebuilding of rural England 1570–1640', *Past and Present* 4, 44–59

Hoskins, W.G. 1955. *The Making of the English Landscape*, Hodder & Stoughton

Howard, M. 1997. 'Civic buildings and courtier houses: new techniques and materials for architectural ornament', in Gaimster, D. and Stamper, P. (eds), *The Age of Transition. The Archaeology of English Culture 1400–1600*, Oxbow Monograph 98, 105–13

Howard-Davis, C. 1987. 'The tannery, Rusland, south Cumbria', *Transactions of the Cumberland and Westmorland Antiquarian and Archaeological Society* 87, 237–50

Howes, L. 1991. 'Archaeology as an aid to restoration at Painshill Park', in Brown, A.E. (ed.), *Garden Archaeology*, CBA Research Report 78, 73–82

Hughes, P.M. 1980. 'Houses and property in post-reformation Worcester', in Carver, M.O.H. (ed.), 'Medieval Worcester: an Archaeological Framework', *Transactions of the Worcestershire Archaeological Society*, 3rd ser. vol. 7, 269–92

Hughes, S. 1988. *The Archaeology of the Montgomeryshire Canal*, RCAHMW

Hughes, S. 1990. *The Archaeology of the Early Railway System*, RCAHMW

Hundsbichler, H. 1997. 'Sampling or proving 'reality'? Co-ordinates for the evaluation of historical archaeology research', in Gaimster, D. and Stamper, P. (eds), *The Age of Transition. The Archaeology of English Culture 1400–1600*, Oxbow Monograph 98, 45–59

Hunter, J. and Ralston, I. 1999. *The Archaeology of Britain*, Routledge

Hurst, J.D. 1997. *A multi-period salt production site at Droitwich: excavations at Upwich*, CBA Research Report 107

Hyde, C.K. 1973. *Technological change and the British Iron Industry*, Princeton

Hyde, M. 1997. 'The puzzle of "Churches of the Middle Ages"', *The Victorian Society Annual 1996*, 21–6

Hyde, R. 1994. *A Prospect of Britain: the Town Panoramas of Samuel and Nathaniel Buck*, Pavilion Books

Ince, L. 1989. 'Water power and cylinder blowing in early South Wales coke ironworks', *Historical Metallurgy* 23/2, 108–11

Ince, L. 1991. 'The introduction of coke iron at the Stour forges of the Knight family', *Historical Metallurgy* 24/2, 107–13

Jackson, J.T. 1979. 'Nineteenth-century housing in Wigan and St Helens', *Transactions of the Historic Society of Lancashire and Cheshire* 129, 124–43

Jackson, R.G. and Price, R.H. 1974. *Bristol Clay Pipes: a study of makers and their marks*, Bristol City Museum Research Monograph 1

James, T.B. 1988. *Clarendon: a Medieval Royal Palace*, Salisbury and South Wiltshire Museum

James, T.B. 1990. *The Palaces of Medieval England*, Seaby

Jamilly, E. 1992. 'An introduction to Victorian synagogues', *The Victorian Society Annual 1991*, 22–35

Jarrett, M.G. and Wrathmell, S. 1977. 'Sixteenth- and seventeenth-century farmsteads: West Whelpington, Northumberland', *Agricultural History Review* 25, 108–19

Jenkin, A.H.K. 1948. *The Cornish Miner*, George Allen & Unwin

Johnson, M.H. 1992. 'Meanings of Polite Architecture in Sixteenth-Century England', *Historical Archaeology* 26, 45–56

Johnson, M.H. 1993a. *Housing Culture: Traditional Architecture in an English Landscape*, UCL Press

Johnson, M.H. 1993b. 'Rethinking the Great Rebuilding', *Oxford Journal of Archaeology* 12:1, 117–24

Johnson, M.H. 1996. *An Archaeology of Capitalism*, Blackwells

Johnson, M.H. 1997. 'Rethinking houses, rethinking transitions: of vernacular architecture, ordinary people and everyday culture', in Gaimster, D. and Stamper, P. (eds), *The Age of Transition. The Archaeology of English Culture 1400–1600*, Oxbow Monograph 98, 145–55

Johnson, M.H. 1999a. 'Reconstructing castles and refashioning identities in Renaissance England', in Tarlow, S. and West, S. (eds), *The Familiar Past? Archaeologies of later historical Britain*, Routledge, 69–86

Johnson, M.H. 1999b. 'The new post-medieval archaeology', in Egan, G. and Michael, R.L. (eds), *Old and New Worlds*, Oxbow Books, 17–22

Johnson, M.H. 1999c. *Archaeological Theory*, Blackwell

Johnson, N. 1991. *Eighteenth-Century London*, Museum of London

Jones, E.L. 1968. 'The reduction of fire damage in southern England, 1650–1850', *Post-Medieval Archaeology* 2, 140–9

Jones, W. 1996. *Dictionary of Industrial Archaeology*, Sutton Publishing

Kaufman, M. 1907. (repub 1975). *The Housing of the Working Classes and of the Poor*, EP Publishing

Kelsall, A.F. 1974. 'The London house-plan in the later 17th century', *Post-Medieval Archaeology* 8, 80–91

Kenyon, J.R. 1977. 'Wark castle and its artillery defences in the reign of Henry VII', *Post-Medieval Archaeology* 11, 50–60

Kenyon, J.R. 1982. 'The Civil War earthworks around Raglan Castle, Gwent', *Archaeologia Cambrensis* 131, 139–42

Kenyon, J.R. 1986. *Kidwelly Castle*, Cadw

Kenyon, J.R. 1990. *Medieval Fortifications*, Leicester University Press

Kerridge, E. 1951. 'Ridge and furrow and economic history', *Economic History Review* 2.4, 14–36

Kiernan, D. 1989. *The Derbyshire Lead Industry in the 16th century*, Derbyshire Record Society

King, P.W. 1996. 'Early Statistics for the iron industry: a vindication', *Historical Metallurgy* 30/1, 23–46

King, P.W. 1997. 'The Development of the iron industry in South Staffordshire in the 17th century: history and myth', *Transactions of the Staffordshire Archaeological and Historical Society* 38, 59–76

Kingsley, N.W. 1981. *The Country House in Gloucestershire*, Gloucestershire County Council

Knox, S.A. 1985. *The Making of the Shetland Landscape*, John Donald Publishers

Laithwaite, M. 1984. 'Totnes houses 1500–1800', in Clark, P. (ed.), *The Transformation of English Provincial Towns*, Oxford University Press, 62–98

Lake, J., Cox, J. and Berry, E. 1997. 'The stronghold of Methodism: a survey of chapels in Cornwall', *Church Archaeology* 1, 26–34

Leah, M., Wells, C.E., Stamper, P., Huckerby, E. and Welch, C. 1998. *The Wetlands of Shropshire and Staffordshire*, Lancaster Imprints 7, Lancaster University Archaeological Unit

Leech, R.H. 1996. 'The prospect from Rugman's Row: the Row House in late 16th and early 17th century London', *Archaeological Journal* 153, 201–42

Leech, R.H. 1999a. 'The Processional City: some issues for historical archaeology', in Tarlow, S. and West, S. (eds), *The Familiar Past? Archaeologies of Later Historical Britain*, Routledge, 19–34

Leech, R.H. 1999b. 'Row and terrace – urban housing in the 17th and 18th century English city', in Egan, G. and Michael, R.L. (eds), *Old and New Worlds*, Oxbow Books, 41–50

Lelong, O. and Wood, J. 2000. 'A township through time: excavation and survey at the deserted settlement of Easter Raitts, Badenoch, 1995–1999', in Atkinson, J.A., Banks, I. and MacGregor, G. (eds), *Townships to Farmsteads. Rural Settlement Studies in Scotland, England and Wales*, BAR Brit. Ser. 293, 40–9

Leone, M.P. and Potter, P.B. (eds), 1988. *The Recovery of Meaning in Historical Archaeology*, Smithsonian

Leone, M.P., Potter, P.B. Jr and Shakel, P.A. 1987. 'Toward a critical archaeology', *Current Anthropology* 28(3), 823–902

Lewis, J., Martin, C., Martin, P. and Murdoch, R. (ed. Yeoman, P.) 1999. *The Salt and Coal Industries at St Monans, Fife, in the 18th & 19th Centuries*, Glenrothes: Tayside and Fife Archaeological Committee, Monograph 2

Li Bing-Wu. Nd. *Emperor Qin Shihuang's Eternal Terracotta Warriors and Horses*, Shaanxi Sanqin Publishing House

Lloyd-Jones, R. and Lewis, M. 1993. 'Housing factory workers: Ancoats in the early nineteenth century', *Manchester Region History Review* 7, 33–6

Locock, M. 1994. 'Spatial analysis of an eighteenth-century formal garden', in Locock, M. (ed.), *Meaningful Architecture: Social Interpretations of Buildings*, 231–52

Locock, M. 1995. 'Excavations behind Bank Street, Chepstow', *Monmouthshire Antiquary* 11, 57–70

Locock, M. 1996. 'Bethel Square, Brecon: excavations in the medieval town', *Brycheiniog* 28, 35–79

Lowe, J. 1977. *Welsh Industrial Workers Housing 1775–1875*, National Museum of Wales

LUAU. 1996a. 'Central Building Hatton Hospital, Warwickshire: Fabric Survey', unpubl. client report

LUAU. 1996b. 'Lyme Park, Cheshire: Archaeological Survey', unpubl. client report

LUAU. 1996c. 'Rufford Old Hall, Lancashire: Fabric Survey', unpubl. client report

LUAU. 1997a. 'Newland Park, Normanton, West Yorkshire: Archaeological Evaluation', unpubl. client report

LUAU. 1997b. 'North West Water's Forest of Bowland Estate, Lancashire: Archaeological Survey Report', unpubl. client report

LUAU. 1998. 'Lancashire Extensive Urban Archaeological Survey Assessment Report', unpubl. client report

LUAU. 1999. 'Telford's Holyhead Road (A5), North Wales: Archaeological Survey Report', unpubl. client report

LUAU. 2000a. 'Queens Park Hospital, Blackburn, Lancashire, Archaeological Assessment', unpubl. client report

LUAU. 2000b. 'Darwen Street and Church Street, Blackburn, Lancashire: Archaeological Assessment', unpubl. client report

Lucas, R. 1998a. 'Neo-Gothic, Neo-Tudor, Neo-Renaissance: The Costessey Brickyard', *The Victorian Society Journal 1997*, 25–37

Lucas, R. 1998b. 'Dutch pantiles in the county of Norfolk: architecture and international trade in the 17th and 18th centuries', *Post-Medieval Archaeology* 32, 75–94

Lydon, J. 1993. 'Task differential in historical archaeology: sewing as material culture', in Du Cros, H. and Smith, L. (eds), *Women in Archaeology. a Feminist Critique*, Australian National University Press

Lynch, M. 1991. *Scotland: a New History*, Pimlico

McDonnel, J. 1988. 'The role of transhumance in Northern England', *Northern History* 24, 1–17

McGlade, J. 1995. 'Archaeology and the ecodynamics of human modified landscapes', *Antiquity* 69, 113–32

McInnes, A. 1988. 'The emergence of a leisure town: Shrewsbury 1660–1760', *Past and Present* 120, 53–87

McKean, C. 1991. 'The House of Pitsligo', *Proceedings of the Society of Antiquaries of Scotland* 121, 369–90

MacKie, E.W. 1997. 'Some eighteenth-century ferryhouses in Appin Lorn, Argyll: the development of the single-storeyed mortared stone cottage', *Antiquaries Journal* 77, 243–89

McWilliam, C. 1979. 'Castles and mansions of Scotland', in Fedden, R. and Kenworthy-Browne, J. (eds), *The Country House Guide* (Jonathan Cape), 353–8

Machin, R. 1977. 'The Great Rebuilding: a reassessment', *Past and Present* 67, 35–6

Magnusson, G. (ed.), 1995. *The Importance of Ironmaking: Technical Innovation and Social Change*, Stockholm

Malcolm, G. 1997. 'Excavations at Island Site, Finsbury Pavement, London EC2', *Transactions of the London and Middlesex Archaeological Society* 48, 33–58

Mandler, P. 1997. 'Against "Englishness": English culture and the limits to rural nostalgia, 1850–1940', *Transactions of the Royal Historical Society*, 6th ser. 7, 155–75

Margeson, S. 1993. *Norwich Households: Medieval and Post-Medieval Finds from Norwich Survey Excavations 1971–78*, East Anglian Archaeology Series 58

Markus, T. 1993. *Buildings and Power. Freedom and Control in the Origins of Modern Building Types*, Routledge

Marsden, D.E. 1997. 'The development of Kirkcudbright in the late 18th century. Town planning in a Galloway context', *Transactions of the Dumfries and Galloway Natural History and Archaeological Society* 72, 89–96

Marshall, G. 1995. 'Redressing the balance – an archaeological evaluation of North Yorkshire's coastal alum industry', *Industrial Archaeology Review* 18.1, 39–62

Marshall, J.D. 1980. 'Agrarian wealth and social structure in pre-industrial Cumbria', *Economic History Review*, 2nd ser. 33, 503–21

Marshall, Y. and Maas, A. 1997. 'Dashing dishes', *World Archaeology* 28.3, 275–90

Martell, H. and Gill, M.C. 1992. 'Lead smelting in Welsh furnaces at Pontesford, Shropshire', *Bulletin of the Peak District Mines Historical Society* 11/2, 297–312

Matthews, K.J. 1999. 'Familiarity and contempt. The archaeology of the "modern"', in Tarlow, S. and West, S. (eds), *The Familiar Past?*, Routledge

Maxwell-Irving, A.M.T. 1994. 'The tower-houses of Kirtleside', *Transactions of the Dumfries and Galloway Natural History and Archaeological Society* 72, 55–67

Mercer, E. 1954. 'The Houses of the Gentry', *Past and Present* 5, 11–72

Mercer, E. 1975. *English Vernacular Houses: a Study of Traditional Farmhouses and Cottages*, HMSO

Mercer, E. 1990. 'Time and chance: a timely rejoinder', *Vernacular Architecture* 21, 1–3

Middleton, R., Wells, C.E. and Huckerby, E. 1995. *The Wetlands of North Lancashire*, Lancaster Imprints 4 Lancaster University Archaeological Unit

Miller, H.M. 1999. 'Archaeology and town planning in early British America', in Egan, G. and Michael, R.L. (eds), *Old and New Worlds*, Oxbow Books, 72–83

Miller, I. Forthcoming. 'The Netherhall blast furnace, Maryport', *Journal of Historical Metallurgy*

Millward, R. and Robinson, A. 1977. *Landscapes of Britain*, David & Charles

Mitchell, S. 1984. 'The development of urban retailing 1700–1815', in Clark, P. (ed.), *The Transformation of English Provincial Towns*, Hutchinson

Mitchell, W.R. 1996. *The Lost Shanties of Ribblehead*, Castleberg

Mitson, A. and Cox, B. 1995. 'Victorian estate housing on the Yarborough estate, Lincolnshire', *Rural History* 6, 1, 29–45

Monckton, A. 1995. 'Environmental archaeology in Leicestershire', *Transactions of the Leicestershire Archaeological and Historical Society* 69, 32–41

Moore, N.J. 1994. 'Arlington Row, Bibury, Gloucestershire, early conversion of an industrial building', *Vernacular Architecture* 25, 20–4

Moorhouse, S. 1995. 'A late medieval water-powered ironworking complex at the head of Bishopdale, North Yorkshire', in Crew, P. and Crew, S. (eds), *Iron for Archaeologists*, Plas Tan y Bwlch

Morgan, K. 1993. *Bristol and the Atlantic Trade in the 18th Century*, Cambridge University Press

Morgan, N. 1993. *Deadly Dwellings*, Preston Borough Council

Morley, B., Brown, P. and Crump, T. 1995. 'The Elizabethan gardens and Leicester's stables at Kenilworth Castle: excavations between 1970 and 1984', *Birmingham and Warwickshire Archaeological Society Transactions* 99, 81–116

Morris, M. 1994. 'Towards an archaeology of navvy huts and settlements of the industrial revolution', *Antiquity* 68, 573–84

Morris, R. 1989. *Churches in the Landscape*, J.M. Dent & Sons

Morris, R.J. 1981. 'Materialism and tenements', *Scottish Economic and Social History* 1

Morris, R.J. 2000. 'The Industrial Town', in Waller, P. (ed.), *The English Urban Landscape*, Oxford University Press, 175–208

Morrison, K. 1999. *The Workhouse – a Study of Poor-Law Buildings in England*, RCHME

Mott, R.A. (ed. Singer, P.) 1983. *Henry Cort: the Great Finer*, The Metals Society

Muir, R. 1998. 'Figures in the landscape', in Jones, M. and Rotherham, I.D. (eds), *Landscapes – Perception, Recognition and Management: reconciling the impossible?*, The Landscape Conservation Forum and Sheffield Hallam University, 1–6

Murdoch, T. 1991. *Treasures and Trinkets. Jewellery in London from Pre-Roman Times to the 1930s*, Museum of London

Muthesius, S. 1982. *The English Terraced House*, Yale University Press

Mytum, H. 1994. 'Language as symbol in churchyard monuments: the use of Welsh in nineteenth- and twentieth-century Pembrokeshire', *World Archaeology* 26, 252–67

Mytum, H. 1999. 'Welsh cultural identity in nineteenth-century Pembrokeshire: the pedimented headstone as a graveyard monument', in Tarlow, S. and West, S. (eds), *The Familiar Past?*, Routledge, 215–30

Mytum, H. forthcoming. 'Gravestones and burial grounds: how nonconformist were they?', in Newman, R. (ed.), *The Archaeology of NonConformity*, LUAU

Mytum, H., Dunk, J. and Rugg, J. 1994. 'Closed urban churchyards in England and Wales: some survey results', *Post-Medieval Archaeology* 28, 111–14

Naismith, R.J. 1985. *Buildings of the Scottish Countryside*, Victor Gollancz

Nash, G.D. 1989. 'Up at Dawn. The experimental erection of a squatter's cabin', *Folk Life* 27, 57–70

Neale, R. 1974. 'Society, belief and the building of Bath, 1700–1793', in Chalklin, C. and Havinden, M. (eds), *Rural Change and Urban Growth 1500–1800*, Longman

Nenadic, S. 1994. 'Middle-rank consumers and domestic culture in Edinburgh and Glasgow 1720–1840', *Past and Present* 145, 122–56

Neustupný, E. 1993. *Archaeological Method*, Cambridge University Press

Nevell, M. 1997. *The Archaeology of Trafford*, Trafford Metropolitan Borough Council

Nevell, M. and Walker, J. 1999. *Tameside in Transition: The Archaeology of the Industrial Revolution in Two North-West Lordships, 1642–1870*, Tameside Metropolitan Borough Council

Newman, C. 1992. 'Small town trade: evidence for international and local exchange from Romsey, Hampshire', *Exchange and Trade*, Medieval Europe 1992 pre-printed papers 5, 99–104

Newman, R. 1983. 'The effect of orcharding and the cider industry on the landscape of West Gloucestershire *c.* 1600–1800', *Transactions of the Woolhope Naturalists and Antiquarian Society* 44, 202–14

Newman, R. 1987. 'Cosmeston: a medieval village reborn', *Archaeology Today*, April 1987, 38–45

Newman, R. 1988. 'The Development of the Rural landscape of West Gloucestershire, *c.* 1550–1800', unpubl. PhD thesis, University of Wales, Cardiff

Newman, R. 1996. 'Medieval rural settlement', in Newman, R. (ed.), *The Archaeology of Lancashire*, Lancaster University Archaeological Unit

Newman, R. 1999. 'Current trends in the archaeological study of post-medieval landscapes in England: context, character and chaos', in Egan, G. and Michael, R. (eds), *Old and New Worlds*, Oxbow Books, 390–6

Newman, R. 2000. 'Landscape study in farm survey', in Fairclough, G.J., Lambrick, G. and McNab, A. (eds), *Yesterday's Landscape, Tomorrow's World: The English Heritage Landscape Project*, English Heritage

Newman, R. and Wilkinson, P. 1996. 'Excavations at Llanmaes, near Llantwit Major, South Glamorgan', *Post-Medieval Archaeology* 30, 187–233

Newton, G.D. 1976. 'Single-storey cottages in West Yorkshire', *Folk Life* 14, 65–74

Newton, R. 1977.'Exeter, 1770–1870', in Simpson, M.A. and Lloyd, T.H. (eds), *Middle Class Housing in Britain*, David & Charles, 12–43

Noël Hume, A. 1968. 'Some ceramic milestones of use to the archaeologist', *Post-Medieval Archaeology* 2, 163

Noël Hume, I. 1969. *A Guide to the Artifacts of Colonial America*, 1st Vintage Books

Noël Hume, I. 1978. 'Into the jaws of death walked one!', in Bird, J., Chapman, H. and Clark, J. (eds), *Collectanea Londoninensis: Studies in Archaeology and History Presented to Ralph Merrifield*, London and Middlesex Archaeological Society, 7–22

Norris, M. 1992. 'Later medieval monumental brasses: an urban funerary industry and its representation of death', in Bassett, S. (ed.), *Death in Towns. Urban Response to the Dying and the Dead 100–1600*, Leicester University Press

Northcote Parkinson, C. 1952. *The Rise of the Port of Liverpool*, Liverpool University Press

Oram, R., Griffiths, W.B. and Hodgson, N. 1998. 'Excavations at Wallsend Colliery B Pit, 1997', *Archaeologia Aeliana* 26, 115–60

Orser, C.E. 1996. *A Historical Archaeology of the Modern World*, Plenum Press

Orser, C.E. Jr and Fagan, B.M. 1995. *Historical Archaeology*, HarperCollins, New York

Orton, C., Tyers, P. and Vince, A. 1993. *Pottery in Archaeology*, Cambridge University Press

Oswald, A. 1975. *Clay Pipes for the Archaeologist*, British Archaeological Reports 14

Page, R. and Page, C. 1995. 'The excavation of a disused military road at Buchlyvie, Central Region', *Glasgow Archaeological Journal* 19, 101–5

Palmer, M. and Neaverson, P. 1998. *Industrial Archaeology. Principles and Practice*, Routledge

Pantin, W.A. 1963. 'Medieval English town-house plans', *Medieval Archaeology* 7, 202–39

Papworth, M., Grace, N., Watts, M. and Brebner, B. 1995. 'Watermills on the Kingston Lacy Estate', *Industrial Archaaeology Review* 18.1, 106–16

Parker Pearson, M. and Richards, C. (eds), 1993. *Architecture and Order: approaches to social space*, Routledge

Parkinson, A.J. 1996. 'Reformation, restoration and revival: churches and chapels in Wales, 1600–1900', in Blair J. and Pyrah, C. (eds), *Church Archaeology. Research Directions for the Future*, Council for British Archaeology, 144–58

Parnell, G. 1983. 'The refortification of the Tower of London 1679–86', *Antiquaries Journal* 63, 337–52

Parry, S. and McGrail, S. 1989. 'The Tredunnoc boat', *International Journal of Nautical Archaeology and Underwater Exploration* 18.1, 43–9

Pattison, P. (ed.), 1998. *There by Design*, RCHME

Pawson, E. 1977. *Transport and Economy: the Turnpike Roads of Eighteenth Century Britain*, Academic Press

Pawson, E. 1979. *The Early Industrial Revolution*, Batsford

Pearce, J. 1998. 'A rare Delftware Hebrew plate and associated assemblage from an excavation in Mitre Street, City of London', *Post-Medieval Archaeology* 32, 95–112

Pearson, S. 1994. *The Medieval Houses of Kent: An Historical Analysis*, HMSO

Pearson, S. 1998. 'Vernacular buildings in the landscape', in Everson, P. and Williamson, T. (eds), *The Archaeology of Landscape*, Manchester University Press, 166–82

Pennell, S. 1999. 'The material culture of food in early modern England', in Tarlow, S. and West, S. (eds), *The Familiar Past? Archaeologies of Later Historical Britain*, Routledge, 35–50

Perry, D.R. 1999. 'Excavations at 77–79 High Street, Arbroath', *Tayside and Fife Archaeological Journal* 5, 68–71

Pevsner, N. 1969. *The Buildings of England: North Lancashire*, Penguin

Phillips, C.B. and Smith, J.H. 1994. *Lancashire and Cheshire from AD 1540*, Longman

Phillpotts, C. 1999. 'Landscape into townscape: an historical and archaeological investigation of the Limehouse area, east London', *Landscape History* 21, 59–76

Philpott, R.A. 1988. *Historic Towns of the Merseyside Area: a survey of urban settlement to c. 1800*, National Museums & Galleries on Merseyside Occasional Papers 3

Pickford, C. 1996. 'From ruin to rebuilding: a study of Pulloxhill church after the fall of the steeple in *c*. 1653 to its rebuilding in 1845–6', *Bedfordshire Archaeology* 22, 155–62

Platt, C. 1976. *The English Medieval Town*, Secker & Warburg

Platt, C. 1994. *The Great Rebuilding of Tudor and Stuart England*, UCL Press

PMA. 1973. 'Post-Medieval Britain in 1972', *Post-Medieval Archaeology* 7, 100–17

PMA. 1985. 'Post-Medieval Britain in 1984', *Post-Medieval Archaeology* 19, 159–91

PMA. 1986. 'Post-Medieval Britain in 1985', *Post-Medieval Archaeology* 20, 333–60

PMA. 1992. 'Post-Medieval Britain in 1991', *Post-Medieval Archaeology* 26, 95–156

PMA. 1993. 'Post-Medieval Britain in 1992', *Post-Medieval Archaeology* 27, 205–96

PMA. 1996. 'Post-Medieval Britain in 1995', *Post-Medieval Archaeology* 31, 245–320

PMA. 1998. 'Post-Medival Britain and Ireland in 1997', *Post-Medieval Archaeology* 32, 145–206

Porter, J. 1978. 'Waste land reclamation in the sixteenth and seventeenth centuries: the case of south-eastern Bowland, 1550–1630', *Transactions of the Historic Society of Lancashire and Cheshire* 127, 1–23

Porter, J. 1980. *The Making of the Central Pennines*, Ash Grove Books

Porter, S. 1994. *Destruction in the English Civil Wars*, Sutton Publishing

Portman, D. 1966. *Exeter Houses 1400–1700*, Phillimore

Potter, P.B. Jr. 1992. 'Critical archaeology: in the ground and on the street', *Historical Archaeology* 26, 118–29

Priestley, U. and Corfield, P.J. 1982. 'Rooms and room use in Norwich housing 1580–1730', *Post-Medieval Archaeology* 16, 93–124

Prince, H.C. 1989. 'The changing rural landscape 1750–1850', in Mingay, G.E. (ed.), *The Agrarian History of England and Wales. Vol. VI: 1750–1850*, Cambridge University Press, 7–85

Pringle, T.R. 1988. 'The privation of history: Landseer, Victoria and the Highland myth', in Cosgrove, D. and Daniels, S. (eds), *The Iconography of Landscape*, Cambridge University Press 142–61

Rackham, O. 1976. *Trees and Woodland in the British Landscape*, Dent

Rackham, O. 1980. *Ancient Woodland: its History, Vegetation and Uses in England*, Edward Arnold

Rackham, O. 1986. *The History of the Countryside*, Dent

Raistrick, A. 1972. *Industrial Archaeology*, Eyre Methuen Ltd

Ramm, H.G., McDowell, R.W. and Mercer, E. 1970. *Shielings and Bastles*, HMSO

Ransom, P.J.G. 1984. *The Archaeology of the Transport Revolution*, World's Work Ltd

RCAHMS. 1986. *Monuments of Industry*, HMSO

RCAHMS. 1996. *Tolbooths and Town-Houses. Civic Architecture in Scotland to 1833*, HMSO

RCAHMW. 1988. *An Inventory of the Ancient Monuments in Glamorgan. Vol. IV: Domestic Architecture from the Reformation to the Industrial Revolution. Part II: Farmhouses and Cottages*, HMSO

RCHME. 1964. *Newark: the Civil War Siege Works*, HMSO

RCHME. 1981. *Early Industrial Housing: the Trinity area of Frome*, Supplementary Series 3, HMSO

RCHME. 1985a. *Rural Houses of the Lancashire Pennines 1560–1760*, Supplementary Series 10, HMSO

RCHME. 1985b. *Workers' Housing in West Yorkshire 1750–1920*, Supplementary Series 9, HMSO

RCHME. 1986. *Rural Houses of West Yorkshire 1400–1830*, Supplementary Series 8, HMSO

RCHME. 1987. *Churches of South East Wiltshire*, HMSO

RCHME. 1991. *Whitehaven*, RCHME

RCHME. 1997. *English Farmsteads 1750–1914*, RCHME

Reed, M. 1983. *The Georgian Triumph 1700–1830*, Routledge & Kegan Paul

Reed, M. 1986. *The Age of Exuberance 1500–1700*, Paladin

Rees, G. 1980. *Early Railway Prints. A Social History of the Railways from 1825 to 1850*, Phaidon

Reeve, J. 1998. 'A view from the metropolis: post-medieval burials in London', in Cox, M. (ed.), *Grave Concerns: Death and Burial in England 1700–1850*, CBA Research Report 113, 213–23

Rehder, J.E. 1987. 'The change from charcoal to coke in iron smelting', *Historical Metallurgy* 21/1, 37–43

Rice, P.M. 1989. *Pottery Analysis, a Source Book*, University of Chicago

Richardson, H. (ed.), 1998. *English Hospitals 1660–1948*, RCHME

Richardson, J.S. 1995. *Sweetheart Abbey*, Historic Scotland

Richens, R. 1997. 'Changes in the physical and social landscape of three Lanarkshire farms during the eighteenth-century agricultural reorganisation', *Review of Scottish Culture* 9, 98–112

Riden, P. 1992. *John Bedford and the Ironworks at Cefn Cribwr*, privately published

Riden, P. 1993. *Gazetteer of Charcoal-fired Blast Furnaces in Great Britain in use since 1660*, 2nd edn, University College, Cardiff

Riden, P. 1994. 'The final phase of charcoal iron-smelting in Britain, 1660–1800', *Historical Metallurgy* 28/1, 14–26

Rimmington, N. 1999. 'Stone crosses of County Durham', *Church Archaeology* 3, 44–5

Rippon, S. 1997. *The Severn Estuary: Landscape Evolution and Wetland Reclamation*, Leicester University Press

Roberts, E. 1977. 'Working-class housing in Barrow and Lancaster 1880–1930', *Transactions of the Historic Society of Lancashire and Cheshire* 127, 109–31

Roberts, J. 1986. 'The provision of housing for the working classes in Manchester 1780–1914', *Journal of the Manchester Literary and Philosophical Society* 124, 48–67

Roberts, J. 1999. 'Cusworth Park: the making of an eighteenth-century designed landscape', *Landscape History* 21, 77–93

Rogers, G. 1981. 'Social and Economic Change in Lancashire Landed Estates during the Nineteenth Century with Special Reference to the Clifton Estate 1832–1916', unpubl. PhD thesis, Lancaster University

Rolt, L.T.C. 1985. (rev. edn). *Navigable Waterways*, Penguin

Rotman, D.L. and Nassaney, M.S. 1997. 'Class, gender and the built environment. Deriving social relations from cultural landscapes in southwest Michigan', *Historical Archaeology* 31.2, 42–62

Rowlands, M.B. 1975. *Masters and Men*, Manchester University Press

Rudling, D. and Barber, L. 1993. 'Excavations at the Phoenix Brewery site, Hastings, 1988', *Sussex Archaeological Collections* 131, 73–113

Rugg, J. 1998. 'A new burial form and its meanings: cemetery establishment in the first half of the 19th century', in Cox, M. (ed.), *Grave Concerns: Death and Burial in England 1700–1850*, CBA Research Report 113, 44–53

Rushton, S. 2000. 'Between the walls: new discoveries from Brucegate, Berwick-upon-Tweed', *Archaeology in Northumberland 1999–2000*, 9

Ryder, P.F. 1992. 'Bastles and bastle-like buildings in Allendale, Northumberland', *Archaeological Journal* 149, 351–79

Ryder, P.F. 1993. *Medieval Churches of West Yorkshire*, WYAS

Ryder, P.F. and Birch, J. 1983. 'Hellifield Peel – a North Yorkshire tower-house', *Yorkshire Archaeological Journal* 55, 73–94

Sacks, D.M. 1991. *The Widening Gate. Bristol and the Atlantic Economy*, University of California Press

Saunders, A.D. 1989. *Fortress Britain*, Liphook

Schama, S. 1995. *Landscape and Memory*, Fontana

Schelereth, T.J. 1985. *US40: A Roadscape of the American Experience*, Indiana Historical Society

Scheuer, L. 1998. 'Age at death and cause of death of the people buried in St Bride's Church, Fleet Street, London', in Cox, M. (ed.), *Grave Concerns: Death and Burial in England 1700–1850*, CBA Research Report 113, 100–11

Schmidt, B. 1997. 'Mapping and empire: cartographic and colonial rivalry in seventeenth-century Dutch and English North America', *The William and Mary Quarterly*, 3rd ser. 56.3, 549–78

Schnapp, A. 1993. *The Discovery of the Past*, British Museum Press

Schofield, J. 1984. *The Building of London from the Conquest to the Great Fire*, British Museum Press

Schofield, J. (ed.), 1987. *The London Surveys of Ralph Treswell*, London Topographical Society

Schofield, J. 1993a. 'Building in religious precincts in London at the Dissolution and after', in Gilchrist, R. and Mytum, H. (eds), *Advances in Monastic Archaeology*, British Archaeological Reports 227, 29–41

Schofield, J. 1993b. 'The capital rediscovered: archaeology in the City of London', *Urban History* 20:2, 211–24

Schofield, J. 1997. 'Urban housing in England, 1400–1600', in Gaimster, D. and Stamper, P. (eds), *The Age of Transition. The Archaeology of English Culture 1400–1600*, Oxbow Monograph 98, 127–44

Schofield, J. 1999. 'City of London Gardens, 1550–c. 1620', *Garden History*, 27:1, 73–87

Schofield, J. and Vince, A. 1994. *Medieval Towns*, Leicester University Press

Schofield, M.M. 1985. 'Shoes and ships and sealing wax: eighteenth-century Lancashire exports to the colonies', *Transactions of the Historical Society of Lancashire and Cheshire* 135, 61–82

Schubert, H.R. 1947. 'Housing conditions of ironworkers in the sixteenth century', *Journal of the Iron and Steel Institute* 155, 371–2

Scurfield, G. 1986. 'Seventeenth-century Sheffield and its environs', *Yorkshire Archaeological Journal* 58, 147–71

Shammas, C. 1993. 'Changes in English and Anglo-American consumption from 1550–1800', in Brewer, J. and Porter, R. (eds), *Consumption and the World of Goods*, Routledge, 177–205

Sharpe, A. 1989. *The Minions Survey*, 2 vols, Cornwall Archaeological Unit

Sharpe, A. 1992. *St Just: An Archaeological Survey of the Mining District*, 2 vols, Cornwall Archaeological Unit

Sharpe, A., Lewis, R., Massie, C. and Johnson, N. 1991. *Engine House Assessment: Minerals Tramway Project*, Cornwall Archaeological Unit

Sheail, J. 1996. 'Town wastes, agricultural sustainability and Victorian sewage', *Urban History* 23.2, 189–210

Shennan, S. 1986. 'Toward a critical archaeology?', *Proceedings of the Prehistoric Society* 52, 327–56

Sherlock, S.J. 1999. 'Nineteenth-century workers' houses in Redcar, Cleveland', *Durham Archaeological Journal* 14–15, 177–86

Silber, A.M. and Flemming, N.H. 1991. *The Victorian Catalogue of Household Goods*, Studio Editions

Simmons, J. 1959. 'Brooke Church, Rutland, with notes on Elizabethan church building', *Transactions of the Leicestershire Archaeological and Historical Society* 35, 36–44

Simpson, M.A. 1977. 'The West End of Glasgow 1830–1914', in Simpson, M.A. and Lloyd, T.H. (eds), *Middle-Class Housing in Britain*, David & Charles, 44–85

Smiles, S. 1874. *Lives of the Engineers. 3: Metcalfe and Telford*, John Murray

Smith, J.R. 1988. *The Luxulyan Valley*, Cornwall Archaeological Unit

Smith, J.T. 1983. 'Short-lived and mobile houses in late seventeenth-century England', *Vernacular Architecture* 16, 33–4

Smith, J.T. 1992. *English Houses 1200–1800. The Hertfordshire Evidence*, HMSO

Smith, P. 1975. *Houses of the Welsh Countryside*, HMSO

Smith, P. 1990. 'Time and chance: a reply', *Vernacular Architecture* 21, 4–5

Smith, R. 1994. 'Copper Metallurgy at Keswick, 1567–1602', in Ford, T.D. and Willies, L. (eds), *Mining before Powder*, Peak District Mines Historical Society, 116–23

Smith, V.T.H. 1993. 'Cockham Wood Fort', *Archaeologia Cantiana* 112, 55–75

Smith, V.T.H. 1994. 'Trinity Fort and the defences of the Anglo-Dutch War at Gravesend in 1667', *Archaeologia Cantiana* 114, 39–50

Smith, V.T.H. 1996. 'The rear defence walls of New Tavern Fort, Gravesend, 1795', *Archaeologia Cantiana* 116, 283–92

Smith, W.J. 1959. 'Blackpool: a sketch of its growth, 1740–1851', *Transactions of the Lancashire and Cheshire Antiquarian Society* 69, 70–103

Smith Pryde, G. 1965. *The Burghs of Scotland*, Oxford University Press

Smout, C. 1996. 'Pre-improvement fields in upland Scotland: the case of Loch Tayside', *Landscape History* 18, 47–55

Soulsby, I. 1983. *The Towns of Medieval Wales*, Phillimore

SPMA. 1988. *Research Priorities for Post-Medieval Archaeology*, SPMA

Start, H. and Kirk, L. 1998. '"The bodies of Friends" – the osteological analysis of a Quaker burial ground', in Cox, M. (ed.), *Grave Concerns: Death and Burial in England 1700–1850*, CBA Research Report 113, 167–77

Stead, G. 1999. *The Moravian Settlement at Fulneck 1742–1790*, Thoresby Society, 2nd ser. 9

Stell, C. 1994. *Nonconformist chapels and meeting houses in the north of England*, RCHME

Stell, C. 1998. *Great meeting houses*, The Chapels Society Miscellany 1, 33–49

Stell, G. 1993. 'Pre-Clearance settlement: evidence of standing buildings', in Hingley, R. (ed.), *Medieval or Later Rural Settlement in Scotland*, Historic Scotland and Ancient Monuments Division Occasional Paper 1, 13–14

Stell, G. 1996. *Dumfries and Galloway*, The Stationery Office

Stewart, J.H. and Stewart, M.B. 1988. 'A Highland longhouse, Lianach, Balquhidder, Perthshire', *Proceedings of the Society of Antiquaries of Scotland* 118, 301–17

Stobart, J. 1996. 'The spatial organization of a regional economy: central places in north-west England in the early eighteenth century', *Journal of Historical Geography* 22, 147–59

Stobart, J. 1998. 'Shopping streets as social space: leisure, consumerism and improvement in an eighteenth-century county town', *Urban History* 25, 3–21

Stock, G. 1998a. 'Quaker burial: doctrine and practice', in Cox, M. (ed.), *Grave Concerns: Death and Burial in England 1700–1850*, CBA Research Report 113, 129–42

Stock, G. 1998b. 'The 18th and 19th century Quaker burial ground at Bathford, Bath and North-East Somerset', in Cox, M. (ed.), *Grave Concerns: Death and Burial in England 1700–1850*, CBA Research Report 113, 144–66

String, T.C. 1996. 'A neglected Henrician decorative ceiling', *Antiquaries Journal* 76, 139–57

Symonds, J. 1999. 'Toiling in the Vale of Tears: everyday life and resistance in South Uist, Outer Hebrides, 1760–1860', *International Journal of Historical Archaeology* 3.2, 101–22

Tabraham, C. 2000. (rev. edn). *Scottish Castles and Fortifications*, Historic Scotland

Tabraham, C. and Grove, D. 1995. *Fortress Scotland and the Jacobites*, Batsford/Historic Scotland

Tarlow, S. 1998. 'Romancing the stones: the graveyard boom of the later 18th century', in Cox, M. (ed.), *Grave Concerns: Death and Burial in England 1700–1850*, CBA Research Report 113, 33–43

Tarlow, S. 1999. 'Wormie clay and blessed sleep. Death and disgust in later historic Britain', in Tarlow, S. and West, S. (eds), *The Familiar Past?* , Routledge, 183–98

Tarlow, S. and West, S. 1999. *The Familiar Past? Archaeologies of Later Historical Britain*, Routledge

Tarn, J.N. 1971. *Working-class Housing in 19th-century Britain*, Architectural Association Paper Number 7

Taylor, A.J. 1950. *Raglan Castle*, HMSO

Taylor, C. 1975. (1987 edn). *Fields in the English Landscape*, Alan Sutton

Taylor, C. 1983. *Village and Farmstead*, George Philip & Son

Taylor, C. 2000. 'Fenlands', in Thirsk, J. (ed.), *The English Rural Landscape*, Oxford University Press 167–87

Taylor, J. 1996. 'The architectural image of the asylum', *The Victorian Society Annual* 1995, 14–20

Taylor, R. 1992. 'Population explosions and housing, 1550–1850', *Vernacular Architecture* 23, 24–9

Taylor, R.F. 1974. 'Town houses in Taunton 1500–1700', *Post-Medieval Archaeology* 8, 63–79

Thacker, A. 1995. 'The reuse of the monastic buildings at Chester, 1540–1640', *Transactions of the Historic Society of Lancashire and Cheshire* 145, 21–43

Thirsk, J. 1985. 'Agricultural policy, public debate and legislation', in Thirsk, J. (ed.), *The Agrarian History of England and Wales. Vol. V: 1640–1750. II Agrarian Change*, Cambridge University Press

Thomas, H. 1997. (1998 corrected edn). *The Slave Trade. The History of the Atlantic Slave Trade: 1440–1870*, Macmillan

Thomas, R.W. 1984. 'The building of Barry', in Moore, D. (ed.), *Barry The Centenary Book*, The Barry Centenary Book Committee Ltd, 333–65

Thompson, A., Grew, F. and Schofield, J. 1984. 'Excavations at Aldgate, 1974', *Post-Medieval Archaeology* 18, 1–148

Thompson, M.W. 1987a. *The Decline of the Castle*, Cambridge University Press

Thompson, M.W. 1987b. 'The abandonment of the castle in Wales and the Marches', in Kenyon, J.R. and Avent, R. (eds), *Castles in Wales and the Marches*, University of Wales Press

Thornber, Revd W. 1837. *History of Blackpool and its Neighbourhood*, privately published

Thornes, R. 1994. *Images of Industry: Coal*, RCHME

Thornton, D. and Cowell, M. 1996. 'The "Armada Service": a set of late Tudor dining silver', *Archaeological Journal* 76, 152–76

Thurley, S. 1993. *The Royal Palaces of Tudor England*, Yale University Press

Thurley, S. 1997. 'Whitehall Palace and Westminster 1400–1600: a royal seat in transition', in Gaimster, D. and Stamper, P. (eds), *The Age of Transition: The Archaeology of English Culture 1400–1600*, Oxbow Monograph 98, 93–104

Tilley, C. 1994. *A Phenomenology of Landscape*, Routledge

Timmins, J.G. 1977. *Handloom Weavers' Cottages in Central Lancashire*, CNWRS Occasional Paper 3, University of Lancaster

Timmins, J.G. 1979. 'Handloom weavers' cottages in central Lancashire: some problems of recognition', *Post-Medieval Archaeology* 13, 251–72

Timmins, J.G. 1993. 'Healthy and decent dwellings: the evolution of the two-up and two-down house in nineteenth-century Lancashire', in Crosby, A.G. (ed.), *Lancashire Local Studies*, 101–22

Tolan-Smith, C. 1997. 'Landscape archaeology', in Tolan-Smith, C. (ed.), *Landscape Archaeology in Tynedale*, Tyne-Solway Ancient and Historic Landscapes Research Programme Monograph 1, University of Newcastle upon Tyne, 1–10

Treble, R. 1971. 'Liverpool working-class housing 1801–1851', in Chapman, S.D. (ed.), *The History of Working-Class Housing*, David & Charles

Trinder, B. 1982. *The Making of the Industrial Landscape*, Dent

Trinder, B. (ed.), 1992. *The Blackwell Encyclopedia of Industrial Archaeology*, Blackwell

Trinder, B. 1999. 'The social and economic impact of Telford's Road', in LUAU, 'Telford's Holyhead Road (A5)', unpubl. Report

Tulket, M. 1821. *A Topographical, Statistical, and Historical Account of the Borough of Preston*, P. Whittle

Turner, M. 1987. 'Post-medieval Colonisation in the Forests of Bowland, Knaresborough and Pickering', unpubl. PhD thesis, University of Hull

Tylecote, R.F. 1987. *The Early History of Metallurgy in Europe*, Longman

Tylecote, R.F. and Cherry, J. 1970. 'The 17th-century bloomery at Muncaster Head', *Transactions of the Cumberland and Westmoreland Antiquarian and Archaeological Society* 70, 69–109

Tyler, K. 1996. 'Excavation of an early modern site at the German Hospital Dalston, London Borough of Hackney', *Transactions of the London and Middlesex Archaeological Society* 47, 157–71

Tyson, B. 1993. 'Low-cost housing in Cumbria 1665–1721: documentary evidence for three cottages', *Vernacular Architecture* 24, 20–8

van der Porten, E.P. 1965. *The Porcelains and Terra Cottas of Drake's Bay*, Point Reyes

Vandervell, A. and Coles, C. 1980. *Game and the English Landscape*, Debrett

Verhaeghe, F. 1997. 'The archaeology of transition: a continental view', in Gaimster, D. and Stamper, P. (eds), *The Age of Transition. The Archaeology of English Culture 1400–1600*, Oxbow Monograph 98, 25–44

Vernon, R.W., McDonnell, G. and Schmidt, A. 1998. 'An integrated geophysical and analytical appraisal of early iron-working: three case studies', *Historical Metallurgy* 32/2, 67–81

Vickery, A. 1993. 'Women and the world of goods: a Lancashire consumer and her possessions 1751–81', in Brewer, J. and Porter, R. (eds), *Consumption and the World of Goods*, Routledge, 274–304

Wade Martins, S. 1998. 'A century of farms and farming on the Sutherland estate 1790–1890', *Review of Scottish Culture* 10, 33–54

Walker, B. and McGregor, C. 1993. 'Evidence from vernacular building studies', in Hingley, R. (ed.), *Medieval or Later Rural Settlement in Scotland*, Historic Scotland and Ancient Monuments Division Occasional Paper 1, 4–10

Walton, J.K. 1998. *Blackpool*, Edinburgh University Press

Warnes, A.M. 1970. 'Early separation of homes from work-places and the urban structure of Chorley 1780–1850', *Transactions of the Historic Society of Lancashire and Cheshire* 122, 105–35

Watson, I. 1993. 'From West Heath to Stepney Green: building development in Mile End Old Town 1660–1820', *London Topographical Record* 27, 231–56

Weatherill, L.M. 1983. 'The growth of the pottery industry in England 1660–1818', *Post-Medieval Archaeology* 17, 15–46

Weatherill, L.M. 1993. 'The meaning of consumer behaviour in late seventeenth- and early eighteenth-century England', in Brewer, J. and Porter, R. (eds), *Consumption and the World of Goods*, Routledge, 206–27

Weatherill, L.M. and Edwards, R. 1971. 'Pottery-making in London and Whitehaven in the late seventeenth century', *Post-Medieval Archaeology* 5, 160–81

Webster, E. 1998. 'William Ranger's report on the sanitary condition of Halifax 1850–1', *Transactions of the Halifax Antiquarian Society* new ser. 6, 55–78

West, S. 1999. 'Social space and the English country house', in Tarlow, S. and West, S. (eds), *The Familiar Past? Archaeologies of Later Historical Britain*, Routledge, 103–22

White, A. 2000. (rev. edn). *The Buildings of Georgian Lancaster*, CNWRS, Lancaster University

White, A. 1993. 'Setting the scene 1193–1500', in White, A. (ed.), *A History of Lancaster 1193–1993*, Keele University Press, 9–47

White, J.F. 1962. *The Cambridge Movement. The Ecclesiologists and the Gothic Revival*, Cambridge University Press

Whittington, G. 1983. 'Agriculture and society in Lowland Scotland 1750–1870', in Whittington, G. and Whyte, I.D. (eds), *An Historical Geography of Scotland*

Whittle, E. 1989. 'The Renaissance gardens of Raglan Castle', *Garden History* 17, 83–94

Whyte, I.D. 1995. *Scotland before the Industrial Revolution. An Economic and Social History* c. 1050–c. 1750, Edinburgh University Press

Whyte, I.D. 1999. 'The historical geography of Britain from AD 1500', in Hunter, J. and Ralston, I. (eds), *The Archaeology of Britain*, Routledge, 264–79

Whyte, I.D. and Whyte, K.A. 1991. *Scotland's Changing Landscape*, Routledge

Wiliam, E. 1978. 'Yr Aelwyd: the architectural development of the hearth', *Wales Folk Life* 16

Wiliam, E. 1988. *Home-made Homes. Dwellings of the Rural Poor in Wales*, National Museum of Wales

Wiliam, E. 1995. '"Home-made homes": dwellings of the rural poor in Cardiganshire', *Ceredigion* 12.3, 23–40

Wilk, R.R. 1990. 'The built environment and consumer decisions', in Kent, S. (ed.), *Domestic Architecture and the Use of Space*, Cambridge University Press, 34–42

Wilkinson, P.F., Locock, M. and Sell, S. 1998. 'A 16th-century saltworks at Port Eynon, Gower', *Post-Medieval Archaeology* 32, 3–32

Willan, T.S. 1980. *Elizabethan Manchester*, Manchester University Press

Williams, M. 1970. *The Draining of the Somerset Levels*, Cambridge University Press

Williamson, T. 1995. *Polite Landscapes: Gardens and Society in Eighteenth-Century England*, Sutton Publishing

Williamson, T. 1997. 'Fish, fur and feather: Man and nature in the post-medieval landscape', in Barker, K. and Darvill, T. (eds), *Making English Landscapes*, Oxbow Monograph 93, 92–117

Williamson, T. 1998. 'Questions of preservation and destruction', in Everson, P. and Williamson, T. (eds), *The Archaeology of Landscape*, Manchester University Press, 1–24

Williamson, T. 2000. 'Understanding Enclosure', *Landscapes* 1.1, 56–79

Williamson, T. and Bellamy, L. 1987. *Property and Landscape*, George Philip

Wilson, A. 1988. 'The excavation of Clydach Ironworks', *Industrial Archaeology Review* 11/1, 16–36

Wilson, E. 1983. 'Swedish limestone paving in 17th and 18th century English buildings', *Post-Medieval Archaeology* 17, 95–110

Wilson, J. 1995. *The Archaeology of Shakespeare*, Sutton Publishing

Winstanley, M. 1993. 'The town transformed 1815–1914', in White, A. (ed.), *A History of Lancaster 1193–1993*, Keele University Press, 145–98

Withers, C. 1990. '"Give us land and plenty of it": the idealogical basis to land and landscape in the Scottish Highlands', *Landscape History* 12, 45–54

Wohl, A. 1971. 'The housing of the working classes in London', in Chapman, S.D. (ed.), *The History of Working-Class Housing*, David & Charles

Wood, J. 1996. 'Castles and monasteries', in Newman, R. (ed.), *The Archaeology of Lancashire*, LUAU, 139–56

Woodforde, J. 1978. *Georgian Houses for All*, Routledge & Kegan Paul

Woodhouse, E. 1999. 'Spirit of the Elizabethan Garden', *Garden History* 27:1, 10–31

Worsdall, F. 1979. *The Tenement. A Way of Life: A Social History and Architectural Study of Housing in Glasgow*, Chambers

Wrathmell, S. 1984. 'The vernacular threshold of northern peasant houses', *Vernacular Architecture* 15, 29–33

Wrathmell, S. 1989. *Wharram: A study of settlement on the Yorkshire Wolds. Vol. 6: Domestic Settlement 2: Medieval Peasant Farmsteads*, York University Archaeological Publications 8

Wrathmell, S. 1990. 'Why the archaeologist cannot be a camera', *Scottish Archaeological Review* 7, 37–40

Yates, M. 1996. 'Medieval or later deserted rural settlements in Wales', *Medieval Settlement Research Group Annual Report* 11, 13–15

Yelling, J.A. 1982. 'Rationality in the common fields', *Economic History Review*, 2nd ser. 35, 409–15

Yentsch, A.E. 1991. 'Chesapeke artefacts and their cultural contexts: pottery and the food domain', *Post-Medieval Archaeology* 25, 25–72

Yentsch, A.E. 1993. 'Man and vision in historical archaeology', in Yentsch, A.E. and Beaudry, M.C. (eds), *The Art and Mystery of Historical Archaeology: Essays in Honor of James Deetz*, Baton Rouge, 23–47

Yeoman, P. 1995. *Medieval Scotland*, Batsford/Historic Scotland

INDEX